This is the first comprehensive study of the group of avant-garde Soviet writers active in Leningrad in the 1920s and 1930s who styled themselves OBERIU, 'The Association for Real Art.' Graham Roberts re-examines commonly held assumptions about OBERIU, its identity as a group, its aesthetics, and its place within the Russian and European literary traditions. He focuses on the prose and drama of group members Daniil Kharms, Aleksandr Vvedensky, and Konstantin Vaginov; he also considers work by Nikolay Zabolotsky and Igor' Bakhterev, as well as the group's most important 'fellow-traveller', Nikolay Oleinikov, and he places OBERIU in the context of the aesthetic theories of the Russian Formalists and the Bakhtin Circle. Roberts concludes by showing how the self-conscious literature of OBERIU – its metafiction – occupies an important transitional space between modernism and postmodernism.

CAMBRIDGE STUDIES IN RUSSIAN LITERATURE

THE LAST SOVIET AVANT-GARDE

Recent titles in this series include

Nabokov's early fiction
JULIAN W. CONNOLLY

Iurii Trifonov
DAVID GILLESPIE

Mikhail Zoshchenko
LINDA HART SCATTON

Andrei Bitov
ELLEN CHANCES

Nikolai Zabolotsky
DARRA GOLDSTEIN

Nietzsche and Soviet culture
edited by BERNICE GLATZER ROSENTHAL

Wagner and Russia
ROSAMUND BARTLETT

Russian literature and empire
Conquest of the Caucasus from Pushkin to Tolstoy
SUSAN LAYTON

Jews in Russian literature after the October Revolution
Writers and artists between hope and apostasy
EFRAIM SICHER

Contemporary Russian satire: a genre study
KAREN L. RYAN-HAYES

Gender and Russian literature: new perspectives
edited by ROSALIND MARCH

A complete list of books in this series is
given at the end of the volume

THE LAST SOVIET AVANT-GARDE

OBERIU – fact, fiction, metafiction

GRAHAM ROBERTS

Lecturer in Russian studies
University of Strathclyde

PUBLISHED BY THE PRESS SYNDICATE OF THE UNIVERSITY OF CAMBRIDGE
The Pitt Building, Trumpington Street, Cambridge CB2 IRP, United Kingdom

CAMBRIDGE UNIVERSITY PRESS
The Edinburgh Building, Cambridge CB2 2RU, United Kingdom
40 West 20th Street, New York, NY 10011–4211, USA
10 Stamford Road, Oakleigh, Melbourne 3166, Australia

First published 1997

Printed in the United Kingdom at the University Press, Cambridge

Typeset in Baskerville no.2 11/12½

A catalogue record for this book is available from the British Library

Library of Congress cataloguing in publication data

Roberts, Graham.
The last Soviet avant-garde: OBERIU – fact, fiction, metafiction / Graham Roberts.
p. cm. – (Cambridge studies in Russian literature)
Includes bibliographical references and index.
ISBN 0 521 48283 6
1. Oberiu. 2. Literature, Experimental – Soviet Union.
3. Russian literature – 20th century – History and criticism.
I. title. II. series.
PG3026.024R63 1997
891.709'0042–dc20 96–21152 CIP

ISBN 0 521 48283 6 hardback

In memory of my parents

l'histoire est entièrement vraie,
puisque je l'ai imaginée d'un bout à l'autre.

Boris Vian, *L'écume des jours*

Contents

Acknowledgements   *page* xi
Notes on transliteration and conventions   xiii

Introduction: OBERIU – the last Soviet
avant-garde   1

1 Authors and authority   22
    The art of public speaking: Russian modernism and the
      avant-garde   22
    Literature as system: Russian formalism and the Bakhtin
      circle   27
    OBERIU – Nikolay Zabolotsky, Nikolay Oleinikov, and
      Igor' Bakhterev   31
    Carnivalizing the author? Daniil Kharms   33
    Writing for a miracle: Kharms's *The Old Woman* as menippean
      satire   38
    What a time to tell a story: Aleksandr Vvedensky   44
    Dialogues of the dead: Vvedensky's *Minin and Pozharsky* 46
    The artist as hermit: Konstantin Vaginov   57
    The author loses his voice: the novels of Konstantin Vaginov 63

2 Rereading reading   75
    Addressing the reader: Russian modernism and the
      avant-garde   75
    Text as dialogue: from Russian formalism to the Bakhtin
      circle   80
    OBERIU and the reader: Zabolotsky, Oleinikov, Bakhterev 82
    Stop reading sense: the prose of Daniil Kharms   85
    Picture this: *Christmas at the Ivanovs'* by Aleksandr Vvedensky 94
    The reader in the text: *The Labours and Days of Svistonov*
      by Konstantin Vaginov   105

3   **Language and representation**   120
       From realism to 'real' art: Russian modernism and the
           avant-garde   120
       Neighbouring worlds, imaginary realities: the *chinari* 125
       OBERIU: The Association for *Real* Art   127
       From the authority of language to the languages of
           authority: Daniil Kharms   131
       Language games and power play: *Elizaveta Bam*   139
       Time, death, God, and Vvedensky   145
       The poverty of language: Vvedensky's *A Certain
           Quantity of Conversations*   151
       Worlds beyond words: Konstantin Vaginov   157
       Art as play: Konstantin Vaginov's *Bambocciade*   159

    Conclusion: OBERIU – between modernism and
    postmodernism?   171

Notes   179
Bibliography   237
Index   268

Acknowledgements

This book began life as a D.Phil. thesis. It has undergone considerable revision, partly in an attempt to appeal to non-Slavists as much as to those with a specialist interest in the subject.

My thanks are due first and foremost to my D.Phil. supervisor at Oxford University, Gerry Smith, to whom I am deeply indebted. I am also grateful to Billy Clark, Neil Cornwell, Ann Jefferson, Catriona Kelly, Robin Milner-Gulland, Mike Nicholson, and Ann Shukman for their helpful comments at various stages of my D.Phil. I am particularly obliged to David Shepherd for kindling my initial interest in OBERIU, and to Pierre Dubois for continuing to inspire me. I would also like to express my deep gratitude to staff from the Bodleian Library and the Taylor Institution in Oxford, and the British Library in London, for assistance above and beyond the call of duty.

While at Oxford, I received financial help from New College, the British Council, and the Oxford University Ilchester Fund committee towards a research trip to Moscow and Leningrad in the autumn of 1990. During that trip, I received the full co-operation of the staff at the Saltykov-Shchedrin library in Leningrad. Special thanks must also go to a number of people whom I was fortunate enough to meet during that trip, namely Anatoly Aleksandrov, for his thoughts, Mikhail Levitin, for three fascinating evenings at the theatre, Vladimir and Natasha Glotser, for their hospitality and inspiration, and Daniil Kharms's sister, Elizaveta Ivanovna Gritsyna, simply for her time.

This book could not have been started without funding from

the British Academy, which was generous enough to grant me a postgraduate studentship (1988–91). While revising my manuscript, I benefited greatly from a period of six months' research leave awarded to me in the first half of 1995 under the auspices of the Academy's Humanities Research Board. I am grateful to the University of Strathclyde for their support during this period, and especially to my colleagues in the Russian division for graciously taking on my teaching and administrative duties. I am also obliged to my editors at Cambridge University Press, namely Kate Brett and, in the latter stages, Linda Bree. Thanks are also due to my colleagues Svetlana Akotia, Phil Cooke, and Sheelagh Graham who were kind enough to read and comment on a near-final draft of this manuscript, and to Martin Dewhirst of Glasgow University for his invaluable bibliographical information.

Some readers may feel that in the pages which follow conventions are broken far too often. In an attempt to redress the balance, I would like to follow convention by thanking the one person who has been my constant companion throughout the seven years which this book has taken to write. For all Kharms's belief in the 'power of words', there are none I can find to thank Nathalie sufficiently for her patience, her encouragement, and her support.

Notes on transliteration and conventions

I have used the *Oxford Slavonic Papers* system of transliteration, which renders final -yi, -ii, or -i in proper names as -y (in, for example, Nikolay Zabolotsky). The only exceptions to this occur in references containing an already transliterated word or name (for example, Vsevolod Meyerhold, *Meyerhold on Theatre*, where I would normally write 'Meyerkhol'd').

All translations are my own, except where stated otherwise. I have chosen to convey the literal meaning of the poetry extracts, rather than attempt a poetic equivalent in English.

In preparing the manuscript, I have adhered to the guidelines in the *Modern Humanities Research Association* Style Book (fourth edition) as closely as possible.

Complete publication details for works cited in the notes can be found in the relevant section of the bibliography.

Introduction: *OBERIU* – the last Soviet avant-garde

OBERIU (an abbreviated form of 'Ob"edinenie real'nogo iskusstva', meaning 'The Association for Real Art'), was the last, certainly the most outlandish, and arguably the most important, manifestation of the Soviet literary avant-garde of the late 1920s.[1] This loose association of Leningrad writers, founded by Daniil Kharms, Aleksandr Vvedensky, Nikolay Zabolotsky, Igor' Bakhterev, and Konstantin Vaginov, lasted, in various forms and under a variety of names from 1926 to 1930.[2] During this relatively short time they achieved a good deal of notoriety, not least for their eccentric behaviour and their generally riotous public performances. Their refusal to conform to accepted notions of good taste earned these writers the opprobrium of the Soviet press, which branded them all manner of things, from 'Dadaists' to 'the class enemy'. The group was soon forced to curtail its activities, its individual members seemingly reduced to silence, thereby signalling what one critic has described as 'the end of Russian futurism'.[3] As we shall see, however, not only did they keep on writing, but the significance of what they produced extends way beyond their own time and space.

What makes OBERIU interesting today? One might begin to answer that question by pointing out that the group was part of the general experimental wave which crashed against the rocks of European literature and the arts in the 1920s and 1930s. OBERIU was more, much more, than just a Russian version of Futurism, Dadaism, or Surrealism, however. Many of the artistic devices employed by members of the group prefigured those used by subsequent aesthetic movements, such as the

I

Theatre of the Absurd, Antonin Artaud's Theatre of Cruelty, the French New Novel, and Anglo-American postmodernism. There is no doubt, too, that the group's intellectual under-pinnings were impressive; as we shall see, there are important analogies between the literature produced by Kharms, Vve-densky, and Vaginov, on the one hand and the thought of mainstream European philosophers such as Wittgenstein and Heidegger, on the other.

Within Russia, OBERIU belonged to the same Leningrad intellectual current as the Formalists and the group of thinkers centred around Mikhail Bakhtin in the late 1920s. Like Osip Brik and other 'left' theorists of the time, the group was vociferously irreverent towards the notion of 'genius' in art. Not for these writers the cult of the artist as Romantic martyr, so beloved of other 'internal émigrés' such as Mikhail Bulgakov or Anna Akhmatova. In this and other respects, OBERIU antici-pated trends in later Russian fiction. Experimental writers who belonged to the Russian émigré movements of the 1960s, 1970s, and 1980s – writers such as Andrey Amal'rik and Vladimir Kazakov – liked to claim a direct link between their own work and the fiction of Kharms and Vvedensky. The fictional tradi-tion to which OBERIU belonged (if the notion of an 'OBERIU tradition' is not itself an oxymoron) has recently been revived and developed in Russia itself by, amongst others, the Con-ceptualist poets of the 1980s, and prose writers such as Tat'yana Tolstaya, Vladimir Sorokin, and Valeriya Narbikova. However, rather than identify what OBERIU has in common with other literary trends, in Russia or in the West, we still need to ask what was unique about the movement – indeed, whether one can talk about OBERIU as a 'movement' at all – and what, if anything, united those writers who belonged, however fleet-ingly, to its ranks.

The best known of all the *Oberiuty*, Nikolay Zabolotsky (1903–58) represents something of an anomaly within the group. Although he spent almost eight years in Soviet labour camps (from March 1938 to January 1946), Zabolotsky has been more or less continually published in his homeland. His first collection, *Scrolls (Stolbtsy)* appeared in 1929 (shortly after he had parted company with OBERIU).[4] His reputation, both in Russia and in the West, is very much that of a 'classic' Soviet poet, although opinions differ as to the relative importance of his 'Formalist' verse of the late 1920s and his subsequent, stylistically more conventional poetry.[5]

Like Zabolotsky, Daniil Kharms (1905–42) and Aleksandr Vvedensky (1904–41) earned a living in the 1930s writing for children.[6] Indeed, until the mid 1960s, Kharms and Vvedensky were known in their own country exclusively as children's writers.[7] Their reputation, and ever-growing popularity as authors of fiction 'for adults' is relatively recent. It began in 1967, when they were 'rediscovered' by two young Soviet scholars at a student conference in Tartu.[8] A number of recent publications have helped their work reach a far wider audience, both in their native land and abroad, and ensured something approaching cult status for Kharms.[9]

A marked contrast to this is provided by the reception of another one-time member of this group, the poet and prose writer Konstantin Vaginov (1899–1934).[10] Although Vaginov's literary rehabilitation began at the very same conference which introduced Kharms and Vvedensky to a broader public,[11] he has remained relatively obscure. Furthermore, his name has not become associated with OBERIU in the same way that Vvedensky's, Kharms's, and, increasingly, Zabolotsky's have.[12] Two international OBERIU conferences recently held in Moscow, for example, have concentrated on Kharms and Vvedensky, and have practically ignored Vaginov.[13]

The complexity of OBERIU pre-history has meant that accounts of the group's formation have tended to be at times fragmentary, at others contradictory. What is certain is that by the time Vaginov met Kharms and Vvedensky in 1926, he had been involved in a number of Leningrad literary groups. These included: the 'Sounding Shell' ('Zvuchashchaya rakovina'); Nikolay Gumilev's second 'Guild of Poets' ('Tsekh poetov'); Nikolay Tikhonov's 'Islanders' ('Ostrovityane'); the 'Brotherhood of Fools' ('Abbatstvo gaerov'); Konstantin Olimpov's 'Ring of Poets in Honour of K. M. Fofanov' ('Kol'tso poetov imeni K. M. Fofanova'); and the 'Emotionalists' ('Emotsiona-

listy'), a relatively loose group centred around Mikhail
Kuzmin.[14] Vaginov had also attended courses at the Leningrad
Institute of Art History given by the Formalists Eikhenbaum
and Tynyanov, and had begun, in 1924, to move in Mikhail
Bakhtin's circle of friends.[15] He was well-known and, although
reserved, well-liked by members of the literary community in
Leningrad. By 1925 his reputation as a poet was sufficient for
him to be participating in a literary evening at the Leningrad
Capella alongside Anna Akhmatova, Mikhail Zoshchenko,
Konstantin Fedin, and Fedor Sologub, among others.[16]

As for Vvedensky, he had worked between 1923 and 1926
with the Futurist poet and theatre director Igor' Terent'ev,
researching the nature of poetic language at the phonology
section of Malevich's Institute of Artistic Culture in Leningrad,
which Terent'ev directed.[17] This was not Vvedensky's first
incursion into matters literary, however. In 1922, a year earlier
than his first meeting with Terent'ev, Vvedensky together with
Leonid Savel'ev (Lipavsky), and Yakov Druskin founded a
philosophical circle which was to play a significant role in all
their lives.[18] Vvedensky had known Lipavsky, who had attended
the same school as he had, since 1917 or 1918, when the two of
them had composed a parody of Futurism, entitled 'The Ox of
Buddah' ('Byk Buddy').[19]

The group comprising Vvedensky, Lipavsky, and Druskin,
which met from 1922 on a regular and frequent basis to discuss
various literary and philosophical issues, saw its numbers swell
in the summer of 1925 with the arrival of Kharms.[20] Later that
same year they were joined by Zabolotsky and the poet Nikolay
Oleinikov (Zabolotsky – never a regular attender – finally
parted company with the group in 1934, Oleinikov remained
until his arrest and death in 1937,[21] while Vvedensky stayed
until settling definitively in the Ukraine in 1936, and Kharms
was a member until his second arrest in autumn 1941).[22]
Between 1925 and 1927 they called themselves the *chinari*, a
neologism apparently invented by Vvedensky, which Druskin
asserts comes from the Russian word 'chin', meaning 'rank',
probably in a spiritual sense (Druskin, ' "Chinari" ', p. 103).[23]

Kharms had first met Vvedensky and Druskin in the spring

or early summer of 1925, at a poetry recital given at Yevgeny Vigilyansky's flat[24] by the group of poets known as the 'Order of the *zaumniki* DSO' ('Orden zaumnikov DSO'). Kharms and Vigilyansky[25] were both members of the 'Order', as was one of the main practitioners of *zaum'* ('trans-rational' poetry), Aleksandr Tufanov.[26] Kharms and Vvedensky took to each other immediately, and, just as Vvedensky was moved to invite Kharms to join the *chinari*, so Kharms suggested that Vvedensky become a member of Tufanov's group. Both invitations were accepted. Over the next few months, the 'Order of the *zaumniki* DSO' now renamed by Kharms and Vvedensky as the 'Left Flank' ('Levyi flang'), would either meet at Tufanov's flat, or give readings at student hostels or factory clubs.[27] In the summer or autumn of the same year, the two young poets met Zabolotsky, reading some of his poetry at a meeting organized by the Leningrad branch of the Union of Poets, which he was hoping to join (Nikita Zabolotsky, *The Life of Zabolotsky*, pp. 45–6). Both were impressed with his verse, and although no formal collaboration resulted at this stage, they became good friends. Zabolotsky's application to join the Union of Poets was successful, and he was joined in the spring of 1926 by Kharms and Vvedensky, who became members after irreconcilable differences had forced Tufanov's 'Left Flank' to disintegrate.[28]

Shortly afterwards, Kharms met Igor' Bakhterev at a poetry recital at which Bakhterev was one of the performers (Nazarov and Chubukin, 'Poslednii iz Oberiu', p. 39). Bakhterev, pleased at Kharms's favourable reception of his verse, invited him to join his 'Radiks' group (ibid.).[29] This experimental theatre group, which aimed at achieving 'pure' theatre, had recently been founded by Bakhterev (the group's artist), and three other students from the drama department of the Leningrad Institute of Art History, namely Georgy Katsman, Boris ('Doivber') Levin and Sergey Tsimbal.[30] In the middle of 1926, Kharms and Vvedensky began to participate in the group's rehearsals which took place in a room lent to them by Malevich at his Institute of Artistic Culture. Zabolotsky also became involved.[31] The result of this collaboration between Kharms, Vvedensky, and 'Radiks' was 'My Mum is Covered in Watches' ('Moya

mama vsya v chasakh'), a syncretic collage of some of their
early poems. Sadly, like all the other 'Radiks' projects, 'My
Mum is Covered in Watches' was never staged (ibid.).[32]

After 'Radiks' collapsed, Kharms and Vvedensky suggested
to Bakhterev and Zabolotsky in the autumn of 1926 that they
continue working together as a group.[33] In this way was formed
the nucleus of what was later to become OBERIU; indeed, a
number of others, including Vigilyansky, Levin, and Tsimbal,
were also eventually to join OBERIU from 'Radiks', and it
could be said that OBERIU really began as 'Radiks'. Vaginov
joined them very shortly afterwards, on Bakhterev's suggestion
(Bakhterev, 'Kogda my byli molodymi', p. 76). Vaginov, like
Bakhterev a graduate of the Leningrad Institute of Art History,
had met Bakhterev while attending 'Radiks' rehearsals. From
the end of 1926 to late 1927, this group called itself either 'Flank
of Left [Forces]' ('Flang levykh'), 'Left Flank [of the Union of
Poets]' ('Levyi flang'), or 'The Academy of Left Classics'
('Akademiya levykh klassikov').[34]

The group with Vaginov, Vvedensky, Kharms, Zabolotsky,
and Bakhterev at its core gave a number of collective, and
generally theatricalized, poetry readings throughout the
autumn of 1926 and the whole of 1927, generally accompanied
by a ballerina and a magician (Nikita Zabolotsky, *The Life of
Zabolotsky*, p. 57). They appeared in places as diverse as 'The
Circle of Friends of Chamber Music', student hostels, and the
barracks where Zabolotsky spent a year doing his military
service from November 1926.[35] On one such occasion, in the
Red Room of the Institute of Art History, the group read a
selection of its work to the Formalists Tynyanov, Eikhenbaum,
Shklovsky, and Tomashevsky.[36] A 'manifesto' of aesthetic
principles was drafted by Zabolotsky and Vvedensky and read
out at the 'dispute' following a poetry reading by Mayakovsky
at the Leningrad Capella in late 1927.[37] Mayakovsky was
sufficiently impressed by the group's performance to commission an article on them for his journal *New LEF* (*Novyi LEF*).
The article was duly written by Vasily Klyuikov, but opposed
by erstwhile Formalist Osip Brik at the editorial stage.[38] It was
also after this show that Oleinikov and Evgeny Shvarts

suggested that the group join the team of children's writers working under Samuil Marshak. Vvedensky, Kharms, and Zabolotsky accepted, and thus began more than ten years of children's writing, including very many contributions to the journals *The Hedgehog* and *The Finch*.

In the autumn of 1927 the group was invited by A. A. Baskakov to become a section of the Leningrad Press Club.[39] Here was, in effect, an offer of formal recognition and the chance, sooner or later, to publish. The only condition was that the group change its name; the word 'left' (rendered politically incorrect by Stalin's recent attack on the Party's 'left opposition') would have to disappear. After much collective thought, Bakhterev eventually came up with the name 'OBERI' which Kharms, for no apparent reason, altered slightly by changing the 'e' to 'э' and adding final 'y' (thereby giving 'Обэриу', instead of 'Объери').[40] The one and only performance which the group gave at the Press Club, on 24 January 1928, is by far the best known of all their appearances, and has, like the OBERIU episode as a whole, acquired a meaning which some scholars argue is far greater than its actual significance for the literary development of those involved.[41] That the show, in spite of Baskakov's warnings about the word 'left', was called 'Three Left Hours' ('Tri levykh chasa') is an irony which appears to have escaped many commentators.

As its title suggests, the performance was split into three parts. These were punctuated by bizarre slogans such as 'Poems Aren't Pies' and 'We Aren't Herring', and followed by a 'dispute' which was led by Vvedensky. During the first 'hour', each group member read out some of his poetry. Each recital was staged differently: while Vaginov read his verse, for example, the ballerina Militsa Popova danced around him; Vvedensky preceded his recital by riding across the stage on a tricycle; Kharms read sitting on top of a cupboard; and Zabolotsky stood next to a large trunk, dressed in an old military jacket and soiled boots (Vaginov and Zabolotsky were apparently the most popular). The second 'hour' contained Kharms's play, *Elizaveta Bam*, while a film was shown during the third part of the performance. The evening as a whole was prefaced by a reading of the article describing OBERIU aesthetic principles which appeared in the second issue of the Press Club journal for 1928.[42] If Bakhterev is to be believed, neither Kharms, Vvedensky, nor Vaginov appears to have had much to do with drafting the article (frequently referred to as the group's 'declaration', or 'manifesto'), although they may well have taken part in the group discussions which led up to it. According to Bakhterev, Zabolotsky wrote the introduction and the section on poetry, while Levin and Bakhterev wrote the section on OBERIU theatre. Once each section of the article had been written, the other members of the group made some minor changes (Bakhterev, 'Kogda my byli molodymi', p. 88).[43]

The article sought to present OBERIU as an artistic avant-garde, profoundly and directly involved in the process of social change. The introductory section of the article was an attempt, reminiscent of early left art, to clothe aesthetic innovation in half-hearted Marxist rhetoric. More than that, it sought to square the circle between, on the one hand, experimentation in the arts and, on the other, the officially encouraged and increasingly strident calls from Soviet 'proletarian' groups for artists to appeal directly to a mass audience. 'The great revolutionary shift in culture and the conditions of everyday life so characteristic of our age', it declared:

is being held back in the arts by a number of abnormal phenomena. We have yet to understand fully that indisputable truth that as far as the arts are concerned the proletariat cannot be satisfied by the aesthetic method of the old schools, that its aesthetic principles go much deeper and undermine old art at its very roots. [...] We believe, and we know, that only left art can lead us to the path of the new proletarian artistic culture.

задерживается в области искусства многими ненормальними явлениями. Мы еще не до конца поняли ту бесспорную истину, что пролетариат в области искусства не может удовлетвориться художественным методом старых школ, что его художественные принципы идут гораздо глубже и подрывают старое искусство до самых корней. [...] Мы верим и знаем, что только левый путь искусства выведет нас на дорогу новой пролетарской художественной культуры. (Milner-Gulland, '"Left Art"', pp. 69–70)

The fact that this circle was, by 1928, beyond squaring was ironically underlined elsewhere in this section, by a direct reference to the difficulties then being experienced by other experimental artists: 'We do not understand why Filonov's School has been expelled from the Academy, why Malevich cannot carry out his architectural work in the USSR, nor why Terent'ev's [production of] *The Government Inspector* was given such an absurdly poor reception' ('Nam ne ponyatno pochemu Shkola Filonova vytesnena iz Akademii, pochemu Malevich ne mozhet razvernut' svoei arkhitekturnoi raboty v SSSR, pochemu tak nelepo osvistan "Revizor" Terent'eva?'; ibid., p. 70).[44]

The next section, on poetry, contained a vehement rejection of *zaum'* and general abstractness in art.[45] Instead, it affirmed a belief in the 'concrete object' which, 'once its literary and everyday skin has been peeled away, becomes a property of art' ('konkretnyi predmet, ochishchennyi ot literaturnoi i obikhodnoi shelukhi, delaetsya dostoyaniem iskusstva'; ibid.). There were already tensions within OBERIU, most notably between Zabolotsky and Vvedensky. In 1926, Zabolotsky had confided to Kharms, 'I can't accept Vvedensky's methods', and had actually written an open letter to Vvedensky in which he declared, 'your verses do not grow on the same soil as we do'.[46] This may have been what lay behind the rejection in the article of *zaum'*, a literary mode which Kharms and Vvedensky had previously embraced, but which Zabolotsky had never accepted.[47] This was also, no doubt, what prompted Zabolotsky to lay the emphasis on individuality within the group, thereby creating a private space for himself, as well as for the others:

... each of us has his own creative personality, and this fact has frequently left some people confused. [...] They obviously assume that a literary school is something like a monastery, where the monks have one and the same personality. Our association is free and voluntary, and it unites masters, not apprentices – artist-painters, not painter-decorators. Each one of us knows his own artistic self, and each knows how that self is connected to the others.

... у каждого из нас есть свое творческое лицо и это обстоятельство кое-кого часто сбивает с толку. [...] Видимо полагают, что литературная школа – это нечто вроде монастыря, где монахи на одно лицо. Наше объединение свободное и добровольное, оно соединяет мастеров, а не подмастерьев, – художников, а не маляров. Каждый знает самого себя и каждый знает – чем он связан с остальными. (Milner-Gulland, ' "Left Art" ', p. 71)

Perhaps because Zabolotsky was trying to reconcile so many opposites, there is a certain vague and impressionistic quality about much of what is written here. This is also the case in the summaries of the aesthetics of each individual OBERIU writer where (except in the case of prose writer Boris Levin, who had also by now joined the group) there is a constant tension between the abstractness of the description and the references to the '[concrete] object':

A. Vvedensky (on the extreme left of our association) breaks the object down into parts, but the object does not thereby lose its concreteness. [...] **K. Vaginov**, whose phantasmagoria passes before our eyes as though shrouded in mist and in trembling. But through this mist one can feel the proximity of the object, and its warmth. [...] **Igor′ Bakhterev** [...] The object and the action, split into their component parts, spring into life once more, revitalized by the spirit of new OBERIU lyricism. [...] **N. Zabolotsky** – a poet of naked concrete figures brought close to the eyes of the spectator. [...] **Daniil Kharms** – a poet and dramatist, whose attention is concentrated, not on a static figure, but on the collision of a number of objects, on their interrelationships. At the moment of action, the object assumes new concrete traits full of real meaning.

А. Введенский (крайняя левая нашего объединения), разбрасывает предмет на части, но от этого предмет не теряет своей конкретности. [...] **К. Вагинов**, чья фантасмагория мира проходит перед глазами как бы облеченная в туман и дрожание. Однако через этот туман вы чувствуете близость предмета и его теплоту [...] **Игорь Бахтерев** [...] Предмет и действие, разложенные на свои составные, возникают обновленные духом новой обэриутской лирики. [...] **Н. Заболоцкий** – поэт голых конкретных фигур, придвинутых вплотную к глазам зрителя. [...] **Даниил Хармс** – поэт и драматург, внимание которого сосредоточено не на статической фигуре, но на столкновении ряда предметов, на их взаимоотношениях. В момент действия

предмет принимает новые конкретные очертания, полные
действительного смысла. (ibid.)

The emphasis on fragmentation and collision which characterized the 'poetry' section of the article is also found in the
sections on OBERIU drama and cinema. Much of the drama
section of the article is devoted to the play *Elizaveta Bam*, which
constituted the second part of the 'Three Left Hours'. The play
itself was devised by Bakhterev (who also decorated the
scenery), Levin, and Kharms, while it was Kharms who actually
wrote the final version. 'The play's *dramatic* plot is shattered', it
was affirmed, 'by many seemingly extraneous subjects' (*'drama-
turgiicheskii* syuzhet p'esy, rasshitan mnogimi, kak by postoron-
nimi temami'). It was replaced by 'a *scenic* plot which arises
spontaneously from all the elements of our spectacle' ('syuzhet
stsenicheskii, stikhiinovoznikayushchii iz vsekh elementov nashego spektaklya'; ibid., p. 73).

Following Baskakov's invitation, there had been a move,
initiated by Zabolotsky, although resisted by Vvedensky and
Levin, to expand the membership of OBERIU even further.
This had resulted in the recruitment of two cinema students,
Klementy Mints and Aleksandr Razumovsky.[48] They co-pro-
duced 'Film No. 1', subtitled 'Meatgrinder' ('Myasorubka'),
shown during the third 'Left Hour'. 'The plot is not important
to us' ('Nam ne vazhen syuzhet'), Razumovsky explained in the
article. 'Separate elements of the film may be completely
unconnected to each other' ('otdel'nye elementy fil'ma mogut
byt' nikak ne svyazany mezhdu soboi'; ibid., p. 72). The film has
been lost, but we do know that it began with a shot of an
interminably long train passing in front of the camera and was
accompanied in the Press Club showing by Bakhterev on the
piano, kettledrum and double bass.

Mints and Razumovsky were not the only new members of
OBERIU to participate in 'Three Left Hours'. There was also
a merchant seaman named Nikolay Kropachev, who was
announced in the Press Club, but whose poetry reading actually
took place some distance away, on Nevsky Prospect. According
to the publicity poster which was drawn up for the 'Three Left

Hours' show, the 'dispute' which was to follow the show was to have been organized by '*Oberiut* Sergey Tsimbal' (like Levin, a co-founder of 'Radiks').[49] In the event, however, the discussion was led by Vvedensky, and there is no reference anywhere to Tsimbal's active collaboration with OBERIU, either on this, or any subsequent occasion.[50] Of the many who were proposed to join OBERIU, Bakhterev maintains that only three may be regarded as genuine members: Levin, Razumovsky and Yury Vladimirov, a prose writer who joined the group in 1929.[51]

Although OBERIU continued working and performing under this name for another two years, Vaginov ceased collaborating with the group shortly after the 'Three Left Hours' evening. And by the end of that same year Zabolotsky had voluntarily left, partly in order to concentrate on his first poetic cycle, *Scrolls*, and partly because of irreconcilable aesthetic and personal differences between himself and the rest of the group (Bakhterev, 'Kogda my byli molodymi', pp. 98–9).[52] In October 1928, Kharms already considered that there were only four genuine members of OBERIU, namely himself, Vvedensky, Bakhterev, and Levin (Vvedensky, *PSS*, vol. II, p. 247). As it was, Vaginov had taken virtually no part in the preparations of the performances, or in the discussions on aesthetic principles between the other members of the group, generally conducted at Kharms's flat. Bakhterev explains this absence by pointing out that at the time, Vaginov was constantly engaged in writing his first novel, *The Goat's Song* ('Kogda my byli molodymi', pp. 85 and 90). As for the remaining members of OBERIU, 1928 also saw a performance, at the newly relocated Press Club, of a one-act play written by Kharms and Bakhterev, entitled 'A Winter Stroll' ('Zimnyaya progulka'), a work which, like so many others, has since been lost.[53]

By now, however, the writing was on the wall for such experimental literary groups as OBERIU. On 8 April 1930, a performance at a student hostel of Leningrad university was followed by a particularly vicious denunciation in the press:

The Obereuty [...] despise the struggle in which the proletariat is engaged. *Their withdrawal from life, their nonsensical poetry, their* zaum' *trickery – all this is a protest against the dictatorship of the proletariat. Their poetry is therefore counterrevolutionary. It is the poetry of people alien to us, the poetry of the class enemy* – such was the judgement expressed by the proletarian students.

Обереуты [*sic*] [...] ненавидят борьбу, которую ведет пролетариат. *Их уход от жизни, их бессмысленная поэзия, их заумное жонглерство – это протест против диктатуры пролетариата. Поэзия их поэтому контрреволюционна. Это поэзия чуждых нам людей, поэзия классового врага,* – так заявило пролетарское студенчество.[54]

This vitriolic, overtly political attack on OBERIU was by no means the first adverse review the group had received, however. A damning press review of a performance given by the group on 28 March 1927 (before it became known as OBERIU), had elicited an explanation of their activities from Kharms and Vvedensky to the executive of the Union of Poets (they were eventually expelled from the Union in 1929, along with a number of others, including Mandel'shtam).[55]

   Almost immediately after the publication of the *Smena* article, OBERIU – or what was left of it – disbanded, its members too fearful of the consequences to continue working together as a group.[56] As they correctly sensed, the *Zeitgeist* in the Soviet Union was now entirely antithetical to their brand of avant-garde literature, indeed to anything which appeared to deviate from the brand of 'proletarian' art of the Party-backed literary organization, the 'Russian Association of Proletarian Writers' (RAPP).[57] The previous year had seen the vituperative press campaign waged against Pil'nyak and Zamyatin, and in an article which appeared in *Literaturnaya gazeta* in January 1930, Shklovsky had apparently rejected his Formalist past.[58] It was in such an atmosphere that on 14 April 1930, less than one week after OBERIU gave their last performance, Mayakovsky shot himself in Moscow. There are no records of any post-OBERIU collaboration between Vaginov, on the one hand, and Kharms and Vvedensky, on the other. They may have continued, however, to meet in the early 1930s, at Mikhail Kuzmin's flat, which they all apparently visited at this time.[59] As for Zabolotsky, after temporarily breaking off all contact with OBERIU in 1929, he appears to have continued attending *chinari* meetings until 1934.[60]

The demise of OBERIU in no way signalled an end to the literary activity of its various members. Virtually all of Kharms's prose, as well as a substantial amount of his verse, dates from the 1930s, while most of Vvedensky's extant 'unofficial' work was written after the breakup of OBERIU. Between 1930 and his death from tuberculosis in 1934, Vaginov wrote two collections of poetry and a short story, and worked on three novels (of which at least one was finished).[61] He collaborated on a history of the frontier post at Narva (a small town on the border between Russia and Estonia), entitled *Four Generations* (*Chetyre pokoleniya*, 1933), and ran a writers' group for factory workers (Chertkov, 'Poeziya Konstantina Vaginova', p. 227). Kharms and Vvedensky also produced a good deal of children's literature during the 1930s. But even this activity did not guarantee immunity from persecution. The first wave of arrests of children's writers came at the end of 1931.[62] Although both Kharms and Vvedensky were released shortly afterwards, the ever-intensifying politicization of children's literature meant that a second arrest was inevitable.[63] It came for both of them in 1941. Vvedensky died on a prison train in December of that year, and Kharms met his death in captivity in early 1942.[64]

As well as his memoirs concerning the group, Bakhterev wrote in 1948 a phantasmagorical short story, in which he celebrated the memory of his erstwhile companions. 'The Shop with a Hole in it, or the *Chinar'-Molvoka*. A True Story' ('Lavka s dyroi, ili chinar'-molvoka. Byl').[65] In this oneiric tale, which contains a number of allusions to works by other members of OBERIU, the narrator enters what appears to be a junk shop, and describes a pit located in the middle of the shop, in which he, and only he can see something. What he makes out is a procession of eight rather eccentric figures, who are anonymous in the text itself, but who are identified by Bakhterev in his introduction to the story as Kharms, Vvedensky, Zabolotsky, Oleinikov, Levin, Vaginov, Vladimirov, and Tufanov. That Bakhterev is a radically different writer from Zabolotsky is clear from a comparison of 'The Shop' with Zabolotsky's own

literary reminiscence of OBERIU, his moving elegy 'Farewell
to Friends' ('Proshchanie s druz'yami', 1952). The opening
stanza of this poem, almost certainly addressed to his erstwhile
companions in OBERIU, sets the tone:

> In broad-brimmed hats and long jackets,
> With notebooks full of your poems,
> Long ago you crumbled to dust,
> Like windfallen lilac branches.

> В широких шляпах, длинных пиджаках,
> С тетрадями своих стихотворений,
> Давным-давно рассыпались вы в прах,
> Как ветки облетевшие сирени.[66]

As far as the critical reception of OBERIU is concerned,
most scholars have tended to discuss Kharms and Vvedensky
together, despite their undoubtedly very different personalities.[67] There is virtually unanimous agreement as to the central
role of both writers in OBERIU (indeed, the impression is
sometimes given in scholarly literature that what is meant by
OBERIU is no more than Kharms and Vvedensky). Others,
such as Goldstein and Björling, have assumed that Zabolotsky
was a key member of the group. While there is broad agreement among scholars on the historical facts concerning
OBERIU, its formation, and the importance within the group
of Kharms, Vvedensky, and Zabolotsky, there is less consensus
when it comes to interpreting the nature and significance of
Vaginov's collaboration.

There are those, clearly in the minority, who argue that
Vaginov's work is aesthetically close to the writings of the other
OBERIU members. Victor Terras, for example, maintains that
Vaginov's later novels 'follow the Oberiu aesthetic, featuring
the grotesque, travesty, language games, verbal collage, an
everpresent literary subtext, and pervasive romantic irony'.[68]
Similarly, Milner-Gulland argues that Vaginov's 'phantasma-
goric novels are a major contribution to OBERIU literature'
("Left Art", p. 75). Nina Perlina, noting the element of the
burlesque, the absurd, the macabre, and the carnivalesque in
OBERIU literature, affirms that it is from such a perspective

that Vaginov's fourth novel, *Harpagoniana* is best read (Perlina, 'Konstantin Vaguinov', p. 479).[69] As regards Vaginov's poetry, Viktor Shirokov claims that the writer's last published collection of verse contains 'quite a few of what one might call "OBERIU" poems'.[70] Then there were the opinions of contemporaries. Bakhterev recalls that Zabolotsky was particularly favourable to Vaginov's candidature for OBERIU membership ('Kogda my byli molodymi', p. 76). Moreover, one contemporary critic held the view that once Kharms moved away from *zaum'*, his work became closer to Vaginov's.[71]

On the other hand, Kharms himself implied, in a note made at some time in 1928, that only he himself, Bakhterev, Levin, and Vvedensky were to be counted as genuine members of OBERIU. His comment, 'it is better to have three people, in full agreement with each other, than more who are in constant disagreement' ('luchshe tri cheloveka, vpolne svyazannykh mezhdu soboi, nezheli bol'she, da postoyanno nesoglasnykh'; Vvedensky, *PSS*, vol. ii, p. 247), suggests he did not believe that either Vaginov or Zabolotsky shared the group's aesthetic principles. Amongst Vaginov scholars, David Shepherd has spoken out in perhaps the strongest terms against seeing any real link between Vaginov's aesthetics on the one hand, and those of Kharms and Vvedensky on the other:

the bizarre world of Vaginov's fiction, in which, nevertheless, events occur, plot develops, and characters behave largely in accordance with conventional expectations, is very different from the fragmented world of the two best-known *oberiuty*, Daniil Kharms and Aleksandr Vvedenskii, where logic, sequentiality, and motivation, both fictional and 'real-life', are radically undermined.[72]

Nikol'skaya believes that although Vaginov shared Kharms's interest in eccentrics, neither his works nor his life contained what she calls the 'conceptualism' ('kontseptual'nost'') characteristic of the other OBERIU members, and of the Leningrad avant-garde in general.[73]

Most scholars, however, base their arguments against Vaginov's importance in OBERIU on biographical and historical factors, rather than on aesthetic grounds. Many argue that

Vaginov was an individualist who had little regard for group programmes, and consequently took little notice of them.[74] Nikol'skaya notes, for example, that Gumilev was constantly exasperated by Vaginov's apparent unwillingness to write like the rest of the members of his 'Guild of Poets' (Nikol'skaya, 'Kanva biografii i tvorchestva', p. 70).[75] Such a refusal to align himself aesthetically or intellectually might explain why in the late 1920s Vaginov participated both in OBERIU and in a small circle of Hellenists known as ABDEM, two groups whose interests, according to Nikol'skaya, were radically different (ibid., p. 76).[76] Vaginov is seen by many as at best a 'loyal ally' of OBERIU.[77] Jaccard describes him as the group's 'outsider *par excellence*' (*Daniil Harms*, p. 586).[78] This notion of Vaginov as literary individualist is, moreover, reinforced by a comment he himself made in a letter as early as 1922: 'I have passed through all the poetic circles and organizations. I have not needed them for a long time now. [. . .] I want to work alone' ('Ya prokhodil cherez vse poeticheskie kruzhki i organizatsii; teper' mne eto davno ne nado [. . .] Ya khochu rabotat' odin').[79] Vaginov's lack of interest in his membership of OBERIU might explain why he did not attend the group meeting called to discuss his candidature, and why he left the group shortly after the 'Three Left Hours' evening.[80]

The central aim of this book is to determine whether one can identify an OBERIU aesthetic which its members shared, or whether Robin Milner-Gulland, for example, is justified in claiming that the main contributory factor to the formation of OBERIU was 'certain practical purposes connected with the Soviet cultural situation of the 1920s' (Milner-Gulland, ' "Kovarnye stikhi" ', p. 17).[81] In so doing, I hope to reinscribe Vaginov within the OBERIU equation in a sustained and systematic manner. At the same time, I intend to challenge a number of commonly held critical assumptions concerning the group, not least the following: first, that Vaginov is peripheral to the OBERIU equation; second, that Zabolotsky's early poetry is an important aspect of OBERIU literature; third, that there is a close relationship between Oleinikov's verse and the OBERIU aesthetic; and fourth, that there is seamless coherence between the theory expounded in the group's 'declaration', read out on the evening of 24 January 1928, and the aesthetic principles of the group's individual members as they developed in practice. Most importantly, by determining just what was distinctive about OBERIU, I hope to be able to place the group within the broader contexts of Russian and Western literature. As and when appropriate, I shall borrow certain critical or philosophical terms from groups with which the *Oberiuty* came into contact, specifically the Formalists, the Bakhtin circle, and the *chinari*. Whether or not these groups had a direct influence on OBERIU, they clearly shared common concerns, and were products of the same intellectual climate.

What, it is hoped, will emerge is that Kharms, Vvedensky, and Vaginov, and (to a lesser extent) Bakhterev, all wrote essentially self-conscious fiction, all produced texts which constitute explorations of the nature of fiction *in fictional form*. Moreover, it is my contention that it is precisely as writers of such fiction – or 'metafiction' – that they can best be distinguished from Zabolotsky and Oleinikov.[82]

This study is divided into three chapters, which focus respectively on the author ('speaker'), the reader ('listener'), and the text ('utterance'). Each chapter is split into five sections. The first section deals with contemporary literary theorists and artists (writers, filmmakers, visual artists), while the second focuses on the minor *Oberiuty*, namely Zabolotsky, Bakhterev, and the group's 'fellow-traveller', Oleinikov. The three remaining sections concentrate on, first, Kharms (since he appears to have been the driving force behind the group), second, on Vvedensky (as he is generally compared with Kharms), and third, on Vaginov.

Chapter 1 explores the ways in which these writers question certain conventional assumptions concerning the function of the story-teller (writer/author/narrator) in the cultural and textual economy. In some of his poetry and much of his prose Kharms appears both to subvert canonical writers from the history of Russian literature, and to challenge the authority of the writer, a process which culminates in his most 'carnivalesque' work, the 1939 novella *The Old Woman*. In his pseudo-historical pseudo-drama *Minin and Pozharsky*, which contains a plethora of stories told by its various characters, Vvedensky questions the validity of any narrative endeavour based upon a conventional understanding of time. Furthermore, by its fragmentary structure and the series of intertextual allusions which it contains, *Minin and Pozharsky*, like *The Old Woman*, undermines the humanist notion of the author as unified centre of the text. The discussion of Vaginov's first and last novels, *The Goat's Song* and *Harpagoniana*, traces his evolution from cultural élitist to cultural materialist, a transformation best measured by his changing attitude towards the author as originator and centre of the text. The process of subverting the author's authority is concluded in *Harpagoniana*, in which the author's voice disappears behind the 'heteroglot' mass of embedded narratives.

Chapter 2 highlights the different ways in which Kharms, Vvedensky, and Vaginov each explore the nature of reading. In many of Kharms's miniature prose pieces Kharms either gives information apparently irrelevant to the story, or seems to withhold details which might be deemed relevant. This manipulation of the reader's expectations underlines the fact that reading, like any act of communication, conventionally involves constructing a context, based on an assumption of relevance. By the same token it forces us to question not just how we read, but why. In the course of his late play *Christmas at the Ivanovs'*, Vvedensky breaks a number of conventions, pertaining both to drama and to 'real life'. What such 'defamiliarization' suggests is that the dramatic text, like any other text, is an utterance oriented towards an 'addressee', whose 'horizon of expectations' will impinge upon the very articulation of that utterance. By repeatedly disrupting the theatrical illusion, Vvedensky can be said to be parodying the naturalist assumptions underpinning Socialist Realist art, and drama in particular. In his second novel, *The Labours and Days of Svistonov*, Vaginov creates a tension in the novel between two notions of reading; on the one hand, as the passive contemplation of a meaning already entirely present in the text, and on the other, as the active recreation of meaning achieved by bringing one's own social and historical context into play with the text. In this way,

Vaginov can be said to underline the 'dialogic' nature of reading as 'active understanding' in the Bakhtinian sense.

Coming after chapters focusing on, respectively, writing and reading, chapter 3 deals with the text itself, both the language of the text, and the relationship between the text and that which it purports to represent. In his non-fictional writing of the 1930s, and some of his prose, Kharms explores the notion, elaborated by Druskin, Lipavsky, and the *chinari* group to which he belonged, of the interdependence of language and reality, of words and the world. Towards the end of the 1930s, however, Kharms's prose reveals an awareness of the political ramifications of such a notion, the chilling fact that the 'authority of language' can so easily be exploited by the 'languages of authority'. Such an awareness, moreover, is already present in Kharms's 1927 play, *Elizaveta Bam*, which dramatizes the use and abuse of language for political ends. The word and its materiality (in a literal sense) is central to Vvedensky's *oeuvre*, where it complements the tripartite theme of time, death, and God. In particular, Vvedensky's *A Certain Quantity of Conversations* calls to mind Heidegger's views on language, specifically the notion that as humans we must reject our 'fallen logos' and achieve a pure state of holy silence if we are to have access to Being, and that the only means by which we can do this is madness and death. Vaginov's early poetry contains images of words-as-things in support of the notion of the force of art, its power to guarantee the artist immortality. However, in his third, and most personal novel, *Bambocciade*, Vaginov appears to reject his previous artistic credo, emphasizing the fundamental ontological distinction between aesthetic representation and the thing represented in a way which looks forward to his own death.

Some may argue that to concentrate on the prose and drama of these three writers is to narrow one's focus to an unacceptable degree. Obversely, others may point out that to discuss, in a study of OBERIU, works written up to ten years after the OBERIU episode is to be guilty of excessively broadening one's scope. In answer to the first objection it should be made clear that I do not claim to be writing a comprehensive account of

OBERIU (such a study could run into several volumes), rather I am attempting to analyse the group's most significant 'common denominator'. As far as the second charge is concerned, it is quite clear, as I hope to show, that the homologies between the fictions of Kharms, Vvedensky, and Vaginov extend way beyond the short period (possibly no more than the 'Three Left Hours' performance itself) during which all three were official, active members of the association.[83] It is a major contention of this present study that such homologies existed, regardless of how the writers themselves may have perceived their work, and irrespective, also, of the extra-aesthetic (personal *and* political) pressures which were undoubtedly the most important factor in the group's eventual disintegration in April 1930.

CHAPTER I

Authors and authority

THE ART OF PUBLIC SPEAKING: RUSSIAN MODERNISM
AND THE AVANT-GARDE

In this chapter I shall first make a number of general comments concerning Russian modernism and the avant-garde, and its challenge to elevated notions of the artist, before discussing the nature of that challenge in OBERIU fiction.

The year in which OBERIU definitively collapsed also marks the end of the period generally referred to as 'modernism' (approximately 1900–30). This was an era of seemingly apocalyptic upheaval, both in Russia and in the West, during which time, in the wake of the intellectual revolution effected in the previous century by thinkers such as Darwin, Marx, and Nietzsche, all 'truths' were questioned, all authorities subverted. The poet Guillaume Apollinaire was speaking both literally and figuratively when he declared in 1913, 'Hommes de l'avenir souvenez-vous de moi / Je vivais à l'époque où finissaient les rois'.[1]

One of the 'kings' which a number of trends within modernism sought to do away with was the Romantic figure of the artist as an 'inspired genius', whose 'creations' are 'original'.[2] The modernist tendency to question such conventional, 'elevated' notions of art and the artist can be traced back in the West to the last years of the nineteenth century, and can be said to have culminated in the 'Dada' movement (1916–22), which was nothing less than an attempt to destroy art as an institution.[3] In Russia, on the other hand, the early modernist period saw the reaffirmation of such notions, with Lev Tolstoy's

22

treatise 'What is Art?' ('Chto takoe iskusstvo?', 1897–8), in which he expressed his belief that the artist is primarily concerned with articulating nothing less than the meaning of life in language which ordinary mortals can understand. Tolstoy's views on art were rapidly superseded, however, by those of the Russian Symbolists, and in particular Symbolism's 'second generation', whose conception of the artist as mystical visionary and conduit for the transcendental Word combined elements of Romanticism and Realism.[4]

It was not until well into the first decade of the twentieth century that such models of art even began to be challenged in Russia, with the primitivist paintings of Goncharova and Larionov replacing Vrubel''s Symbolist tableaux.[5] 1910 saw the formation of two (very different) Russian literary movements, namely Acmeism (in St Petersburg), and Futurism (in Moscow).[6] Broadly speaking, both were a reaction to the crisis in Russian Symbolism. The Acmeist poets, grouped around Nikolay Gumilev, Osip Mandel'shtam, and Anna Akhmatova, likened the poet not to a high priest, but to a 'craftsman', and questioned accepted notions of artistic originality with their emphasis on intertextuality. Russian Futurism went much further, subordinating the poet to the free play of lexical and phonetic units in the text, in its celebration of 'the self-sufficient word' ('samovitoe slovo') and 'the word as such' ('slovo kak takovoe').[7] Its most radical form was the 'trans-rational' poetry, or *zaum'* of poets such as Kruchenykh, Khlebnikov,[8] and Tufanov, which was essentially an attempt to eradicate all traces of the writer as a rationally cognizing subject (amply illustrated by Kruchenykh's poem 'Dyr bul shchyl', published in 1913).[9]

In the theory and practice of Suprematism, the most famous manifestation of Russian Futurism in the visual arts, just as radical a challenge to the centrality of the artist was posed. Suprematism was founded by Kazimir Malevich, whose first Suprematist work, a black square on a white background (1913), Malevich described as 'no empty square, but rather the experience of non-objectivity [. . .] the supremacy of pure feeling'.[10] This downplaying of the cognitive-expressive function of art in

favour of the emotional charge of pure form links Malevich
with the poets of *zaum'*, and indeed he collaborated with
Kruchenykh and Khlebnikov as early as 1913, designing the
costumes and sets for their opera *Victory over the Sun* (*Pobeda nad
solntsem*). Malevich also painted a number of works which he
described as '*zaum'* realism' ('zaumnyi realizm'), including his
'Englishman in Moscow' ('Anglichanin v Moskve', 1914) and
'Cow and Violin' ('Korova i skripka', 1913), which features a
cow superimposed onto a violin, with proportion and perspective suitably distorted.[11] In his short treatise on poetry written
in 1919, Malevich applied his convictions as to the necesarily
abstract nature of art to the verbal medium, equating the
essence of poetry with rhythm, tempo, and movement, rather
than with any cognitive function.[12]

In the early 1920s, once the Bolsheviks' hold over the country
was reasonably secure, the Party's leading ideologues began to
spell out the Party's own views on aesthetics. The emphasis now
shifted in favour of a predominantly utilitarian ethos, with the
accent on 'production', rather than 'creation'. Such rhetoric
represented a much more radical attack on Romantic notions
of art and the artist than anything which had gone before. The
most extreme voice was that of Marxist critic P. S. Kogan:

To search for the author in a work of art is to talk about secondary
matters. It's the same thing as trying to explain the location of a
railway or a bridge in a certain place as due to the inspiration of the
engineer, instead of a complex of economic conditions.[13]

Mayakovsky's 'Left Front of the Arts' ('Levyi front iskusstv'),
founded in 1923, was an ill-fated attempt to apply such
principles to avant-garde artistic praxis. For Mayakovsky, the
realm of poetry was no longer the inner space of the emotions
or the alternative world of metaphysics, but rather the very
public places of the square and the city streets: 'In order to
write about the tenderness of love, take bus no. 7 from
Lubyansky Square to Nogin Square. The appalling jolting will
serve to throw into relief for you, better than anything else, the
charm of a life transformed.'[14] In some poems, such as 'Home-

ward!', ('Domoi!', 1925), Mayakovsky explicitly equated authorship with industrial production.

Of course, Mayakovsky's tendency to suppress his own
personal, authorial voice stemmed largely from his belief in his
ability as poet to speak on behalf of the people as a whole.[15]
Other, more mainstream proletarian literary groups, such as
'Proletkul't' (short for 'Proletarian culture', 'Proletarskaya
kul'tura'), 'The Smithy' ('Kuznitsa'), 'October' ('Oktyabr''), and
'On Guard' ('Na postu'), went further than Mayakovsky in their
rejection of the notion of the 'genius-poet', and their advance-
ment of a strictly utilitarian aesthetic. Few were more strident
than 'Proletkul't' writer Aleksey Gastev, who wrote in 1921:

Cram technics down the people's throats,
Energize them with geometry,
Beat them with logarithms,
Kill their romanticism![16]

'Proletkul't' also had a theatre section, in which the future
cinema director Sergey Eisenstein first developed his technique
known as the 'montage of attractions'. As Eisenstein subsequently made clear, this technique was predicated upon a
radical challenge to artist-oriented aesthetics:

Whether the individual elements of the effect [produced by a film] are
devoid of plot in the conventional sense or whether they are linked
together by a 'plot carcass', as in my *Potemkin*, I see no essential
distinction. [...] Provoking the necessary effect is 'a purely mathema-
tical affair' and it has nothing whatsoever to do with the 'manifestation of creative genius'.[17]

With its preference for industrial and scientific metaphors,
'Proletkul't' had much in common with the branch of the arts
known as 'Constructivism'. Fired by the Futurist cult of the
machine, the Constructivists declared art to be dead, and
likened the artist to an engineer.[18] Such a principle united, for
example, the architect Vladimir Tatlin, who had begun to
make 'Relief Constructions' in Moscow from glass, iron, and
wood as early as 1913, and the theatre director Vsevolod
Meyerkhol'd, whose theory of 'biomechanics' effectively transformed the actor into a machine.[19] The tendency, characteristic

of Constructivism, to replace the notion of 'creative genius' with one which saw the artist as simply reworking already existing materials, was particularly evident in the photo-collages of the photographer Aleksandr Rodchenko, or the films of Dziga Vertov. Indeed, Vertov's most famous film, *Man with a Movie Camera* (*Chelovek s kinoapparatom*, 1928), constructed as a montage of documentary material, explicitly likens the cameraman to a factory worker, and foregrounds the editing process itself.[20] In literature, this view of artist as production worker led to the genre of the 'Production Novel', including Fedor Gladkov's *Cement* (*Tsement*, 1925–), Leonid Leonov's *The River Sot'* (*Sot'*, 1930), and Marietta Shaginyan's *Hydrocentral* (*Gidrotsentral'*, 1930–1), forerunners of Socialist Realist classics such as Nikolay Ostrovsky's *How the Steel was Tempered* (*Kak zakalyalas' stal'*, 1934).

However, one did not have to be a Bolshevik, or even a Bolshevik sympathizer to question lofty notions of the 'inspired' artist-genius. The artist Pavel Filonov, who was closely acquainted with Zabolotsky, talked about the artist as a 'master-inventor', and used metaphors to describe his paintings which were taken from the natural or physical sciences.[21] In prose, Boris Piln'yak's novel *Materials for a Novel* (*Materialy k romanu*), published in 1924, is constructed as a collage of pages from diaries, letters, anecdotes, dramatic monologues, and fragments of conversation, in such a way that the authorial voice virtually disappears behind a mass of already-quoted discourses.[22] The most famous 'fellow-travellers' in literature, the 'Serapion Brothers' ('Serapionovy brat'ya', a loose collective, active between 1921 and 1928, which included Venyamin Kaverin, Mikhail Zoshchenko, Vsevolod Ivanov, Konstantin Fedin, Viktor Shklovsky, and Lev Lunts) explicitly rejected utilitarianism in literature.[23] Yet their plea for the writer's freedom of creation, articulated in their 'manifesto' of 1922[24], was ironically undercut by the belief, held by a number of the group's members, that literature was a 'craft', the techniques of which could be learnt.[25] Moreover, in the works of so many Serapions, verbal play and other narrative strategies worked either to mask the author's individual voice (as with Zoshchenko's use of oral speech, or *skaz*), or question the very possiblity that that voice might produce anything truly original (in the prose of Kaverin or Shklovsky, for example).[26] To quote from Shklovsky's fiction-cum-autobiography, *The Third Factory* (*Tret'ya fabrika*, 1926), 'The dimensions of a book have always been dictated to its author. [...] It is the necessity of including specified material, absence of freedom generally, that gives rise to creative work.'[27]

LITERATURE AS SYSTEM: RUSSIAN FORMALISM AND THE BAKHTIN CIRCLE

Although a number of scholars have suggested homologies between Serapion practice and Formalist theory,[28] the Formalists went much further than the Serapions in their attack on notions of the author as creative genius. That they did so may have something to do with Formalism's roots as a descriptive poetics of Russian Futurism, beginning with Shklovsky's 1914 essay, *The Resurrection of the Word*.[29] The Formalists polemically downplayed the importance of the author in the text, in favour of the artistic 'device' ('priem').[30] According to Formalist theory, a work of literature functioned not to express the writer's 'message' about the world, but simply to draw attention to itself, and to its own stylistic devices. Similarly, the Formalists rejected the concept of originality in art. Poetic craft, according to Shklovsky, involved arranging pre-existing images far more than it entailed the creation of new ones.[31] Such an attitude was based upon the notion of literature as a self-generating system (rather as the individual text was itself held to be a system of devices).[32] Eikhenbaum, in an essay designed to rebuff the ever more vehement attacks on Formalism after 1925, may have claimed that the question of 'how to write' had been replaced by another – 'how to be a writer';[33] in reality, however, he still believed in what he called the 'dialectical *self-generation* of new [literary] forms'.[34] For Tynyanov, the primary Formalist theorist of literary evolution, 'creative freedom' was nothing more than 'an optimistic slogan which does not correspond to reality', and it would be more accurate to talk about 'creative necessity' (Tynyanov, 'On Literary Evolution', p. 74).

The Formalist who had from the beginning maintained the most strident anti-author stance was Osip Brik (1888–1945). He may well have had his tongue planted firmly in his cheek when he claimed that, if Pushkin had not written *Evgenii Onegin*, somebody else would have.[35] Nevertheless, he was quite clear where OPOYAZ (the Leningrad Formalists, or 'Society for the Study of Poetic Language') stood on the question of authorship: '*Opoyaz* proposes that *there are no poets or literary figures, there is poetry and literature*' (Brik, 'The So-Called Formal Method', p. 90). Brik played an important editorial role on the journal of the late left-art movement in Moscow, *New LEF* (*Novyi LEF* 1927–8). By this time the movement had rejected its Futurist credentials, and was now advocating a 'literature of fact' ('literatura fakta'), in the form of reports – newspaper articles, sketches – describing industrial projects.[36] A number of articles from *New LEF* outlining the theory of 'literature of fact' were published collectively in a volume edited by Nikolay Chuzhak in 1929.[37] In his numerous contributions to the volume, Osip Brik was particularly dismissive of the author's significance in the creative process. The following statement is typical:

Any work of art is the result of the complex interrelationship of separate elements of artistic creativity. The author's role is to make use of these elements and to incorporate them into a definite artistic product. These elements, from which the work of art is created, are external to the author and exist independently of him. The author simply makes use of them for his work, with a greater or lesser degree of success.[38]

Chuzhak himself summed up the group's position on the question of the author in an even more assertive tone:

There are still some naive eccentrics who would have us believe that the so-called work of art, or of *belles-lettres*, is somehow *created* by the writer-artist, and not *worked* in just the same way as all other products, that is to say, from sources: from others' materials in print, from one's own papers, from old and new notes.[39]

Although the left-art movement was based in Moscow, there is some evidence of collaboration with writers and artists in Leningrad.[40]

The views elaborated by Brik and Chuzhak might not, at first sight, appear to have much in common with those of Bakhtin and the other members of the Bakhtin circle, also based in Leningrad during the last years of the 1920s. Left art's call for writers to abandon the novel in favour of newspaper articles and sketches stands in direct opposition to Bakhtin's declared preference for the novel above all other literary forms.[41] On the other hand, if left-art rhetoric resembled an amalgam of Formalism and Marxism, then so, in many ways, did the ideas of Bakhtin and his associates.[42] Like the theorists of those two groups, Bakhtin radically decentred the author. This process began with Bakhtin's first major essay, 'Author and Hero in Aesthetic Activity' ('Avtor i geroi v esteticheskoi deyatel′nosti', 1924). According to Bakhtin, in order to have an authentic sense of my 'self', I need the other to complete that self, since I need to see my self as the other sees me. Subjectivity for Bakhtin is always and inevitably *inter*subjectivity, whether between self and other, or between the author of the text, and the hero in the text. While this essay was concerned with 'authorship' to a certain extent as a paradigm of human relations, *The Formal Method in Literary Scholarship* (*Formal′nyi metod v literaturovedenii*, 1928) focused its attention on literature. It was in effect an attempt to marry Marxism and Formalism, by retaining the notion of literature as a system, but by emphasizing the social nature of that system: 'Every literary phenomenon (just like any ideological phenomenon) [...] is determined simultaneously by external and internal factors; internally, by literature itself, and externally, by the other spheres of social life' ('Kazhdoe literaturnoe yavlenie (kak i vsyakoe ideologicheskoe yavlenie) [...] opredelyaetsya odnovremenno i izvne i iznutri. Iznutri – samoi literaturoi, izvne – drugimi oblastyami sotsial′noi zhizni').[43] No text, according to Bakhtin, is ever fully its author's, since no utterance can be understood independently of its social context. This is expressed particularly clearly in the critique of Freudianism, published in 1927 under Voloshinov's name:

No verbal utterance can be attributed entirely to the person articulating it. Every utterance is *the product of interaction between speakers* and, more broadly, of the complex *social situation* in which the utterance emerges.[44]

Bakhtin's book on Dostoevsky, first published in 1929[45], and his essay 'Discourse in the Novel', were further attempts to decentre the author from the text. In these works, Bakhtin uses terms such as 'polyphony' ('polifoniya') and 'heteroglossia' ('raznorechie') to describe the rich, multi-voiced texture of the modern novel, in which the author's discourse is just one among many. Bakhtin's exposition of a profoundly dialogic model of textuality may be said to have culminated in his study of Rabelais (written in the late 1930s and early 1940s). Here Bakhtin focuses on the popular tradition of carnival, and discusses the ways in which the voices of carnival temporarily subvert *all* authority, not just the author's.[46]

OBERIU's broadly anti-authoritarian, anti-convention posturing has prompted a number of critics to claim that the group was the modern embodiment of the carnival spirit as understood by Bakhtin. The first to do so was the Soviet scholar A. Dorogov, who suggested looking at OBERIU as reflecting not just carnival but a number of Bakhtin's ideas in their textual practice.[47] More recently, Robin Milner-Gulland has explicitly linked OBERIU and Bakhtin's notion of carnival when he claims, 'Bakhtin himself knew of the Oberiuty and apparently welcomed the carnivalistic element which their lives and work contributed to the atmosphere of the city' ('Beyond the Turning-Point', p. 265). Milner-Gulland's tantalizing, but unattested comment echoes those of other scholars. Lars Kleberg has described the 'parodical and carnivalesque aspect [of the Soviet avant-garde], which in the 1920s flourished mainly in Leningrad (among the OBERIU poets, the director Igor Terentev, and others)'.[48] That Bakhtin's theories – and especially his concepts of dialogism and carnival – have serious ramifications for author-centred models of literature (whether Romantic, Realist, or Symbolist) hardly needs to be emphasized.[49] Having outlined the various challenges posed by Russian modernism and its theorists to the author's authority over her/his text, I shall now turn my attention to the *Oberiuty* themselves.

OBERIU – NIKOLAY ZABOLOTSKY, NIKOLAY OLEINIKOV, AND IGOR' BAKHTEREV

As Shepherd has observed (*Beyond Metafiction*, p. 117), the poetry section of the OBERIU article, with its reference, for example, to Vaginov warming the poetic object with his very breath, appears actually to *reinforce* a number of Romantic clichés concerning the importance of the artist in the literary process, and the 'inspired', 'creative' nature of that process. This should not surprise us, however, if we remember that this section of the article was written by Zabolotsky. Although the poet's 'I' might be said to 'hide' behind the mask of the city in Zabolotsky's *Scrolls*, or the kaleidoscope of narrative voices in his long poem, 'The Triumph of Agriculture' ('Torzhestvo zemledeliya', 1933), Zabolotsky ultimately had no interest in subverting the figure of the poet. For he held a life-long sense of the poet's mission to perfect the world, and effect a harmonious co-existence between humanity and nature. This can be sensed even in some of his early poems, such as 'Art' ('Iskusstvo', 1930):

> But I, a monotonous man,
> Put a long, shining flute to my mouth,
> And blew, and, obeying my breath,
> Words flew out into the world, becoming objects.

> The cow cooked me porridge,
> The tree read a fairy-tale,
> And the dead little houses of the world
> Jumped about, as if alive.

> Но я, однообразный человек,
> Взял в рот длинную, сияющую дудку,
> Дул, и, подчиненные дыханию,
> Слова вылетали в мир, становясь предметами.

> Корова мне кашу варила,
> Дерево сказку читало,
> А мертвые домики мира
> Прыгали, словно живые.[50]

Such a utopian understanding of his function as an artist, expressed in what is a rare excursion for Zabolotsky into the metaliterary, is fully consistent with the view which Zabolotsky expressed in a lecture in 1957: 'As a poet I live in a world of bewitching mysteries. [...] With my assistance both Nature and humanity will transform themselves, are perfecting and bettering themselves.'[51] It would seem that Zabolotsky's unshakeable belief in his messianic role as poet allows him no room to question his authority as author. Indeed, it is precisely his Romantic notion of the artist which sets Zabolotsky apart, both from the mainstream of Russian modernism, and from the other members of OBERIU.

Oleinikov's short, irreverent poems, generally written as either bawdy declarations of love, ruminations on the connection between food and sex, or odes to insects, provide a sharp contrast with Zabolotsky's verse.[52] The 'vulgar' style in which much of Oleinikov's poetry is written serves to challenge precisely those lofty notions of art and the artist on which Zabolotsky's verse is ultimately predicated.[53] Occasionally this challenge is achieved through a self-conscious stylistic device. For example, the trailer which Oleinikov wrote for the film *The Wedding* (*Zhenit'ba*) contains the line 'perhaps you're tired of me' ('mozhet byt', naskuchil vam').[54] However, although Oleinikov's irreverent tone links him with contemporary practitioners of *skaz* such as Zoshchenko, the general absence of self-consciousness in his verse sharply distinguishes him from Kharms, Vvedensky, and Vaginov.

Closer to these three is Bakhterev, who not only subverts the figure of the author or story-teller (unlike Zabolotsky), but does so by means of self-reflexive narrative strategies (unlike either Zabolotsky or Oleinikov). For example, in the strangely named 'Koloborot', subtitled 'A Short Announcement' ('Kratkoe soobshchenie'), the narrator tells us about his habit of walking backwards.[55] The story, related in an oral style or *skaz*, and peppered with asides addressed to the reader, continues somewhat aimlessly until the narrator unexpectedly interrupts his story in order to talk about moustaches, a theme which, as he himself admits, has nothing to do with what he has said so far (but which reads like a parody of the opening of Gogol''s 'Nevsky Prospect'). A similarly metafictional device is used by Bakhterev in his story 'An Incident in "The Crooked Stomach"' ('Sluchai v "Krivom Zheludke"').[56] This story, about an alarm clock belonging to the narrator's brother, which eats a meal in the 'Crooked Stomach' restaurant, is told in a consistently self-conscious, oral style. The narrator eventually abandons his narrative, however, first declaring it uninteresting, then admitting incomprehension as to a number of issues raised by his narrative (and suggesting that it is precisely his *failure* to understand which prompts him to tell stories): 'No, all this, put quite simply, is impossible to explain. As are a lot of other things. Forgive me, but I refuse to understand. [...] That's the way I live, you see: I ask questions, and tell myself stories' ('Net, vse eto, poprostu skazat', neob"yasnimo. Da i mnogoe drugoe. Ya, prostite, ponyat' otkazyvayus'. [...] Tak ya, ponimaete li, i zhivu: zadayu voprosy, rasskazyvayu samomu sebe istorii'; Aleksandrov (ed.), *Vanna Arkhimeda*, p. 432).

In this section, I have looked at how Russian modernism and particularly the Soviet avant-garde posed a radical challenge to those 'elevated' notions of the artist which had underpinned Romanticism, Realism, and Symbolism. This tendency to decentre the author from the literary text was also an important feature of Russian Formalism and the theories of the Bakhtin Circle. While Zabolotsky ultimately sought to reaffirm the authority of the author (of himself as poet), Oleinikov and Bakhterev tended in their own work to subvert that authority. Bakhterev, moreover, did so by means of self-reflexive narrative devices. In this respect, Bakhterev is closer to Kharms, Vvedensky, and Vaginov, who all question the authority of the story-teller, and all resort to a plethora of metafictional devices. In order to see how close, it is now necessary to focus on these three authors, beginning with Kharms.

CARNIVALIZING THE AUTHOR? DANIIL KHARMS

There are two points to note concerning the way in which Kharms subverts the figure of the author in his fiction. First, despite the references in the OBERIU article to the proletariat and to left art, Kharms's attitude towards the artist (and in particular the writer) contains none of the explicitly political rhetoric found in earlier proletarian literature. Second, Kharms challenges certain conventional images of the writer in a much more radical way than any other Russian modernist, whether proletarian, 'fellow-traveller', or *Oberiut*.[57]

Both points are aptly demonstrated in the miniature dramatic work entitled 'Four Illustrations of how a New Idea disconcerts a Man Unprepared for it' ('Chetyre illyustratsii togo, kak novaya ideya ogorashivaet cheloveka, k nei nepodgotovlennogo'). This text contains four brief exchanges in which a figure of authority is debased, beginning with 'the writer':

WRITER: I am a writer.
READER: Well in my opinion, you're s**t!

Писатель: Я писатель.
Читатель: А по-моему, ты г...о![58]

At times, Kharms subverts specific notions concerning literary authorship. For example, in 'A Fairy Story' ('Skazka'; pp. 275–8), originally written for children, Kharms mocks belief in the possibility of originality in literature (rather as left-art theorists had). This text is essentially a story about Vanya's series of attempts to compose a fairy story, before having this story-about-a-story-about-other-stories published in a children's magazine (the very magazine, and edition, in which the story actually appeared).[59] As Vanya tries repeatedly to compose something original, however, Lenochka rejects every suggestion with the assertion that 'there is already a story like that' ('takaya skazka uzhe est''), before relating the tale in question. In this way, Vanya's endeavours at literary creativity are doomed to failure at every turn.

Two other prose pieces which focus on the act of writing are 'Knights' ('Rytsari') and the untitled story which begins 'They Call me the Capuchin' ('Menya nazyvayut kaputsynom').[60] If the writers in these stories succeed in producing something original, they are, on the other hand, ethically suspect. In this way they constitute a challenge to the concept of the writer as a

superior caste (a belief which underpinned much pre-revolutionary Russian literature, from the Romantics to the Futurists),
a challenge entirely consonant with the kind of rhetoric produced by the Moscow left-art movement in the late 1920s.
'Knights' begins with description of the violence that goes on in
a house full of old women.[61] Suddenly the narrative breaks off
– the narrator turns out to be a writer, who cannot find his ink-
pot. From being a story about sadism, 'Knights' becomes a tale
about a sadistic writer, getting his kicks by writing about
violence against women. The act of writing, and the writer's
unethical attitude towards his subject matter, is also the subject
of 'They call me the Capuchin'. In this story, the narrator
reveals his depraved state of mind by describing in gruesome
detail how he would like to obliterate children and give young
girls away in marriage. He too is suddenly forced to interrupt
his narrative, and his writing of that narrative, in order to go
and buy some tobacco.[62]

If the writers in 'Knights' and 'They Call Me the Capuchin'
are to be condemned for their excessive, prurient fascination
with the subject of their narratives, other Kharmsian story-
tellers appear singularly uninterested in the stories they tell.
Each time the narrator of 'Five Unfinished Narratives' ('Pyat'
neokonchennykh povestvovanii') begins a story he abandons his
narrative after only a few lines, arbitrarily concluding that his
(exceedingly banal) subject matter is exhausted (pp. 498–9).[63]
Although the narrator of 'Symphony No. 2' ('Simfoniya No. 2')
pretends to take an interest in his characters, he is in fact
interested in no-one but himself:

SYMPHONY No. 2

Anton Mikhailovich spat, said 'ekh', spat again, said 'ekh' again,
spat again, said 'ekh' again, and left. To hell with him. I'd do better
to tell you about Il'ya Pavlovich.

Il'ya Pavlovich was born in 1893, in Constantinople. [...] And to
hell with him, too. I'd do better to tell you about Anna Ignat'evna.

Except that telling you about Anna Ignat'evna is not that easy. First
of all, I don't know anything about her, and secondly, I've just fallen
off my chair, and I've forgotten what I wanted to tell you about. I'd
do better to tell you about myself.

I'm tall, not stupid, I dress elegantly and with good taste, don't drink, and don't go to the races, although I'm fond of the ladies.

СИМФОНИЯ № 2

Антон Михайлович плюнул, сказал «эх», опять плюнул, опять сказал «эх», опять плюнул, опять сказал «эх», и ушёл. И Бог с ним. Расскажу лучше про Илью Павловича.

Илья Павлович родился в 1893 году, в Константинополе. [...] Ну и Бог с ним. Я лучше расскажу про Анну Игнатьевну.

Но про Анну Игнатьевну рассказать не так-то просто. Во-первых, я о ней ничего не знаю, а во-вторых, я сейчас упал со стула, и забыл, о чём собирался рассказывать. Я лучше расскажу о себе.

Я высокого роста, неглупый, одеваюсь изящно и со вкусом, не пью, на скачки не хожу, но к дамам тянусь. (Kharms, *Sluchai*, p. 4)[64]

Both in 'Five Unfinished Narratives' and in 'Symphony No. 2', Kharms appears to question the idea that story-tellers are motivated by an interest in the subject of their tale.

Whereas in 'Symphony No. 2' the narrator confesses at one point that he cannot remember what he was going to talk about, memory loss is itself the subject of another work by Kharms. The narrator sets out to tell the story of an Englishman who could not remember the name of a particular bird. It soon transpires, however, that the narrator too has forgotten, and so, after trying desperately to jog his own memory, finally admits defeat and brings his narrative to an abrupt and premature conclusion with the embarassed statement: 'I have forgotten what this bird is called. If I hadn't forgotten, I would have told you the tale of this cockadoodle-doodlecluckaduck' ('Zabyl ya, kak eta ptitsa nazyvaetsya. A uzh esli b ne zabyl, to rasskazal by vam rasskaz pro etu kirikurku-kukrekitsu').[65]

In a number of texts, Kharms presents a far from conventional image of specific authors from the Russian literary tradition.[66] 'Anecdotes from Pushkin's Life', ('Anekdoty iz zhizni Pushkina'), is a collection of seven anecdotes in which the man traditionally regarded as the father of modern Russian literature is depicted as a half-wit who cannot grow a proper beard, holds his nose when walking past smelly peasants, spends much of his time throwing stones, and cannot sit on a chair without falling off it (pp. 392–3).[67] In 'Pushkin and Gogol'' ('Pushkin i Gogol'') the two writers mentioned in the title are bungling buffoons who spend their whole time tripping over each other and cursing in the manner of Laurel and Hardy, or circus clowns (p. 360). Kharms also lampoons Lev Tolstoy in 'The Fate of the Professor's Wife' ('Sud'ba zheny professora'), in which the wife in question dreams of the author of *War and Peace* holding out his chamber pot, eager to show her its freshly deposited contents (pp. 328–30).[68]

Nor does Kharms spare figures from contemporary Soviet literature. The targets of the untitled text which begins 'Ol'ga Forsh went up to Aleksey Tolstoy and did something' are quite explicit.[69] They are the writers mentioned in this opening sentence, along with another major Soviet writer, Konstantin Fedin. Instead of writing, however, they give way to apparently unmotivated violence, with Fedin smashing Forsh in the face with a shovel, before Tolstoy runs along the street neighing loudly like a horse. As he does so, passers-by look on bemused at the antics of what they recognize as 'a major contemporary writer'.

Why does Kharms parody story-telling and story-tellers? Stalin's henchmen clearly interpreted his work as politically subversive, and it could be argued that Kharms was courting danger by subverting the 'centre' of the text in a society where the centre (Stalin and the Party) claimed absolute authority for itself. It is in this specifically political sense that the Russian medieval figure of the 'holy fool in Christ' ('yurodivyi'), in whose antics Kharms's contemporaries saw a pre-echo of his own eccentric behaviour, is so appropriate.[70] For, as Soviet cultural historians D. S. Likhachev and A. M. Panchenko observe, it was only by mocking themselves as 'authors', by undermining the authority of their own narrative discourse, that these 'holy fools' could reveal the stupidity of the world (and particularly the society) in which they lived:

Authors pretend to be fools, 'play the fool', create nonsense and feign incomprehension. In actual fact they believe themselves to be clever, and only portray themselves as fools in order to be free in their laughter. Their 'authorial image' is necessary for their 'comic work', which consists in both 'making nonsense' ['durit''] and "nonsensifying" ['vozdurit''] the whole world.[71]

There remains, however, a good deal of ambiguity surrounding Kharms's author-fool. For the point about the 'holy fools', as about the medieval carnivals with which they are associated, is that their mocking laughter signalled nothing more than a *temporary* suspension of power structures, which they ultimately served to reinforce. So is Kharms, by depicting the writer as a 'fool', endeavouring in a carnivalesque manner to reassert the author's authority? To use Formalist parlance, is he 'defamiliarizing' the image of the writer only to renew it in a positive, productive sense? Is Susan Scotto, for example, justified when she implies that Kharms is essentially rearticulating the Romantic concept of the artist as gifted outcast: 'Kharms seems to be saying that there is no room for the truly creative but non-conformist writer in the society he presents' ('Daniil Xarms's Early Poetry', p. 181)? Or is Kharms in fact intent on debasing the writer/author absolutely and definitively? To put it plainly, is Kharms extending the modernist challenge to the authority of the writer, or is he parodying it by caricaturing its worst excesses? For much of Kharms's *oeuvre* this question remains unclear; it is just as possible, for example, to read 'Anecdotes from Pushkin's Life' either as lampooning Pushkin, or as ridiculing those Philistines who belittle the great man by recounting all sorts of trivia about his life.[72] It is only in one of his last works, the novella *The Old Woman*, that Kharms even begins to provide us with a clear answer to this question.

WRITING FOR A MIRACLE: KHARMS'S *THE OLD WOMAN* AS MENIPPEAN SATIRE

The central irony of *The Old Woman* (*Starukha*) is that, while it is Kharms's most thoroughly carnivalesque work, it is the text in which Kharms finally resolves his carnivalesque ambivalence towards the authority of the writer.[73]

There is a remarkable discrepancy between the kind of writer generally found in Kharms's fiction, and the image which he sought to project of himself as a writer, in his letters and diaries. In October 1933, in a letter to the actress K. V. Pugacheva, Kharms declared himself to be a 'world-creator' ('tvorets mira'), and affirmed unequivocally his belief in the power of 'true' art to effect a 'purity of order' ('chistota poryadka').[74] By the late spring of 1939, when he wrote *The Old Woman*, Kharms's material situation had seriously deteriorated.[75] He and his second wife Marina were soon penniless and close to starvation, a situation exacerbated in 1937, with the censor's refusal to allow publication of even his children's stories following the appearance of his poem, 'Out of a House walked a Man' ('Iz doma vyshel chelovek').[76] The same man who in 1933 had had such unshakeable confidence in his powers as a writer was, by April 1937, bemoaning his absolute creative entropy: 'No thoughts have entered my head during the last few days, and so I have not written anything down, either here [Kharms's diary] or in my blue notebook' ('Nikakikh myslei za eti dni v golovu ne prikhodilo, a potomu ni syuda, ni v golubuyu tetrad' ya nichego ne zapisyval'; ' "Bozhe, kakaya uzhasnaya zhizn'..." ', p. 215).[77]

The fact, of course, that Kharms produced *The Old Woman* (by far his longest work in prose) just over two years later suggests that he succeeded in overcoming this lack of inspiration, if only temporarily. In this deceptively fragmentary tale, narrated in the first person, a man trying to write a story about a miracle-worker who never actually commits miracles, experiences a major crisis when confronted with the presence of an old woman's corpse in his Leningrad flat.[78] After trying to forget about her (he visits his friend Sakerdon Mikhailovich[79], and tries to talk to a young woman about God while waiting in a bread queue) he eventually crams the body into a suitcase. While attempting to flee the city on a train, he is forced to rush to the lavatory with a dose of diarrhoea, and has the suitcase stolen from him. Apparently thankful for this 'miracle', the narrator descends from the train at the next station, goes into the woods, kneels down, and makes the sign of the cross. At this point the narrative comes to an abrupt end.

If 'Anecdotes from Pushkin's Life' carnivalizes the figure of

Pushkin, then by the same token *The Old Woman*, with its plethora of parodic allusions to the 'classics' of nineteenth-century Russian prose can be said to carnivalize the Petersburg literary tradition.[80] The various motifs which the tale contains reinforce its carnivalesque thrust.[81] These include: the return and renewal of the body on the border between life and death, as the old woman's corpse appears to come to life; the black humour concerning death (especially the anecdote which the narrator relates concerning an incident when a corpse escapes from a mortuary and terrorizes women at a maternity ward, provoking one to give birth prematurely (p. 419));[82] and the 'carnivalesque *mésalliance*' which prompts the story's dénouement, based on the notion that the narrator's bout of diarrhoea is the pretext for the 'miraculous' disappearance of the suitcase.[83]

But what is the relationship between the carnivalesque element of *The Old Woman* and the image of the writer which Kharms projects? Answering that question will necessitate a close examination of the kind of carnival text which *The Old Woman* constitutes. Kharms's story demonstrates, in fact, many of the characteristics of 'menippean satire', a genre which, Bakhtin asserted, 'has been, in the literature of the modern era, the main vehicle for the most concentrated and vivid forms of carnivalization' ('v literaturakh novogo vremeni byla preimushchestvennym provodnikom naibolee sgushchennykh i yarkikh form karnavalizatsii'; Bahktin, *PPD*, p. 233).[84] According to Bakhtin, the most important characteristic of menippean satire is 'its extremely bold and unrestrained element of the fantastic[85] and adventure' ('samaya smelaya i neobuzdannaya fantastika i avantyura') devoted to 'the creation of *extraordinary situations* in order to provoke and test a philosophical idea – a discourse, a *truth*, embodied in the image of a wise man, the seeker of this truth' ('sozdavat' *isklyuchitel'nye situatsii* dlya provotsirovaniya i ispytaniya filosofskoi idei – slova, *pravdy*, voploshchennoi v obraze mudretsa, iskatelya etoi pravdy'; Bahktin *PPD*, p. 193). This is precisely what lies at the heart of *The Old Woman*: an extraordinary situation (the presence of a corpse – and a 'live' one at that – in the narrator's bedroom), which is the catalyst for an exploration undertaken by a wise man who merely feigns stupidity. The 'truth' which he tests ostensibly concerns the existence of God and the possibility of miracles. He also seeks, however, the answer to another, more personally relevant question, concerning the writer's authority, both ethical[86] and epistemological.

In order to explore this issue of the writer's authority, *The Old Woman* is constructed in a manner which calls to mind what Bakhtin describes as the paradigmatic carnival narrative, namely the 'mock crowning and subsequent uncrowning of the carnival king' ('shutovskoe uvenchanie i posleduyushchee razvenchanie karnaval′nogo korolya'), through which 'a new crowning glimmers' ('prosvechivaet novoe uvenchanie'; Bakhtin, *PPD*, pp. 210–11). At the beginning of *The Old Woman*, as has been shown, Kharms's character/narrator decides to write a story.[87] The problems begin for the narrator, however, when he finds himself unable to write. This realization comes in a passage which, with its triumphalism shot through with irony, can be read as a 'mock crowning' of the writer as 'carnival king':

Now I feel sleepy, but I'm not going to sleep. I'll take paper and pen and I'll write. I feel tremendous strength inside me. I thought it all out yesterday. It's going to be a story about a miracle worker who lives in our time and does not work miracles. He knows he is a miracle worker and can work any miracle he wants, but he doesn't. [...]

Sakerdon Mikhailovich will burst with envy. He thinks I'm no longer capable of writing a work of genius. Quickly, quickly to work. Away with all sleep and laziness! I'll write for eighteen hours straight!

Теперь мне хочется спать, но я спать не буду. Я возьму бумагу и перо и буду писать. Я чувствую в себе страшную силу. Я все обдумал еще вчера. Это будет рассказ о чудотворце, который живет в наше время и не творит чудес. Он знает, что он чудотворец, и может сотворить любое чудо, но я этого не делает. [...]

Сакердон Михайлович лопнет от зависти. Он думает, что я уже не способен написать гениальную вещь. Скорее, скорее за работу! Долой всякий сон и лень! Я буду писать восемнадцать часов подряд! (p. 400)

Once he has 'crowned' his writer (who resembles Kharms

himself in a number of ways), Kharms begins to uncrown him, debunking him and his project by means of irony:

I tremble all over with impatience. I can't figure out what to do. I needed to get a pen and paper, but I've picked up all kinds of objects, not at all the things I needed. [...]

I stand in the middle of the room. Whatever am I thinking about? Why, it's already twenty past five. I've got to write. I push the table toward the window and sit down at it, squared paper in front of me, pen in hand. [...]

The sun hides behind the chimney of the building opposite. The shadow from the chimney runs along the roof, flies across the street, and settles on my face. I ought to take advantage of the shadow and write a few words about the miracle worker. I pick up my pen and write:

'The miracle worker was tall.'

I can't write anything else.

От нетерпения я весь дрожу. Я не могу сообразить, что мне делать: мне нужно было взять перо и бумагу, а я хватал разные предметы, совсем не те, которые мне были нужны. [...]

Я стою посередине комнаты. О чём же я думаю? Ведь уже двадцать минут шестого. Надо писать. Я придвигаю к окну столик и сажусь за него. Передо мной клетчатая бумага, в руке перо. [...]

Солнце прячется за трубу противостоящего дома. Тень от трубы бежит по крыше, перелетает улицу и ложится мне на лицо. Надо воспользоваться этой тенью и написать несколько слов о чудотворце. Я хватаю перо и пишу:

«Чудотворец был высокого роста.»

Больше я ничего написать не могу. (pp. 400–1)

This process of abasement, by which the writer is uncrowned, continues at Sakerdon Mikhailovich's flat. The conversation which the narrator has with his friend centres precisely on the narrator's status as a writer, which is once more debunked by means of irony:

'You know, the last time I ate was yesterday, when I was with you in the cellar bar, and I haven't eaten since', I said.

'Oh aye', said Sakerdon Mikhailovich.

'Since then I've spent all my time writing', I said.

'Get away!' Sakerdon Mikhailovich exclaimed in an exaggerated tone. 'It's a pleasure to behold a genius.'

'You bet!', I said.

'Scribbled much?' asked Sakerdon Mikhailovich.

'I have', I said. 'I've got through masses of paper.'

'Here's to a genius of our time', said Sakerdon Mikhailovich, raising his glass.

- Ведь я последний раз ел вчера, с вами в подвальчике, и с тех пор ничего еще не ел, – сказал я.

- Да, да, да, – сказал Сакердон Михайлович.

- Я все время писал, – сказал я.

- Черт побери! – утрированно вскричал Сакердон Михайлович. – Приятно видеть перед собой гения.

- Еще бы! – сказал я.

- Много поди наваляли? – спросил Сакердон Михайлович.

- Да, – сказал я, – исписал пропасть бумаги.

- За гения наших дней, – сказал Сакердон Михайлович, поднимая рюмку. (p. 412)

It is not until the closing scene of *The Old Woman* that the story's carnivalesque ambiance is finally, and definitively dissipated, however.[88] As the narrator crosses himself, thanking God for the miracle from which he has just benefited, it is obvious that he is not to be 'recrowned'. This is because the miracle has provided the answer to both questions which this deceptively wise man has been trying to answer throughout Kharms's menippean satire. On the one hand, it has shown him that God exists, and can even perform miracles (God does indeed move in mysterious ways!). On the other, it reinforces the fact that even as a writer, he is at the mercy of God, the Word with which everything began, and the ultimate author who alone has the power to determine the end of the story.[89] Since by definition the menippean satire has universal significance, the dual truth disclosed at the end of *The Old Woman* has ramifications not just for Kharms, but for all writers, including all those to which Kharms has alluded throughout his tale.

With *The Old Woman*, then, Kharms bangs the final nail into the coffin of authorial authority. He subverts the notion of the author as creative subject in a less overtly political, but far more radical way than that advocated by the left-art movement with which OBERIU had appeared to be allying itself in January 1928; theorists such as Brik and Chuzhak never questioned the writer's ethical or epistemological credentials, and prescribed a rigidly realist, 'journalistic' mode of writing entirely alien to Kharms. Perhaps it was because he sensed that he had now definitively 'uncrowned' the figure of the writer, that Kharms wrote relatively little after *The Old Woman*. The reasons for his virtual silence as a writer after 1939 remain unclear. Something which can be said with far greater certainty is that by interweaving the themes of time, death, God, and story-telling in *The Old Woman*, Kharms calls to mind his fellow *Oberiut*, Aleksandr Vvedensky. It is Vvedensky, and his brand of metafiction, which I shall now discuss.

WHAT A TIME TO TELL A STORY: ALEKSANDR VVEDENSKY

Just as in Kharms's fiction, many of Vvedensky's characters also tell stories. Only occasionally, however, are these characters also *writers*. One such is 'Griboedov', who appears in Vvedensky's dramatic poem 'The Eyewitness and the Rat' ('Ochevidets i krysa').[90] This text in fact gives a clue to a major difference between Kharms and Vvedensky; whereas the former focuses on story-tell*ers*, the latter explores story-tell*ing*.

In particular, Vvedensky challenges the way in which many stories are conventionally narrated, since they are based on the assumption that time is linear and finite.[91] It is this notion of time which is parodied in 'The Eyewitness', not so much in the figure of the writer, as in that of the 'historian'. When one of the characters attempts to establish whether or not a murder has just taken place,[92] the answer which she receives reads like a caricature of the historian's view of time, as a blind succession of years (with an irrelevant concluding comment added for good measure):

KOSTOMAROV (HISTORIAN).
    Thirteen years.
    Twelve years.
    Fifteen years.
    Sixteen years.
    All around is nothing but shrubbery.

Костомароб (историк).
   Тринадцать лет.
   Двенадцать лет.
   Пятнадцать лет.
   Шестнадцать лет.
   Кругом одни кустарники.

This response is followed immediately by a passage of incoherent babble from the 'writer' Griboedov, who seems to make no more sense than the historian:

GRIBOEDOV (WRITER).

   There's no question about it,
   It's clear he's a thief.
   Thick magical visions
   are visiting my soul.
   Inexplicable aching pleasures
   Are what they promise me.
   They have my mind in a whirl,
   I myself am now like a squirrel in a wheel.
   Otherworldly creations, go away,
   I am leaving for Georgia today like everyone else.

Грибоедов (Писатель)

   О чем тут быть может разговор,
   ясно что он вор.
   Крутые волшебные виденья
   мне душу посещают.
   Неизъяснимые больные наслажденья
   они мне обещают.
   Мой ум они вскружили,
   я сам теперь как белка в колесе.
   Создания нездешние уйдите,
   я еду в Грузию сегодня как и все.   (p. 122)[93]

The nature of time is a question to which, as we shall see, Vvedensky returns throughout his *oeuvre*. For Vvedensky, an adequate, non-linear understanding of time is essential if we are fully to comprehend the world and tell the right kind of narratives about that world (whether as stories or as *histories*). Such understanding, he maintains, is clearly not guaranteed by the conventional ways in which we think and talk. As he put it in his 'Grey Notebook', in one of the many comments concerning the nature of time which the notebook contains: 'Our human logic and language do not correspond to time, not in any sense, basic or complex. Our logic and language slide over the surface of time' ('Nasha chelovecheskaya logika i nash yazyk ne sootvetstvuyut vremeni ni v kakom, ni v elementarnom, ni v slozhnom ego ponimanii. Nasha logika i nash yazyk skol'zyat po poverkhnosti vremeni'; p. 184).[94]

For Vvedensky, the key to comprehending existence is to realize that human time is in fact annulled, made meaningless, by the inevitability of death and the eternal life to which it leads.[95] As the tsar expresses it, in Vvedensky's play _All Around Maybe God_ (_Krugom vozmozhno Bog_): 'It really is a heavy blow / To think that you are steam. / That you will die and [therefore] do not exist' ('Eto deistvitel'no tyazhelyi udar / podumat' chto ty par. / Chto ty umresh' i tebya net').[96] Such an understanding of time was precisely what Vvedensky felt distinguished him from others (as a thinker, rather than as a writer). As he expressed it, in a comment made at one of the _chinari_ meetings:

I have understood how I am different from previous writers, and from people in general. They would say: life is an instant in comparison with eternity. I say: life is in an absolute sense an instant, even in comparison with an instant.

Я понял, чем отличаюсь от прошлых писателей, да и вообще людей. Те говорили: жизнь – мгновение в сравнении с вечностью. Я говорю: она вообще мгновение, даже в сравнении с мгновением. (Vvedensky _PSS_, vol. II, p. 251)

Vvedensky's assertion has ramifications not just for human history, but for all the stories which his characters relate and which we as humans tell. It is in his early dramatic work, _Minin and Pozharsky_, that Vvedensky most systematically explores those ramifications.

DIALOGUES OF THE DEAD: VVEDENSKY'S _MININ AND POZHARSKY_

One of Vvedensky's earliest surviving pieces, _Minin and Pozharsky_ (_Minin i Pozharsky_) was written shortly after its author first met

Kharms (the manuscript is dated May–July 1926).[97] As is the case with much of Vvedensky's *oeuvre*, *Minin and Pozharsky* is written in dialogue, approximately half of which is also in verse. Vvedensky presents the reader with a number of characters belonging to different cultures and historical periods, who appear to co-exist, and engage in dialogue, on an extra-temporal plane.[98] These characters include the Roman emperor Nero (AD 37–68), who converses with a tsarist Russian officer; Boris Godunov (*c.* 1552–1605); the Indian poet and philosopher Rabindranath Tagore (1861–1941); a certain 'Prince Men'shikov' (perhaps Prince Aleksandr Danilovich Menshikov, 1673–1729, or Prince Aleksandr Sergeevich Menshikov, 1787–1869)[99]; a torch-bearer; and the driver of a steam train. Also mentioned are: the medieval Russian prince Vladimir Monomakh (1053–1125); Catherine the Great (1729–96); a certain 'Ermolov', who may be General Aleksey Ermolov (1777–1861); Prince Andrey Kurbsky (1528–83; he fled to Poland during the reign of Ivan the Terrible); and 'the second son of Count Sheremet'ev' (the Sheremet'evs were a Russian noble family, the most famous member of which was Boris Petrovich Sheremet'ev, 1652–1719, a military commander and diplomat). There is, finally, a character named 'Petrov' (perhaps an oblique reference to Peter the Great), who is mentioned four times in what could be section headings: 'Petrov in civilian dress', 'Petrov in military dress', 'Petrov in judge's dress', and 'Petrov in spiritual dress' ('Petrov v shtatskom plat'e', 'Petrov voennom plat'e', 'Petrov v sudeiskom plat'e', and 'Petrov v dukhovnom plat'e'; pp. 5, 9, 14, and 18 respectively).

The eponymous heroes call to mind two important figures of seventeenth-century Russian history.[100] Kuz'ma Minin (date of birth unknown) was a butcher who settled in Yaroslavl, where he died in 1616.[101] Dmitry Mikhailovich Pozharsky (1578–1642), on the other hand, was a prince and a commander in the tsar's army. Together they led the Second People's Militia, which succeeded in the summer of 1611 in forcing the Polish, Swedish, and Lithuanian forces out of Moscow, where they had massed in order to crown Vladislav, son of the Polish king Sigismund

III, as Tsar of Russia. Their statue stands in front of St Basil's at one end of Red Square in Moscow.[102] Although *Minin and Pozharsky* does actually contain characters with these names, the events for which they are famous are nowhere even mentioned in the text. What Vvedensky gives us, furthermore, is a text very different from anything resembling a piece of orthodox historical writing.

Any summary of *Minin and Pozharsky* can only be severely reductive. The text is highly fragmented; various characters and situations are introduced, only to disappear as unexpectedly as they appear. The text begins with a pie-seller calling for certain (unnamed) individuals to be strangled, after which a character named Veechka wonders whether women wear trousers. This is followed by the arrival of Prince Men'shikov, who informs us that he will not be needing his usual lullaby, before a certain Grekov recounts the circumstances surrounding his own death. It is not long before we are introduced to Minin, who declares he knows 'the law of the hours' ('zakon chasov'), and Pozharsky, who tells us, in a statement which runs contrary to his apparent social status as recorded in the history books, how depressing he finds life as a farm labourer (p. 6).[103] The reader's suspicion that these characters are all dead seems to be confirmed as Minin announces his incorporeality (p. 7). A 'governor' ('gubernator') subsequently describes himself lying dead on a battlefield, a scene elaborated upon by a civil servant, himself speaking 'the morning after his death' ('na sleduyushchee utro posle smerti').[104] After a seemingly incongruous reference to penguins, Grekov begins a long narrative featuring a dead nanny. His story, which also mentions an apparently androgynous English person ('nash anglichanka'), includes all sorts of language games and images (including an anecdote about a headless Pushkin). The mood then changes abruptly, with the stage direction, 'A district in the Urals. Hell.' ('Ural'skaya mestnost'. Ad.'; p. 9). The ambiance is immediately transformed once more, however, as a 'plebeikin' (from 'plebei', a 'plebeian') sings a folk song and engages in a brief and bawdy conversation with a woman named Varvarova. The musical theme continues, as a certain Nentsov sings a couple of

ditties and a 'brown-eyed cockerel' ('petukh kareglazyi') sings
about the second son of Count Sheremet'ev. The opening
theme of *Minin and Pozharsky* is then restated, as a military
ensign recounts a tale containing a reference to his own death.
He is answered by the Emperor Nero, who proceeds to engage
in conversation with a character called Portupeev, a fisherman,
and some 'country aunts' ('derevenskie teti') and 'country
muzhiks' ('derevenskie muzhiki'). Next comes mention of the
death of Nentsov, another dialogue consisting of a series of
apparent non-sequiturs, a long monologue by a character
called 'Courier-courier' ('Gonets-gonets'), and an anecdote
recounted by a certain Pershchebaldaev. To end, there is a very
short execution scene, in which Boris Godunov participates, a
brief conversation between some of the characters from
Gogol''s *The Government Inspector* (*Revizor*, 1836), a monologue in
unpunctuated verse by Minin (sitting on a shelf), a very short
discussion between Minin and Pozharsky about an unidentified
corpse, a short piece of dialogue in which it transpires that a
woman ('mummy') has been eaten by a crocodile, an exchange
of apparently unconnected comments by a number of different
characters, and, finally, another monologue, this time by
Pozharsky (perched on top of a cupboard). The theme of death
is maintained until the end of the text – Minin is described as
'half-killed' ('poluubityi'; p. 17), and 'mummy' declares 'now we
are not alive' ('nynche my ne zhivy'; p. 19).

Despite appearances, there are important connections
between *Minin and Pozharsky* and Kharms's *The Old Woman*.
Vvedensky's text (and much of the rest of his *oeuvre*) is constructed as a 'dialogue of the dead', an ancient dialogic genre
linked historically to menippean satire.[105] More importantly
Vvedensky's *Minin and Pozharsky* contains, like *The Old Woman*, a
number of parodical references to the works of canonical
Russian writers. As Anatoly Vishevsky has observed, for
example, there is an allusion to Pushkin's fairy-tales, 'Ruslan
and Lyudmila' ('Ruslan i Lyudmila') and 'The Golden Cockerel' ('Zolotoi petushok'), in the lines: 'the candle goes out and
Ruslana / lies in the grass like a cockerel' ('gasnet svechka i
Ruslana / petushkom v trave lezhit'; p. 13).[106] As in Kharms's

anecdotes, so in *Minin and Pozharsky* the image of Pushkin himself is debunked, with the character Grekov's comment, 'that [particular] Pushkin was headless' ('tot Pushkin byl bez golovy'; p. 8) – which hints at a multitude of different Pushkins – and the same Grekov's mock-plaintive, 'O Pushkin, Pushkin' (p. 7). Vvedensky also alludes to certain works by Gogol', including *Taras Bul'ba* (1835; p. 20), and *The Government Inspector* (pp. 16–17).[107] In his treatment of these texts, Vvedensky goes much further than pastiche or parody, altering them to such an extent that virtually nothing remains of the original. The (practically unrecognizable) conversation between characters purportedly from *The Government Inspector* demonstrates this particularly well:

The mayor, Khlestakov, and Mar'ya Antonovna with a flute (conversing on a hill in the Urals).

MAR'YA ANTONOVNA (*spitting at the flute*): And I will tell you dear Grigory and Yakovlevich Grigory, that you are a white-bearded and hefty man, as muscular as this terrain, although you click-clack your teeth, and I am leprous. I am hanging just like a gob of spittle.

MAYOR: Do not be afraid dear Fortepianushka, one way or the other, but if everything turns out alright I shall present you with a muff and the seventh little fire. You hold this fire in a subordinate position. They are making you a blouse there.

KHLESTAKOV: I am splitting my sides with laughter. Let us sit down for a while. I feel a little dizzy.

MAR'YA ANTONOVNA: You are far too fussy.

KHLESTAKOV: Play a little. And I will cover you in slobbery kisses.

MAR'YA ANTONOVNA: He like my flute is squeaking at her.

MAYOR (*runs about like a goat looking for a blade of grass*): I am curly-haired, curly-haired, take care of me little children. I am eating a ladies' man.

COMMANDANT: Enough of this. When in Rome, keep your mouth shut.[108]

Городничий, Хлестаков и Марья Антоновна с флейтой (разговаривают на уральской горке).

Марья Антоновна (*поплевавши на флейту*): И скажу вам дорогой Григорий и Яковлевич Григорий, что мужчина вы белобородый и осанистый, мускулистый как эта местность, но зубами вы щелк-щелк, и я опрокажена. Прямо как слюна повисаю.

Городничий: Не бойтесь дорогая Фортепьянушка, уж ли или нет не уж ли, а уж ли подарю я вам муфту и седьмой огонек. Вы держите сей огонек в придаточном положении. Там шьют вам кофту.

Хлестаков: Как смешно печенкам. Присядем. Я чуть качаюсь.

Марья Антоновна: Вы чересчур разборчивы.

Хлестакоб: Поиграйте. А я вас почмокаю.

Марья Антоновна: Он как моя флейта пищит ей.

Городничий (*бегает козлом ищет травки*): Курчавый я, курчавый, поберегите меня детки. Я ем ловеласа.

Комендант: Довольно. С волками жить, рот не разевай.
    (pp. 16–17)

As well as these literary references (if 'literary' is what they are!), *Minin and Pozharsky* also contains echoes of the ballad, the folk song, children's counting rhymes,[109] proverbs, march songs, Russian *balagan* and Greek tragedy, which makes it closer to Kharms's pseudo-historical play *The Comedy of the City of Petersburg* (see Vishevsky, 'Tradition in the Topsy-Turvy World of Two Oberiu Plays' pp. 357–8). Indeed, by their intertextual, fragmentary, and discontinuous nature, texts such as *Minin and Pozharsky* and *The Comedy of the City of Petersburg* radically decentre the 'author' as unified writing subject, in a way which looks forward, not just to Bakhtin's dialogism, but to the post-structuralist theories of authorship espoused by Roland Barthes and Michel Foucault. In particular, they appear to bear out Barthes' definition of the quintessential 'text':

a text is not a line of words releasing a single 'theological' meaning (the 'message' of the Author-God) but a multi-dimensional space in which a variety of languages, none of them original, blend and clash. The text is a tissue of quotations drawn from the innumerable centres of a culture.[110]

There is more to *Minin and Pozharsky*, however, than endless intertextual play. For Vvedensky is primarily concerned, not with historical writers, nor with the writer as a figure in the text, nor even with the activity of writing *per se*; rather he explores the human activity of story-telling in a general, abstract sense (albeit one which has far-reaching ramifications for the kind of writing and speaking practices to which he alludes in *Minin and Pozharsky*). Furthermore, what Vvedensky has to say about stories and story-telling in this text is intimately connected with his presentation of death and time.

Vvedensky's characters, though separated in space and time, are all brought together by death, and are presented languishing in what resembles the pre-Christian Underworld where some of them recount their own deaths, apparently awaiting Judgement Day ('we will meet there, in heaven', as the narrator himself declares; 'Tam v rayu uvidimsya', p. 19). Death, as the tsar in *All Around Maybe God* ruefully observes, is indeed a great leveller – of history, as much as of historical figures. It is only in death that Nero, for example, can talk with a tsarist Russian officer, for death means that time is irrelevant.

Since they are all dead, these historical characters can no longer do what made them famous, that is, act, and instead find themselves condemned to 'do' nothing but talk. As they speak, they all, and none more so than the eponymous heroes, narrate mini-texts, embedded stories which appear just as discontinuous as the text which embeds them (the macro-text of *Minin and Pozharsky* itself). Indeed, in their role as tellers of stories, the description of Minin speaking from up on a shelf, and Pozharsky, once he has found his pouch of pipe tobacco, declaiming from on top of a cupboard, may be a veiled reference to Vvedensky and Kharms themselves; Kharms liked to declaim his poetry at literary evenings sitting on a cupboard smoking a pipe (as he did, for example, at the 'Three Left Hours' show).[111] The only thing, in fact, that happens in *Minin and Pozharsky* is that stories are told: context is subsumed by, and disappears behind, text.

Yet the subject of so many of these narratives is death. The suggestion here is that nothing else but death – the moment when we pass from the infinitely brief time of life to the infinitely vast time of the after life – really exists. For Vvedensky, as the following extract from his 'Grey Notebook' indicates, death renders time meaningless: 'A miracle is possible at the moment of death. It is possible because death is the stopping of time' ('Chudo vozmozhno v moment smerti. Ono vozmozhno potomu chto smert′ est′ ostanovka vremeni'; p. 185). Death means that time, properly speaking, does not exist, neither now, nor in the future, nor in the past. As time is non-existent it is ineffable, and the only thing that we can hope to be able to express in language is death, since death is, for Vvedensky, that which stands outside time, that 'miraculous' moment when time stops, and yet, paradoxically, the only time we have: 'a person dying at eighty, and a person dying at ten years old both have just a second in which they die' ('umir-ayushchii v vosem′desyat let, i umirayushchii v 10 let, kazhdyi imeet tol′ko sekundu smerti'; p. 187).

The notion that life can be measured in units of time is ridiculed at one important moment in *Minin and Pozharsky*. Pointing to a corpse, Pozharsky asks Minin about the man's life:

POZHARSKY: How many years did he live?
MININ: Nines of years he lived.
POZHARSKY: How many years did he live?
ANSWER: And we ourselves are like thoughts.

Пожарский: Сколько лет жил?
Минин: Девятки лет жил.
Пожарский: Сколько лет жил?
Ответ: И сами мы словно мысли. (p. 18)

The repetition of the semantic unit 'let zhil', which appears in both questions and in the first reply; the reiteration of the question, even as it seems to have been answered; the use of the word 'skol′ki' instead of 'skol′ko', and 'devyatki' for the stan-dard 'desyatki' ('tens'); and the 'absurd' prospect of an answer uttering itself (a common feature of Vvedensky's dialogues): all this points to the meaninglessness of questions such as Pozhars-ky's and the the stupidity of the linear, sequential view of time (life) which informs them.[112]

Instead of strictly linear time, we have in *Minin and Pozharsky* a number of different contexts, of places and times, which appear to exist simultaneously. One way in which Vvedensky achieves a sense of simultaneity is by presenting the reader with contradictory situations or statements which appear to be true at the same time. The character Varvarova, for example, appears as sexually mature while still in fact a baby, as she crawls out of her cot to implore:

> Give me a boy
> a child of love
> so that the boy with his finger
>
> мне дайте мальчика
> дитю любви
> чтоб мальчик пальчиком   (p. 8)

Similarly, in the song which the 'brown-eyed cockerel' sings, one of the characters, a certain Shpazhetsky, is at the same time his own grandson: 'And Shpazhetsky would run onto the bridge / and he was Shpazhetsky's grandson' ('I begal Shpazhetsky na most / i byl on Shpazhetskogo vnuk'; p. 12).

More generally, a sense of simultaneity also arises from the fragmentary structure of the text of *Minin and Pozharsky*. The absence of any teleological plot means that each segment of the text, each scene or dialogue, is given equal status. The disruption of communication, so central a feature of Vvedensky's *oeuvre*, is instrumental here in creating an impression of a number of different conversations all taking place at once. To give detailed accounts of these dialogues would serve little practical purpose here. It is worth, however, quoting just one in order to give an idea of the extent of discursive discontinuity underpinning Vvedensky's dialogues and the sense of simultaneity – of different, isolated conversations occurring at the same time – which textual disruptions inevitably create:

PORTUPEEV: It's the serving girls who gave birth to them.

COMMANDANT: I am reading the cards; she loves me, she loves me not. Let's go to bed.

FISHERMAN (*sitting down on a sweep-net*): I shall not give you a fish. I shall find my own lot in life. Not on the mountain, not on the watermeadow.

VILLAGE AUNTS: Well, the war started there.

VILLAGE MUZHIKS: And was it that particular regiment which passed through.

BEAR-CUBS ON LITTLE WHEELS (*the whole Bottle family*): Goodbye we are leaving now.

Портупеев: Это горничные девки их нарожали.
Комендант: Гадаю, Люба я или нет? Давайте спать ложиться.
Рыбак (*садясь на невод*): Я вам рыбы не дам. Я свою долю найду.
  Не на горе, не на лугу в воде.
Деревенские Тети: Что ж там и война началась.
Деревенские Мужики: Да тот ли полк прошел.
Медвежата На Колесиках (*вся семья Бутылкиных*): Прощайте вот
  мы уходим. (p. 13)

As well as constituting a good example of the seemingly
arbitrary way in which Vvedensky constructs his dialogues and
narratives, this excerpt also serves to demonstrate the way in
which deictic markers are often used to refer to elements of the
context to which the reader never has any access. What is
meant, for example, by 'them' ('ikh'; line 1), or by 'there' ('tam';
line 5)? Such language creates an impression not just of a
multitude of simultaneous dialogues, but also of a plethora of
contexts/intertexts relevant at any one time, contexts to which
the reader has only partial, intermittent access.[113]

Linearity is displaced in *Minin and Pozharsky* not just by the
suggestion of simultaneity, however, but also by the sense of
infinity which Vvedensky at times evokes. This effect is achieved
by the erasure of context, and particularly of any sense of
narrative beginning and ending, which such displacement
inevitably produces. This absence of a beginning or end is
reinforced in the text linguistically; the word 'them' ('ikh') in
the very first line of *Minin and Pozharsky* sends the reader to a
context which precedes this line, while the absence of either
a verb or a full stop in the final two lines of the text creates a
sense of continuation.

There are also, however, specific discursive features of *Minin
and Pozharsky* which help produce this sense of infinity. In
particular, Vvedensky manipulates grammar, and especially the
system of verbal tenses. Verbs, as words implying action taking
place in time, hold a particularly important place in Vvedensky's
poetics. As Vvedensky himself asserted in his 'Grey Notebook',
in a comment on his own writing: 'Verbs are dying out before
our very eyes. In art the plot and action are in the process
of disappearing. Those actions which appear in my own verse

are illogical and serve no purpose. They should not even be called actions' ('Glagoly na nashikh glazakh dozhivayut svoi vek. V iskusstve syuzhet i deistvie ischezayut. Te deistviya, kotorye est' v moikh stikakh, nelogichny i bespolezny, ikh nel'zya nazvat' deistviyami'; p. 186).

Tenses seem to be used arbitrarily in *Minin and Pozharsky*, as the narrator switches unexpectedly and bewilderingly between past, present, and future (thereby further problematizing the temporal relationship between the act of narration and the object of narration). One of the very first stage directions reads: 'the nuns are silent and have left' ('monashki molchat i ushli'; p. 6). Elsewhere, the narration switches between the present and the future: 'the wayfarers [...] will sit down and there they go on and on about their affairs' ('putniki [...] syadut i tam sverlyat svoi dela'; p. 16). The corollary of everything happening or simply standing outside of time is, of course, nothing taking place, or even existing, within time. This concept is expressed particularly succinctly by the absence of a verb, in a phrase such as 'The commandant one day.' ('Komendant odnazhdy.'; p. 13).

Why does Vvedensky disrupt temporality so extensively? He may be said to be subverting not just isolated texts, but all discursive practices which rely on a linear understanding of time, be they the works of Pushkin and Gogol', the *balagan*, Greek tragedy, folk songs, or children's counting rhymes.[114] Beyond this, the paradox at the heart of Vvedensky's pseudo-historical play is that only the dead can hope to produce authentic narratives, since only their words, expressed in a timeless realm, and expressing an event taking place outside time (their own death) can escape time and its vice-like grip on human cognition. It is not so much that death is the end of the story; rather, death means that there can be no story, since there is no time, at least not in any 'reasonable' sense. With its fragmentary, discontinuous structure and its otherworldly chronotope, *Minin and Pozharsky* both suggests this and puts itself forward as an alternative discursive practice.

Vvedensky's dead story-tellers have brought us a long way from Mayakovsky's bus-journeying poets, Bakhterev's Gogolian

narrators, or even Kharms's sadistic scribblers. While
Vvedensky echoes Kharms in his use of intertextuality to
decentre the authoring subject, his metafiction is considerably
more abstract. Whereas Kharms, in his explicit challenge to the
authority of the writer, appears to echo certain aspects of late
left art, Vvedensky's metafiction looks back to the heady
experimentalism of early left art, and beyond that, to
Kruchenykh's Futurist opera, *Victory over the Sun*. This may well
have been what Zabolotsky had in mind when he referred to
Vvedensky, in the OBERIU article, as standing on the 'extreme
left' of the association (*Minin and Pozharsky*, written in the
previous year, will presumably have been one of the works upon
which Zabolotsky based his judgement). However, in order to
complete my study of the images of authorship which emerge in
OBERIU metafiction, I must now turn to Vaginov. As with
Kharms, but not Vvedensky, Vaginov's characters are themselves frequently writers. Unlike either Kharms or Vvedensky,
Vaginov's view of the writer evolves from something resembling
Romanticism to a brand of cultural materialism which the
theorists of late left art would surely have welcomed.

THE ARTIST AS HERMIT: KONSTANTIN VAGINOV

If, as Tat'yana Nikol'skaya has observed, 'the central theme of
Vaginov's *oeuvre* remained constantly that of art and art's place
in the modern world', then an intrinsic element of that theme
was the artist himself.[115] The paralysing fear experienced in the
early 1920s by the poet as a member of the Soviet *intelligentsia*
(and one formerly close to the executed Gumilev)[116] is given
stark expression in an early poem:

> It is morning once again. Once again a piece of dawn on
>   the sheet of paper.
> Only my heart is not beating. It would seem to be tired.
> It is not beating at all. . . I have even grown afraid,
> And have fallen.
>
> The table on the right – is breathing, the chair on the left
>   – is breathing.

That's funny! But I am not laughing.
I am calm once more.

Снова утро. Снова кусок зари на бумаге.
Только сердце не бьется. По-видимому устало.
Совсем не бьется... даже испугался,
Упал.

Стол направо – дышит, стул налево – дышит.
Смешно! а я не смеюсь.
Успокоился.[117]

In a poem from a collection dated four years later, Vaginov
appears to have overcome such anxiety, as his heart beats with
renewed strength, filled with love for the god of poetry himself:

> Glory to you, Apollo, glory!
> My heart is full of great love.
> [...]
> I was weak, but now I am stronger than a young ox,
> [...]
> In the evenings I listen to the muses' singing.
> Glory to you, Apollo, glory!

> Слава тебе, Аполлон, слава!
> Сердце мое великой любовью полно.
> [...]
> Слабым я был, но теперь сильнее быка молодого,
> [...]
> По вечерам слушаю пение муз.
> Слава тебе, Аполлон, слава![118]

Despite this expression of confidence, however, the image of
the artist most frequently found in Vaginov's early work is one
of a poet alienated, desperately trying to survive and preserve
his art against appalling adversity, in the midst of a city ravaged
by revolution and civil war. At times Vaginov appears defiant,
such as in this poem, written in 1922:

> I live as a hermit at 105 Ekaterina canal.
> Outside the windows camomile and wild clover are
>   growing,
> From beyond the smashed stone gates
> I can hear the cries of Georgia and Aizerbaidzhan.

[...]
I have nothing to do, and I shall go and pray awhile
And kiss the cypress cross.
[...]
I have no need of anything – I am young
And proud of my troubled soul [...]

Живу отшельником Екатерининский канал 105.
За окнами растет ромашка, клевер дикий,
Из-за разбитых каменных ворот
Я слышу Грузии Азербайджана крики.
[...]
Мне делать нечего, пойду и помолюсь
И кипарисный крестик поцелую.
[...]
Мне ничего не надо – молод я
И горд своей душою неспокойной [...][119]

Such pride is coupled with a muted optimism in the ability of the 'true', non-conformist writer to survive all kinds of oppression, if not physically, then at least through his words (inspired by a higher, transcendent authority):

O, make into a ringing statue
My shell, Lord,
So that after its open captivity
It might stand and sing
About its beloved life,
About its marvellous [female] friend,
Under the protection of the emerald night,
By the gates of the Babylon wall.

О, сделай статуей звенящей
Мою оболочку, Господь,
Чтоб после отверстого плена
Стояла и пела она
О жизни своей ненаглядной,
О чудной подруге своей,
Под сенью смарагдовой ночи,
У врат Вавилонской стены. [120]

The vision of the indomitable artist, contained in these lines, is given further expression in another early poem, 'Art' ('Iskusstvo'):

I do not love the stars. I love remote houses
And town squares as red-gold as the night.
I am not yet dead and buried. Not for me have the bells
    wheezed
And lashed the night with their tongues.

I know, I am an island in the midst of the scarlet
    thunderstorm
Of Venus, of the Muses and of eternal fire.
I am strong, I am not to be broken by a rebellious storm.
Gardens still ring in my eyes.

Я звезды не люблю. Люблю глухие домы
И площади червонные, как ночь.
Не погребен. Не для меня колокола хрипели
И языками колотили ночь.

Я знаю, остров я среди кумачной бури
Венеры, Муз и вечного огня.
Я крепок, не сломать меня мятежной буре.
Еще сады в моих глазах звенят.

(p. 82)

In his early poetry Vaginov appears to have faith in art –
'true' art, rather than the red, Bolshevik kind – as an autonomous, timeless cultural force.[121] The subject of one poem dated
February 1923, for example, is the 'vine-like verse' ('vinogradnyi
stikh'):

Like a fierce bull hurtling over walls,
The vine-like verse fell onto the town square.
What must we do, with what harsh retribution
Shall we return to it the sparkle of its glory?
We will forge into it sombre tunes,
Ancient, iron words,
So that it might chime, so that its veins might swell,
So that its blood might flow like thick gold.
It will not die, but will become wild and dark.
And the words will reside in its breast,
And it raises its voice, and with its voice it will resemble
A tidal wave, destroying buildings.

Крутым быком пересекая стены,
Упал на площадь виноградный стих.
Что делать нам, какой суровой карой
Ему сиянье славы возвратим?

Мы закуем его в тяжелые напевы,
В старинные чугунные слова,
Чтоб он звенел, чтоб надувались жилы,
Чтоб золотом густым переливалась кровь.
Он не умрет, но станет дик и темен.
И будут жить в груди его слова,
И возвышает голос он, и голосом подобен
Набегу волн, сбивающих дома.   (p. 127)

Despite the instrumental role played by the poet in reviving the verse, Vaginov's faith in art does not, ultimately, extend to the artist. In the third stanza of 'Art', Vaginov subjugates his artistic persona to universal 'Man'. And in the later work, 'The Song of Words' ('Pesnya slov', 1927), it is words themselves – 'old' words, 'young' words, and 'the word in a theatrical costume' ('slovo v teatral'nom kostyume')[122] – which engage in their own struggle for supremacy, while the poet cowers in his cellar with his books (pp. 171–4). Works such as 'The Song of Words' seem to suggest that it is poetry and the poetic word which will rise again like the phoenix – independently of the poet.

Despite the occasional expressions of defiant optimism to be found in his verse written up to the mid 1920s, Vaginov's loss of confidence in the power of the artist, and his eventual shift to a radically different view of art can be said to have begun as early as 1922. In that year he composed two works in prose, namely 'The Star of Bethlehem' ('Zvezda Vifleema'), and 'The Monastery of our Lord Apollo' ('Monastyr' Gospoda nashego Apollona').[123] Implicit to a greater or lesser extent in each is the analogy between the destruction of pagan culture by the first Christians in ancient Rome, and the attacks on Christian culture perpetrated by the Bolsheviks in post-revolutionary Russia. 'The Star of Bethlehem', made up of thirty-seven short prose segments (numbered 1–5 in the introduction, and 1–32 in the main body of the text), describes Peter's city in the grip of a 'new religion'. The narrator, himself a poet, weaves a highly fragmentary, episodic narrative which conflates different places and times, mixing together Imperial Rome, ancient Greece, medieval Spain, Renaissance Italy, France, and Soviet

Petrograd (in a manner which calls to mind Vvedensky's *Minin and Pozharsky*, albeit with a different emphasis). Vaginov, for example, describes an 'Athenian night' on a 'Finnish shore' ('Finskii breg, Afinskaya noch''; segment no. 17, p. 496), and depicts three contemporary Russian poets as members of the seventeenth-century Italian literary academy, 'Arkadiya' (segment no. 18, ibid.). The figure of Philostratus (the biographer of Apollonius of Tyana, ardent defender of the pagan world and its culture against the onslaught of Christianity in first-century Greece) is described walking around Petersburg and its environs – the empty streets, the Summer Garden, and Pavlovsk.[124] Despite the overlap between different places and eras, what this text suggests is that there can be no return to the past; Philostratus cries for the cities 'which will never return' ('kotorye nikogda ne vernutsya'; section no. 30, p. 499). The poet is helpless to prevent change; all he can do is chronicle it, albeit as a privileged observer, one whose stature, like Philostratus', fills the sky.

'The Monastery of our Lord Apollo', which is also structured as a series of numbered segments, is a text which blurs the distinction between myth and reality. It constitutes a call-to-arms addressed by the narrator to his fellow artists, to restore the glory of the god of poetry through poetic creativity in an age when, as he observes, science has gained precedence over the arts. At first the narrator and his brotherhood of monks appear to succeed in curing the body of Apollo of the ills of modernity, namely the motor cars and rail tracks sticking out of his broken leg, the oil in his blood, and syphilis. One by one, however, the narrator's brothers die in their cells, as does Apollo himself. Despite the narrator's earlier strictures on the skills the poet needs, he finds it 'terrifying' to live, 'a dead man among the living' ('strashno zhit' mertvetsu sredi zhivykh'; p. 487). If he strives to preserve a hackneyed, Romantic notion of the poet by adopting the persona of a wandering minstrel with his lyre, he admits that his soul can no longer hear what he sings. This less than optimistic view of the poet's role in the new society is complete when the narrator abandons his song to give a scientific lecture on peonies, and, at the very end, describes himself and his fellow poets selling bundles of their poems in order to eat (an image reminiscent of Pushkin's poet in his 'Conversation between a Bookseller and a Poet').

These two prose works were followed, three years later, by the dramatic poem, 'The Year 1925' ('Tysyacha devyat'sot dvadtsat' pyatyi god').[125] In this work, Vaginov pits both Philostratus and Apollo, as upholders of the cultural tradition, against representatives of the new, Philistine society, in the guise of a character called Teptelkin, and a factory foreman. Teptelkin tells Philostratus that he should concern himself with politics, while the foreman promises that the new regime will crush those who put art above industry. Philostratus remains defiant, however, in his efforts to uphold the values of the 'old world', while Apollo and the other gods look on apparently helplessly.

'The Year 1925' is not just, as Anemone has claimed, a transitional work between Vaginov's poetry and his prose. In the way in which it inscribes radically divergent ideological discourses, and particularly in the fact that the foreman's words go unchallenged, this text signals a further shift in Vaginov's conception of the artist. Essentially, this shift takes Vaginov from Romanticism (a view of the artist as an individual inspired by a higher authority, whose tormented creativity sets him apart from the society in which he lives) to cultural materialism (in which art offers no prospect of transcendence, and the artist's voice is just another social discourse). To see how Vaginov's view of art and the artist develops through his middle period to his final years, I shall now take a closer look at his novels.

THE AUTHOR LOSES HIS VOICE: THE NOVELS OF KONSTANTIN VAGINOV

Vaginov's first novel, *The Goat's Song* (*Kozlinaya pesn'*), was written between 1926 and 1927, approximately at the time that he became acquainted with the Bakhtin circle and the future members of OBERIU (Vaginov revised it slightly in 1929). Indeed, it has been read as a *roman à clef* satirizing, *inter alia*, the activities of those two groups.[126] As well as gently lampooning real-life writers, Vaginov turns his attention in *The Goat's Song* both to the role of the writer in post-revolutionary Russia and, on a more abstract plane, to the place of the author in the text.

The story concerns the plight of members of the old Russian *intelligentsia* in the aftermath of the Bolshevik Revolution. Vaginov's heroes cling desperately to lofty and increasingly outmoded notions of art and the artist. In general, they believe that art is a purely personal matter, the result of a creative impulse and as such untainted by social reality. In a similar vein, their concept of the artist is of an autonomous and apolitical subject. They imagine themselves to be a cultural élite, 'the last island of the Renaissance' ('poslednii ostrov Renessansa'), as one of them puts it.[127] Vaginov's first novel shows these characters' 'tragic' fate (the title, 'Goat's Song', is a literal translation of the Ancient Greek word for 'tragedy'), as their cultural ideology becomes increasingly anachronistic in the new Soviet era.

One of the most important characters in the group, Teptelkin, is a writer and bibliophile with a passion for classical antiquity and Renaissance Italy. He feels so out of place in Soviet Leningrad, so cut off from the world in which he lives, that he isolates himself on the outskirts of Leningrad in his dacha, which he refers to as his 'tower'.[128] Teptelkin and his closest friend, the so-called 'unknown poet' ('neizvestnyi poet'), compare the wanton, barbarous destruction of pagan culture by the first Christians with the annihilation of pre-revolutionary art and society by Lenin and the Bolsheviks, (thereby echoing an important theme of Vaginov's earlier writing).[129] Teptelkin is dismissive of 'new' writers in the Soviet era as soulless Philistines, while the unknown poet still clings to the view that literature (in his case, poetry) is a particular cultural practice which stands above the merely social, political, or economic, and offers the true poet real transcendence: 'Poetry is a special business [...] you take a few words, put them together in an unusual way [...] and you are swallowed up in the completely new world revealed beyond those words' ('Poeziya – eto osoboe

zanyatie [...] voz'mesh' neskol'ko slov, neobyknovenno sopos-
tavish' [...] i pogloshchaet tebya sovershenno novyi mir,
raskryvayushchiisya za slovami'; pp. 82–3).

In *The Goat's Song* Vaginov appears to draw a stark contrast
between these righteous upholders of literary and cultural
tradition and the shallow, unprincipled conformists of the new
régime. For example, the sincerity of the unknown poet's views
is contrasted with the superficiality of the poet called 'September', who composes Symbolist verse without knowing the
first thing about Symbolism, and subsequently proclaims
himself a Futurist. Then there is the critic Asfodeliev (whose
name may come from 'asphodel', the flower of death in Greek
legend), who confesses to the unknown poet that the critical
articles which he writes for literary journals amount to no more
than intellectual prostitution: '[...] I turn out journal articles
under a pseudonym. [...] I praise proletarian literature, I write
not just that it will flourish, but that it already is flourishing. I
[...] get paid for that' ('[...] stateiki v zhurnalakh pod psevdo-
nimom popisyvayu. [...] Khvalyu proletliteraturu, pishu, chto
ee rastsvet ne tol'ko budet, no uzhe est''. Za eto [...] den'gi
platyat'; p. 81). No wonder Teptelkin and the others continually
curse modernity and, sequestered in their 'tower', turn their
utopian gaze to the distant Renaissance. The unknown poet
expresses their disgust and disillusionment at the new régime
and its representatives: 'What a generation is growing up now!
They have no humanism, they are future true representatives of
the middle ages, fanatics, barbarians, unenlightened by the
humanities' ('Ekoe pokolenie rastet, bez vsyakogo gumanizma,
budushchie istinnye predstaviteli srednevekov'ya, fanatiki,
varvary, ne prosveshchennye svetom gumanitarnykh nauk';
p. 36).

Such reactionary views expressed by Vaginov's characters
are echoed by the so-called 'author', who intervenes in the
novel at various stages (interventions which led a number
of scholars to view *The Goat's Song* either as a novel about its
own creation, or as a text depicting the process of literary
creation in general).[130] As he remarks in his 'foreword' ('predislovie'): 'I do not like Petersburg, my dream is over' ('Ne lyublyu

ya Peterburga, konchilas' mechta moya'; p. 12). The present is
of no consequence or interest to this author figure; he can only
write about that which is now dead: 'Now there is no Petersburg. There is only Leningrad; but Leningrad does not concern
us – the author is by profession a maker of coffins, not cradles'
('Teper' net Peterburga. Est' Leningrad; no Leningrad nas ne
kasaetsya – avtor po professii grobovshchik, a ne kolybel'nykh
del master'; p. 13).[131]

Vaginov, then, seems to be reacting in *The Goat's Song*
against modernity (and especially the Bolshevik variety),[132]
reasserting the importance of the writer in society, and, in an
analogous move, reinserting the author at the centre of the
text. Yet in this novel, Vaginov undercuts such lofty notions of
art and the artist, and he does so through irony. In this way,
the 'tragedy' of Teptelkin and the unknown poet unfolds into a
'tragicomedy'.[133]

Vaginov subverts his 'islanders'' cultural élitism in a number
of ways, but primarily through the figure of the unknown poet.
For this character, art means creation through inspiration,
which in turn necessitates complete abandonment of the self to
alcohol, sex, and madness. During his meeting with students of
literature, he expresses (if only to himself) his artistic credo in a
key passage which explicitly links libidinal self-indulgence,
mythological heroism, and literary creativity and just as explicitly marks off such 'knowledge' as inaccessible to the youth of
the Soviet era:

'I'm trapped', thought the unknown poet, turning to the window.
'This is not the place to talk about the affinity between poetry and
drunkenness', he thought. 'They won't understand anything if I start
to talk about the need to shape the world anew by means of the word,
about the descent into the hell of the absurd, into a hell full of wild
noises and wild howling, in order to find a new melody for the world.
They won't understand that, at all costs, the poet must be Orpheus
and descend into hell, albeit an artificial hell, enchant it and return
with Eurydice-art, and that, like Orpheus, he is condemned to turn
round and see the sweet vision disappear. Those who believe that art
is possible without a descent into hell are wrong.

'The means by which one isolates oneself and descends into hell are
alcohol, love, madness. . .'

Попался, – повернулся к окну неизвестный поэт. – Здесь нельзя
говорить о сродстве поэзии с опьянением, – думал он, – они
ничего не поймут, если я стану говорить о необходимости заново
образовать мир словом, о нисхождении во ад бессмыслицы, во ад
диких и шумов, и визгов, для нахождения новой мелодии мира.
Они не поймут, что поэт должен быть во что бы то ни стало
Орфеем и спуститься во ад, хотя бы искусственный, зачаровать
его и вернуться с Эвридикой-исскуством и что, как Орфей, он
обречен обернуться и увидеть, как милый призрак исчезает.
Неразумны те, кто думает, что без нисхождения во ад возможно
искусство.

Средство изолировать себя и спуститься во ад: алкоголь,
любовь, сумасшествие... (p. 72)

The unknown poet's posturing, and the Romanticism which
underpins it, are undercut by what follows, however. The poet
imagines himself at the court of Lorenzo the Magnificent, where
he is brought to account by writers such as Dante, Gogol', and
Juvenal for his activities as a poet during his own lifetime. It soon
emerges, moreover, that he is unworthy to be counted amongst
these 'greats'. As Dante puts it: 'There is no place for you among
us, in spite of all your art' ('Net tebe mesta sredi nas, nesmotrya
na vse tvoe iskusstvo'; p. 73). It is this sense of inferiority which
prompts Teptelkin's subsequent comment to the poet: 'It is not
worth grieving [...] I also believed that I would be able to carry
the flame of the Renaissance right to the end, and now look how
things have turned out' ('Ne stoit gorevat' [...] Ved' ya tozhe
dumal donesti ogonek vozrozhdeniya, a ved' vot chto polu-
chaetsya'; ibid.). This is one of the clearest admissions by any of
Teptelkin's circle of their inevitable failure to maintain and
perpetuate the cultural tradition which they hold so dear.

Vaginov also suggests that the persona which the unknown
poet seeks to cultivate is in no sense natural, but rather the
product of an artificial desire to emulate those cultural figures
of previous eras of whom he is in fact unworthy. Just like the
poet 'September', the unknown poet gets drunk in a conscious
effort to induce a particular state of mind. The poet's 'inspiration' turns out to be nothing but a sham, however. Instead of
providing a stimulus to his creativity, drunkenness makes the
poet sense his lack of creativity:

Even in his drunkenness he felt that he was a nonentity, that he was not visited by any great idea, [...] that there was no pedestal beneath his feet. He no longer treated wine properly, with self-respect, with the consciousness that he was doing a great deed, with the presentiment that he was about to discover something so beautiful that the world would be astonished. Wine now revealed to him his creative impotence, his inner baseness, his spiritual desolation

И в опьяненье он чувствовал свое ничтожество, никакая великая идея не осеняла его, [...] никакой пьедестал не появлялся под его ногами. Уже не чисто он подходил к вину, не с самоуважением, не с сознанием того, что он делает великое дело, не с предчувствием того, что он раскроет нечто такое прекрасное, что поразится мир, и вино теперь раскрывало ему собственное его творческое бессилие, собственную его душевную мерзость и духовное запустение (p. 132)

This is perhaps why the unknown poet eventually rejects his former poetry, and stops writing altogether, a detail made much more explicit in sections added in the later version of the novel contained in Vaginov, *Romany* (pp. 123 and 128–9, and 107 respectively).

In *The Goat's Song*, then, Vaginov adopts an ironic attitude towards his characters' Romantic vision of their role as writers and aesthetes in the new society. Similar ambivalence surrounds the figure of the author, whose voice is heard in the novel's prologue and reasserts itself at various stages in the novel. Just as Vaginov questions the cultural role which Teptelkin and the unknown poet ascribe to themselves, so he questions the author's textual authority.

It appears, for example, that the author shares the same world as his characters. This is suggested when the author converses with the unknown poet, who complains at having his name blackened for all posterity. Towards the end of the novel, he even has his characters over for dinner. Moreover, the author claims (although perhaps a little ironically) to share his characters' values: 'Like Teptelkin, I am an idealist. I have Kostya Rotikov's fine taste, the unknown poet's ideas, [the writer] Troitsyn's simple-mindedness. I am made out of the stuff of my heroes' ('ya po-Teptelkinski prekrasnodushen. Ya obladayu tonchaishim vkusom Kosti Rotikova, kontseptsiei neizvestnogo poeta, prostovatost'yu Troitsyna. Ya sdelan iz testa moikh geroev').[134]

In other ways, however, the implied author of *The Goat's Song* seems actually subordinate to the novel's characters, or at least to one of them. At one point, for example, the poet berates the author for being a 'professional man of letters' ('professional'nyi literator'; p. 40). During his conversation with Dante, the unknown poet declares 'I allowed the author to immerse us in the sea of life and laugh at us' ('Ya pozvolil avtoru pogruzit' v more zhizni nas i nad nami posmeyat'sya'; p. 73). (It is this, more than anything else, which prompts condemnation from Dante.) In fact, if the unknown poet is to be believed, it is he who brought the author into existence, and not the other way round: 'I engendered the author' ('ya porodil avtora'; ibid.), he affirms in the same speech. The impression which the unknown poet gives here is of a dialogically relative relationship between author and character. The question, 'who is authoring whom?', evoked here, may well be an allusion to Bakhtin's views on the author–hero relationship, which he expressed in an essay written shortly before *The Goat's Song* was begun:

Author and hero come together in life, entering lived-life, cognitive-ethical relations with each other, and contending with each other. This event ['co-being'] of their life, of their intensely serious relations and of their contention, crystallizes in an architectonically stable, but dynamically living and aesthetically significant relationship between author and hero. This relationship is extremely important for understanding the life of a work.[135]

In much the same way that the author's voice is determined by the characters which it articulates – or who now appear to articulate *it* – so the author's very status as 'author' is a function of the text which he writes. Whereas the author who pronounces the two 'prologues' is described as '*appearing*' ('*poyav-lyayushchi[i]sya*' (my italics); pp. 12–13), the pre-penultimate chapter (at least in the first version of the novel) is entitled 'Interword of the *Established* Author' ('Mezhduslovie *ustanovivshe-gosya* avtora'; Vaginov, *KP*, p. 177, my emphasis). This would appear to underline the fact that it is only by producing the novel that the writer can fully call himself 'author'. The author needs a text to author, very much as consciousness needs something to be conscious of, a point aptly made by Bakhtin in his 'Author and Hero' essay. In this very concrete sense, the author appears as a 'product' of the text, 'authored' by it despite his reference to 'my novel'. Significantly, the author does not appear to establish himself at all in the later version of the novel, in which all reference to the author is omitted from the title of the 'Interword' (Vaginov, *Romany*, p. 148).

The author's place at the centre of the creative process is thus questioned by Vaginov. By the end of *The Goat's Song*, the image of the author is not so much as a creator but as just one of many important elements in the production process. This is made more explicit in the first version of the novel, when, in the 'afterword' ('posleslovie'), the work is likened to a play, and the author described as joining the actors/characters on stage after a performance, before drinking a toast to high art with them (Vaginov, *KP*, pp. 194–5). In the second version, there is no afterword, merely a brief section appended to the final chapter, in which the author promises to tell another 'Petersburg fairy tale' ('peterburgskuyu skazku') very soon – if, that is, he can find anyone to listen (Vaginov, *Romany*, p. 161).

Whichever ending one takes, however, *The Goat's Song* appears to conform to Bakhtin's archetypal carnival narrative, in which, as we saw earlier, the author-carnival king is first crowned and then uncrowned, only for a recrowning to be glimpsed at the end of the story. What Vaginov would appear to be doing in *The Goat's Song*, then, is to 'carnivalize' Romantic notions of art and the artist, in other words to bring them *temporarily* 'down to earth' precisely in order that they may be renewed in a positive, regenerative fashion (however faint).[136] In his subsequent prose works, however, Vaginov increasingly rejects such notions, further liberating the text from the authority of the author by packing the text with alternative discourses, saturating it with other texts. It is in the last of Vaginov's four 'completed' novels, *Harpagoniana* (1934), that the author finally loses his 'voice' altogether.

The title of *Harpagoniana* (*Garpagoniana*)[137] is an allusion to Harpagon, the character at the centre of Molière's play *The*

Miser. However, the Leningrad which Vaginov depicts in this novel is inhabited not so much by misers, as by people who hoard or trade all kinds of kitsch and other manifestations of the banality of Soviet life, from toenails to wine labels, from May Day posters to enemas.

Structurally, *Harpagoniana* contains embedded within it a multitude of discourses, including a number of self-contained stories.[138] Many of these mini-narratives are uttered by an identified speaker, and are realistically motivated in the text. For example, chapter 13 begins with the description of the picture on one of the Japanese matchboxes belonging to the character Punshevich (the self-styled president of the 'Society for the Collection of Trivia'):

'That is the Sun, a goddess, the founder of Japan, the mother of the first emperor. Her younger brother offended her by throwing the pelt of an unclean animal into her chamber!'

Punshevich lit up a cigarette and continued:

'At that moment the goddess was weaving. She became angry and hid behind a rock. Then eternal night fell. The gods, her vassals, assembled and began to ponder how they might persuade her to come out from behind the rock, so that the Sun might appear once more. They arranged a banquet in front of the rock. They danced and sang there for a long time. Among their number was a beautiful young woman, a goddess. She began to dance in such a funny way that the garments slipped from her, revealing her bosom. The gods burst into laughter. The Sun-Goddess could not contain her curiosity as to what had made the gods laugh like that. She moved the rocks slightly. Then the strongest gods threw themselves at the rocks and, pushing them completely aside, forced the goddess to come out. And the Sun appeared once more on the earth. She was the last female representative of the patriarchal order, the last goddess to reign!

– Вот Солнце – богиня, основательница Японии, мать первого императора. Ее обидел младший брат, бросил шкурку нечистого животного в ее спальную!

Пуншевич закурил и продолжал:

– Богиня в это время ткала. Она рассердилась и скрылась за скалой. Наступила вечная ночь. Боги – ее вассалы – собрались и принялись думать, как поступить, чтобы вызвать ее из-за скалы, чтобы снова появилось Солнце. Устроили пир перед скалой. Долго пели они там и танцевали. Среди них была молодая красавица – богиня. Она принялась танцевать так смешно, что даже обнажилась, появились груди. Боги рассмеялись. Богиня-Солнце не выдержала, ей захотелось узнать, что рассмешило так богов. Она слегка раздвинула скалы. Тогда самые сильные боги бросились и совсем раздвинули скалы и ее заставили выйти. И опять на свете появилось Солнце. Она была последней представительницей патриархального быта, она была последней царствовавшей богиней! (p. 464)

Some of the secondary narratives embedded in *Harpagoniana* take over the story entirely. In chapter 7, for example, the character Anfert′ev, descending rapidly into terminal alcoholism, finds himself in a bar. Entering the lavatory, he overhears a conversation between a number of men on drunkenness. Each man has his own anecdote on the subject, and each narrative is reproduced verbatim in the text.[139] These embedded narratives are represented in such detail that they totally obscure the immediate context in which they are told. Indeed, once the third story has been recounted, the chapter immediately comes to an end; just as we have not followed the character Anfert′ev into the bar, so we do not see him leave. Much the same occurs in the penultimate chapter, which focuses initially on the character Kleshnyak as he travels on a train to see his brother in Baku, but transforms itself into an apparently random series of anecdotes told by his fellow-passengers.[140]

The proliferation of embedded narratives, some realistically motivated, others much less so, means that the centre of discourse (the authorial 'voice') is to a significant degree erased from the text. This brings us back once again to Bakhtin, since with its plethora of social discourses, *Harpagoniana* bears not a little resemblance to Bakhtin's definition of the modern novel. In 'Discourse in the Novel', an essay written within a year of *Harpagoniana* (1934–5), Bakhtin described the novel as the 'heteroglot' site of conflict between a given society's orthodox, 'centripetal' discourses and that society's heterodox, 'centrifugal' discourses, which ultimately triumph:

While the main types of poetic genre develop along a path determined by the unifying, centralizing, centripetal forces of literary-ideological life, the novel and those artistic-prose genres which gravitate towards it have historically joined the path taken by the decentralizing, centrifugal forces. (Bakhtin, 'Slovo v romane', p. 86)[141]

Adapting (however crudely) Bakhtin's model to *Harpagoniana*, one might say that in Vaginov's novel the conventionally central space occupied by the unified authoring subject and that subject's words is usurped by the characters and their stories. Moreover, there is a parallel between the displacement of the author's language in *Harpagoniana* and the way in which the novel marginalizes official Soviet discourse in favour of a whole host of politically 'centrifugal' discourses.[142] Even those discourses which at first appear reasonably orthodox turn out to be very different. For example, one story told by an ex-foreman about the construction of a factory by workers overfulfilling labour targets turns into a tale of how an American hairdresser gets a job at the factory by fooling the management into thinking he is an engineer (p. 541).

The embedded stories contained in Vaginov's novel *Harpagoniana* represent precisely the kind of 'decentralizing, centrifugal forces' which Bakhtin speaks of. The plethora of alternative, traditionally marginalized discourses represented in *Harpagoniana*, serves to relativize and decentre the discourse of the author. At the end of the revised version of *Harpagoniana* the secondary character Mirovoy sings a song, the last line of which is 'And my feeble voice has disappeared' ('Propal i tonkii golos moi', p. 543). This is, in fact, what has happened to the figure of the author over Vaginov's *oeuvre* as a whole.[143] By the end of *Harpagoniana* the author is not, as he was in *The Goat's Song*, an 'established author'; he is now, like his character Mirovoy, merely a 'voiceless figure' ('bezgolos[aya] figur[a]', ibid.).[144] Reading Vaginov through Bakhtin, and specifically Bakhtin's model of 'carnival' and 'heteroglossia', it is far easier to concur with Shepherd's view that Vaginov's subversion of elevated notions of art and the artist can be read as a positive assertion of the need to challenge them, than with Segal's more pessimistic conclusion to the effect that Vaginov shows 'the impossiblity of preserving the old forms of culture and life'.[145]

To conclude, Vaginov moves from his early verse, through

The Goat's Song to *Harpagoniana*, from an ambivalently Romantic view of the artist as an inspired genius belonging to a privileged minority to a far more materialist attitude towards literary authorship. This evolution might help explain, moreover, why Vaginov turned increasingly from poetry to prose.[146] By his fourth novel he would seem to be suggesting that books no longer afford access to timeless realms where authors might enjoy real immortality, that they are nothing more or less than an amalgam of a multitude of social discourses. Literature is no privileged discourse, merely one discursive practice among many. Writers are no longer original creators, since to write means to rewrite already-available discourses. Despite their undoubted differences in perspective and emphasis, Kharms, Vvedensky, and Vaginov can each be said to decentre the writer from the cultural and textual equation. Exactly what they put in the author's place is what I shall now examine.

CHAPTER 2

Rereading reading

ADDRESSING THE READER: RUSSIAN MODERNISM AND THE AVANT-GARDE

As well as decentring the creative subject from the text, many Russian modernists sought to re-evaluate the role of the reader/spectator in the aesthetic process. The high-Symbolist, egocentric concept of the author as solitary discoverer of higher realities gave way to the Acmeist principle of the text as communication with the reader. The communicative nature of Acmeism was emphasized in theoretical essays by Mandel′shtam and Gumilev, respectively entitled 'On the Addressee' ('O sobesednike', 1913) and 'The Reader' ('Chitatel′').[1] Mandel′shtam was particularly critical of the Symbolists' refusal to ask the 'extremely modern' question, 'just whom is the poet speaking to?' ('s kem zhe govorit poet?'; 'O sobesednike', p. 234). He compared a poem to a message in a bottle, maintaining that while neither was written with a specific reader in mind, both were addressed to someone (the poem's addressee being 'the reader in posterity', 'chitatel['] v potomstve'; p. 235). But despite Mandel′shtam's insistence on the importance of the reader as 'interlocutor' (the literal meaning of 'sobesednik'), the Acmeists fell short of advocating a genuine dialogue between poet and reader. Ultimately, the Acmeists' concept of a 'good' reader was one who would be somehow changed by the poem; there was no suggestion that the presence of the reader should have any effect on the composition of the poem itself.

The Russian Futurists were also conscious of their audience, although in a very different way. In particular, by disrupting all sorts of linguistic, aesthetic, psychological, and even ethical conventions, the Futurists were deliberately challenging that audience's assumptions, going beyond what they perceived to be its collective 'horizon of expectations'.[2] Moreover, while the attempt by Mayakovsky, Khlebnikov, Kruchenykh, and others to deliver a 'slap in the face of public taste' had the effect of alienating many readers or spectators, there are those who have argued that their art turned its audience into co-producers, free to interpret the text as it wished. To quote G. M. Hyde, 'the Futurist theatre in Russia as in Italy [...] demanded the total participation of the audience in a spectacle by no means tied to a text; similarly their poetry demanded the active collaboration of the reader in *making* the text' (Hyde, 'Russian Futurism', p. 264). 'Defamiliarizing' words and the world, the Futurists may be said to have anticipated Barthes' 'writerly' text in which the reader is afforded access to 'the pleasure of writing'.[3] Such was also one of the effects of Meyerkhol'd's theatrical excursions into pantomime and *commedia dell'arte*. Deliberately foregrounding theatrical convention, Meyerkhol'd aimed at ending theatre's segregation of actors and spectators, hitherto guaranteed by the proscenium arch. Meyerkhol'd went so far as to describe the spectator as the 'fourth creator' in the theatre, in addition to the author, the director, and the actor. As a result of the emphasis which he placed in his productions on theatrical convention, he argued, 'the spectator is compelled to employ his imagination *creatively* in order *to fill in* those details *suggested* by the stage action'.[4]

However, many artists before the 1920s sought to limit 'meaning' to the artist's intentions, even as they insisted on the communicative function of art. For example, the theory behind Nikolay Evreinov's 'monodramas', developed in the first decade of the twentieth century, was based on the principle that the spectator was to co-experience the actor's emotions as fully as possible.[5] Similarly, in an essay published in 1913, Vasily Kandinsky appeared to characterize the 'successful' work of art as an egocentric and monologic process:

A work of art consists of two elements, the inner and the outer. The inner is the emotion in the soul of the artist; this emotion has the capacity to evoke a similar emotion in the observer. [...]

The two emotions will be like and equivalent to the extent that the work of art is successful. In this respect painting is in no way different from a song: each is communication.[6]

After the Revolution, the Party's emphasis on art as propaganda left no room for the spectator/reader to arrive at an understanding of the artefact independently of the artist's will. The Party's view was shared by a number of prominent left artists in the early 1920s. Typical of this trend was Eisenstein, whose 'montage of attractions', while based on the principle that 'the spectator himself constitutes the basic material of the theatre', aimed at imposing the director's point of view on that spectator.[7] As Eisenstein himself put it, a film should 'embody the author's relation to the content, at the same time compelling the spectator to relate himself to the content in the same way'.[8] Similarly, in 1924 the Constructivist playwright Sergey Tret'yakov insisted 'the theatre show is to be replaced by the theatre blow, by the direct processing of the audience'.[9] It was for such propagandistic reasons that most proletarian groups in the arts vehemently argued for accessibility in art, a call which subsequently became one of the pillars of Socialist Realism.

Throughout the 1920s, however, a notion of the reader/spectator as more active was also given expression. In fiction, this trend was most clearly seen in the short stories of Mikhail Zoshchenko, a number of which featured 'readers', in the form of a spectating public which intervenes actively in the scenes which it observes. As Cathy Popkin astutely notes: 'by stressing the discriminating role of the receiver, the stories raise again and again, explicitly and implicitly, the question of what makes something worth the reader's effort' (a point which, as we shall see, is also applicable to Kharms's prose).[10] Another artist whose work implied an active audience was Dziga Vertov. Like Eisenstein, Vertov had spent the first years of the Bolshevik régime on agit-trains, bringing cinema – and the Party's message – to uneducated peasants throughout the Soviet Union.[11] The 'Cine-Eye' ('Kino-glaz') method of filming documentaries, which Vertov developed in the early 1920s (and which the Party increasingly attacked) implied a passive audience, observing and interpreting Soviet reality in the manner determined by the eye of the camera: '[Cine-Eye is] the decoding of life as it is. Using facts to influence the workers' consciousness.'[12] In practice, however, Vertov's films required a very different kind of spectator. For example, by the unusual juxtaposition of particular scenes, and its numerous special effects, his pseudo-documentary *Man with a Movie Camera* draws attention to itself as an artefact in ways which force the spectator to take a more active role in the production of the text, and of that text's meaning.[13] Indeed, the film includes, alongside shots of the cameraman filming in the streets and the film editor working in the cutting room, a sequence wherein a cinema audience takes its seats, thereby suggesting the importance of all three elements in the creative process.[14]

Vertov's fellow-Constructivist El Lissitsky was another whose output after the Revolution evolved from direct propaganda aimed at eliciting a specific, concrete response from the spectator, to art which engaged the viewer in a genuinely productive sense. The call for action addressed to the viewer by his geometrical design entitled 'Beat the Whites with a Red Wedge' ('Krasnym klinom bei belykh', 1919–20), produced at the height of the Civil War, was as unambiguous as it was explicit. Throughout the 1920s, however, Lissitsky's art, as Alan C. Birnholz has pointed out, was increasingly designed to stimulate the observer's *inter*action – both mental and physical. One of the most interesting examples of this was his *Abstract Cabinet* (*Abstrakte Kabinett*, 1927), a so-called 'Proun Room' installed in Berlin, in which the viewer had no choice but to walk past a series of vertical slats from behind which light was emitted, thereby changing the patterns of light and dark on the opposite wall.[15] Lissitsky went further than most in calling for a radical shift in attitudes towards aesthetic reception: 'The private property aspect of creativity must be destroyed [since...] all are creators and there is no reason of any sort for this division into artists and non-artists.'[16]

While some Soviet artists were, like Lissitsky, beginning to see the reader/observer as 'co-creator', others saw themselves first and foremost as 'readers' (thereby echoing a point about the writer first made by Gumilev in 'The Reader'). Engaging in a creative dialogue with the cultural heritage, they sought to 'reread' it, to adapt it to the new, post-revolutionary era. In music, for example, Shostakovich radically reinterpreted Leskov's short story 'Lady Macbeth of the Mtsensk District' ('Ledi Makbet Mtsenskogo uezda', 1865), with his opera of the same name (premiered in 1934; subsequently retitled as *Katerina Izmailova*).[17] In the theatre, the 1920s saw two radically new interpretations of Gogol''s *The Government Inspector*, namely Meyerkhol'd's famous 'biomechanical' production of 1926, and the *zaum'* version, premiered in the Leningrad Press Club on 25 March 1927, produced by Igor' Terent'ev.[18] One contemporary review of the latter reveals that the actors, dressed in particularly gawdy costumes, read out all the stage directions themselves, interspersed their lines with passages in French, German, Polish, Ukrainian, and *zaum'*, crawled around on the floor or else rushed armed with toilet paper to the cubicles stationed in the middle of the stage, while during one particular pause a number of white mice were set free, promptly causing panic among the audience. At the end of the six-hour performance, it transpired that the real inspector was none other than Khlestakov himself, thereby turning Gogol''s play on its head.[19]

In Soviet prose fiction, it was the 'Serapion Brothers' who most systematically developed this concept of writing as rereading/reinscribing already existing discourses. As Erika Greber has contended, the group's very name, suggesting a model of creativity as collective, 'symbolises the attempt to realize a utopia, a model world of communication in which production and reception, writing and reading, theory and practice meet in professional dialogue'.[20] The Serapions explicitly foregrounded their own writing as an imitative, intertextual 'palimpsest' through which the traces of earlier discourses can be discerned. One of Kaverin's early prose works was in fact called *The Purple Palimpsest* (*Purpurnyi palimpsest*, 1921).[21] Blurring the distinction between originality and copy, the Serapions sought to affect a positive re-evaluation of the concept of literary influence and imitation. As their chief theorist Lev Lunts observed, 'epigones of an alien ['chuzhoi'] literature are initiators of a new trend in their own, national literature'.[22]

TEXT AS DIALOGUE: FROM RUSSIAN FORMALISM TO THE
BAKHTIN CIRCLE

The Serapions' interest in readers and reading – and their tendency to defeat the reader's expectations through verbal and textual play – was perhaps not surprising, given their close association with the Formalists. While so much Serapion literature consisted of parodic rereadings of earlier texts, Shklovsky and Tynyanov were among the first to suggest that parody should in fact be considered a *constructive* literary device.[23] The Formalists insisted on the cognitive force of the literary text. In a now much-rehearsed comment, Shklovsky maintained that 'the process of perception in art is an end in itself and should be prolonged' ('vosprinimatel'nyi protsess v iskusstve samotselen i dolzhen byt' prodlen').[24] Such insistence, together with their concept of 'defamiliarization' ('ostranenie') has led the Formalists to be seen as precursors of more recent reader-centred theories of literature.[25] On the other hand, Peter Steiner maintains that the Formalists' emphasis on literature as system meant that 'the perceiving subject [wa]s either treated as an appendix of this impersonal system or ignored' (Steiner, *Russian Formalism: A Metapoetics*, p. 137).[26] According to Steiner, despite Tynyanov's claim that 'it is utterly impossible to separate the author of literature from the reader because they are essentially the same',[27] Formalist aesthetics implicitly expunged both author and reader from the literary system.

In the final analysis, 'meaning' for Tynyanov, Eikhenbaum, and Shklovsky was dependent neither on a text's readers nor on its author, but on the cultural context of its production. To quote Carol Any, 'in general, Formalist theory and practice were concerned not with new or variant readings but with establishing a "baseline" reading of works by reconstituting the literary conventions in force at the time of writing' (Any, *Boris Eikhenbaum*, p. 70). If we are looking for a positive and meaningful re-evalution of aesthetic reception in the Soviet Union in the 1920s and early 1930s, then we must turn, once again, to Bakhtin.

As David Shepherd has pointed out, although no full-blown theory of reading can be found in Bakhtin's work, there is nevertheless a specific kind of reader implied by Bakhtin's notion of dialogism, one which can be traced back to Bakhtin's earliest writing.[28] In his 'Author and Hero' essay, Bakhtin specifically criticized those who adhered to the view that the text could be reduced to the expression of the author's intention alone: 'The aesthetic *whole* is not something co-experienced, but something actively created both by the author and by the contemplator' ('Esteticheskoe *tseloe* ne soperezhivaetsaya, no aktivno sozdaetsya i avtorom i sozertsatelem'; Bakhtin, 'Avtor i geroi', pp. 60–1). Bakhtin's critique of 'expressive' aesthetics was developed in a series of subsequent essays by members of the Bakhtin circle. In *The Formal Method in Literary Scholarship*, for example, the following point is made:

The poet's audience, the readers of a novel, the audience in a concert hall – these are all collective organizations of a particular type, sociologically distinctive and exceptionally important. Without these distinctive forms of social intercourse there are no poems, no odes, no novels, no symphonies. Specific forms of social intercourse are constituent to the meaning of the works of art themselves. (Bakhtin, *Formal'nyi metod*, p. 21)

Bakhtin went further in *The Formal Method* than in 'Author and Hero', insisting that every artistic text is in part shaped by its addressee, towards whom, as an utterance, it is oriented: 'Every utterance is oriented on intercourse, on the hearer, on the reader, in a word, on another person, on some form of social intercourse, whatever it may be' ('Vsyakoe vyskazyvanie ustanovleno na soobshchenie, na slushatelya, na chitatelya, odnim slovom, na drugogo cheloveka, na kakuyu-to formu sotsial'nogo obshcheniya, kakova by ona ni byla'; ibid., p. 129). This 'dialogic' principle was given fuller expression in one of the most frequently quoted passages from *Marxism and the Philosophy of Language*:

The fact that a word is oriented toward the addressee is extremely significant. In essence, *a word is a two-sided act*. It is determined equally by *whose* word it is and *for whom* it is meant. As word, it is precisely *the product of the interrelationship between speaker and listener*. [...] A word is a bridge thrown between myself and the other.[29]

Bakhtin further elaborated upon the dialogic nature of the utterance in 'Discourse in the Novel'. In this essay he introduced the concept of 'active understanding' ('aktivnoe ponimanie'), by which he meant that the speaker's 'orientation towards the listener [...] introduces totally new elements into his discourse' ('ustanovka na slushatelya [...] vnosit sovershenno novye momenty v ego slovo'; Bakhtin, 'Slovo v romane', p. 95).[30] This concept of the text-utterance as the subject of limitless dialogic exchange between speaker and listeners was one to which Bakhtin returned in an important late essay:

There is no first or last word and there are no limits to the dialogic context (it extends into a boundless past and a boundless future). Even *past* meanings, that is, meanings born in the dialogue of past ages, can never be stable (finalized, determined once and for all); they will always change (thereby renewing themselves) in the process of the subsequent, future development of the dialogue. At any moment in the development of the dialogue there are immense, boundless masses of forgotten contextual meanings, but at certain moments of the dialogue's subsequent development along the way they are recalled and brought back to life in renewed form (in a new context).[31]

OBERIU AND THE READER: ZABOLOTSKY, OLEINIKOV, BAKHTEREV

Few scholars have explored what OBERIU literature has to say about the nature of reading and aesthetic reception. Furthermore, those critics who have addressed the issue have tended to restrict themselves to tantalizing generalizations. Aleksey Medvedev places OBERIU (by which he means Kharms and Vvedensky) in the context of the literary avant-garde of the first quarter of the twentieth century which, he maintains, relegated the author from his superior position *vis-à-vis* the reader in order to make a point about the invalidity of subject-centred discourse. As Medvedev observes, in a general statement which he unfortunately does not substantiate, 'in their art Kharms and Vvedensky free both the text and the reader from the monologic diktat [of the author-creator]'.[32] The American scholar Anthony Anemone has suggested that the model of dialogue which Vaginov inscribes in his novel *The Labours and Days of Svistonov* bears some resemblance to recent Reader-Reception Theory (Anemone, 'Carnival in Theory and Practice', p. 10). S. N. Chumakov has suggested that Kharms's miniature dramatic works serve to stimulate the 'active co-creation of the receiver' ('aktivnoe sotvorchestvo retseptora').[33] Darra Goldstein, in her recent monograph on Zabolotsky, believes that the *Oberiuty* were interested not in the word as such but in 'its effect on the reader' (Goldstein, *Nikolai Zabolotsky*, p. 26). Elsewhere in her study she claims that 'Zabolotsky challenged his readers not only to discern his eternal presence through his verse, but also to *participate* in the unfinished act of creation' (ibid., p. 126). Finally, in an article on Zabolotsky, Robin Milner-Gulland quotes the poet's statement 'I count upon the intelligent reader', to conclude that Zabolotsky was hoping for a reader 'who was ready to use his mind as well as his feelings in the appreciation of poetry'.[34]

Works such as Vaginov's *The Labours and Days of Svistonov*, and Vvedensky's play *Christmas at the Ivanovs'* explore dialogic models of reading close to Bakhtin's, as we shall see. The OBERIU article, however, gestured not towards Bakhtin (whose concept of 'active understanding' had yet to be formulated), but in the direction of Formalism, with its talk of renewing the reader's perception (even if it promised not so much to foreground the 'literariness' of the object, as 'strip away' the object's literary shell).

Zabolotsky demonstrates an awareness of the reader in the OBERIU article, where he describes himself as 'a poet of naked concrete figures brought close to the eyes of the spectator'. A number of Zabolotsky's poems of the late 1920s contain examples of what appears to be Formalist-inspired defamiliarization.

As Goldstein has demonstrated, Zabolotsky's 'Dinner' ('Obed', 1929) defamiliarizes its subject both in a 'literary' sense (by playfully deconstructing the stock nineteenth-century tone of the opening lines) and in an 'everyday' sense (by transforming a description of meat and vegetables as they are cooked into a grotesque, almost surreal vision).[35] Similarly, Fiona Björling, in a perceptive close reading of Zabolotsky's 'Football' ('Futbol', 1926), has analysed how the description of a game of football is 'made strange' through a whole host of allusions to mock-heroic poetry, and particularly to Pushkin's 'Ruslan and Lyudmila'.[36] In 'An Evening Bar' ('Vechernii bar'), written in 1926, Zabolotsky plays with the reader by interrupting his description of a window reflected in a beer glass with a Gogolian 'But I cannot talk about this' ('No eto rasskazat' nel'zya'; Zabolotsky, *Stolbtsy i poemy*, p. 15). On the whole, however, Zabolotsky does not explore the reading process in his poetry, since the reader on whom Zabolotsky counts is a largely passive contemplator of his poetic visions, be they utopian, as in the early 'The Mad Wolf' ('Bezumnyi volk', 1931), or more personal, as in 'The Thistle' ('Chertopolokh', 1956).[37]

As with Zabolotsky's pre-1930 urban verse, some of Oleinikov's poems also provide the reader with an unfamiliar perspective on the world. One of the best examples of this is the bittersweet 'The Cockroach' ('Tarakan'), in which the reader shares the insect's viewpoint as it lies in a glass waiting to be dissected by scientists.[38] Like Zabolotsky, however, Oleinikov cannot be said to explore the question of aesthetic reception in any genuine sense. As if to emphasize this, the matter-of-fact descriptions of paintings contained in the cycle *In an Art Gallery* (subtitled *Reflections on Art*) imply a detached, passive observer.[39]

Bakhterev, on the other hand, forces the reader to work very hard, especially in his prose, some of which is as oneiric as anything produced by OBERIU. The mystifying short story 'Only a Pintle' ('Tol'ko shtyr'') changes direction a number of times, as Bakhterev uses a series of narrative techniques resembling what Shklovsky defined as 'retardation devices'.[40] The narrative of 'Only a Pintle' begins with the description of a boating accident, observed by the narrator, in which a woman is decapitated (the title comes from the enigmatic assertion made by the narrator's companion, that 'only a pintle will save her'; 'pomozhet ei tol'ko shtyr'', p. 418). As the story continues, however, this accident appears to be merely a device to delay the main narrative, since the narrator suddenly asks a passing decorator to paint him a portrait of a goat (p. 419). The narrative switches back, however, to the woman's head, which is now being used as a football by a group of boys (p. 421). As part 2 begins, the narrator asks self-consciously 'what else should I talk about?' ('o chem govorit' dal'she?'), before going on to describe himself waking up in his flat, wondering whether or not the accident and the decorator had been a dream (ibid.). Following a brief conversation with a woman who lives in his block, the decorator arrives with his assistants, thereby confirming the reality of the first part of the story. The narrator then leaves home, visits a bar, and spends time with some acquaintances, before returning home, at which point the narrative ends.

What does 'Only a Pintle' tell us about reading? Negotiating one's way through the text and its numerous shifts in direction, the reader is made aware of, and obliged to challenge the assumptions underpinning the reading process. The oneiric structure of this text forces us to ask how we make meaning as readers, how we conventionally distinguish between 'significance' and 'insignificance', 'relevance' and 'irrelevance'. What is an occasional feature of Bakhterev's *oeuvre* is, however, central to Kharms's prose, as we shall now see.

STOP READING SENSE: THE PROSE OF DANIIL KHARMS

The most explicit way in which Kharms draws attention to the (f)act of reading is by including among his characters a reader figure. In what may be an allusion to the concern with readers characteristic of much avant-garde art of the 1920s, Kharms's play *The Comedy of the City of Petersburg* (1927) contains a 'spectator' ('zritel'') among the characters. At one moment during the action, the 'Komsomol member Vertunov' ('Komsomolets Vertunov') asks this member of the audience for his opinion on another character, Famusov (the latter bears a certain resemblance to his namesake in Griboedov's play *Woe From Wit* (*Gore ot uma*, 1824)). The spectator gives an enigmatic answer, 'seek where you will' ('ishchite gde khotite'), and Vertunov's impatience eventually forces the spectator to leave, threatening to complain to his 'mummy' as he goes (Kharms, *Sobranie proizvedenii*, vol. 1, pp. 94–5).[41] This somewhat pusillanimous reader figure provides a stark contrast with the reader in 'Four Illustrations of how a New Idea disconcerts a Man Unprepared for it', who, as was shown in my previous chapter, directly challenges the writer's authority by calling him 'shit'.[42]

Such reader figures rarely appear in Kharms's texts, however. Generally, Kharms makes us aware of our own status as readers, by prompting us to engage actively with his text (particularly in his prose of the 1930s). He does this in two ways. First, as Shukman has noted, he questions the implied social and cultural values of his potential readership.[43] Kharms shocks us by the cruelly detached, ironic attitude towards violence and death demonstrated by his narrators in such stories as 'What they're Selling in the Shops these Days' ('Chto teper' prodayut v magazinakh'), and 'The Plummeting Old Women' ('Vyvalivayushchiesya starukhi').[44] The latter story, which describes the deaths of six old women as they fall consecutively from a window, ends with the comment: 'Once the sixth old woman had fallen out, I became tired of looking at them, and set off for Mal'tsevsky market where a blind man had apparently been given a knitted shawl' ('Kogda vyvalilas' shestaya starukha, mne nadoelo smotret' na nikh, i ya poshel na Mal'tsevskii rynok, gde, govoryat, odnomu slepomu podarili vyazanuyu shal''; Kharms, *Polet*, p. 356).

Second, and more importantly, Kharms disrupts the equilibrium between relevance and irrelevance, a cornerstone of realism, including the 'Socialist' variety.[45] This aspect of his fiction explains perhaps more than any other why his work has so often been termed 'absurd',[46] since it involves playing on the reader's assumptions of 'common sense'.[47] The tentative definition of 'common sense' offered by Susan Stewart in her study of nonsense in literature underlines the importance of assumptions concerning relevance:

Accomplishing common sense has to do with an agreement regarding the horizon of the situation, an agreement regarding what is relevant or appropriate to the situation in light of this horizon, and a mutual procedure for achieving an appropriate outcome of the situation – a procedure that [...] depends upon typifications and relevance structures. (Stewart, *Nonsense*, p. 9)

Stewart continues by arguing that the more self-conscious a text, the more it will disrupt the information equilibrium of common sense, either by withholding information relevant to the situation, or by including an excess of irrelevant detail.[48] Both strategies feature prominently in Kharms's prose, and both have ramifications for notions of reading.

At times, Kharms's narrator withholds information relevant to the context, only revealing it at a later moment in the text, thereupon forcing the reader to recontextualize, to revise his/her interpretation of the situation.[49] The result can be particularly comic. For example, in 'Fedya Davidovich' (Kharms, *Polet*, pp. 390–1), Fedya and his wife engage in a dispute as to whether Fedya has stolen the butter from the kitchen (he has in fact just popped the whole block into his mouth with a view to selling it to a mysterious neighbour). It is only about half-way through the text, however, that an important (i.e. immediately relevant) element of the context is given to the reader: as Fedya rushes out of the flat to escape his incensed spouse, the narrator suddenly reveals that she cannot chase after him because she is naked. As a result of this new information, the reader has to 'repicture' the scene, as it were, to recontextualize, mentally undressing Fedya's wife before the reading process can continue successfully. The unexpectedness of the revelation, and the sense of the gratuitous which surrounds it, foregrounds it as a narrative device, while at the same time reminding us of our own constitutive role, as readers, in the communicative act that is the text.

In other works by Kharms, what Stewart calls 'gaps or tears in the performance' (Stewart, *Nonsense*, p. 103), are not, as they are in 'Fedya Davidovich', resolved by the text. At times, for example, Kharms denies the events which he depicts any prior cause. This is particularly true of those texts which feature unrestrained violence, such as 'The Beginning of a Beautiful Summer's Day (A Symphony)' ('Nachalo ochen' khoroshego letnego dnya (Simfoniya)'), 'Grigor'ev and Semenov' ('Grigor'ev i Semenov'), and 'Incidents' ('Sluchai').[50] These, and many other prose works, present 'stories' with no apparent beginnings, since we never see what has motivated the violence (if the violence is unmotivated, why aren't we told so?).

Generally, Kharms omits not just the causes which have led to a particular context, but also important elements of that context itself (although the distinction between the two may at times be blurred). In the starkly disturbing 'Mashkin Killed Koshkin' ('Mashkin ubil Koshkina'), for example, we are told nothing about the characters' identities or whereabouts, and little which might help illuminate their psychological state:

Comrade Koshkin danced around comrade Mashkin.
　　Comrade Mashkin followed comrade Koshkin with his eyes.
　　Comrade Koshkin waved his arms about offensively and stuck his legs out repulsively.
　　Comrade Mashkin frowned.
　　Comrade Koshkin twitched his belly and stamped his right foot.
　　Comrade Mashkin cried out and hurled himself at comrade Koshkin.
　　Comrade Koshkin tried to run away, but tripped and was overtaken by comrade Mashkin.
　　Comrade Mashkin punched comrade Koshkin on the head.
　　Comrade Koshkin cried out and fell onto his hands and knees.
　　Comrade Mashkin kicked comrade Koshkin under the stomach and gave him another punch on the back of his head.
　　Comrade Koshkin spread himself out on the floor and died.
　　Mashkin killed Koshkin.

Товарищ Кошкин танцевал вокруг товарища Машкина.
　　Товарищ Машкин следил глазами за товарищем Кошкиным.
　　Товарищ Кошкин оскорбительно махал руками и противно выворачивал ноги.
　　Товарищ Машкин нахмурился.
　　Товарищ Кошкин пошевелил животом и притопнул правой ногой.
　　Товарищ Машкин вскрикнул и кинулся на товарища Кошкина.
　　Товарищ Кошкин попробовал убежать, но споткнулся и был настигнут товарищем Машкиным.

Товарищ Машкин ударил кулаком по голове товарища Кошкина.

Товарищ Кошкин вскрикнул и упал на четвереньки.

Товарищ Машкин двинул товарища Кошкина ногой под живот и еще раз ударил его кулаком по затылку.

Товарищ Кошкин растянулся на полу и умер.

Машкин убил Кошкина. (p. 383)

Such stories are important, of course, for the questions they ask of human psychology and behavioural patterns, for the way in which they invite us to provide the characters with a psychology or set of motivating criteria that might accord with the particular situation in which they find themselves. More significantly, however, they produce, through their indeterminacies, a general sense of unease at the way in which we define terms such as 'situation', or 'context'.[51]

In other works it is the ending of the story which Kharms erases.[52] On a few occasions, the ending is ambiguous. In other words, there is certainly a sense of resolution as concerns the main plot, but whether this resolution is to have positive or negative consequences for the central character(s) remains unclear; the reader is not given enough information to find out. In one story the narrator is pursued by children and old men and women, apparently for having raised dust. He finds his way eventually into a bath-house, and as he runs through it we are suddenly told that 'a mighty repose stopped my heart' ('moguchii otdykh ostanovil moe serdtse').[53] It is far from clear how we are to interpret this ending from the point of view of the main character's fortunes (and thereby of the main plot). Have the children succeeded in killing him by inducing a heart attack? Or does the word 'relaxation' imply a positive attitude towards his physical condition, as if welcoming a saving miracle from God? Indeed, is the narrator dead at all? If so, how could he now be narrating (assuming that he is not speaking to us, like many of Vvedensky's characters, from a mythical space beyond the grave)? Kharms prompts us to ask these questions, but leaves them unanswered.

Many of Kharms's stories are devoid of any kind of resolution, ambiguous or otherwise. 'The Story of the Fighting Men'

('Istoriya derushchikhsya'), for example, which concerns a fight between a certain Aleksey Alekseevich and Andrey Karlovich, ends in the following way: 'Andrey Karlovich gave his dentures a rub, put them back in his mouth and clicked his teeth. Having satisfied himself that his dentures were in place, he took stock of his surroundings and, not seeing Aleksey Alekseevich, set off to look for him' ('A Andrey Karlovich proter svoyu vstavnuyu chelyust', vstavil ee sebe v rot, poshchelkal zubami i, ubedivshis', chto chelyust' prishlas' na mesto, osmotrelsya vokrug i, ne vidya Alekseya Alekseevicha, poshel ego razyskivat''; p. 366).[54] 'The Bronze Look' ('Mednyi vzglyad') ends in the middle of a conversation with the question: 'Do you have a watch?' ('U vas est' chasy?'; Kharms, *Sluchai*, pp. 9–10).[55] And in 'Petrakov's Problem' ('Sluchai s Petrakovym'), Petrakov spends the whole time trying to get to sleep, and is still trying when the story ends (p. 365).

Occasionally, Kharms draws the reader's attention to a gap in the text. In 'The Career of Ivan Yakovlevich Antonov' ('Kar'era Ivana Yakovlevicha Antonova'), for example, certain people have cuckoos fly into their mouths when they yawn (Kharms, *Sluchai*, p. 5). The Ivan of the title proves adept at extracting the birds, a feat which earns him public recognition. Yet the reader never finds out how he does this, for each time he rescues a bird the text merely tells us that he acts 'in the most cunning manner' ('samym ostroumnym sposobom'). The text functions as a lipogram, with one particular contextual element automatically replaced in the text by the same cryptic phrase. This is underlined by the ironic last line: 'And now it is clear how Ivan Yakovlevich Antonov got himself a career' ('I vot teper' stanovitsya yasnym, kakim obrazom Ivan Yakovlevich Antonov sdelal sebe kar'eru').

Just as Kharms frustrates the reader's desire for more information, so at times he *includes* in his stories apparently irrelevant material. Sometimes Kharms plays with the reader's assumptions concerning relevance. In 'The Connection' ('Svyaz''), written in 1937, what appears irrelevant is eventually revealed to have been significant (pp. 500–2).[56] In this story a series of bizarre incidents and coincidences link the characters, unbeknown to them, over a number of years. The text, divided up into twenty short numbered sections, includes an assault on a violinist by hooligans, a bus driver who sells a coat for some tomatoes, an old woman who is buried in a cemetery, and a church destroyed by fire. As the characters who were present in the opening section find themselves 'reunited' in the final scene, unwittingly travelling together on the same tram, the narrator concludes: 'They ride along and don't know what connection there is between them, and they won't find out until the day they die' ('Oni edut i ne znayut, kakaya mezhdu nimi svyaz', i ne uznayut etogo do samoi smerti'; p. 502). The ending of the text posits an alternative, unconventional order behind the apparent disorder in the body of the text.[57]

In other texts, the relevance of certain details is a good deal harder to ascertain. Sometimes Kharms begins a story with information which appears to function as a gratuitous appendage to the rest of the story. Such is the case in the tale which commences with the words 'Ivan Yakovlevich Bobov woke up' ('Ivan Yakovlevich Bobov prosnulsya'; pp. 319–22). The text, written between 1934 and 1937, opens with Ivan waking up one morning in a particularly good mood. As he looks up at the ceiling, we are given a lengthy description of a coloured blob which covers part of it. The reader may imagine that this detail has some relevance to the rest of the story, or merely assume that the description of the blob means that Ivan is looking at it. Both assumptions turn out to be erroneous, since the description ends with the revelation that 'Ivan Yakovlevich looked at the ceiling, not in that place where the blob was, but somewhere else, although it's not clear where' ('Ivan Yakovlevich posmotrel na potolok, no ne v to mesto, gde bylo pyatno, a tak, neizvestno kuda'; p. 319). The blob is never mentioned again by the narrator, who proceeds to tell a story about Ivan's purchase of an odd-coloured pair of trousers.[58]

In other stories what appears to be irrelevant information comes not at the beginning, but somewhere in the middle, momentarily rupturing the textual fabric. It is perhaps not completely coincidental that one such breach should occur in a story entitled 'On Equilibrium' ('O ravnovesii', 1934; Kharms,

Sluchai, pp. 28–9). This story concerns one Nikolay Ivanovich Serpukhov, and the time that a fairy godmother appeared to him, promising to fulfil his every wish, while he was sitting having a quiet meal in a restaurant. The mention of Nikolay comes with a particular detail which, given the text's subject matter, and its length, creates, once again, an impression of irrelevance: 'He was called Nikolay Ivanovich Serpukhov, and he smoked "Rocket" cigarettes at thirty-five copecks a packet, and always said that they made him cough less than those costing five roubles which, he used to say, "always make me choke"' ('Zvali ego Nikolay Ivanovich Serpukhov, a kuril on papirosy "Raketa", 35 kop. korobka, i vsegda govoril, chto ot nikh on men'she kashlem stradaet, a ot pyatirublevykh, govorit, ya vsegda zadykhayus''; ibid. p. 28).

On occasion Kharms saturates the entire text with superfluous detail. The writer of the letter addressed to a certain Nikandr Andreevich, for example, uses virtually the whole of his missive to say the same thing over and over again, namely how happy he was when he realized that the letter which he has just received was in fact from Nikandr (Kharms, *Sluchai*, pp. 8–9).[59] And in the playlet 'The Mathematician and Andrey Semenovich' ('Matematik i Andrey Semenovich'), each line of dialogue is spoken three or four times (pp. 368–9).

Sometimes the reader has the impression that the text as a whole – rather than one of the details which goes to make up that text – is superfluous. This impression is particularly strong in those texts which are merely two or three lines in length. One wonders, for example, what the point is of a text such as 'A Meeting' ('Vstrecha'):

One day a man set off for work, and on the way met another man, who, having bought a Polish loaf, was on his way home.
That's it, really.

Вот однажды один человек пошел на службу, да по дороге встретил другого человека, который, купив польский батон, направлялся к себе во-свояси.
Вот, собственно, и все. (р. 378)[60]

If something, however trivial, happens in 'A Meeting', then in another miniature text, we are specifically told that 'nothing happened'.[61] Ultimately, Kharms forces the reader to ask questions of the text and its context as much by what he tells us as by what he doesn't.

In a story written in 1938, entitled 'The Artist and the Watch' ('Khudozhnik i chasy', Kharms, *Sluchai*, p. 32), the narrator underlines the utter pointlessness of his story in an outburst which alludes quite clearly to the reader's desire for relevance. He begins his tale by introducing us to an artist named Serov, and informing us that one day Serov went to the Obvodny Canal. The narrative suddenly breaks off: 'Why did he go there? To buy some rubber. What did he want rubber for? To make himself a rubber band. And what did he want a rubber band for? In order to stretch it' ('Zachem on tuda poshel? Pokupat' rezinu. Zachem emu rezina? Chtoby sdelat' sebe rezinku. A zachem emu rezinka? A chtoby ee rastyagivat''). The superfluousness of the character's action mirrors the pointlessness of the narrator's discourse. This is further emphasized almost immediately afterwards, when the narrator tells us that Serov broke his watch, and then adds, directly addressing the reader: 'What else? Nothing else. Nothing, that's all there is to it! Don't go poking your filthy snout where it's not wanted!' ('Chego eshche? A bole nichego. Nichego, i vse tut! I svoe poganoe rylo kuda ne nado ne sui!').

If we accept Jonathan Culler's contention that 'the meaning of the work is what it shows the reader, by the acrobatics in which it involves him, about the problems of his condition, as homo significans, maker and reader of signs',[62] then what, we might ask, do Kharms's texts tell us about the way in which we read? The information imbalance characteristic of so much of Kharms's prose can be interpreted ('read') in one of two ways: either the 'common sense' reader will always miss the point, or we should not read for the point at all, but rather revel in the Barthesian 'pleasure of the text' for its own sake.[63] Stories such as 'The Connection' and Kharms's letter to Pugacheva would seem to suggest the former,[64] while works such as 'A Meeting' and 'The Artist and the Watch' may be said to imply the latter.

Either way, by transcending the boundaries of relevance,

Kharms is underlining the fact that when we read, we will always look for 'the point', according to criteria based on our 'common sense' notions of what is relevant and what is not.[65] Reminding us how we read, Kharms forces us to ask questions concerning the way we construct contexts and how we decide what is and is not relevant to them.[66] Furthermore, by refusing time and time again to 'make sense', Kharms suggests that we should stop reading 'sense'. It is thus on the question of reading that the absurd (the world's incoherent narratives) and the metafictional (our difficulty in reading those narratives) in Kharms's texts/contexts collide.

Kharms goes much further than writers such as Gogol', Chekhov, Zoshchenko (the three mentioned in Popkin's study), or even Bakhterev, in his challenge to 'common sense' reading strategies. This is why critics such as Ellen Chances have compared him unfavourably with Chekhov, accusing him of attempting to achieve 'the destruction of literature' (Chances, 'Čexov and Xarms', p. 191). My reading of Kharms suggests, however, that he seeks not to destroy literature, but to renew it, to tear up the contract between writer and reader in order to begin the search for another. Subverting the narrative conventions of realism, Kharms forces us as readers to engage actively with the text, and to re-examine the assumptions which we make in reading. Another who breaks conventions in order to address the issue of aesthetic reception is Vvedensky, and he does this nowhere more consistently than in his play *Christmas at the Ivanovs'*.

PICTURE THIS: *CHRISTMAS AT THE IVANOVS'* BY ALEKSANDR VVEDENSKY

The 1930s, the decade in which Kharms wrote most of his prose fiction, saw the emergence in the Soviet Union of a radically different attitude towards the reader from that which had prevailed before the onset of Socialist Realism. Whereas a number of Soviet artists (in various branches of the arts) had previously tried to foster a notion of the reader/spectator as 'an independent, reflective and productive subject',[67] by 1938, when Vvedensky came to write *Christmas at the Ivanovs'* (*Elka u Ivanovykh*),[68] the only view of the audience which was now allowed any currency was as a uniform mass passively receptive to the artist's (i.e. the Party's) message. As Spencer Golub has astutely observed:

Pre- and post-revolutionary avant-gardists (e.g., Meyerhold, Nikolay Evreinov and Nikolay Okhlopkov) originally saw the curtainless stage as a way to *unmake* the Procrustean bed of bourgeois-fed and mimetically encoded pictorial realism. Under Stalin, however, the absorption of the spectator and the audience *en masse* into performance, like the attack on formalism, was part of a larger program to eliminate difference. Socialist Realist art re-defined dramatic character as the blueprint for audience identity construction.[69]

A measure of how much things had changed in the theatre is given by Meyerkhol'd's attitude towards the spectator. While Meyerkhol'd had, before the Revolution, sought to break the barrier between stage and auditorium in order to encourage the spectator to 'co-create' the play, in his 1931 production of Vsevolod Vishnevsky's *The Final Battle* (*Poslednii reshitel'nyi*, 1931) he sought to manipulate his audience by planting a 'weeper' in one of the front rows of the theatre (a ruse which achieved the desired effect of moving the whole audience to tears at the play's tragic end).[70]

That the audience should be encouraged to be passively receptive was underscored at a conference on the theatre organised in 1931[71] by the soon-to-be-defunct RAPP, and finally enshrined in Zhdanov's oft-quoted formulation of Socialist Realism in 1934:

Socialist Realism, being the basic method of Soviet literature and criticism, requires from the artists truthful, historically concrete representation of reality in its revolutionary development. Moreover, truth and historical completeness of artistic representation must be combined with the task of ideological *transformation and education* of the working man in the spirit of Socialism.[72]

While the practice of Socialist Realism often diverged from this – and other – expressions of the theory,[73] many novels, films, or plays purporting to belong to the genre featured a

linear narrative structure, positive heroes, and a contemporary, or near-contemporary setting.[74] Nothing could be
further from Vvedensky's *Christmas at the Ivanovs'*, a play written
in 1938, at a time when the war waged in the Soviet press
against the 'formalists' and 'decadents' in the theatre was at its
height.[75]

The play's setting is not the Leningrad of the early Soviet
period, but a bourgeois household in the Russia of the 1890s.
The story is split into nine scenes or tableaux ('kartiny'), which
together follow the fate of a family whose name is Puzyrev (and
not, as the title of the play might suggest, Ivanov) one Christmas
eve. The action begins with the seven Puzyrev children (aged
between one and eighty-two) being given a bath by their nanny
and eagerly discussing the forthcoming festivities. One of the
girls, the thirty-two-year-old Sonya, begins to indulge in sexual
innuendo, which offends her nanny so much that she promptly
decapitates the 'child'. The police immediately arrive to arrest
the murderess and the scene ends. Scene 2 takes us to a nearby
forest, where the nanny's fiancé, Fedor, is one of a number of
woodcutters chopping down Christmas trees. As they finish
their work and leave, three animals (a giraffe, a wolf, and a lion)
enter, and hold a brief conversation about time and death. The
next scene concerns the discovery of Sonya's murder, both by
her parents (who, undeterred, proceed to copulate in front of
the corpse), and by the woodcutters delivering the tree. The
scene, the final one in this act, ends with all of them leaving the
room, and a brief verbal exchange between the dead Sonya's
head and the rest of her body. The beginning of the second act
takes us to the police station, where a policeman tries to cheer
the nanny up by telling her a story about a group of Greek
horsemen which he once saw while on guard duty, before she is
taken off to a lunatic asylum. The scene which follows takes
place in the asylum, where the doctor tells her to go and have
herself executed, while in the same breath declaring there is
nothing wrong with her. Act 2 ends with the sixth scene, which
takes us back to Fedor, who is sleeping with the Puzyrevs' maid
while his fiancée is in the asylum. The third act includes just
two scenes, the seventh, in which the Puzyrevs' dog Vera

delivers a monologue about life and death, and the eighth, which ostensibly concerns the nanny's 'trial', but which includes an account of the case of a certain Kozlov and Oslov (as well as the sudden death of two judges). The ninth and final scene, the only scene in act 4, returns us to the Puzyrev household, only to see their Christmas celebrations cut short, as one by one each member of the family suddenly and unexpectedly dies. As the last of them keels over the play runs out of characters, and so comes to an abrupt end.

By and large *Christmas at the Ivanovs'* has been discussed either as a parody of the classics of Russian literature, or as a forerunner of the Western Theatre of the Absurd.[76] Both views have much to support them; the play is littered with thinly disguised allusions to the works of Dostoevsky and Chekhov (and Ibsen), and animals have the gift of speech and rational thought while humans babble incoherently. What advocates of both approaches tacitly agree upon is that the play subverts a plethora of literary and extra-literary conventions associated with realist drama (the genre to which it most appears to conform as it begins). Indeed, it is this tendency to draw attention to the established codes of realist drama by disrupting them[77]which holds the key to *Christmas at the Ivanovs'* and to what it says about reading and the reception process. For by defamiliarizing the word, the text, and the world, Vvedensky's play underlines the fact that the dramatic text, like any utterance, is 'co-created' by the addressee towards whom it is oriented, however much it might try to pass itself off as an objective 'picture' of reality.

According to theatre semiotician Keir Elam, the conventions, or 'codes' at work in a dramatic text/theatrical performance fall into three broad categories: 'theatrical' codes, 'that permit us to apprehend [the theatrical performance] in its own terms and not as, say, a spontaneous and accidental event or piece of film'; 'dramatic' codes, which depend upon our 'knowledge of the generic, structural, stylistic and other rules [...] relating to the drama and its composition'; and other 'more general cultural, ideological, ethical and epistemological principles which we apply in our extra-theatrical activities'.[78] Conventions

from each of these three classes are subverted by Vvedensky in
Christmas at the Ivanovs'.

The most important 'theatrical' code which Vvedensky's play
subverts is the 'mimetic' nature of drama itself (as 'showing'
rather than 'telling'), which goes back to Aristotle. This was
central to the naturalism of directors such as Konstantin
Stanislavsky at the Moscow Art Theatre,[79] just as it was to the
Symbolists. As Andrey Bely had opined:

In drama the format of art seeks to expand until it achieves the
possibility of being life, in both the literal and figurative senses of the
word.
   That is why performance on stage is a necessary precondition of
dramatic art. The drama cannot be read. What sort of drama would
that be? The action portrayed must be viewed ocularly, the words
enunciated must be heard.[80]

The use of the word 'kartina' ('picture', or 'tableau') to
describe the individual scenes of a play, opera, or ballet,
thereby reinforcing this mimetic illusion, is not unusual in
Russian.[81] Yet Vvedensky problematizes this notion of drama
as picture or tableau – and the idea, which underpins it, of
drama as mimesis – at the very start of *Christmas at the Ivanovs'*.[82]
The description of the opening scene makes it far from clear
whether we are dealing with a three-dimensional scene, or with
a two-dimensional world. For the children appear to be bathing
in a bath-tub which is 'drawn' on stage ('narisovana'):

In the first picture is drawn a bath-tub. The children are bathing on
Christmas Eve. There is also a chest of drawers. To the right of the
door, cooks are slaughtering hens and slaughtering piglets. Nannies,
nannies, nannies are washing the children. All the children are sitting
in one big bath-tub, but the one-year-old boy Petya Perov is bathing
in a wash-basin standing directly opposite the door. On the wall to
the left of the door hangs a clock. The clock reads nine o'clock in the
evening.

На первой картине нарисована ванна. Под сочельник дети
купаются. Стоит и комод. Справа от двери повара режут кур и
режут поросят. Няньки, няньки, няньки моют детей. Все дети
сидят в одной большой ванне, а Петя Перов годовалый мальчик

купается в тазу, стоящем прямо против двери. На стене слева от двери висят часы. На них 9 часов вечера. (p. 157)

If the bath-tub is drawn, and the characters are bathing in it, then does that not mean that they, too, must be drawn? On the other hand, the children say and do things as if they belonged to a three-dimensional world modelled on our own. This question is left unanswered by Vvedensky.

Vvedensky further undermines the mimetic illusion by inscribing a (subjective) narrative voice into his text.[83] This voice is foregounded first and foremost linguistically. The 'stage directions' in the description of the opening scene, for example, contain unconventional language, where words are for no apparent reason repeated, such as 'rezhut' ('are slaughtering'), or 'nyan'ki' ('nannies'). At the start of the third scene, the narrator's syntax breaks down, as sentences are replaced by single words/phrases, once again suggesting the (male?) subjectivity of the narrative voice: 'Night. A coffin. Candles floating down a river. Father-Puzyrev. Spectacles. A beard. Saliva. Tears. Mother-Puzyrev. She is wearing women's armour. She is beautiful. She has a bust.' ('Noch'. Grob. Uplyvayushchie po reke svechi. Puzyrev-otets. Ochki. Boroda. Slyuni. Slezy. Puzyreva-mat'. Na nei zhenskie dospekhi. Ona krasavitsa. U nee est' byust.'; p. 161).[84] As in Kharms's prose, Vvedensky's narrative voice is foregrounded not just linguistically; it is also perversely voyeuristic and calmly detached towards suffering, and never more so than in the matter-of-fact description of Sonya's corpse: 'A table. On the table is a coffin. In the coffin is Sonya Ostrova. In Sonya Ostrova is a heart. In the heart is congealed blood. In the blood are red and white corpuscles. And, of course, ptomaine.' ('Stol. Na stole grob. V grobu Sonya Ostrova. V Sone Ostrovoi serdtse. V serdtse svernuvshayasya krov'. V krovi krasnye i belye shariki. Nu konechno i trupnyi yad.'; p. 167).

Another 'theatrical' code which Vvedensky subverts is the (naturalist) illusion which depends on our bridging the ontological gap between our own world and the world of the play. This was such a central feature of Soviet Socialist Realist drama that in Nikolay Okhlopkov's productions at the Moscow 'Realistic Theatre' between 1930 and 1937, he constantly attempted to break down the ontological division between stage and auditorium by, for example, throwing 'snow' on actors and audience alike.[85] As Okhlopkov himself put it in an essay written some years later:

Do you know the smell of a soldier's cape that has many times been exposed to wind and rain? Do you know the smell of saddles and leather straps, or the scent of hay? Do you know the taste of soldier's porridge, reheated over a campfire? Can you imagine in a flash that you are by the sea in the early morning, and feel the light morning breeze on your face? Many are the beautiful and wonderful things a man can feel, if he loves and knows nature and life. So I wanted to do all this, as far as possible, in the theatre, so that the audience should forget completely that it was watching a play and feel totally in the midst of the men of the Taman Regiment in *The Iron Flood*.[86]

Vvedensky, however, breaks the theatrical illusion very succinctly, by means of a clock which he inserts into scenes where there would not normally be one. For example, the stage directions for scene 2, which takes place in a forest, mention the clock hanging on the stage wall to the left of a door, and showing 9 o'clock. Focusing our attention on the clock is just one of the ways in which Vvedensky shatters the theatrical illusion.

In *Christmas at the Ivanovs'*, Vvedensky subverts not just theatrical codes, but what Elam refers to as 'dramatic', and 'extra-theatrical' codes, too. As far as the dramatic codes are concerned, the clock is once again important, for it is foregrounded not only spatially, but also temporally. Each scene, according to the time shown on the clock at its beginning and end, takes up much more time than the text, and the context, would otherwise suggest. For example, the first scene, which covers just two pages of text, apparently lasts from nine o'clock in the evening until midnight. This apparent incongruity between story time and text time could be partly explained by arguing that it may have taken some time for the children to recover from the shock of Sonya's murder before calling the police, who, in their turn, may not have arrived immediately.

Yet nothing else in the text suggests that this is in fact the case; no reference to time passing is made in the text during the scene itself, and everything is presented as if happening without any temporal ellipses:

NANNY (*seizes the axe and chops off her head*): You deserved this death.
The children shout: Murderess, she is a murderess. Save us. Stop bathing.
The cooks stop slaughtering hens and slaughtering piglets. At two paces from the body lies the bloody, desperate head. The dog Vera barks behind the door. The police enter.
POLICE: Where are the parents?

Нянька (*хватает топор и отрубает ей голову*): Ты заслужила эту смерть.
Дети кричат: Убийца, она убийца. Спасите нас. Прекратите купанье.
Повара перестают резать кур и резать поросят. Удаленная на два шага от тела лежит на полу кровавая отчаянная голова. За дверями воет собака Вера. Входит полиция.
Полиция: Где же родители? (p. 158)

The policemen do indeed appear to arrive immediately. Yet their arrival seems unmotivated, marked with a haste and apparent prescience usually associated not with realist drama, but with the silent movie, the cartoon strip, or the *balagan*.[87] There are similar temporal discrepancies in each of the other scenes, between the initial and final time, as shown on the clock. The clock, then, oscillates throughout the play between the foreground (as, for example, in non-domestic settings or at the end of each scene) and the background (in those scenes where the presence of a clock does not appear incongruous). It is thus implicated in that continual process of frame-making/frame-breaking which contributes to the play's overall self-consciousness.[88]

Another set of extra-theatrical codes which Vvedensky's play appears to subvert concerns our epistemological principles; in other words, there is frequently a discrepancy between what it is reasonable to assume an audience might know about the world, and what actually happens in the world of the text (this, of course, also has a bearing on the ontological illusion). For example, one searches in vain for a creditworthy psychological explanation for many of the characters' actions, much as one does in so many of Kharms's texts. Pseudo-explanations are sometimes given. For instance, the policeman in the courtroom tells a story about the time he was on guard duty and a group of Greek horsemen rode by. When he is asked to explain the point of his story, he simply replies 'I wanted to distract the murderess from her gloomy thoughts' ('Ya khotel otvlech' ubiitsu ot ee mrachnykh myslei'; p. 164). Most often, however, the play offers no explanation whatever as to why the characters behave in the way they do; it is up to the spectator to judge, rather as Kharms's 'spectator' is asked to pass judgement in *The Comedy of the City of Petersburg*.

On other occasions, it is far from clear *how* they act in the way they do. At the end of act 1, for example, the body and head of the recently defunct Sonya appear to engage in conversation (although the lack of ears apparently means the body, by its own admission, cannot hear, the absence of a mouth seems to be no obstacle to its talking).[89] *Christmas at the Ivanovs'* contains many instances of this kind of behavioural 'nonsense', centred mainly on the question of who has the ability to talk and who does not. Apparently 'dumb' woodcutters, animals, and infants all speak, while human adults make noises like animals or use the phonemes 'A o u e i ya B G R T' instead of recognizable words (p. 173).[90] These, and other details of the play, such as the suggestion that an eighty-two-year-old can still be called a 'child', all serve to establish an *asymmetrical* relationship between the world of the text and our world, the world of the audience.[91]

Another, final category of extra-theatrical codes which Vvedensky subverts concerns not knowledge but what Elam refers to as behavioural/ethical and ideological codes. There is a discrepancy between certain things which happen in *Christmas at the Ivanovs'*, and the values which it is reasonable to assume most readers or spectators confronted by the play are likely to hold. The nanny's sudden murder of Sonya, and her less than credible attempt to justify the deed; the sight of Mr. and Mrs. Puzyrev copulating in front of their daughter's corpse, their eagerness for the Christmas celebrations undampened by her tragic end; the doctor's indifferent dismissal of the nanny, which is both a reassurance that she is sane and an exhortation to go and get herself executed; Fedor's apparently total lack of concern over the fate of his fiancée: all this shocks and alienates us, very much like the violence which fills Kharms's prose.

By parodying canonical dramatic texts and well-established theatrical conventions, *Christmas at the Ivanovs'* reminds us that writing is always rereading. At the same time, subverting a number of 'extra-theatrical' codes, Vvedensky's play underlines that, as readers, we will always bring to the text what Jauss has termed a 'horizon of expectations'. *Christmas at the Ivanovs'*, while appearing full of Formalist-inspired defamiliarizing strategies, points in fact to the quintessentially Bakhtinian notion of the dialogic nature of the word/utterance/text – a concept which Bakhtin had expressed just a few years before Vvedensky wrote his play,[92] in his essay 'Discourse in the Novel':

The word is born in dialogue, as a living answer in that dialogue. The word is shaped in dialogic interaction with an alien word already in the object. The word forms a concept of its own object in a dialogic way.

But this does not exhaust the internal dialogism of the word. It is not only in the object that it encounters an alien word; every word is oriented towards an answer and cannot escape the profound influence of the answering word which it anticipates.[93]

Furthermore, by breaking so many rules, by defeating the reader's expectations so consistently, at so many moments, *Christmas at the Ivanovs'* reminds us that 'all speech is dialogic speech, directed at another person, at his *understanding*, and at his real or potential *response*'.[94] Put another way, Vvedensky's play, by flouting so many conventions (both literary and extra-literary), underlines the fact that there can be no text without context, that the listener's purview is as important in shaping the speaker's utterance as either that speaker's intention or the object spoken about, that, ultimately, 'discourse is a skeleton which is fleshed out only in the process of creative perception, consequently, only in the process of real social interaction'.[95]

Furthermore, Vvedensky's play points to the fact that such rules also apply to works of drama, that dramatic texts – 'plays' – constitute just as much an utterance – in the Bakhtinian sense of the word – as any other discursive genre. *Christmas at the Ivanovs'*, then, underlines the fact that 'it is with the spectator, in brief, that theatrical communication begins and ends' (Elam, *The Semiotics of Theatre and Drama*, p. 97), and it does so in a way which has important ramifications for the way in which drama as a genre represents reality.[96]

Christmas at the Ivanovs' can be read not only as a commentary on the reception process, but also – and perhaps primarily – as part of Vvedensky's critique of the naturalist and monologic assumptions of Socialist Realism, and Socialist Realist drama in particular.[97] If the dramatic text/performance is truly an utterance, then it is a 'telling', rather than a 'showing' – with all that that implies for its status as 'truth' – and, moreover, it is constructed with its addressee's answer in mind as much as the speaker's intention. Naturalism – in the broad sense – is a lie, since it works to conceal the fact that a dramatic text is never seamlessly imitative of reality; if it were, we would see Petya going to the toilet, instead of hearing his nanny exhorting him to pretend that he is going (p. 172).[98] This means that drama, like any other artistic medium, cannot simply be monolithically monologic, but depends on the audience's 'aesthetic interaction', since only this can ensure 'the creation of the artistic work and [...] its continual recreations in cocreative perception' (Voloshinov, 'Discourse in Life', p. 9).

In a recent overview of OBERIU, Anatoly Aleksandrov has described *Christmas at the Ivanovs'*, as 'a drama to be read' (Aleksandrov, 'Evrika Oberiutov', p. 32).[99] Yet this is surely oversimplifying matters; for there is still much in the play that can be shown, in however stylized a way (as recent productions and adaptations of the play have demonstrated).[100] It would surely be possible to produce the play on a stage, in which case it might resemble a gruesome pantomime/circus show with a narrator figure situated off stage, in a way reminiscent of Fedor Sologub's 'Theatre of a Single Will' ('Teatr odnoi voli') performances, in which a reader, representing the author, and sitting to one side of theatre would read all the stage directions.[101]

Whether or not *Christmas at the Ivanovs'* was written to be read, or performed, is in the final analysis irrelevant. What can be said with a greater degree of certainty is that in this play Vvedensky foregrounds the process of aesthetic reception, and specifically the addressee-oriented nature of drama. Moreover, Vvedensky thereby questions the Aristotelian notion of drama as mimesis, a notion which united Naturalist, Symbolist, and (Socialist) Realist dramatic models. Ultimately, the question of aesthetic reception is secondary to Vvedensky, who makes us aware of the assumptions behind our own reception in order to underline the dialogic nature of all discourse, the fact that all utterances are oriented both towards previous utterances, and towards a future answer. Vvedensky's play with conventions, like Kharms's, forces the reader to engage with the text actively, rather than passively (in this sense both writers were subverting contemporary orthodox textual pragmatics). Refuting the mimetic nature of drama in favour of a dialogic theatricality, *Christmas at the Ivanovs'* is reminiscent of Marinetti's Futurist theatre, which similarly sought to do away with 'photographic reproductions of our daily life', aiming instead at 'entertaining and amusing its public with effects of comedy, erotic excitement and imaginative shock'.[102] It must be said, however, that my own reading of Vvedensky's play is in many ways a rewriting, since I am in effect making explicit that which is generally implicit in the text. To see a more explicit, thematic (rather than merely formal) treatment of the dialogic relationship between text and reader, I shall now turn to Vaginov, and in particular to his novel *The Labours and Days of Svistonov*.

THE READER IN THE TEXT: *THE LABOURS AND DAYS OF SVISTONOV* BY KONSTANTIN VAGINOV

The Labours and Days of Svistonov was first published in 1929,[103] shortly after the rise of RAPP, and just before the start of the Party's vituperative press campaign against 'fellow-travellers' such as Pil'nyak and Zamyatin. This was a time when it was still just possible to hope for a genuine dialogue between writer and reader. Such a dialogue, based on Bakhtin's 'dialogic' model of reading as 'active understanding', is itself the subject of Vaginov's second novel.[104]

Like *The Goat's Song* before it, this novel portrays a writer (this time Svistonov) and a circle of acquaintances living in post-revolutionary Leningrad. These characters appear just as pretentious and sham as the unknown poet and his friends. There is Kuku, who spends his time cultivating a Pushkin image (complete with sideburns!); the self-styled 'mystic' Psikhachev, who holds pseudo-occult evenings while claiming to be several hundred years old; and Deryabkin with his 'crusade against Philistinism', based on the belief that hygiene is synonymous with culture and on an obsession with calligraphy.[105] One important difference between the two novels, however, is that whereas in *The Goat's Song* these secondary characters are themselves mostly artists, Svistonov's companions serve as material for his own book. Svistonov 'translates' them all – and, eventually, himself – into the novel which he writes, the creation of which lies at the centre of Vaginov's own novel. Indeed, the only reason Svistonov cultivates his various friendships is in order to cull material for his novel. These people appear to be no more important to him than the countless seemingly unconnected newspaper cuttings, advertisements, secondhand books and anecdotes which he also collects, and which are destined also to find their way, in annotated and refracted form, into his book. So powerful is Svistonov's obsession with things bookish that he eventually introduces a writer into his own book, a writer, furthermore, who writes in much the same way that he himself does and bears a name ('Vistonov') more than a little resembling his own. If Svistonov and Vistonov share virtually the same name, they ultimately appear to inhabit the same world; *The Labours and Days of Svistonov* ends with Svistonov utterly incapable of distinguishing between the world of his novel and the world in which he lives, to such an extent that he feels 'locked' ('zapert') inside his own text.[106] For him there will be no possibility, as there was for the author figure in *The Goat's Song*, to come back out of the book into the Petersburg night air.

A number of Vaginov's contemporary Soviet readers, in the guise of the leading journals' literary critics, were vehemently hostile to *The Labours and Days of Svistonov* for its apparent lack of concern with the problems of socialist reconstruction. One critic, writing for the pro-proletarian journal *Pechat' i revolyutsiya*, went so far as to call for the 'ruthless ideological extermination of Vaginovism ['vaginovshchina']'.[107] More recently, Russian and Western scholars alike have focused on the novel's metafictional characteristics. It has been suggested, for example, that in Svistonov, who composes his novels by juxtaposing all kinds of disparate material, Vaginov is caricaturing Formalist theory and practice.[108] However, it is once again the relationship between Bakhtin's thought and Vaginov's artistic praxis which has proved potentially the most fruitful line of enquiry. As was shown in chapter 1, David Shepherd has argued persuasively that Vaginov 'carnivalizes' authorial authority, subverting the author's conventional position in the textual hierarchy in a manner in line with contemporary left-art theory (in this respect, *The Labours and Days of Svistonov* stands approximately mid-way between *The Goat's Song* and *Harpagoniana*).[109] Anthony Anemone has also examined *The Labours and Days of Svistonov* from a Bakhtinian perspective, if only to suggest that the novel represents a rejection by Vaginov of Bakhtin's concept of 'dialogism' ('Carnival in Theory and Practice', pp. 9–10).

What the discussions of *The Labours and Days of Svistonov* offered by Shepherd and Anemone no more than hint at is that this novel has just as much to say about reading as it does about writing.[110] In this work Vaginov foregrounds the issue of reading in two ways; first, by making reading difficult (rather as Kharms and Vvedensky do); and second, by making reading one of the central themes of his novel.

How does Vaginov make reading difficult in *The Labours and Days of Svistonov*? In a manner which calls to mind Vvedensky's *Christmas at the Ivanovs'*, Vaginov begins the novel by 'showing' the audience a 'picture', only subsequently to blur that picture quite considerably. The opening pages of the novel contain a description of the view which Svistonov can see as he looks out of the window of his flat. The moderate semantic charge which the theme of seeing is given in this opening section of the novel, with phrases such as 'In the window *could be seen*' ('V okne *vidnelis'*'), and 'Svistonov *looked* out of the window' (Svistonov *smotrel* iz okna' (p. 162; my emphasis), is considerably increased in the description of Svistonov's dream which immediately, and rather unexpectedly, follows. The account of this dream contains a series of verbs indicating, or implying, a visual activity: Svistonov *recognizes* ('uznaet') himself in a man hurrying along the street; another man is described as *looking* ('smotrya') at his own face reflected in a samovar; children *stare* ('glyadyat') for hours at a lamp, a stove, or a corner of the floor; a clerk sits for hours smoking a pipe and *watches* ('smotrit') the smoke swirling around; Svistonov *sees* ('vidit') himself *peeping* ('zaglyanet') into a cellar; and he enters a little shop and *looks around* ('osmotrit'; p. 163).

If Svistonov's reading of the world amounts to a leisurely observation of material and phenomena which are relatively stable, then it differs quite considerably from the kind of reading one must apply to Vaginov's text. For the initial ease with which the reader is drawn into the novel's diegesis, in a narrative technique reminiscent of much nineteenth-century realism, is in stark contrast to the difficulty of recovering that diegesis throughout much of the rest of the novel. Vaginov, rather like Kharms, deprives the reader of much information which may be said to be relevant to the world inhabited by his characters. We see far more, for example, out of Svistonov's window than we do of Svistonov and his wife, Lenochka – or any of the other characters to whom we are introduced throughout the novel. Very rarely are we ever given any physical depiction of these characters, Vaginov generally preferring to tell us what they read rather than what they look like.

This is just one kind of textual 'gap' which Vaginov obliges the reader to fill in for her/himself. The inter-personal relationships between some of these characters are similarly left unclear. Why does Lenochka leave home, and where does she go? From where does she write her letter to Svistonov (p. 214)? What is the precise relationship to Svistonov of the deaf mute Trina Rublis, with whom Svistonov appears at one point in the text to be co-habiting? The answers to these and other questions are never provided; we never see nearly enough of the context behind the text. Like Lenochka, all the characters in Svistonov's life, and Vaginov's novel, initially appear central to the book, only to fade suddenly into the background and appear much more peripheral and episodic as the novel develops. It is as if Vaginov is constantly questioning the relative importance of the characters which people his own novel, much as Svistonov appears to hesitate before deciding to include certain of his acquaintances in his own text.

Just as we are so often prevented from seeing the relationships between these characters, so it is sometimes unclear as to how the events in which they take part are connected. At the end of chapter 2, which deals with holidays among the dacha community, the narrator suddenly introduces the reader to a character called 'Psikhachev'. Psikhachev goes to see another character to whom the reader has not been introduced, a certain Zoya Fedorovna, who is busy entertaining guests on her birthday. There then follows a sketchy description of Psikhachev, and of a game of forfeits which they all play. The relevance of this scene to the main story only gradually emerges, however; after a number of paragraphs mention is made of two characters to whom we have already been introduced, namely Kuku and Naden'ka, and a little further still Psikhachev is described asking Svistonov to include him in his novel (pp. 200–2). The relevance of the passage to the rest of the novel is thus delayed, and revealed only indirectly to the reader.

At times the *fabula* disappears altogether. By no means insignificant (as we shall see later) is the fact that so little of Svistonov's text is presented to us, compared with the time he spends in the novel gathering material for it. At the end of chapter 6 in particular, Svistonov's announcement to the character Iya that he wants to read her his latest chapter is followed immediately in the text by her reaction to the chapter – the framed novel is omitted (and explicitly so) from the framing novel. The narrator actually admits at one point to withholding from the reader information concerning the *fabula*; commenting on a night which Psikhachev and Svistonov spend in conversation, he tells us, 'of what guest and host discussed that night, the reader has no need to know' ('o chem govorili v etot vecher gost' i khozyain, chitatelyu znat' ne nado'; p. 225).

Ironically, Vaginov's novel comes to resemble the same kind of collage of materials and devices that Svistonov's text constitutes. Leonardo Paleari no doubt has in mind textual strategies such as those discussed here when he observes that 'the first chapter [of the novel] ends like it might in any "realist" novel, and yet the reader – even the most unsophisticated reader – feels that behind the entirely real facts there lurks something which breaks the visible order of things, which as it were displaces the usual coordinates [of that order]'.[111] By the various gaps in the *fabula* which the reader is forced actively to fill in, Vaginov's novel, like much of Kharms's prose, anticipates Barthes' notion of the 'writerly' text. These gaps 'actualize'[112] reading, forcing the reader as she/he negotiates them to fluctuate between involvement in the text and awareness of the reading self. This is also the effect of the numerous embedded texts in *The Labours and Days of Svistonov*, and in particular the newspaper cuttings and advertisements which are pasted into Svistonov's notebooks, which Lenochka reads to her husband, and which are reproduced typographically in the novel (pp. 170–1).[113]

By drawing attention to the process of (our) reading, *The Labours and Days of Svistonov* underlines the fact that a literary-fictional text, like any utterance, is dialogically oriented towards an addressee. In fact, the Bakhtinian notion of 'dialogism' is as central to Vaginov's work as it is to Kharms's and Vvedensky's. The difference between Kharms's prose and *Christmas at the Ivanovs'* on the one hand, and *The Labours and Days of Svistonov* on the other, however, is that Vaginov's novel focuses not so much on the dialogic, 'two-sided' word itself, as on the reader, the addressee of that word.

This novel is full of characters who read. At one end of the scale is the minor character Pavel Uronov, who declaims poetry as his contribution to an impromptu talent show during Zoya's birthday party (p. 201). The letter which Lenochka sends to Svistonov contains the results of a mini-survey which she has conducted, on Svistonov's request, on what those around her remember of their reading of the character Liza from Turgenev's novel *A Nest of Gentlefolk* (*Dvoryanskoe gnezdo*, (1859), p. 214). Practically all Vaginov's readers engage in a singularly monologic kind of reading, which involves suppressing their own status as readers, and determining the 'timeless' meaning of what they read. Kuku, for example, likes to 'read' dreams to determine their hidden significance (p. 196). Psikhachev organizes a reading club (described as an 'academic assembly' ('akademicheskoe sobranie')), at which he sits as self-appointed president (complete with spurs and sash), spouting commentaries on selected passages from (for example) the Bible, Seneca, and Confucius (p. 232). Psikhachev gives the clerk Yablochkin a copy of Plutarch's *Cato*, and as Yablochkin reads, he feels himself becoming 'cleverer and cleverer' ('umnee i umnee'; p. 229). For another character, Mashen′ka, reading means searching for the most hallowed thoughts of writers, whom she regards as 'genii' (pp. 253–4). More mundanely, the deaf and dumb Trina Rublis contents herself with reading for the plot, and skips anything superfluous to this, particularly descriptions (pp. 205–6). Biographically-oriented reading is also represented in *The Labours and Days of Svistonov*, whether in Kuku's passion for the details of great people's (viz. writers') lives, or in Lenochka's obsessive habit, on reading Svistonov's poetry, of recalling where he wrote it and what he was wearing (p. 169). A similar kind of reading is that which concentrates on the 'real' lives of a work's characters rather than on details concerning the real author. This type of hermeneutics proves just as obsessive as Lenochka's; as soon as a work by Svistonov is available for consumption his readers begin by looking for clues as to the 'real' identity of the characters portrayed in it. This is not to say that such an approach is not to some extent justified; Svistonov's avowed purpose in life is, as we have seen, to 'translate' those around him into his novel(s).

This last mode of reading appears very convincing here, at least as concerns the reappropriation of Svistonov's work – and judging by the main focus of much Vaginov criticism it seems to have convinced a number of readers that it is valid for

Vaginov's own novels as well. Even Svistonov himself is not averse to taking an object from his own life or from his immediate surroundings and tacking it on to one of the characters in his novel (p. 210). Yet, however much they might all be taken in by this theory of writing (and hence of reading), things are far from that simple. For the idea that specific correspondences can be sought by the reader between the world inside the text and the world outside it is exaggerated to such a degree that it appears as ridiculous as any of the other theories of reading seen in the novel. It is given its most explicit, and most hyperbolized, expression in the foreword to Svistonov's novel, which is almost the last thing Svistonov writes. This foreword, addressed explicitly to the reader, discusses reading as a search for aspects of the world outside the text that are transposed and concretized inside it:

if people are described in such a book, they seem to be alive, as it were, in front of you. You recognize their facial features, their physiognomy, their habits. You have the impression that you would recognize them immediately, if they could appear in front of you.

если описываются в такой книге люди, то они как будто живые перед вами. Вы узнаете черты лица их, физиономию, привычки. Вам кажется, что вы тотчас узнали бы их, если бы они могли явиться перед вами. (p. 257)

Yet the tone of this whole foreword and the examples which it gives undercut any seriousness which it might claim for itself. The opening sentences are ridiculous in their banality and their patronizing tone; 'It's nice to read an interesting book. [...] Isn't that so, dear readers?' ('Priyatno chitat' interesnuyu knigu. [...] Ne pravda li, milye chitateli?'; p. 256). The example of a wood, whose cool shade the reader feels as she/he reads, sounds particularly trite.

The point is not that such correspondences do not exist between the text and the real world in which it is produced; the manifest truth of this fact is mirrored by the obviousness of the transformation of 'Kuku' into 'Kukureku' and 'Svistonov' into 'Vistonov'. It is rather that a hermeneutics which is no more than an obsessive, self-consuming search for correspondences between these two worlds – virtually the only kind of reading to which Vaginov's first novel had been subjected – is shown in *The Labours and Days of Svistonov* to be fundamentally flawed.[114] It is flawed because it fails to take account of the context of reading itself. Like virtually all the other kinds of reading presented in Vaginov's novel, it prevents the reader from entering into a real dialogue with the text. It is by the extent to which they embrace dialogism, or actively recontextualize some of what Bakhtin calls the 'boundless masses of forgotten textual meanings' of what he reads, that Svistonov's readings differ from those of all Vaginov's other characters. It is in this sense also that Svistonov's readings work, like the gaps in Vaginov's own writing, against 'interpretation' as passive and monologic.

At more than one moment in the novel, various characters equate reading with the monologic extraction of meaning already present in its entirety in the text, with no regard for the context of interpretation. Discussing the theory behind his explanation of dreams, for example, Kuku defines it in terms of what it signifies: 'A dream is an omen' ('Son est' znamenie'), he declares (p. 196). When Psikhachev and his occultist circle read ancient texts in order to 'interpret' ('tolkovat'') them, this undoubtedly contributes to Svistonov's feeling bored, awkward and more than a little amused (pp. 232–3). For Svistonov's views on reading could not be further removed from those of Kuku and Psikhachev. For him, constructing a world based on his reading of the 'text' all around him (in much the same incomplete and imperfect way that we construct his world from what we read in Vaginov's text), reading is just as creative a process as writing. Indeed, reading is no different for Svistonov from (re)writing.

Svistonov is obsessed with reading, whether literally or metaphorically. He obviously takes reading very seriously, as is witnessed by the meticulous, painstaking way in which he reads: 'He read slowly, as if walking around a nice neighbourhood. He loved to think about each phrase, to sit down a little, and have a smoke' ('On chital medlenno, kak by shel peshkom po prelestnym okrestnostyam. On lyubil nad kazhdoi frazoi podumat', posidet', pokurit''; p. 210). But his reading extends

beyond the printed page; for him, everyone he meets is a text to
be read: ' "People are also books", thought Svistonov as he
rested. "It's nice to read them" ' (' "Lyudi – te zhe knigi, –
otdykhaya, dumal Svistonov – Priyatno chitat' ikh" '; p. 239).
For Svistonov, furthermore, there is no essential difference
between reading and writing. When he feels the urge to write,
for example, he does not pick up a notebook ('(zapisnuyu)
knizhku') and start to write ('pisat''); instead, he picks up a book
('knigu') and starts to read ('chitat''; p. 165). Reading is so
important for Svistonov that he actually equates it with writing:
'Svistonov lay in bed and read, that is he wrote, since for him
they were one and the same thing' ('Svistonov lezhal v posteli i
chital, t.e. pisal, tak kak dlya nego eto bylo odno i to zhe'; ibid.).

The point is that what separates Svistonov's reading from
everyone else's in the novel is that his reading is creative, and it
is creative because it is a rewriting, 'perepisan'e', not simply as
copying (one meaning of the word), but as redrafting (another
possible sense):

He felt the urge to write. He took a book and began to *read*. Svistonov
was not methodical in the way he *created* [...] On the contrary, all his
material arose from vague comments in the margins of books, from
stolen similes, from skilfully *rewritten* pages, from overheard conversations, from distorted gossip.

Ему захотелось писать. Он взял книгу и стал *читать*. Свистонов
творил не планомерно [...] Напротив, все его вещи возникали из
безобразных заметок на полях книг, из украденных сравнений,
из умело *переписанных* страниц, из подслушанных разговоров, из
повернутых сплетен. (ibid., my emphasis)

To say that reading has, or should have, the same status as
writing is neither to claim, as Stanley Fish does, that the text
only comes to exist as a written artefact while it is being
read,[115] nor to suggest, *pace* Derrida, that the reader 'writes' the
text by unlocking the signified's multitude of traces.[116] Rather,
Svistonov's reading is creative to the extent that, like Bakhtin's
reader/listener, he brings his own situation (historical and
social) to bear on the texts which he reads, and thus engages in
a real dialogue with those texts.

In one sense, of course, Svistonov appears to reject his own historical context, rather like the characters of *The Goat's Song*. Perhaps one of the main reasons why Soviet critics such as Raisa Messer felt the need to take Vaginov so vehemently to task over *The Labours and Days of Svistonov* was his portrayal of Svistonov himself. In an age in which 'modernity' should have been swallowing up all that lay in its path, Vaginov had created a hero who whiled away the hours reading Old French literature by candlelight, and writing with a quill.[117] Details such as this have led Shepherd to remark that Svistonov 'rigorously rejects the recognizably contemporary in favour of the eccentric or outlandish' (Shepherd, *Beyond Metafiction*, p. 101). Shepherd is, of course, justified in pointing out that Svistonov in many respects eschews what Soviet writers were increasingly expected to embrace. Yet just as Svistonov's attempt to preserve and extend the 'high' cultural tradition leads to the dissolution of that same tradition, as Shepherd observes, so his apparent rejection of his own historical situation is undercut by the ways he brings that situation into his reading.

This situation, however much this goes against the grain of his own particular world view, is revealed in much of what he (re)writes. As Nikol'skaya observes, one particular 'layer' of Vaginov's novel is formed by the theme of the reception of the literature of the past by a modern consciousness, or reader (Nikol'skaya, 'Tragediya chudakov', p. 14). Many of Svistonov's source texts are historically, or geographically, or both, far removed from his own Leningrad. His reading matter includes a text on ancient Russian cooking utensils, an account of Wilhelm de Rubrik's oriental travels in 1253, a St Petersburg calendar for 1754, and a children's book written in 1842. Even the newspaper cuttings which Svistonov collects (and which are reproduced typographically in Vaginov's novel) all come from before the Revolution, a radically different world from Svistonov's own. Yet for much of the novel Svistonov's reading constitutes a creative redrafting in which these historical texts serve as the skeletal context in which he places his own – inevitably 'Soviet' – characters.

At one moment we see a fragment of a text in Old French

which Svistonov has written down. There seems to be nothing particularly relevant to Svistonov's (literary) time or (linguistic) space in this piece, which is a story about a wizard and a great feast. Yet what immediately follows the extract reveals that Svistonov's reception of this text is to be productive, dialogic (while also looking back to the recent reception of Vaginov's own novel, *The Goat's Song*); he is going to use it to reflect certain truths about his own society, and those who people it:

Svistonov began to reflect. What would happen to those men and women when they read his book? Now they happily and festively came to meet him, but then there would perhaps be such a confused din of voices, of offended *amour-propre*, of betrayed friendship, and of derided fantasies.

Свистонов стал раздумывать. Что будет со всеми этими женщинами и мужчинами, когда они прочтут его книгу? Сейчас они радостно и празднично выходят ему навстречу, а тогда, быть может, раздастся смутный шум голосов, оскорбленных самолюбий, обманутой дружбы, осмеянных мечтаний. (p. 229)

This passage, perhaps more than any other in Vaginov's novel, points out the inadequacy of the *roman à clef* theory of reading, if such a theory is not placed within the broader context of the issue of dialogism.

A similar refraction of an overtly historical text occurs in the novel's final chapter, where Svistonov 'modifies' (the verb Vaginov uses to describe his activity, 'pereinachival', sounds very much like 'perenachal', 'recommenced') the pages of the children's book of 1842, by including characters contemporaneous to himself and, indeed, himself. If Svistonov is personally, as well as historically, situated in the reading (and writing) that is his novel, then this is further underscored by the way in which he includes in an episode about Psikhachev not just historical details such as the character Chavchavadze, but also material from his own immediate physical surroundings, namely the bar in which he sits while he writes.[118]

Yet this is not the final word. Just as no text, in Bakhtin's most challenging formulation, is *inherently* either dialogic or monologic, but is the site of an endless struggle between the two, so Svistonov is himself torn between these two orientations. The tension which exists between his complicity in his own context and denial of that context is most succinctly shown in his reading/rewriting of the passage on the town of Telav from a guide book (pp. 166–7). On the one hand, Svistonov's reworked text contains a trace of politicization, as his character Chavchavadze inveighs against a merchant in terms fully consonant with Soviet propaganda of Svistonov's own period; 'Chavchavadze looked with disgust at the merchant sitting next to him [...] "Money-grubber", muttered Chavchavadze, "base tribe, lackey"' ('Chavchavadze s otvrashcheniem posmotrel na sidevshego ryadom kuptsa [...] "Torgash, – probormotal Chavchavadze, – podloe plemya, lakei"'; p. 166). Yet, as Shepherd points out, Svistonov rejects the idea of making Chavchavadze an engineer in Moscow, and portrays him instead as a prince. His denial of history leads him, like Vvedensky in *Minin and Pozharsky*, to seek to include in this text real characters from different eras and geographical locations, such as a Pole, and 'an illegitimate son, one of the Bonapartes, who commanded a Russian regiment in the 1880s' ('nezakonnogo syna, odnogo iz Bonapartov, komandovavshego v 80-kh godakh russkim polkom'; p. 167). Similarly, when in Vaginov's last chapter Svistonov goes into the 'Workers' Garden' in search of material for his novel, he cannot make up his mind whether to include, on the one hand, the (tsarist) Admiralty Building, or, on the other, the (proletarian) 'people' ('narod'; p. 257). The dichotomy in Svistonov's readings is succinctly expressed by Iya, who exclaims to him 'vy proglyadeli sovremennost'' (p. 238). Although Iya means that Svistonov has *overlooked* his own society by referring intertextually to Balzac and Hoffmann in his writing, her sentence could also mean that Svistonov has *looked through* his own society, while reading.

The ambiguity with which Svistonov relates to 'the other' is only resolved in his relationship to his own self. For if, however incompletely, he does bring his own context as a reader to bear on the texts which he reads, then he seeks to deny the possibility of subsequent dialogical exchange between his own text and any future reader. He fears that, just as Psikhachev's 'perepiska' (i.e. 'correspondence'), is eventually read by a reader for whom they were not intended (Svistonov himself), so a similar fate might befall his own 'perepiski' (i.e. 'rewritings'). This is why he finds in Trina Rublis the perfect reader. She is a deaf mute, yet Svistonov insists on reading aloud his text to her himself, secure in the knowledge that in this way she will have no access to it, and will therefore be unable to engage in any kind of dialogue – metaphorically or literally – with it: 'He felt safe. She would not overhear his thoughts, and would reveal to no-one the details of his creation. He could talk to her about whatever he liked. She was the ideal listener' ('On chuvstvoval sebya v bezopasnosti. Ona ne podslushaet ego myslei, nikomu ne peredast podrobnostei ego tvorchestva. S nei on mog govorit' o chem ugodno. Eto byl ideal'nyi slushatel''; p. 206).[119] Svistonov's attitude, so succinctly expressed here, underscores the irony of his view of art as something existing 'beyond the grave'. For Svistonov, this metaphor signifies eternity and therefore immortality; for Bakhtin, on the other hand, such images imply a refusal of time, and a denial of the text's dialogic possibilities. For Bakhtin, such art is dead art: 'The text lives only by coming into contact with another text (context). Only at the point of this contact between texts does a light flash, illuminating both the past and the future, joining a given text to a dialogue' ('Tekst zhivet tol'ko soprikasayas' s drugim tekstom (kontekstom). Tol'ko v tochke etogo kontakta tekstov vspykhivaet svet, osveshchayushchii i nazad i vpered, priobshchayushchii dannyi tekst k dialogu'; 'K metodologii gumanitarnykh nauk', p. 364).

Svistonov's acceptance, at the end of the novel, of an exclusively text-bound existence stems, ultimately, from a rejection of reading as 'based on dialogic relations between reader and text, and text and context' (Shepherd, 'Bakhtin and the Reader', p. 98). However, the dichotomy between openness and closure which characterizes much of Svistonov's reading/writing means that if, as Perlina and Anemone argue, Vaginov is engaging in his own dialogue with Bakhtin's notion of the novel as an open, dialogic text, then this dialogue is by no means as straightforward as they both suggest.[120]

The irony is that Svistonov's ultimate refusal of dialogism comes from a character whose whole existence has so far been nothing if not a series of dialogues. If, as the narrator suggests, each person's life is punctuated by a night of momentous doubt, which is followed either by victory or defeat (p. 223), then *The Labours and Days of Svistonov* is in one sense the story of Svistonov's doubt about the nature of reading. Svistonov eventually eradicates all doubt, but Vaginov's novel makes it abundantly clear that in so doing he makes the 'wrong' choice; and the monologism which he embraces is no better than that ultimate defeat, death. Perhaps it is because he dialogically accepts for so much of the novel his own socio-historical situation, that Svistonov has ultimately to accept everything which that situation implies, including, and especially, the monologism dominant within it. To say that such a paradox stands metaphorically for Vaginov's own situation, reading and writing as he was in a society where the vehement imposition of state control on literature increasingly made the writer's choice between monologism and dialogism an irrelevance, would perhaps be to impose on *The Labours and Days of Svistonov* the kind of finalizing interpretation against which the novel itself at least partly militates. What can be said with greater certainty, however, is that Vaginov's second novel contains a tension between two types of reading, one passive and timeless, the other creative and historically determined.

To conclude, Vaginov's *The Labours and Days of Svistonov*, like Kharms's prose and Vvedensky's *Christmas at the Ivanovs'*, lays bare the dialogic nature of reading as 'active understanding'. Unlike Kharms or Vvedensky, Vaginov also thematizes reading by including in the text itself a plethora of readers and different images of reading. Whatever their differences, however, Kharms, Vvedensky, and Vaginov go much further than most other Russian modernists in their affirmation of reading as an active process which both helps to shape the text-utterance, and involves the making of meaning.[121] While foregrounding the issue of aesthetic reception, all three writers also raise questions concerning language and representation. It is to this problem that I shall devote my third chapter on OBERIU metafiction.

CHAPTER 3

Language and representation

In my first two chapters I have examined OBERIU metafiction
from the point of view, first, of the writer, and second, of the
reader. If writer and reader may be said to stand at opposite
ends of the 'horizontal' axis of the text, then the focus of this
chapter will shift to what might be described as the 'vertical'
axis, namely the relationship between the text itself and the real
world. The exact nature of that relationship – what Vaginov
refers to in *The Labours and Days of Svistonov* as 'the correlation
between the imaginary and the real' ('sootnoshenie [...] pridu-
mannogo i real'nogo'; p. 211) – was a constant concern of
Russian modernism and of the Soviet avant-garde alike. As we
shall see, it was a question which also exercised the minds of the
Oberiuty and their associates.

For many artists, interest in the nature of aesthetic representation amounted to an obsession with language, with the
relationship between words and the world. The Symbolists, for
example, believed that their words offered access to a higher,
more authentic 'reality', *A realibus ad realiora*, to quote the title of
a cycle of poems by Blok. Indeed, one of Russian Symbolism's
foremost theorists, Andrey Bely, believed that the poet could
use the word to create an alternative, and better world:

Language is the most powerful instrument of creation. [...] If words
did not exist, then neither would the world itself. [...] In the word is
given the original act of creation. The word connects the speechless,
invisible world swarming in the subconscious depths of my individual

consciousness with the speechless, senseless world swarming outside my individual ego. The word creates a new, third world: a world of sound symbols by means of which both the secrets of a world located outside me and those imprisoned in a world inside me come to light. [. . .] In the word and only in the word do I recreate for myself what surrounds me from within and from without, for I *am* the word and only the word.[1]

While the Symbolists maintained that the word afforded access to a higher reality, the Acmeists reacted strongly against such a view, asserting that poetry 'represented' nothing but itself. Comparing a poem, in his essay 'The Morning of Acmeism' ('Utro akmeisma', 1913), to the stone fashioned by a mason, Mandel'shtam declared, 'the only reality is the work of art itself' ('edinstvenno real'noe – eto samo proizvedenie').[2]

Futurist aesthetic theory combined elements of Acmeism (the notion of the 'self-sufficient word' which represents only itself) and of Symbolism (the utopian belief in the possibility of transforming the world by means of the word). The type of *zaum'*, or 'trans-rational' poetry which Khlebnikov sought to cultivate, for example, was to be a kind of cosmic, organically formed (rather than artificially imposed) Esperanto, a pre-Babel common tongue which, if accepted, would somehow put an end to all war.[3] Comparing his own verbal play to the charms and invocations of pagan rites, and what he called the 'trans-rational language of folklore', Khlebnikov asserted: 'attributed to these incomprehensible words is the greatest power over man, spells of sorcery, a direct influence on man's destiny. The greatest charms are concentrated in them. They are regarded as having the power to control good and evil.'[4] Taking as their point of departure Kruchenykh's dictum that 'a new verbal form creates a new content' ('novaya slovesnaya forma sozdaet novoe soderzhanie'),[5] the Futurists indulged in all kinds of verbal play, displacing, and reorganizing phonetic, semantic, and syntactical units in their search for the abstract linguistic forms which might result in a broader, more authentic (more *real*) representation of the real world.

It was only a short step from the belief that art could actively transform the world, create an alternative reality (a view which ran counter to the Party's notion of art as essentially cognitive)[6] to the idea that art was itself an alternative reality. Such a view began to be vehemently asserted after 1917, in the name of the Revolution and social progress. Whereas the Symbolists had talked about the need to make one's life a work of art, many left artists now claimed that art – utilitarian art, as distinct from 'decadent', 'bourgeois', 'decorative' art – created its own reality, and in doing so was indistinguishable from life. The Futurist newspaper *Art of the Commune* (*Iskusstvo kommuny*) which appeared between December 1918 and April 1919, defined art as 'action', and the 'direct material creation of things' (Maguire, *Red Virgin Soil*, pp. 151–2). Ironically, this belief in the ontological autonomy of art – in art's 'thingness' – was echoed in statements made by the 'Serapion Brothers', who represented the ideological antipode of left art. The hermit Serapion, the Hoffmann character from whom the group took its name, believed in the absolute reality of his artistic visions. As Lev Lunts expressed it in the group's manifesto of 1921: 'We are with hermit Serapion. We believe that literary chimeras are a special reality, and we do not want any utilitarianism. [...] Art is as real as life itself. And, as life, it is without aim and without meaning: it exists because it cannot help existing.'[7]

The *zaumniki*, or 'trans-rational' poets continued after the Revolution to emphasize the epistemological qualities of their art, as a way of interpreting the world.[8] At the same time, however, they also suggested that the more authentic vision of the world offered by their verse constituted a more 'real' reality. To quote Tufanov:

Zaum' literature is non-objective in the sense that its images do not have their usual relief or outlines. However, if perceived with broadened vision, 'non-objectivity' provides at the same time a fully real image of the world, produced in a 'distorted' way through a fluid outline.[9]

It was in the theatre, however, that the 'reality' of 'trans-rational' art could most tangibly be experienced. One of the most significant attempts to produce *zaum'* theatre in the 1920s was in Terent'ev's 1926 production of Gogol''s *The Government*

Inspector, which was mentioned in chapter 2.[10] After working with Vvedensky at Malevich's Institute of Artistic Culture, Terent'ev ran the theatre at the Leningrad Press Club from the beginning of 1926. As Jaccard points out, Terent'ev's concept of theatre had much in common with Kharms's, and it should not surprise us that at one time there were plans for the two to collaborate on a play (Jaccard, *Daniil Harms*, p. 227). Terent'ev's productions involved fragmentation of the plot, sudden shifts between scenes, an important gestual element, autonomous sounds and musical scores, magic tricks of one sort or another, montage, and techniques borrowed from cinema. The aim of Terent'ev's 'trans-rational' theatre was to create an alternative reality, a 'living object' ('zhivoi predmet') on stage.[11]

In the realm of painting, too, artists such as Malevich and Matyushin (who directed the 'organic culture' section of Malevich's Institute of Artistic Culture) experimented with abstract forms in their search for a new relationship between art and reality.[12] Mikhail Matyushin elaborated the concept of 'broadened vision' ('rasshirennoe smotrenie') in his work on the physiological perception of reality with his 'Zorved' ('Seeknow') group in the 1920s.[13] Matyushin's assertion that in order for the real world to be perceived satisfactorily it must be observed at an angle of 360 degrees rather than 180 degrees stemmed partly from his interest (shared by Malevich and many of his contemporaries) in the possibility of a fourth dimension existing beyond time and space. Influenced by the writings of Charles Hinton, Petr Uspensky, Nikolay Lobachevsky, and Albert Einstein, Matyushin advocated non-Euclidean, non-planar representation: '[One must] practise correctly, seeking the fourth dimension, since it is necessary to train oneself to see everything all around.'[14]

Whereas for Matyushin, art was essentially an *epistemological* tool, Malevich went one step further, affirming the *ontological* primacy of art and its representations over the real world. Arguing that there could be no reality independent of the mind's representation of that reality, Malevich wrote:

Each thought moves, for mental stimulation moves, and in their movements they create real representations, or in their art they produce something as real as reality, and all that which has been produced changes and departs into the eternity of non-becoming, just as it arrived from eternal becoming.[15]

Kharms almost certainly read this, since it was contained in Malevich's *God has not been Cast Down* (*Bog ne skinut*), a copy of which the artist presented to Kharms with the dedication 'go out and stop progress' ('idite i ostanavlivaite progress').[16]

But what of those who were not primarily artists, but theorists? Russian Formalism began in the years immediately preceding the Bolshevik Revolution as a descriptive poetics of Futurist poetry. Some of Shklovsky's earliest articles, for example, were devoted to *zaum'*.[17] Yet although the mechanics of aesthetic representation were of great interest to the Formalists, one thing which distinguished them from the Futurists was their tendency to bracket off the referent, the real world as represented in the text as just another artistic 'device' to be bared. That the purpose of 'defamiliarization' for the Formalists was to renew perception of the word, rather than of the world (a point already made in chapter 1), is particularly clear from an oft-quoted comment by Shklovsky in 'Iskusstvo kak priem': 'Art is a means of experiencing the artfulness of an object. The object itself is not important in art' ('Iskusstvo est' sposob perezhit' delan'e veshchi, a sdelannoe v iskusstve ne vazhno'; Shklovsky, *Gamburgskii schet*, p. 63). As Ann Jefferson has cogently noted, it was 'literariness' – the extent to which a text bared its devices, deformed 'everyday language', and so on – rather than mimesis – the 'imitation', however strange, of reality – which interested the Formalists.[18]

The Formalists were criticized by the Bakhtin circle precisely for their failure to include the real world in all its social concreteness in their textual model.[19] Yet Bakhtin also insisted on a fundamental distinction between art and life, and he did so, moreover, far more explicitly than the Formalists: 'art and life are not one' ('iskusstvo i zhizn' ne odno'), he maintained.[20] Although, in his study of Dostoevsky's poetics, Bakhtin suggests that Dostoevsky's characters, by virtue of the different words which they use, inhabit different 'worlds', this is not meant in any 'real' sense (how could it be?). Even in his study of Rabelais, when Bakhtin enthuses about the absence of footlights in carnival, and the consequent erasure of the distinction between performers and spectators, he makes it clear that this is a feature specific to carnival, and one, furthermore, whose significance is primarily ideological.

Far from revealing affinities with the Formalists or the Bakhtin circle, OBERIU's professed interest in the 'thingness' of art, in art as an alternative, autonomous reality, looks back to early left art. At the same time, however, such an interest suggests the importance of a group with which the *Oberiuty* were much more directly associated, namely the *chinari*. It is to this unofficial circle of friends that I must briefly return.

NEIGHBOURING WORLDS, IMAGINARY REALITIES: THE *CHINARI*

As well as their acquaintance with the Formalists and the Bakhtin circle, a number of *Oberiuty* also took part in the philosophical and literary discussions of the *chinari* group, from the mid-1920s to the late 1930s. As was mentioned briefly in my introduction, a number of scholars maintain that this group, consisting, at various times, of Kharms, Vvedensky, Druskin, Lipavsky, Oleinikov, Zabolotsky, and Tamara Meyer-Lipavskaya, was far more important for the literary careers of each of its members than was OBERIU.[21] Jaccard has been more vociferous than most in this respect, pointing out, for example, that the *chinari* group lasted much longer than OBERIU, that all its members' literary works were read out and discussed at the group's regular meetings, and asserting that the break-up of OBERIU was as much due to immanent, aesthetic differences within the association as it was caused by external, political pressure (Jaccard, *Daniil Harms*, p. 137). In particular, Jaccard sees strong affinities between the group's philosophical concerns and those which appear in Kharms's writing, both fictional and non-fictional.

A detailed discussion of *chinari* philosophy is, unfortunately, beyond the scope of this work.[22] In essence, however, Druskin's claim that the group 'tried to construct a new, non-substantial existential ontology' is an accurate summary of the group's philosophical endeavours taken as a whole.[23] Their essentially anti-Kantian philosophy focused on the dual question of being and time. In their regular conversations, they speculated, for example, on the nature of the present moment as the infinitely brief dividing-line between a non-existent past and an equally non-existent future. They believed that the present moment was that 'point zero' of existence, which, like the zero in the number series, was not nothing (since the continuity of the whole as a series of negative and positive values depended on it), and yet nothing real (since it was neither a negative nor a positive value itself).[24] From this came the (pre-post-structuralist) contention that existence and non-existence are relative terms: 'One should not say that a thing "exists" or "does not exist", but rather one should say that it "exists in relation to this thing, and does not exist in relation to that thing". [...] That is why "to exist" means "to be different"' ('Nel'zya govorit' "sushchestvuet", "ne sushchestvuet", a nado govorit' "sushchestvuet po otnosheniyu k tomu-to i ne sushchestvuet po otnosheniyu k tomu-to". [...] Vot poetomu "sushchestvovat'" znachit "otlichat'sya"').[25] That which guarantees the relative distinction, both between individual elements of the real world, and between the real world and other, imaginary worlds, was given various names by the *chinari*, most importantly Kharms's 'impediment' ('prepyatstvie'), and Druskin's 'minor error' ('nebol'shaya pogreshnost').[26]

This notion was given a religious twist by Druskin, who, alluding to the opening of John's gospel, described God's Word which created the world as a 'pogreshnost'' demarcating the real from the imaginary (Jaccard, 'Chinari', p. 88). Such a view was, however, simply an expression *in extremis* of Druskin's belief in the ontological primacy of language, according to which naming a thing guaranteed its existence, since the word acted to break the equilibrium between the object's existence and its non-existence: 'the naming of an object constitutes that object's beginning' ('nazvanie predmeta est' ego nachalo'), as he expressed it in an essay written in 1933.[27]

The primacy of words over the world and its objects was also a feature of Lipavsky's philosophy, although to a lesser extent. In one of his major essays of the 1930s, 'A Theory of Words' ('Teoriya slov'), Lipavsky indulged in a good deal of amateur etymology in an attempt to determine the relationship between words and the world.[28] Echoing Saussure (almost certainly unknowingly), Lipavsky argues that language 'cuts the world up into pieces, and, consequently, subjugates it' ('razrezaet mir na kuski i, znachit, podchinyaet ego').[29] He goes further, claiming that when words are formed and sounds produced, 'the model of the world [the voice] and the world itself begin to coincide [...] The sound begins to cast upon the world its shadow, namely meaning' ('model' mira i sam mir nachinayut sovpadat' [...] Zvuk nachinaet otbrasyvat' ten' na mir – znachenie').[30] Lipavsky's attempt to blur the distinction between words and the world is particularly relevant, as we shall see, to Vvedensky's fiction.

The three main substrata of *chinari* philosophy, the existential, the theological, and the textual, came together in perhaps the most interesting term produced by the group, namely the *vestniki*. The Russian word 'vestnik', meaning 'herald', is a literal translation into Russian of the Greek 'angelos'. It was first introduced into *chinari* discussions by Lipavsky, and subsequently developed by Druskin.[31] For Druskin, the *vestniki* embodied the possibility of the existence not just of alternative worlds, but of the imaginary world of representation, with all that this implied for the ontological status of literary-fictional discourse (or of any other semiotic system).[32] In a key passage dealing with the *vestniki*, Druskin implies that these beings both exist and do not exist; they do not exist, because their world is 'imaginary' ('voobrazhaemyi'), and yet they must exist, since, echoing Lipavsky's definition of existence as difference, Druskin says that they 'are sharply distinct from us' ('sil'no otlichayutsya ot nas').[33]

OBERIU: THE ASSOCIATION FOR *REAL* ART

The term '*real* art' ('*real'noe*[34] iskusstvo'), encapsulated in the name OBERIU, might in itself be interpreted as the expression of a desire to erase – or at least to blur – the ontological distinction between art and reality. (Such a tendency may also have lain behind the outlandish behaviour of certain members of the group, none more than Kharms, whose own attempts at blurring fact and fiction amounted to passing himself off in public as his non-existent aristocratic half-brother, Ivan Ivanovich.)[35] However, if the poetry section of the OBERIU article contained countless references to the '(concrete) object' ('(konkretnyi) predmet'), and insisted that the group's artistic method involved conveying a 'concrete, materialist sense of the object' ('konkretn[oe] materialistichesk[oe] oshchushcheni[e] veshchi'), this was little more than a call, made in the spirit of Acmeism, to free art from mysticism and excessive sentiment.[36] Indeed, the OBERIU article went so far as to assert that art was *not* like life, since it had 'a logic of its own'.[37]

Yet in their *writing* (as distinct from their theoretical pronouncements) the *Oberiuty* explore the issue of the ontological primacy of the word – the word as thing[38] – and they do so, furthermore, in ways which suggest a dialogue both with the artistic avant-garde and with *chinari* philosophy. Once again, there is an essential distinction to be drawn between Zabolotsky and other members of OBERIU (despite the fact that Zabolotsky was also involved with the *chinari*, if not as closely as Kharms and Vvedensky). This time, that distinction hinges on the fact that Zabolotsky views art almost exclusively in cognitive terms, as a means of knowing the world, while Kharms, Vvedensky, and Vaginov, while not denying the cognitive function of art, also echo – and extend – the avant-garde's belief in art as an alternative, equally authentic reality. As Zabolotsky expressed it in the poetry section of the OBERIU article, 'art has a logic of its own, and that logic does not destroy the object, but helps to *cognize* it' ('U iskusstva svoya logika i ona ne razrushaet predmet, no pomogaet ego *poznat'*'; Milner-Gulland, ' "Left Art" ', p. 71 (my emphasis)).

In one or two of Zabolotsky's poems written during his collaboration with the *chinari*, words do take on a reality of their own. In 'Art' ('Iskusstvo'), words leave the poet's mouth to be transformed instantaneously into 'objects' ('predmet[y]'; Zabolotsky, *Stolbtsy i poemy*, pp. 66–7 (p. 67)). In 'The Face of a Horse' ('Litso konya', 1926, ibid., pp. 55–6), the poet likens words to objects in the real world, as part of his description of a utopian state of existence:

> And if man could see
> The magical face of the horse,
> He would tear out his own impotent tongue
> And give it to the horse. Truly worthy
> Is the magical horse to have a speaking tongue!
>
> We would hear words.
> Words, as big as apples. Thick,
> Like honey or thick, creamy milk.
> Words which shoot up, like a flame,
> And which, flying into man's soul, as fire enters a hut,
> Light up the miserable shack.
> Words which do not die
> And about which we sing songs.

> И если б человек увидел
> Лицо волшебное коня,
> Он вырвал бы язык бессильный свой
> И отдал бы коню. Поистине достоин
> Иметь язык волшебный конь!
>
> Мы услыхали бы слова.
> Слова большие, словно яблоки. Густые,
> Как мед или крутое молоко.
> Слова, которые вонзаются, как пламя,
> И, в душу залетев, как в хижину огонь,
> Убогое убранство освещают.
> Слова, которые не умирают
> И о которых песни мы поем.   (ibid., p. 56)[39]

Another of Zabolotsky's poems, 'The Battle of the Elephants' ('Bitva slonov', 1931), actually features a battle of words – nouns, adjectives, verbs, and conjunctions – which symbolizes the clash between old and new poetic forms in an era of monumental social change (ibid., pp. 92–5).[40] On the whole, however, while Zabolotsky constantly seeks new ways in his poetry to represent (cognize) the real world in time and space,[41] it cannot be said that the poet engages in any sustained metafictional inquiry into the ontological relationship between art and reality.

As for Oleinikov, the only one of his extant works which deals with the relationship between language (or more specifically, the act of naming) and reality is 'A Change of Surname' ('Peremena familii').[42] Yet this poem appears in fact to be a (very witty) parody of the whole concept of the materiality of the word and the primacy of language, as well as a deceptively chilling (Aesopian) reminder of the precarious situation of the individual personality in a totalitarian state. Oleinikov's hero, a certain Aleksandr Kozlov, seeks to change his name to Nikandr Orlov, in the hope that this will change his life for the better. Unfortunately, this act brings with it irrevocable physiological – and existential – consequences; after his new name has been registered, 'Orlov' acquires 'another's face' ('chuzhoe litso'), and his appearance is generally so altered that he fails to recognize himself. At the end of the poem, he is about to commit suicide, and begs his readers, with tragicomic irony, 'friends, pray for us!' ('druz'ya, pomolites' za nas!').[43]

If Zabolotsky and Oleinikov belonged at various times to the *chinari* group, Bakhterev, for reasons which have yet to be clarified, was never a member.[44] Be that as it may, his mysterious, prayer-like incantation 'The Eternally Standing' ('Vechno stoyashchee', 1932) bears some affinity with *chinari* philosophy. For example, its subtitle, 'A real dream' ('Real'noe snovidenie') seeks to erase the distinction between reality and the representations of the mind.[45] This text, which is an abstract description of movement in time, also contains (p. 434) a reference to 'strange planes' ('strannye ploskosti') which arrive 'from other worlds' ('iz drugikh mirov'), which may be an allusion to the *vestniki* and their 'neighbouring worlds'.[46] If 'The Eternally Standing' seeks to conflate, however implicitly, thought and reality, then the action of Bakhterev's 'Tsar Makedon', which was mentioned in chapter 2, is based on the primacy of words over the world. The power game which the two characters play is in essence a language game; it is sufficient to name oneself 'tsar' to achieve supremacy over the other player (Aleksandrov (ed.), *Vanna Arkhimeda*, pp. 434–40). As we shall see, the political ramifications of the very real power of language are central to Kharms's play *Elizaveta Bam*. Indeed, it is to Kharms, and his metafictional inquiry into the authority of language, that I now need to turn my attention.

FROM THE AUTHORITY OF LANGUAGE TO THE LANGUAGES OF AUTHORITY: DANIIL KHARMS

Like his fellow *chinari*, Kharms was especially interested in the relationship between words and the world.[47] To say this is to do much more, however, than to repeat Jaccard's rather predictable assertion to the effect that Kharms shared the 'trans-rational' poets' lack of faith in the adequacy of human language to account for the world in any 'real' sense.[48] Kharms's belief in the power of words – or rather of special kinds of words, what he called 'word machines' – not just to articulate our experience of the world, but actually to change that world in a concretely *physical* sense, is revealed in a note made in 1931:

The power invested in words should be liberated. There exist combinations of words which make more apparent the effect of this power. It is not good to think that this power can force an object to move. I am certain that the power of words can do even this. But the most valuable effect of this power is almost impossible to determine. A vulgar example of this power is provided by the rhythms of metered verse. Those complex examples, like the help afforded by metered verse to anyone trying to move one of their limbs, should not be regarded as mere figments of the imagination. This is [however] the most vulgar and at the same time the weakest manifestation of the power of words. The most extreme examples of the effect of this power are scarcely accessible to our rational understanding. [...] For the moment I know of four types of word machine: poems, prayers, songs and spells. These machines are built not by computation or calculation, but by another method, called the ALPHABET.

Сила заложенная в словах должна быть освобождена. Есть такие сочетания из слов при которых становится заметней действие силы. Нехорошо думать, что эта сила заставит двигаться предметы. Я уверен, что сила слов может сделать и это. Но самое ценное действие силы, почти неопределимо. Грубое представление этой силы мы получаем из ритмов метрических

стихов. Те сложные пути, как помощь метрических стихов при
двигании каким-либо членом тела, тоже не должны считаться
вымыслом. Это грубейшее и в то же время слабейшее
проявление словесной силы. Дальнейшие действия этой силы
вряд-ли доступны нашему рассудительному пониманию. [...]
Пока известно мне четыре вида словесных машин: стихи,
молитвы, песни и заговоры. Эти машины построены не путем
вычисления или рассуждения, а иным путем, название которого
АЛФАВИТ.[49]

What exactly did Kharms understand by 'the power of
words'? One possible answer is suggested in the letter which
Kharms wrote to the actress Pugacheva in October 1931, and
which was mentioned in chapter 1. In this letter, Kharms
distinguishes 'real', creative art (among the practitioners of
which he, not surprisingly, includes himself) from other types of
art and writing in general. The difference, he insists, lies in the
fact that 'real' art articulates/establishes a 'purity of order',
thereby creating a new reality. Furthermore, Kharms is keen to
emphasize the concreteness of the reality created by his words,
inverting (rather than erasing) the conventional ontological distinction between 'fact' and 'fiction' (in what sounds like a
belated counterblast at left art's call for factographic literature):

Now my task is to create the correct order. I am preoccupied by this,
and can think only about this. [...] I am the creator of a world, and
this is the most important thing about me. How on earth could I
prevent myself from thinking about this all the time! In all that I do, I
invest my consciousness of the fact that I am the creator of a world.
[...]
Genuine art is of the same order as primary reality, it creates a
world and constitutes its primary reflection. It is without doubt real.
[... Genuine art] is no longer simply words and thoughts printed
on paper, but a thing just as real as the cut-glass ink bottle standing in
front of me on the table. It seems to me that verses such as these,
having turned into real things, could be lifted straight from the page
and thrown at a window, and that the window would break. That is
what words can do!
On the other hand, how helpless and pitiful those very same words
can be! I never read the newspapers. That is a fictitious world, not a
created one. That is just pitiful, half-erased typographic print on poor
quality, prickly paper.

Теперь моя забота создать правильный порядок. Я увлечен этим и только об этом думаю. [...] Я творец мира, и это самое главное во мне. Как же я могу не думать постоянно об этом! Во все, что я делаю, я вкладываю сознание, что я творец мира. [...]

Истинное искусство стоит в ряду первой реальности, оно создает мир и является его первым отражением. Оно обязательно реально.[...]

Это уже не просто слова и мысли, напечатанные на бумаге, это вещь такая же реальная, как хрустальный пузырек для чернил, стоящий передо мной на столе. Кажется, эти стихи, ставшие вещью, можно снять с бумаги и бросить в окно, и окно разобьется. Вот что могут сделать слова!

Но, с другой стороны, как те же слова могут быть беспомощны и жалки! Я никогда не читаю газет. Это вымышленный, а не созданный мир. Это только жалкий, сбитый типографский шрифт на плохой, занозистой бумаге. (Kharms, *Polet*, pp. 482–4)[50]

But, one might ask, in what way can the writer create an alternative, 'real' world? In a sense, Kharms himself fudges the issue in this letter to Pugacheva, by accompanying his more extreme formulations with the suggestion, for example, that genuine art simply 'reflects' ('otrazhaet') the real world, and that such art is characterized by what he calls its '*proximity* to reality, i.e. to autonomous existence' ('*blizost'* k real'nosti, t.e. k samostoyatel'nomu sushchestvovaniyu'; Kharms, *Polet*, p. 483; my emphasis). What Kharms may also be suggesting in this letter, however, is that the poet's words can stand as the (ontological) 'impediment' between the real and the fictional worlds, in a way which makes the existence of those worlds mutually dependent (for if one were not to exist, neither would the other).[51] To take this interpretation further, one might say that Kharms is doing two things here: first, he is vulgarizing Druskin's notion of The Word (God) as ultimate origin (guarantor) of existence; and second, he is developing Lipavsky's arch-structuralist linguistic philosophy by positing the word – in particular the word of his own, 'true' art – as the 'impediment' between 'this' and 'that', between 'this' world of which the text forms a part, and 'that' world of which the text is an expression. These two worlds, held in tension by the 'impediment', emerge in Kharms's thought as simply parts of *the same world*.

This aspect of Kharms's philosophy is most articulately expressed in an essay written some time in the 1930s, namely 'On Time, Space, and Existence' ('O vremeni, o prostranstve, o sushchestvovanii').[52] Although this piece contains no specific reference to language and aesthetic representation, it can nevertheless be read in such a way as to throw light on Kharms's belief in the ontologically creative function of (his own) words. As Kharms put it in this essay, written in the form of sixty numbered points:

3. An existing world must be heterogeneous and have parts. [...]
7. Let us call the first part *this* and the second part *that* and the transition from one to the other let us call *neither this nor that*.
8. Let us call *neither this nor that* the 'impediment'.
9. So: the basis of existence comprises three elements: *this, the impediment,* and *that.* [...]
13. The impediment is that creator which creates 'something' out of 'nothing'. [...]
18. In this way are created, of their own accord, non-existent parts. [...]
21. Should one of the three basic elements of existence disappear, then the whole would disappear. So: should the 'impediment' disappear, then *this* and *that* would become unitary and continuous and would cease to exist.

3. Существующий мир должен быть неоднородным и иметь части. [...]
7. Назовем первую часть *это,* вторую часть *то,* а переход от одной к другой назовем *не то и не это.*
8. Назовем *не то и не это* «препятствием».
9. Итак: основу существования составляют три элемента: *это, препятствие, и то.* [...]
13. Препятствие является тем творцом, который из «ничего» создает «нечто». [...]
18. Таким образом создаются, сами по себе, несуществующие части. [...]
21. Если бы исчез один из трех основных элементов существования, то исчезло бы и все целое. Так: если бы исчезло «препятствие», то *это* и *то* стало бы единым и непрерывным и перестали бы существовать.[53]

At this point, we are faced with something of a conundrum. Despite Kharms's apparent belief in the creative power of words, it must be said that in his fiction (as opposed to his philosophical essays and letters) examples of such power are few and far between. Indeed, the only texts written in the 1930s which suggest such a link between words and the world appear either to parody the idea, or else to assert the *destructive* force of (his own narrative) discourse. In 'On Equilibrium', for example, the words spoken by Nikolay Ivanovich as he sits in a restaurant have the effect of summoning a fairy godmother:

At this point Nikolay Ivanovich said to himself, 'How a person is put together', Nikolay Ivanovich said to himself, 'is an interesting topic'.
No sooner had he said this than out of nowhere a fairy appeared in front of him and said:
'What do you need, my good man?'

Вот тут-то Николай Иванович и сказал себе: «Интересно, – сказал себе Николай Иванович, как человек устроен».
Только это он себе сказал, откуда ни возьмись, появляется перед ним фея и говорит:
– Чего тебе, добрый человек, нужно? (Kharms, *Sluchai*, p. 28)[54]

Nikolay Ivanovich is unable to cope with such an intrusion into his universe, however, and declines the offer somewhat timorously, before running out of the restaurant in a panic.

In another text written in the same year (1934), and entitled 'On Phenomena and Existences No. 2' ('O yavleniyakh i sushchestvovaniyakh No.2'),[55] Kharms creates a world, before proceeding to destroy it (or virtually all of it) through language:

Here's a bottle of vodka, of the so-called lethal spirit variety. And next to it you can see Nikolay Ivanovich Serpukhov.
From the bottle rise spirit fumes. Observe how Nikolay Ivanovich Serpukhov breathes the fumes in through his nose. Notice how he licks his lips and screws up his eyes. It is obvious that he is enjoying this very much, and that is largely due to the fact that this is the lethal spirit variety.
But now note the fact that behind Nikolay Ivanovich's back there is nothing. That is not to say simply that there is no cupboard, or no chest of drawers, or something like that. Rather it is to say that there is nothing at all, not even any air. Whether you believe it or not is up to you, but behind Nikolay Ivanovich's back there isn't even a

vacuum, or, as they say, any universal ether. Put plainly, there's nothing there.

Вот бутылка с водкой, так называемый спиртуоз. А рядом вы видите Николая Ивановича Серпухова.

Вот из бутылки поднимаются спиртуозные пары. Посмотрите, как дышит носом Николай Иванович Серпухов. Поглядите, как он облизывается и как он щурится. Видно, ему это очень приятно, и главным образом потому, что спиртуоз.

Но обратите внимание на то, что за спиной Николая Ивановича нет ничего. Не то чтобы там не стоял шкап, или комод, или вообще что-нибудь такое, – а совсем ничего нет, даже воздуха нет. Хотите верьте, хотите не верьте, но за спиной Николая Ивановича нет даже безвоздушного пространства, или, как говорится, мирового эфира. Откровенно говоря, ничего нет. (p. 317)

The power of words to destroy, rather than create, a reality is also a feature of what is perhaps Kharms's most famous text, 'Blue Notebook No. 10' ('Golubaya tetrad' No. 10'), which was written three years later (1937), and which deserves to be reproduced in its entirety:

There was once a ginger-haired man who had no eyes or ears. He had no hair either, so he was called 'ginger-haired' as a matter of convention.

He could not speak, since he had no mouth. He had no nose either.

He did not even have any arms or legs. And he had no stomach, and he had no back, and he had no spine, and he had no insides. He had nothing at all! So it's not very clear who we are talking about.

So we'd better not talk about him any more.

Жил один рыжий человек, у которого не было глаз и ушей. У него не было и волос, так что рыжим его называли условно.

Говорить он не мог, так как у него не было рта. Носа тоже у него не было.

У него не было даже рук и ног. И живота у него не было, и спины у него не было, и хребта у него не было, и никаких внутренностей у него не было. Ничего не было! Так что непонятно, о ком идет речь.

Уж лучше мы о нем не будем больше говорить. (p. 353)[56]

How can one account for the apparent incongruity between Kharms's theory and his fiction, between his apparent belief in his ability to create worlds, and his tendency in his fiction to destroy the narrative universe? To answer this question I must reintroduce an element of very real political history. As Stalin's orgy of violence gathered momentum through the 1930s, claiming Kharms himself as victim for a time, along with many of his friends and former colleagues, Kharms may have come to realize that Stalin's terror machine was simply another type of 'word machine', or (to use another metaphor) a language game, in which one's words had the very real power to 'create' alternative truths and at the same time destroy others' realities.[57] In this respect, 'Blue Notebook No. 10' is particularly important, since it, perhaps more than any other prose work by Kharms, is open both to formalist and to historicist readings, and, in fact, shows how the two approaches can, and should, complement each other. Just as Kharms's narrator uses words in order to strip away first the ginger-haired man's physical attributes, and then his very existence, so Stalin's henchmen were using denunciations and 'doublespeak' to liquidate thousands of Soviet citizens.[58]

Examples of language used in power games can be found in three of Kharms's late prose works. In 'Comprehensive Research' ('Vsestoronnee issledovanie', 1937), a doctor plays a game with words, in an eventually successful attempt to get his victim to swallow a fatal pill.[59] At the start of their conversation, Ermolaev tells the doctor of his friend Blinov's tremendous strength. The doctor replies by asking Ermolaev to introduce him to his friend, since he would like to research Blinov's strength by giving him a 'research pill'. The dialogue continues:

ERMOLAEV: And what kind of pill are you intending to give Blinov?
DOCTOR: What pill? I don't intend to give him any pill.
ERMOLAEV: But you just said you wanted to give him a pill.
DOCTOR: No, no, you've got it wrong. I didn't mention any pill.
ERMOLAEV: Well I'm sorry, but I heard you talk about a pill.
DOCTOR: No I didn't.
ERMOLAEV: What do you mean, you didn't?
DOCTOR: I didn't say anything!
ERMOLAEV: Who didn't say anything?
DOCTOR: You didn't say anything.
ERMOLAEV: What didn't I say?

DOCTOR: I don't think you're telling me everything.

ERMOLAEV: I don't understand. What aren't I telling you?

DOCTOR: Your speech pattern is very typical. You swallow your words, you don't finish expressing your thoughts, you hurry and then you stutter.

ERMOLAEV: When did I stutter? I'm speaking perfectly smoothly.

DOCTOR: That's precisely where you are mistaken. Can't you see? You're even starting to be covered with red spots, with all the tension. Aren't your hands getting cold?

Ермолаев: А что зто за пилюля, которую вы собираетесь дать Блинову?

Доктор: Как пилюля? Я не собираюсь давать ему пилюлю.

Ермолаев: Но вы же сами только что сказали, что собираетесь дать ему пилюлю.

Доктор: Нет, нет, вы ошибаетесь. Про пилюлю я не говорил.

Ермолаев: Ну уж извините, я-то слышал, как вы сказали про пилюлю.

Доктор: Нет.

Ермолаев: Что нет?

Доктор: Не говорил!

Ермолаев: Кто не говорил?

Доктор: Вы не говорили.

Ермолаев: Чего я не говорил?

Доктор: Вы, по-моему, чего-то недоговариваете.

Ермолаев: Я ничего не понимаю. Чего я недоговариваю?

Доктор: Ваша речь очень типична. Вы проглатываете слова, недоговариваете начатой мысли, торопитесь и заикаетесь.

Ермолаев: Когда же я заикался? Я говорю довольно гладко.

Доктор: Вот в этом-то и есть ваша ошибка. Видите? Вы даже от напряжения начинаете покрываться красными пятнами. У вас еще не похолодели руки? (Kharms, *Sluchai*, p. 15)

Manipulating his victim's words, and setting himself up as supreme arbiter of the validity of those words, the doctor gains power over Ermolaev, thanks to which he is able to kill him by persuading him to swallow the pill.[60]

In the aptly-entitled 'Power' ('Vlast'),[61] written three years later, Myshin tires of Faol and his increasingly absurd questions, and so destroys him with just two words:

'Shaddup!', shouted Myshin, jumping up off the floor. 'Scram!'
And Faol crumbled, like a lump of bad sugar.

– Хветь! – крикнул Мышин, вскакивая с пола. – Сгинь!
    И Фаол рассыпался, как плохой сахар. (p. 343)

A more subtle, but equally sinister use of language is depicted
in 'The Drawback' ('Pomekha'), also written in 1940.[62] In this
story a stranger, presumably a member of the secret police,
arrests a man, Pronin, and the object of his sexual advances,
Irina. The police agent, flanked by a couple of soldiers, uses
words to ask questions and give orders. Most significantly, he
does not allow his two detainees to talk to each other as he
leads them away: 'all talking is forbidden' ('razgovory zapresh-
cheny'), he insists (p. 350).

Over the course of the 1930s, then, Kharms appears to have
moved substantially away from his earlier position, which was
at least partly inspired by his conversations with the other
chinari, and which conceived of the word as 'impediment'
between the 'this' and 'that' of the text and the world. By the
end of the decade, his faith in the ontological authority of
language had been replaced by an acute, personal awareness of
the very real power of the languages of authority.[63] Yet this
acute sense of the political uses to which language can be put is
a central theme of a much earlier work by Kharms, one which
enjoyed a prominent place in the 'Three Left Hours' show in
January 1928 – the play *Elizaveta Bam*.

LANGUAGE GAMES AND POWER PLAY: *ELIZAVETA BAM*[64]

Elizaveta Bam, rather like the much later piece 'Comprehensive
Research', shows not so much the 'tragedy of language' as the
tragic consequences of language used to shore up oppressive
power structures.[65] The play concerns the arrest of the eponymous heroine by two men, Ivan Ivanovich and Petr Nikolaevich, who at first refuse to reveal anything more about her
crime than that it is 'heinous', but who subsequently suggest to
her that she is guilty 'because you have lost the right to speak'
('potomu, chto Vy lisheny vsyakogo golosa'; p. 224). What the
men subsequently accuse her of is even more 'absurd', however
– the murder of Petr Nikolaevich, the same Petr Nikolaevich
who has come to arrest her.

Of all Kharms's fiction, *Elizaveta Bam* is perhaps the most linguistically self-conscious. The majority of its nineteen sections foreground language in one way or another. For example, the so-called 'Battle of the Two Heroes' ('Srazhenie dvukh bogatyrei') between Elizaveta's 'daddy' ('papasha') and Petr, which constitutes section 15, contains what many critics have interpreted as *zaum'*:[66]

Petr Nik: Kurybýr daramúr
   dýn'diri
   slakatýr' pakarádagu
   da ký chíri kíri kíri
   zandudíla khabakúla
      khe-e-el'
   khánchu aná kudy
   stúm chi na lákudy
   para vy na lýitena
      khe-e-el'
   chápu áchapáli
   chapátali már
   nabalóchíná
      khe-e-el'

П. Н.: Курыбы́р дарамӳр
   ды́ньдири
   слакаты́рь пакара́дагу
   да кы́ чи́ри ки́ри ки́ри
   зандуди́ла хабакӳла
      хе-е-ель
   ха́нчу ана́ куды
   стӳм чи на ла́куды
   пара вы на лы́йтена
      хе-е-ель
   ча́пу а́чапа́ли
   чапа́тали ма́р
   набало́чи́на́
      хе-е-ель (р. 237)

In the subsequent section, entitled 'Chimes' ('Kuranty'), the characters appear to engage in a spontaneous language game:

EL. BAM: Ivan Ivanovich, go down to the halfbar
   and bring us a bottle of beer and some peas.

IVAN IV.: Aha! peas and a half bottle of beer,
    go down to the bar, and from there, back here.
EL. BAM: Not a half bottle, but a bottle of beer,
    and don't go to the bar, go to the peas!
IVAN IV.: Right away I'll hide my fur coat in the halfbar,
    and I'll put halfpeas on my head.

Ел. Б.: Иван Иванович, сходите в полпивную
    и принесите нам бутылуку пива и горох.
И. И.: Ага, горох и полбутылки пива,
    сходить в пивную, а оттудова сюда.
Ел. Б.: Не полбутылки, а бутылку пива,
    и не в пивную, а в горох идти!
И. И.: Сейчас, я шубу в полпивную спрячу,
    а сам на голову надену полгорох. (p. 239)

There is more to *Elizaveta Bam* than unfettered linguistic play, however. With its theme of wrongful arrest, *Elizaveta Bam* is chillingly prophetic of Stalin's Reign of Terror. Indeed, the year before Kharms wrote the play had seen the arrest of Georgy Katsman, who had directed the 'Radiks' shows in which both Kharms and Vvedensky had taken part.[67] And it must not be forgotten that the play itself was premiered at the 'Three Left Hours' show in January 1928, on which occasion political pressure was sufficient to force Kharms and his companions to change the name of their group.

As well as the political relevance, there may well be allusions to the *chinari* in *Elizaveta Bam*. That Kharms was mindful of this philosophical circle when he wrote the play is clear from the title of the twelfth section, 'The *chinar'*-ish bit' ('Kusok chinarskii').[68] This particular scene may well have been meant as a parody of a typical *chinari* conversation, many of which were constructed like language games:[69]

MUMMY (*running after El. Bam*): Have some bread?
EL. BAM: Have some soup?
DADDY: Have some meat? (*running*).
MUMMY: Have some flour? [...]
MUMMY: Oh, my legs are tired!
IVAN IV.: Oh, my arms are tired!
EL. BAM: Oh, my scissors are tired!
DADDY: Oh, my springs are tired!

Мамаша (*бежит за Ел. Б.*): Хлеб ешь?
Ел. Б.: Суп ешь?
Папаша: Мясо ешь? (*бежит*).
Мамаша: Муку ешь? [...]
Мамаша: Ой, ноги устали!
И. И.: Ой, руки устали!
Ел. Б.: Ой, ножницы устали!
Папаша: Ой, пружины устали! (p. 232)[70]

In spite of the references in the play, both to the political context and to the *chinari* group, most criticism of *Elizaveta Bam* has tended to focus on its thematic and formal links with the Theatre of the Absurd, and specifically on the inadequacy of human language as a tool for expressing and communicating concepts related to the real world.[71] On the contrary, however, in *Elizaveta Bam* Kharms explores the notion, implicit in Druskin's and Lipavsky's thought, of the ontological primacy of the word as 'impediment', only to reveal the 'tragic' irony of that notion in a nascent totalitarian state.[72] Language emerges, not as 'impotent' (as Jaccard and others would have us believe), but as supremely *powerful*.

Elizaveta Bam presents us with a world where language shapes reality in a very real sense. As Stelleman has observed, 'the characters create a new situation, a different reality, by their speech' (Stelleman, 'An Analysis of *Elizaveta Bam*', p. 343). The words which the characters use both articulate their own being and mark out the limits of their world. As if conscious of this, Ivan Ivanovich declares (twice), 'I speak in order to be' ('govoryu, chtoby byt''; pp. 229–30).

A suggestion of the power of words is given as early as the second scene, in which Elizaveta tries to turn the tables on the men, accusing one of them of acting without a conscience, like a common crook:

SECOND [MAN]: Who's a crook? Me? Me? Am I the crook?!
FIRST: Now hold on, Ivan Ivanovich! Elizaveta Bam, I'm ordering...
SECOND: No, Petr Nikolaevich, are you telling me that I'm the crook here? [...]
FIRST: Now just hold on a minute before you start taking offence! Elizaveta Bam, I'm order...

SECOND: No, hang on a sec, Petr Nikolaevich, are you trying to tell me that I'm the crook here?

FIRST: Leave it out, will you!

SECOND: So you think I'm a crook, do you?

FIRST: Yes, you're a crook!

SECOND: So that's it, you think I'm a crook! Is that what you said?

El. B. runs around the stage.

FIRST: Get out of here, stupid! You're supposed to be here to conduct a responsible inquiry, and yet the first word that's said to you, you go up the wall. Just what does that make you? Nothing but an idiot!

II-й: Кто мошенник? Это я? Это я? Это я мошенник?!

I-й: Ну подождите, Иван Иванович! Елизавета Бам, приказываю...

II-й: Нет, Петр Николаевич, это я что ли мошенник? [...]

I-й: Да подождите тут обижаться! Елизавета Бам, прика...

II-й: Нет, постойте, Петр Николаевич, Вы мне скажите, это я мошенник?

I-й: Да отстаньте же Вы!

II-й: Это что же, я по-Вашему мошенник?

I-й: Да, мошенник!!!

II-й: Ах так, значит по-Вашему я мошенник! Так Вы сказали?

Ел. Б. бегает по сцене

I-й: Убирайтесь вон! Балда какая! А еще пошел на ответственное дело. Вам слово сказали, а Вы уж и на стену лезете. Кто же Вы после этого? Просто идиот! (р. 224)

Tragically for Elizaveta, not everyone's language in Kharms's play has the potential to articulate new realities. For there is ultimately a dividing line between those who can create alternative worlds and those who cannot, a distinction arbitrarily determined, it would seem, by the (male) ruling élite. The words uttered by Petr and Ivan seem to have all the authority they need to be true, even when they are patently false (Elizaveta cannot have killed Petr Nikolaevich, since he has come to arrest her). Elizaveta's language, on the other hand, affords her only a temporary reprieve before she is silenced once and for all. Until the fateful final scene, her words (and therefore her world) compete for supremacy with those uttered by the men. It is precisely in order to resist the men's version of reality that she in fact initiates the series of 'absurd' language games which take up the bulk of the play's nineteen sections, when she rebuts the men's accusation that she has no voice by telling them to look at the clock:

EL. BAM.: Why am I a criminal?
PETR. NIK.: Because you have lost the right to speak.
IVAN. IV.: Lost the right to speak.
EL. BAM.: No I haven't. You can check by the clock.

Ел. Б.: Почему я преступница?
П. Н.: Потому, что Вы лишены всякого голоса.
И. И.: Лишены всякого голоса.
Ел. Б.: А я не лишена. Вы можете проверить по часам. (pp. 224–5).

The men eventually succeed in silencing Elizaveta, annihilating not just her words, but her very world.

The fact that language has the power to destroy as well as create is emphasized throughout *Elizaveta Bam*. In section 7, for example, Petr Nikolaevich begins to tell the story of how he lived, as a young man, all alone in a little house on a hill. Suddenly, however, Ivan takes over the narrative, assuming not only Petr's story, but his 'I' also, usurping both his language and his space:

PETR NIK.: But one day I wake up...
     (*P.N. and I.I. merge together*)
IVAN IV.: ... and I see the door is open, and in the doorway stands some woman or other.

П.Н.: Но однажды я просыпаюсь...
     Закрывают друг друга.
И.И.: – ...и вижу, дверь открыта, а в дверях стоит какая-то женщина. (p. 229)

Ivan subsequently accuses Elizaveta of Petr's murder. Yet it is Ivan who, for the moment at least, appears to have 'killed' Petr. For by appropriating the other man's language, he has also taken over Petr's space, his 'reality'; by speaking for him, he has in effect annihilated him. Petr in fact reappears only when Ivan addresses him, refers to him in language as that 'other', as 'you' ('ty'), at the very start of the thirteenth section (p. 233). At the end of the 'Battle of the Two Heroes', Petr also falls, apparently vanquished by the power of his adversary's words, rather than by any real weapon (p. 239).

In *Elizaveta Bam* Kharms echoes the linguistic philosophy of Druskin and Lipavsky by suggesting the ontological primacy of words (words divide the world into 'pieces', 'kuski'). He then gives that somewhat abstract concept a terrifyingly real twist, by showing the discursive basis of state-sanctioned terror. The political subtext is particularly evident in the final scene, when the men order Elizaveta to open the door 'in the name of the law' ('imenem zakona'; p. 240). By his use of 'language games' – both literal and figurative – to underscore the ontological primacy of language, Kharms looks forward to Wittgenstein's later linguistic philosophy.[73] At the same time, by virtue of the fact that the power struggle in which Elizaveta and the men engage is first and foremost a struggle over the linguistic sign, *Elizaveta Bam* is one of Kharms's most Bakhtinian works. One could go so far as to say that Elizaveta's 'hysterical' discourse – the series of nonsensical language games which she appears to initiate – represents 'carnivalesque' resistance (in the Bakhtinian sense) to the men's monologic discourse, resistance which subverts that discourse's authority in a radical, if only temporary sense.[74]

In his prose and drama, Kharms shows how language – at least certain languages – can shape, even transform reality. In his fiction words are more powerful than things, yet words are never the same as things (despite Kharms's assertion, in his letter to Pugacheva, that language, or at least poetry, should be capable of smashing windows). In this respect, Vvedensky goes further than Kharms, positing the ontological *co-identity* of words and the world, as we shall now see.

TIME, DEATH, GOD, AND VVEDENSKY

At the very start of his literary career, Vvedensky claimed to be interested in three themes, namely time, death, and God.[75] That Vvedensky was indeed concerned with these issues is borne out by those of his texts which I have so far mentioned. *Minin and Pozharsky*, for example, contains numerous narrative accounts of individuals' deaths, presented in a way which questions our conventional, linear concept of time. Stories about death are also a central feature of 'Four Descriptions' ('Chetyre opisaniya', pp. 112–19). The notion that the inevitability of death makes time meaningless is also evoked in 'The Eyewitness and the Rat'. And even when Vvedensky turns his parodic gaze to the conventions of drama as a literary genre, in *Christmas at the Ivanovs'*, the themes of time and death play an important role in that investigation.

Indeed, it could be argued that time, death, and God lie at the heart of everything which Vvedensky wrote.[76] As far as time is concerned, for instance, the existence of the gods in 'The Gods' Answer' ('Otvet bogov', pp. 27–9) appears to imply that there is no time, or as the gods themselves put it, 'there are no minutes' ('net minut'; p. 29). The question of time, its measurement, and its direction, is central to 'Kupriyanov and Natasha' ('Kupriyanov i Natasha', 1931), in which preparations for the act of copulation between the two eponymous characters are presented, first, as in slow motion, and second, as in reverse (pp. 102–6). At the end of the dialogue, Kupriyanov asks whether time is really more powerful than death, and concludes by admitting that he understands nothing.[77] Another text, entitled '24 Hours' ('Sutki'), which is written as a dialogue in pseudo-question and answer form, has as its subject the passage of time and its measurement (pp. 132–4). *All Around Maybe God*, which deals with the death and afterlife of a certain 'Fomin', contains a conversation between different 'hours' ('beseda chasov'). At the end of the conversation, the eleventh hour tells the twelfth that the hours themselves (and the 'real' nature of time which they articulate) are incomprehensible to the human mind ('the mind cannot reach us', 'do nas ne dobrat'sya umu'; p. 88).

Of the thirty-two finished works contained in the two-volume set edited by Meilakh, more than three-quarters contain at least one reference to death. One of Vvedensky's most personal pieces, which is also the last extant work, 'Where. When.' ('Gde. Kogda.', 1941), in which the poet bids farewell to the world around him, evokes death in the form of the suicide which comes halfway through the piece (pp. 176–8). For

Vvedensky, the theme of death is closely linked to that of time,[78] particularly in the untitled poem which begins, 'I am sorry that I am not a wild beast' ('Mne zhalko, chto ya ne zver'', 1934; pp. 129–31). Here, the poet regrets the fact that, as a human being rather than an animal, a bird, or even an object such as a roof, he is mortal ('Mne ne nravitsya, chto ya smerten') and as such is condemned to an 'instantaneous' ('mgnovenna[ya]') death (p. 129). In Vvedensky's fiction it is only the dead who appear to understand time. As the other-worldly character 'Zumir' puts it, in 'Four Descriptions', 'Now [i.e. after death] for our consciousness / there is no difference in years' ('Teper' dlya nashego soznan'ya / net bol'she raznitsy godov'; p. 119).

God is evoked in four works written in 1930 – one untitled poem, 'The Saint and his Followers' ('Svyatoi i ego podchinennye'), 'Fact, Theory, and God' ('Fakt, teoriya i bog'), and 'The Meaning of the Sea' ('Znachen'e morya'), all of which contain characters who die and subsequently converse with God.[79] As its title suggests, *All Around Maybe God* (Vvedensky's longest extant work) introduces the notion of God, albeit as an absent presence, that which is all around but cannot, it would seem, be represented by/in the text.[80] The final section of this work contains the suggestion – crucial to Vvedensky's entire *oeuvre* – that 'only God can be' ('byt' mozhet tol'ko Bog'; p. 100), and ends with the image of a 'deceased gentleman' silently sending time away ('Vbegaet mertvyi gospodin / Molcha udalyaet vremya'; p. 101).

Given Vvedensky's obsessive interest in the tripartite theme of time, death, and God, it might appear somewhat perverse to insist on the self-conscious aspect of his work. However, there is a close connection between these two strands of Vvedensky's fiction. A clue to the nature of this connection is provided in a comment by the *chinar'* Yakov Druskin, made in a major essay on Vvedenksy.[81] Noting that in a number of Vvedensky's poems words are transformed into *real* objects, Druskin asserts that Vvedensky 'wanted poetry to produce not just a linguistic miracle, but a real one: he called this miracle the *transformation of the word into the object, of one state into another*. [...] This

transformation has for him [...] an eschatological significance'
(Druskin, 'Kommunikativnost'', p. 83).[82]

Before I attempt to determine how the eschatological and the
metafictional might be connected in Vvedensky's *oeuvre*, let us
first examine how Vvedensky materializes the word. The three
examples which Druskin gives from Vvedensky's *oeuvre* are
particularly appropriate. The first is from the long poem 'Two
Little Birds, Grief, the Lion, and Night' ('Dve ptichki, gore, lev
i noch'', 1929; pp. 44–6): 'and the word tribe becomes heavier /
and is transformed into an object' ('i slovo plemya tyazheleet / i
prevrashchaetsya v predmet'; p. 45).[83] Druskin's second
example, taken from 'The Guest on a Horse' ('Gost' na kone'),
involves what is in fact the reverse process, since an object
becomes a word:

> I heard the clatter of horses' hooves
> and did not understand this murmuring,
> I decided that this was an experience
> of the transformation of the object
> from iron into a word, into a rumble,
> into a dream, into unhappiness, into a drop of light.

> Я услышал конский топот
> и не понял этот шепот,
> я решил, что это опыт
> превращения предмета
> из железа в слово, в ропот
> в сон, в несчастье, в каплю света.　　　　(p. 109)[84]

The third example which Druskin gives is from the poem
which begins 'I am sorry that I am not a wild beast'. This is
perhaps the clearest example of the way in which Vvedensky
gives the word a material presence. Moreover, the fact that the
word involved is 'cupboard' ('shkaf') is significant, since it
probably alludes to the OBERIU notion of 'art as a cupboard':

> I see a distorted world,
> I hear the murmur of muffled lyres,
> and here taking hold of the tip of a letter,
> I lift up the word cupboard,
> and now I put the cupboard in its place,
> it is a thick dough of a substance.

Я вижу искаженный мир,
я слышу шепот заглушенных лир,
и тут за кончик буквы взяв,
Я поднимаю слово шкаф,
теперь я ставлю шкаф на место,
он вещества крутое тесто.   (p. 130)[85]

The interchangeability of words and things is evoked at various other moments in Vvedensky's *oeuvre*, although mostly in a less explicit manner than in the examples to which Druskin refers. In 'The Eyewitness and the Rat', for example, Kozalov's words rise up in front of him as he pronounces them (p. 124).[86] It should be pointed out, however, that this interchangeability, while itself highly significant, is in fact part of a more general feature of Vvedensky's work, namely the transformation of objects and phenomena into other objects and phenomena by means of semantic play.[87]

In the dramatic work 'Potets' (1936–7),[88] this involves identifying an animate being with an inanimate object, as one line of dialogue appears to be spoken by 'Pillow, a.k.a. the father' ('Podushka, ona zhe otets'; p. 138). *All Around Maybe God* contains three examples of absolutely (rather than relatively) incompatible transformation. At one point the narrator informs us that 'the duel is transformed into a famous forest' ('duel' prevrashchaetsya v znamenityi les'; p. 86). At another moment in the work, the character Nosov remarks, 'the air into a tiny fish / is transformed through impatience' ('vozdukh v malen'-kuyu rybku / prevrashchaetsya ot neterpen'ya'; p. 94). And, in an even stranger phrase, another character says, 'The night is transformed into a vase' ('Noch' prevrashchaetsya v vazu'; p. 95). Vvedensky's verbal play goes beyond mere semantic substitution, producing a deep sense of dislocation, as in the following example, also from *All Around Maybe God*:

FOMIN: Are you a lantern?
BEGGAR: No I am starving.

Фомин: Ты фонарь?
Нищий: Нет я голодаю. (p. 87)[89]

Vvedensky uses language, then, to erase the distinction

between words and things, between the animate and the inanimate, and between the concrete and the abstract. In a similar vein, Vvedensky's world contains numerous examples of the irruption into the real world of the 'neighbouring' world of the imagination.[90] In the opening scene of *All Around Maybe God*, for example, the character 'Ef' converses with an 'imaginary flying girl' ('voobrazhaem[aya] letayushch[aya] devushk[a]'; p. 77). And in 'An Invitation to Think Me' ('Priglashenie menya podumat''),[91] it is apparently enough to imagine that one is flying for this to be the case: 'And I flew off like a woodpecker, / imagining that I was flying.' ('I ya poletel kak dyatel, / voobrazhaya chto ya lechu.'; p. 128). The world reflected in the mirror at the beginning of 'The Mirror and the Musician' ('Zerkalo i muzykant', 1929)[92] is an autonomous reality; while the 'musician Prokof'ev' stands in front of the mirror, another character, named Ivan Ivanovich, appears in the mirror itself (p. 47).

Is there any sense behind this apparent 'nonsense' (to use Druskin's term, 'bessmyslitsa')? To answer this question, let us return briefly to the themes of time, death, and God. The closing speech of *All Around Maybe God* contains the assertion, 'only God can be' ('byt' mozhet tol'ko Bog'; p. 100). For Vvedensky, only God can exist, since only He is not subject to time or death, only He is both eternal and immortal. Words, objects, products of the imagination, or material phenomena – for Vvedensky all are identical in their non-existence. As Vvedensky expressed it, in a comment made in his 'Grey Notebook': 'objects are a faint mirror-image of time. There are no objects' ('predmety eto slaboe zerkal'noe izobrazhenie vremeni. Predmetov net'; p. 186).

Vvedensky articulates in his 'Grey Notebook' and in his fiction precisely the kind of non-substantial existential ontology which Druskin saw as central to the philosophy of the *chinari*. The one text in which Vvedensky most systematically explores this ontology, and in which his eschatological themes are most closely connected to his metafictional inquiry into the nature of language, is *A Certain Quantity of Conversations* (*Nekotoroe kolichestvo razgovorov*), dated 1936–7.

THE POVERTY OF LANGUAGE: VVEDENSKY'S *A CERTAIN QUANTITY OF CONVERSATIONS*[93]

In *A Certain Quantity of Conversations*,[94] written after Vvedensky had left Leningrad (and the *chinari*) to live in Khar'kov, Vvedensky no longer offers the reader images of the materialized word. Instead of suggesting that words and thoughts are as 'real' as concrete objects, he now explores the corollary of that notion, namely the idea that the real world – things and people – are just as unreal as verbal and mental phenomena.[95] As we shall see, however, behind Vvedensky's metafictional inquiry into the ontology of language there still lies the unspoken omnipresence of God.

Conversations comprises ten conversations, spoken mostly between three anonymous characters. The first conversation ('about a madhouse'; 'o sumasshedshem dome') presents three figures riding in a carriage, and their reflections on a particular 'madhouse', which they eventually appear to enter. The next section contains the recital of a poem, 'about the absence of poetry' ('ob otsutstvii poezii'), at the conclusion of which the poet/singer dies. In the third conversation ('about the remembering of events'; 'o vospominanii sobytii') two, or perhaps three, men recall a previous argument concerning a still earlier event. During the whole of the dialogue which follows this ('a conversation about cards'; 'razgovor o kartakh'), three figures spend their time telling each other of their passion for card games and suggesting that they play, without ever passing from word to deed.[96] The fifth conversation, 'about running in a room' ('o begstve v komnate'), presents the reader with three characters who run around in a series of specific places (first a room, then a garden, then a mountain top, then a shore, before returning to the room). A sudden shift in context appears to occur between this dialogue and the ensuing section of the text ('a conversation about immediate continuation'; 'razgovor o neposredstvennom prodolzhenii'), in which each of the three speakers recounts his suicide. The seventh conversation ('about various activities'; 'o razlichnykh deistviyakh') takes place between three figures (those who have committed suicide?) as they attempt to light a candle on their journey down a river in a rowing boat. The eighth conversation takes place between merchants and a bath-house attendant, in a waterless bath-house. A poem about a World War I battle forms the main subject of the ninth dialogue, entitled 'the penultimate conversation entitled one man and war' ('predposlednii razgovor pod nazvaniem odin chelovek i voina'). In the tenth and final piece (entitled simply 'the final conversation'; 'poslednii razgovor') three characters discuss journeys that they all appear to have made. This conversation comes to an abrupt and unexpected conclusion, which also marks the end of the *Conversations* as a whole.

As might be surmised from its title, and from my summary, *Conversations* foregrounds language. More specifically, it dramatizes the inadequacy of human language and thought to deal with the world: 'Respect the poverty of language. Respect impoverished thoughts', as the narrative voice exhorts in the opening conversation ('Uvazhai bednost' yazyka. Uvazhai nishchie mysli'; p. 142).[97] This sense of the 'poverty of language' is reinforced throughout Vvedensky's text by the various ways in which the characters flout basic rules of everyday conversation.[98] At the very start of the first conversation, for example, a sense of incoherence is created, as questions are left unanswered, or answered inappropriately, and the punctuation system contrives to blur the very distinction between question and answer:

FIRST: I know the madhouse. I have seen the madhouse.
SECOND: What are you saying? i [*sic*] know nothing. What does it look like.
THIRD: Does it look like? Who has seen the madhouse.
FIRST: What is in it? Who lives in it.
SECOND: Birds do not live in it. Clocks go in it.

Первый: Я знаю сумасшедший дом. Я видел сумасшедший дом.
Второй: Что ты говоришь? я ничего не знаю. Как он выглядит.
Третий: Выглядит ли он? Кто видел сумасшедший дом.
Первый: Что в нем находится? Кто в нем живет.
Второй: Птицы в нем не живут. Часы в нем ходят. (р. 142)

At other moments, characters repeat themselves, apparently needlessly. At the end of the sixth conversation, for example, each of the speakers announces his death, only to reiterate the same information in an utterance which, thereby, is now superfluous, not to say impossible, given what they actually say:

FIRST: [I] have died.
SECOND: Have died.
THIRD: Have died.
FIRST: Have died.
SECOND: Have died.
THIRD: Have died.

Первый: Умер.
Второй: Умер.
Третий: Умер.
Первый: Умер.
Второй: Умер.
Третий: Умер. (p. 149)[99]

If the language of the *Conversations* helps to create a deep sense of dislocation and incoherence, then towards the end of the text, the characters' discourse suddenly appears excessively *coherent*. In other words, their dialogue is so constructed as to suggest that these interlocutors are in fact one and the same person.[100] In the penultimate conversation, the discursive boundaries separating the three main characters are definitively deconstructed. The third speaker declares he has written a poem, whereupon the first speaker announces that he will recite it, only for it to be read out, in fact, by the second speaker (p. 153). With the final conversation, the co-identification of the three characters is complete:

FIRST: I left my home and walked a long way.
SECOND: It is clear that I walked along a path.
[...]
THIRD: I sat down under the leaves of a tree and lapsed into thought.
FIRST: Thought about that.
SECOND: About my supposedly enduring existence.
THIRD: I could not understand anything.

Первый: Я из дому вышел и далеко пошел.
Второй: Ясно, что я пошел по дороге. [...]
Третий: Я сел под листьями и задумался.

Первый: Задумался о том.
Второй: О своем условно прочном существовании.
Третий: Ничего я не мог понять. (p. 155)

Given the fact that language is foregrounded to such an extent in the *Conversations*, it is somewhat ironic that nothing appears actually to be said (or, for that matter, to happen). During the first conversation, the narrative voice declares: 'Respect what is happening. But nothing is occurring.' ('Uvazhai to chto sluchaetsya. No nichego ne proiskhodit.'; p. 142). Just as nothing is said to occur in the *Conversations*, so, we are told, the characters' speech is only inner speech: 'Three people were riding in a carriage. They were exchanging thoughts.' ('V karete ekhali troe. Oni obmenivalis' myslyami.'; ibid.). And at the end of the third conversation, the third speaker tells the other two, 'both of you have said nothing' ('vy oba nichego ne govorili'; p. 145).[101]

Language is clearly all that these characters have; their words (whether articulated or merely thought) provide them with no direct access to the world. This may be what is meant by the reference to the 'poverty' of language. But what conclusions should one draw from this? Milner-Gulland sees a strong analogy between Vvedensky's *Conversations* and the later work of Wittgenstein, which 'is suffused by awareness of the limits of the sayable, of the curious but indispensable role of language, its intractibility when required to correspond logically with the phenomenal world' (Milner-Gulland, ' "Kovarnye stikhi" ', p. 33). However, it is the linguistic philosophy of Heidegger, rather than of Wittgenstein, which is most appropriate to Vvedensky's text.[102]

Much as Vvedensky does in the *Conversations*, Heidegger questioned the idea that language is a means of communication:

In the current view, language is held to be a kind of communication. It serves for verbal exchange and agreement, and in general for communicating. But language is not only and not primarily an audible and written expression of what is to be communicated. It not only puts forth in words and statements what is overtly or covertly intended to be communicated; language alone brings what is, as something that is, into the Open for the first time.[103]

The Heideggerean subtext of Vvedensky's conversations involves a journey in consciousness (since nothing is actually said, and nothing really happens) from madness, through death, to God. This journey – a sense of which is given by the references to 'walking' and 'paths' in the tenth conversation – does not end with the last word or full stop of this dialogue. Rather it extends on into that realm of absolute silence which appears to 'close' the text, but which in fact brings being – co-being with God – into the 'Open'.[104] Silence is central to Heidegger's thinking, for silence, rather than our 'fallen logos' is the only 'language' which affords us as humans access to Being, since it alone 'allows the unconcealment that discloses truth and beings', as Thiher puts it (*Words in Reflection*, p. 51).

Following this interpretation, the hierarchical division in the *Conversations* might not be organized, *pace* Nakhimovsky, according to who can speak, but according to who is silent.[105] Only Nature, with its 'soundless forests' ('bezzvuchnye lesa', p. 143) is naturally silent. In its 'silence' lies real poetry: the worms sing 'verses' ('stikhi'), the rivers repeat 'rhymes' ('rifmy').[106] The only way in the *Conversations* for humankind to achieve a (Heideggerean) 'recovery of silence in the midst of idle talk'[107] appears to be madness or death, for these, as we have seen, are the two worlds which Vvedensky's silent characters inhabit. For Heidegger too, madness and death appear to be the only means with which we can accede to the originating logos (the silence which he calls 'poetry'): 'The poet becomes poet only in so far as he follows the "madman" who died away into the time of the beginning.'[108]

This reference to language and beginning, to logos as (ineffable) origin underlines the religious nature, both of Heidegger's thought and of Vvedensky's text. Yet they are not religious in the same sense; whereas the former, to quote Thiher, 'aims at finding those conditions of possibility that [...] once allowed the sacred to appear' (Thiher, *Words in Reflection*, p. 35), the latter is essentially theological, for it posits God as the unsayable and unspeaking beginning and end of all language – the Word made flesh.[109] This is the being, the 'truth' which Vvedensky's silent language ultimately 'unconceals'. The last two conversations present the convergence of three speakers in the same voice and, simultaneously, the erasure of the (extradiegetic) narrative voice. As the characters approach what is both the end of the story and the end of the(ir) world, they become one 'being' in three 'persons'. The analogy with the Holy Trinity is too obvious to be ignored; if, in the fifth conversation, Vvedensky's characters were 'running away to God' ('ya ubegayu k Bogu'; p. 148), this was in order to achieve discursive (and ultimately, ontological) union with Him, for the voice which by the tenth conversation speaks in the text belongs to none other than God Himself. It is God who, for Vvedensky, fills the ontological void at the elusive centre of the shifting signifiers of 'tainted' human discourse, the God who stands outside time and who constitutes the 'hidden' unifying telos of Vvedensky's – and his characters' – subtextual sojourn, the God whose existence we mortals can indeed aspire to share, but only in the timeless, silent realm of the dead.

To conclude, *Conversations* is a text which, while bearing traces of *chinari* philosophy – the word offering transcendence to the neighbouring, non-substantial ontology of the Word[110] – also anticipates elements of Heidegger's linguistic cosmology. Vvedensky focuses on the 'fallen' nature of our logos, and suggests that true existence can be found only in discursive union with God through a rediscovery of holy silence. Unlike his fellow *chinar'* Kharms, who asserts the power of certain modes of human language, only to express horror at the political manifestations of that power, Vvedensky appears to suggest, paradoxically, that only silence offers genuine transcendence.

Works such as *Elizaveta Bam* and *A Certain Quantity of Conversations* are not just metafictional (fiction about fiction), but also, and more specifically, metalinguistic (language about language). That these two forms of metadiscourse are related can also be seen in the work of Vaginov, one member of OBERIU who took no recorded part in any *chinari* meetings, but who has much to say in his fiction about language and its representations.

WORLDS BEYOND WORDS: KONSTANTIN VAGINOV

In his first two novels, as we saw, Vaginov blurs and ultimately erases the ontological distinction between text and reality, words and the world. *The Goat's Song* ends with the 'author' joining his characters for a toast to high art, while in *The Labours and Days of Svistonov*, the reader finds it as difficult as Svistonov does to distinguish between the framing and the framed novels. In his pre-OBERIU work also, such as the prose text 'The Star of Bethlehem' and the dramatic poem 'The Year 1925', Vaginov erases ontological boundaries (of space and time) as part of his cyclical vision of history and his ambivalent attitude towards the cultural 'renewal' offered by the Bolshevik Revolution.[111]

Vaginov also materializes the word in a manner reminiscent of Vvedensky. For example, in the 1924 *poema* 'Hermits' ('Otshel'niki'; pp. 143–5), the poet has a dream in which he finds himself in a wasteland. As he hears a song, which reaches him from within 'high ruins', the words take on a materiality of their own, in stark contrast to the emptiness and ethereality of everything else in the scene: 'Like effigies, words sit with me / More welcome than a feast and quieter than pyramids' ('Kak izvayaniya, slova sidyat so mnoi / Zhelannei pirshestva i tishe piramid'; p. 144).[112] In the third section of 'The Song of Words', entitled 'the word in a theatrical costume' ('slovo v teatral'nom kostyume'), the poet addresses the word as if it were another being, of equivalent ontological status to his own, entreating it to join him in his meanderings around the city of Leningrad:

> Give me your hand, word – one, two, three!
> I walk with you over the earth.
> Behind me walk words in a procession,
> Their tiny wings barely moving.
>
> Дай ручку, слово, раз, два, три!
> Хожу с тобою по земле.
> За мною шествуют слова
> И крылышки дрожат едва.　　　　　(p. 173)[113]

Moreover, images of the objectified word are not confined to

Vaginov's early verse. In a poem from the late cycle *Likeness of Sound* (*Zvukopodobie*), a word is given physical attributes as part of a description of a bleak Leningrad morning:

> Black is the endless morning,
> The streetlights stand like tears.
> The purple, echoing sounds
> Of the distant dawn can be heard.
> And the word burns and grows dark
> On the square outside the window,
> And birds crow and soar
> Above the morning's black oblivion.

> Черно бесконечное утро,
> Как слезы стоят фонари.
> Пурпурные, гулкие звуки
> Слышны отдаленной зари.
> И слово горит и темнеет
> На площади перед окном,
> И каркают птицы и реют
> Над черным его забытьем.   (p. 177)

Such images of the word-made-object are unlikely to have been motivated by an interest in *chinari* philosophy; for one thing, there is no record of Vaginov ever attending a meeting of the *chinari*, and for another, most of these images are contained in works written before Vaginov had even met Kharms and Vvedensky. What is far more likely is that the materialized word is one of many different manifestations of Vaginov's belief (a belief shared by the hermit Serapion) in the reality of the poet's artistic visions, one expression of Vaginov's Romantic faith in the possibility of transcendence – and, ultimately, of immortality – through art and the language of art.[114]

As we saw in chapter 1, such a belief in the reality of the poet's vision is also expressed in *The Goat's Song* by the unknown poet: 'Poetry is a special business [...] you take a few words, put them together in an unusual way [...] and you are swallowed up in the completely new world revealed beyond those words.' There is, however, a fundamental shift in Vaginov's attitude towards the ontological status of language and its representations, from his early verse and prose to his later work (moreover, this evolution runs parallel to Vaginov's changing attitude towards authorship). To appreciate fully the extent to which Vaginov in his late prose refutes his earlier optimism about the reality of art and its representations – and how this relates to the metafiction of Kharms and Vvedensky – I must now look at Vaginov's novel *Bambocciade*.

ART AS PLAY: KONSTANTIN VAGINOV'S *BAMBOCCIADE*

Bambocciade (*Bambochada*) was Vaginov's third novel, and the last to be published during his lifetime (it first appeared in Leningrad in 1931). From the outset, the novel foregrounds the issue of aesthetic representation. The novel's epigraph explains that 'Bambochada' is an approximate transliteration into Russian of the Italian word 'Bambocciata', a term which means a caricature of everyday life, and comes from the sobriquet 'il Bamboccio', given to one of the finest exponents of the art of caricature in painting, the seventeenth-century artist Van Leer.[115] Yet although *Bambocciade* begins by focusing on visual art and its epistemological relation to the real, the novel is equally concerned with verbal art, and is primarily an exploration of the ontological status of representation.

The 'caricature' which *Bambocciade* presents is of the city of Leningrad itself, depicted as a place full of misfits and marginals.[116] The novel's main character is the strangely named Evgeny Felinflein,[117] a former actor, circus performer, and theatre director (to name but a few of his previous professions). As the novel begins, Felinflein finds himself unemployed, following 'eight years spent getting involved in shady deals, travelling from place to place, and lying' ('vosem' let avantyur, puteshestvii i vran'ya'; p. 262). It is not long, however, before Evgeny begins to suffer from a serious respiratory disease and signs himself into a sanatorium, on the outskirts of the city (at Detskoe Selo).[118] His condition steadily deteriorates, however, and by the end of *Bambocciade*, he is in no doubt that his ailment will prove fatal.

The atmosphere of sadness and loneliness which pervades the latter stages of the novel, bears little resemblance to that which accompanies Felinflein through much of the rest of the work. Felinflein is a likeable rogue, a 'merry trickster' ('vesely[i] obmanshchik[...]'; p. 268), the embodiment of the spirit of irony. He feels life to be a game, and is fond of quoting Shakespeare's 'all the world's a stage' (' "Ves' mir – teatr" [*sic*]'; p. 342). His life is entirely devoted to play, in both the ludic and the theatrical senses.[119] He is described more than once as 'immersed in a play world' ('pogruzhennyi v mir igry'; e.g. p. 282), a world which becomes for him more real than life itself. Felinflein surrounds himself with images of play; when he moves into a new flat, virtually the first thing he does is to hang up representations of play, in the form of a Dutch painting of card players, and photographs depicting, variously, a game of back-gammon in a bourgeois household, peasants fighting over a card game and military officers playing cards in a brothel (ibid.).

If the world for Felinflein is a play space, then the sanatorium in which he finds himself is a microcosm of play. At one point, for example, the sanatorium is visited by a theatre troupe, which actually performs a play (p. 361). Most of the numerous games which feature in *Bambocciade* – cards, ping-pong, chess, skittles, snowballs, dominoes, or draughts – are played within the confines of the sanatorium. The grounds around the main building are full of play areas of their own; there is an amusement park, as well as a children's playground (p. 360). Indeed, it is in the sanatorium that one particular 'game' comes to dominate. This mode of play involves the simulation of an alternative world, based to a certain extent on our own world, in whose existence the players must all believe if the game is to be played.[120]

For everything in the sanatorium – the games, the books which they are encouraged to read, the films which are shown – is geared towards encouraging the inmates to simulate an alternative (and illusory) world, where they are not terminally ill, indeed, where diseases such as tuberculosis and the ago-nizing life choices which they impose upon the sufferer do not exist, or at least can be cured, and therefore do not count: 'The sanatorium facilitated the temporary transformation of its inmates into children. The patients forgot about their ailments'

('Sanatoriya sposobstvovala prevrashcheniyu na nekotoroe vremya svoikh postoyal'tsev v detei. Bol'nye zabyvali o svoei bolezni'; p. 360). (Is it coincidence that the 'children's village' which the sanatorium constitutes is situated in Tsarskoe Selo, just outside Leningrad, renamed by the Bolsheviks after the Revolution 'Detskoe Selo'?) As might be expected, Felinflein loses no time in entering into the spirit of things; as the narrator tells us, 'surrounded by a world of play he felt he was the number-one player, a player by nature' ('sredi mira igry on chuvstvoval sebya pervym igrokom, igrokom po prirode'; p. 361).

Yet *Bambocciade* is not just concerned with demonstrating how these characters turn life into a game; the novel shows that fiction, like all forms of art and all means of representation, is analogous to play, precisely because, like one common mode of play it involves the creation of an alternative, but illusory reality.[121] It is art (both visual and verbal), and its 'playful' nature which lies at the heart of *Bambocciade*, rather than play itself.

The novel contains, alongside its various games, numerous examples of *mise en abyme*, various representations (as stories narrated or pictures described) embedded within it.[122] For example, one of the work's secondary characters, Vasily Vasil'evich Ermilov, tells many stories (including a number about his dead daughter), many of which are reproduced in their entirety in Vaginov's text, and at times in an uninterrupted series. At one point the novel contains a lengthy footnote, which tells the story of how in his student days Punshevich (the self-appointed president of the 'Society for the Collection of Trivia')[123] earned a small commission by writing stories advertising various products. One of these stories, an advertisement for face powder, is itself reproduced in its entirety in the footnote (pp. 295–6).

There are also extended descriptions of pictorial representations in *Bambocciade*, such as the painting in Toropulo's room, entitled 'Entertaining the Ambassador' ('Ugoshchenie posla'; p. 285), and the ceiling in the confectioner's into which Toropulo's lodger, nicknamed 'Nunekhiya Usfazanovna', goes to buy a cake (pp. 290–1). The latter deserves to be quoted at length, since it gives a good indication of Vaginov's prose style, while also hinting at the contemporary Soviet debate about the value of pre-revolutionary art:

Nunekhiya Usfazanovna, standing in the queue for the cash desk, wondered which cake she'd like to eat.

A half well-dressed young lady, turning to an elegant young lady, exclaimed:

'Just look at that funny ceiling!'

The elegant young lady had a look.

'Well, it's terribly sweet!'

Nunekhiya Usfazanovna turned to them angrily and said through clenched teeth:

'It's so artistic! They don't paint like that any more. You're young, you've never seen anything nice.'

The well-dressed young lady:

'Well I find the ceiling tasteless, and I can tell you we've seen nicer.'

'Well of course, we've now had twelve years of the revolution, and it's true, this used to be a sumptuous cake shop.'

'As a matter of fact, we've been here when it was a sumptuous cake shop,' replied the well-dressed young lady.

'You don't mean you're thirty?'

'We are.'

Nunekhiya Usfazanovna calmed down. She tried to strike up a conversation:

'Just look how artistically those flowers are painted, with what taste.'

The young ladies sniggered.

Nunekhiya Usfazanovna raised her eyes to the ceiling and began to contemplate it, sharing her impressions: a boy-cherub held a mirror in front of a girl-cherub, in which his face was reflected; a cherub carried a sheaf of wheat, from which red poppies and cornflowers fell; a boy-cherub and a girl-cherub sat on a hill and looked enchantedly into each other's eyes; the same pair, sitting on another hill, listened to the birds singing; they sat on flourishes representing a branch; in the middle of the ceiling a larger angel, with butterfly's wings, played on a lyre, surrounded by roses; a chubby, plump girl-cherub, with dimples in her cheeks, was sitting on an apple and decorating her hair with a pearl necklace, – and everywhere there were roses, and lilac.

A hat, black, and brimless, a coat, wider towards the hem, lips, ready to close up in fright, bought a cream cake, left through mirrored doors, and disappeared into the mist.

Нунехия Усфазановна, стоя в очереди к кассе, раздумывала, какое съесть пирожное.

Полунарядная барышня воскликнула, обращаясь к изящной барышне:

– Смотри, какой здесь забавный потолок!

Изящная барышня посмотрела.

– Да, здорово конфетно!

Нунехия Усфазановна раздраженно обернулась и сквозь зубы проговорила:

– Так художественно! Теперь так не рисуют. Вы молоды, вы хорошего не видели.

Нарядная барышня:

– А я нахожу, что потолок безвкусный, и что мы получше видели!

– Ну да, двенадцать лет революции уже, а здесь была богатая кондитерская.

– Как раз в этой богатой кондитерской мы и бывали, – ответила нарядная барышня.

– Не тридцать же вам лет?!

– Тридцать.

Нунехия Усфазановна успокоилась. Она попыталась завязать разговор:

–Посмотрите, как художественно нарисованы цветы, с каким вкусом.

Барышни хихикнули.

Нунехия Усфазановна стала созерцать, подняв глаза к потолку и делясь впечатлениями: ангелочек-мальчик перед ангелочком-девочкой держит зеркало, в котором отражается его лицо; ангелочек несет сноп пшеницы, со снопа падают красные маки и васильки; ангелочек-мальчик и ангелочек-девочка с восхищением смотрят друг другу в глаза, сидя на холме; они же, сидя на другом холме, слушают пение птиц; сидят на загогулинах, изображающих ветку; посреди потолка более крупный ангел, с крылышками бабочки, играет на лире среди роз; пухлая, сдобная ангелочек-девочка, с ямочками на щеках, сидя на яблочке, украшает волосы жемчужным ожерельем, – и всюду розы, сирень.

Шляпа, черная, без полей, пальто, расширяющееся книзу, губки, готовые сложиться испуганно, купили кремовое пирожное, вышли из зеркальных дверей, скрылись в тумане.[124]

Bambocciade is full of such embedded representations. But what is their meaning? Despite the abundance of kitsch which it contains, *Bambocciade* is much less concerned with themes of modernity and its attendant spiritual and aesthetic decadence (in the manner of, say, *The Goat's Song*), than with people living in that modernity who fail – or refuse – to distinguish between the real and its representations.[125] For example, Nunekhiya rereads her diary, entire extracts from which are reproduced in the text, so as to 'immerse herself in the years of her youth' ('pogruzi[t'sya] v gody svoei molodosti'; p. 292). A more extreme case is Ermilov, who appears to believe that by his own representations of his daughter (the stories which he tells about her) he can literally recreate her verbally as once he created her biologically. In this sense, Ermilov makes little or no distinction between biological and artistic reproduction (sex and representation). Toropulo also appears to believe that to represent a being is to bring that being (back) to life. When his beloved cat dies, he gives both the cat's body and its photograph to a taxidermist: ' "There", he said, "is my favourite cat; and there is its photograph. Give it that pose, so that it looks as if it were alive" ' ('– Vot, – skazal on, – moi lyubimyi kot; vot ego fotograficheskaya kartochka. Pridaite emu etu pozu; pust' on lezhit kak zhivoi'; p. 321).

Felinflein also seems to confuse representation with reality, and never more so than once he is inside the sanatorium. As he looks out into the sanatorium park one morning, he sees a snowman – the Russian term 'snezhnaya baba' literally means 'snow-woman' – in the process of melting. The figure is now so deformed that none of the other inmates even looks at it any more. Yet Felinflein continues to imagine it as a real woman:

the woman was melting; her elegant nose, fashioned by the hand of an ailing sculptor, had completely melted away; her dark eyes had disappeared, her neatly trimmed hair was still in place, but her oval-shaped face was scored by fine streams; yesterday the woman's firm, voluptuous snow-white bosom had grown as soft as jelly and turned grey, while all around her, as she stood melting, green grass and yellow and grey leaves had once more become visible. Now no one paid any attention to this woman; she stood condemned to melt away into nothing.

баба таяла; изящный нос, вылепленный рукой больного скульптора, совсем растаял; темные глаза исчезли, подстриженные волосы еще держались, но овал лица был весь источен мелкими струйками; вчера еще крепкая и пышная белоснежная грудь стала студенистой и серой, а вокруг еще стоявшей, но уже таявшей женщины, опять зазеленела травка, зажелтели и засерели листья. Теперь на женщину никто уже не обращал внимания; она стояла, обреченная на истаивание. (p. 355)[126]

With Felinflein, the theme of representation is subsumed within that of play, however. If Ermilov and Toropulo use representations in an attempt to 'revive' a loved one, Felinflein plays in order to prolong his own life. Once he senses the seriousness of his illness, Felinflein thinks it necessary, not merely to immerse himself in a world of play and games, but somehow to internalize that world, literally to embody the spirit of play, to become nothing but a play space himself. Only this way, he feels, can he 'win the game' and thereby avoid death:

Evgeny sat in the barber's shop and thought about how he might outplay death. Death did not appear before him as an image from an engraving, or as a skeleton carrying a scythe; rather, he felt death inside himself. And it was precisely this which was so difficult; for it meant that he would have to transfer the game to an inner plane, his inner world.

Евгений сидел в парикмахерской и думал, как бы ему обыграть смерть. Смерть не возникала перед ним в образе гравюры, в образе скелета с косой; он чувствовал ее в себе самом; это-то и составляло трудность; приходилось перенести игру во внутренний план, во внутренний мир. (p. 361)

This passage represents the terminal phase of Felinflein's anti-existentialism. For by seeking to make his life nothing but (a) play, both in the ludic and the theatrical senses, Felinflein is in fact attempting to enter the ontology of play, to assimilate a world where all is simulated, represented and consequently not real. In other words, Felinflein wants to reach that 'spatio-temporal *elsewhere*, represented as though actually present',[127] which characterizes both the ontology of drama, and the play world, that 'enigmatic realm that is not nothing, and yet nothing real'.[128]

Timelessness is, of course, the corollary of spacelessness, and if Felinflein has, until the onset of his illness, laboured under the illusion of his own immortality, it is in order to perpetuate this sense of his own extra-temporality that he seeks the refuge of the play space. For, as Eugen Fink puts it, 'in the autonomy of play action there appears a possibility of human timelessness in time. Time is then experienced, not as a precipitate rush of successive moments, but rather as the one full moment that is, so to speak, a glimpse of eternity' (Fink, 'The Oasis of Happiness', p. 21). Felinflein almost wills himself to inhabit the 'fairy-tale' world of play/art, where ontological oblivion alone might guarantee a happy ending, where he could live, if not 'happily', then at least 'ever after'. At one point in the novel, as Felinflein walks through the sanatorium park, the 'fairy-tale' nature of his aspirations is underlined: 'This corner of the park today reminded Evgeny of the stories of Tomcat Murr; he felt that at any moment the puppet prince Iriney would appear and set off around his park' ('Etot ugolok parka segodnya napomnil Evgeniyu skazki Kota Murra; kazalos', vot-vot vyidet kukol'nyi knyaz' Iriney i poidet po svoemu parku'; p. 360).[129] In such a world could Felinflein defer meaning, and notably the meaning of his own mortality. It is this desire to suspend significance which explains his tendency towards irony; for what else is irony, if not a displacement of meaning?

In *Bambocciade* Vaginov explores the ontological relationship between representation and reality. Yet, unlike Kharms and Vvedensky (and unlike Vaginov the poet), Vaginov the novelist insists on drawing an absolute distinction between words and the world. It is in the ontological 'otherness' of its representations that art, whether discursive or pictorial, diegetic or mimetic, is like play.[130] This fact is underlined by the plethora of mirrors contained in *Bambocciade*.[131] By its nature, the mirror offers, not so much knowledge of another world 'out there', as an illusory duplicate of our own world. Like the two halves of Felinflein's name, the real and its mirror image are, and are not, the same thing. For this reason the mirror embodies most succinctly the ambiguities of the (ontological) sameness and difference involved in mimetic reproduction.[132] Vaginov's novel constitutes a veritable hall of mirrors; mirrors are mentioned everywhere: in the painting on the cake shop ceiling; on the same shop's doors; in Ermilov's flat; in Felinflein's apartment (where they help him with his self-imposed speech therapy); in a photograph cut by Felinflein from a German magazine; in Toropulo's flat (his beloved cat likes to sit in front of one and wash himself); in the Palace of Weddings where Felinflein and Laren'ka are married (where mirrors line the walls); in the barber's where Laren'ka's father has his hair cut; in Felinflein's conversation with another character, Ninon, on people who like to kiss their own reflection in mirrors; in the 'mirror-lined boudoirs' ('zerkal'nye buduary'; p. 348) where Felinflein imagines an eighteenth-century version of the same Ninon spending her time; and in the cloakroom/postroom in the sanatorium. The huge mirror in Ermilov's flat offers a slightly different example from the novel's other mirrors, however. It had been installed so that Varen'ka could see herself during her ballet exercises. Yet now she is dead, all it reflects is her representation, in the form of a white statue which occupies the room. If the original mirror image of Varen'ka constituted an imitation of the real thing, what we now have is the real thing twice removed, or an imitation (the image in the mirror) of another imitation (the statue itself). By embedding one representation within another in this way, *Bambocciade* looks back to Plato's definition of art, which is precisely that of an imitation of an imitation. (The same kind of effect is achieved by having the mirror itself the object of representation, such as in the ceiling painting which Nunekhiya Usfazanovna so admires.) Once again, the conclusion to which we are drawn is that the representation of the real is not the same, ontologically, as the real itself; the former is a mirror image of the latter, with all that implies for the relative ontological status of each.

Focusing on the ontological distinction between the world and its representations, *Bambocciade* may be said to participate in what critics such as Christine Brooke-Rose have labelled the 'mimetic crisis' of modern fiction.[133] The novel appears to underline the fact that mimesis (understood in the broader, Aristotelean, sense as either narrative or direct representation of events) is an illusion. Yet there is much more to Vaginov's novel than a mere rehearsal of what, by the early twentieth-century, was already a well-worn truth of much metafiction.[134]

While Vaginov evidently shares Kharms's and Vvedensky's interest in the ontological status of representation, *Bambocciade* can in fact be read as a polemic with the *chinari*, and in particular their assertion that language and reality are somehow interdependent. From an even narrower perspective, it is possible to see in Felinflein's ludic existence a parody of Kharms, whose habit of conflating art and life may well have been experienced by Vaginov at first-hand, during his colla-boration with OBERIU. Vvedensky's comment 'Kharms is art' stemmed from the latter's Felinfleinesque celebration of 'thea-tricality' in life, marked by means of all kinds of stunts, masks (notably that of his fictitious aristocratic brother whom he liked to impersonate) and games.[135] (This raises the interesting prospect that Felinflein represents both Vaginov, who was by the time he wrote *Bambocciade* terminally ill with tuberculosis, and Kharms, who sought to make life as unpredictable and eccentric as his own art.)

There may also be an element of auto-critique in *Bamboc-ciade*.[136] By the way in which it systematically denies the reality of art and its representations, the novel can be said to constitute a rebuttal of Vaginov's earlier belief in the reality of the poet's words, in the possibility of transcendence through art, and in 'the organic relationship between life and art'.[137] Felinflein, Ermilov, and Toropulo all discover what the unknown poet could not see, namely the fact that to 'shape the world anew' requires more than words. Indeed, the faint hope expressed in *The Goat's Song*, that art affords access to another reality 'beyond the grave' is replaced in Vaginov's third novel with the realiza-tion that there is nothing beyond the grave except annihilation, and not even art and its 'playful' representations can save us from this.[138] Unlike the inscribed author of *The Goat's Song*, or

Svistonov, Felinflein has no unmediated, ontological access to his, or anybody else's representations.[139]

If art is no longer seen to afford the artist the possibility of transcendence to another world, what is its relation to reality? One possible answer to this question comes in a brief conversation between Punshevich and Toropulo. As the two men look through their collection of pre-revolutionary menus, Toropulo observes, 'all this was legitimate in its own time and accurately reflected life' ('vse eto bylo zakonomerno v svoe vremya i verno otrazhalo zhizn''; p. 325). Proposing that their Society organize an exhibition of all its kitsch, Punshevich argues that the exhibits (which include sweet wrappers depicting events from the Bolshevik Revolution, political leaders, and examples of Soviet technological progress) will have ideological value. They will, he argues, help provide an impetus towards the formation of the new (socialist) society ('vystavlennye materialy dadut tolchok k obrazovaniyu novogo byta'; ibid.). The suggestion seems to be that if representation affords no ontological access to the real, then it nevertheless has ideological value, since it both reflects the prevailing socio-political order, and can contribute to the further development of that order. As Toropulo says of his countless sweet wrappers, with their images of the Kremlin and their scenes from the Russian Civil War, 'here are politics, and history, and iconography' ('zdes' i politika, i istoriya, i ikonografiya'; p. 297).[140] Of course, it is possible to read such comments as an ironic allusion to those who would wish to conflate the ideological and the aesthetic (including Bakhtin and other members of his circle).[141] For hasn't Toropulo already confessed his tendency towards irony? Yet the fact that Vaginov went on, after *Bambocciade*, to write his most 'heteroglot' work in *Harpagoniana* surely suggests that the remarks made by Toropulo and Punshevich are meant to be taken at least partly seriously.

Whatever the case, it is deeply and tragically ironic that had Vaginov not died of natural causes while trying to revise his fourth novel in 1934, his own 'caricatures' would almost certainly have led to the kind of horrific end suffered by his erstwhile companions in art and life, Kharms and Vvedensky.

That his words, like those of his fellow *Oberiuty*, survived at all suggests that Felinflein may have been more than a little justified in his faith in the power over death of art and its 'playful' representations.

Conclusion: OBERIU – between modernism and postmodernism?

If the OBERIU article sought to draw a fundamental distinction between 'art' and 'reality', 'fiction' and 'fact', then this study of the group as a whole has sought to separate fact from fiction, reality from myth. What it has been attempted to show is that Kharms, Vvedensky, and Vaginov all wrote metafiction, self-conscious literature which posed questions concerning the nature of fiction itself. My reading (especially in chapters 1 and 2) has been self-consciously Bakhtinian not just in the use of terms such as 'carnival', 'dialogism', and 'heteroglossia', but also in the way I have tried to bring my 'active understanding' both to OBERIU fiction and to the concept of 'metafiction' itself. As well as re-examining some of the assumptions conventionally made about OBERIU, the present study may in fact suggest the need to redefine 'metafiction' to take into account the fact that self-consciousness is not an inherent quality of any literary text, but the product of a dialogic exchange between writer, text, and reader.

Be that as it may, Patricia Waugh's reading of some of the salient features of metafiction sounds not unlike a résumé of OBERIU self-consciousness:

a celebration of the power of the creative imagination together with an uncertainty about the validity of its representations; an extreme self-consciousness about language, literary form and the act of writing fictions; a pervasive insecurity about the relationship of fiction to reality; a parodic, playful, excessive or deceptively naive style of writing. (Waugh, *Metafiction*, p. 2)

As part of their search for new aesthetic forms, Kharms,

Vvedensky, and Vaginov all explore three aspects of the literary process: first, the cultural and textual authority of the writer; second, the role of the reader in the production of text and textual meaning; and third, the ontological relationship between words and the world. Paraphrasing Raymond Federman, one might say that Kharms, Vvedensky, and Vaginov engage in the act of searching, in their fiction itself, for the meaning of what it means to write fiction, to read fiction, and to exist as fiction.[1]

Furthermore, most of the devices which Patricia Waugh claims are found in metafictional writing feature at one time or another in the work of Kharms, Vvedensky, and Vaginov: 'the over-obtrusive, visibly inventing narrator'; 'ostentatious typographic experiment'; 'explicit dramatization of the reader'; 'Chinese-box structures'; 'incantatory and absurd lists'; 'over-systematized or overtly arbitrarily arranged structural devices'; 'total breakdown of temporal and spatial organization of narrative'; 'infinite regress'; 'dehumanization of character, parodic doubles, obtrusive proper names'; 'self-reflexive images'; 'critical discussions of the story within the story'; 'continuous undermining of fictional conventions'; 'use of popular genres'; 'and explicit parody of previous texts whether literary or non-literary' (Waugh, *Metafiction*, pp. 21–2).

Such a catalogue of literary devices should not blind us, however, to the fact that the (meta)fictions of OBERIU were inevitably, and intimately connected to the times in which they were written. They were in part a product of the crisis which confronted not just Soviet prose, but Soviet art as a whole in the late 1920s, when faced with the question of how best to reflect, or 'refract', as Bakhtin would put it, the momentous changes which had taken place in Soviet society since the Bolshevik Revolution of 1917. Unfortunately, the *Oberiuty* believed that the best way to achieve this goal was to effect an aesthetic revolution, at a time when those in power were advocating conservatism in all branches of the arts, resorting to increasingly violent means in their efforts to deny anyone else a voice. Yet the deeply social and political nature of much OBERIU metafiction should not surprise us. Critics such as

Waugh and more recently Shepherd have been keen to establish metafiction's 'sociological' credentials, arguing that the genre is first and foremost predicated upon:

the dissociation between, on the one hand, the genuinely felt sense of crisis, alienation and oppression in contemporary society and, on the other, the continuance of traditional literary forms like realism which are no longer adequate vehicles for the mediation of this experience. (Waugh, *Metafiction*, p. 11)

Our study has important ramifications for hitherto widely accepted assumptions concerning OBERIU. First, their (systematic) use of self-reflexive literary devices clearly distinguishes Kharms, Vvedensky, and Vaginov from Zabolotsky, regarded until now as a key member of OBERIU, and Oleinikov, whom many still consider an important 'fellow-traveller' of the group. Consequently, the generally-accepted view of Vaginov's relation to the rest of the group as at best peripheral must surely be questioned. Rather, it is Zabolotsky who should be considered the group's outsider, a fact underlined by his sharp disagreement with Vvedensky over aesthetics, and by his break with the group halfway through 1928 (his reacquaintance with the *chinari* in the early 1930s was to prove remarkably shortlived). Unfortunately, my brief excursions into work by Bakhterev, while revealing interesting similarities with the fiction of Kharms, Vvedensky, and Vaginov, must remain inconclusive, given the dearth of material by this writer currently available. One can only hope that more of Bakhterev's (unofficial) fiction will soon see the light of day.

Second, the relevance to the group's aesthetic practice of the principles outlined in the OBERIU article (much of which was penned by Zabolotsky) would appear to be far less marked than many have hitherto assumed. The systematic exploration, in the works of Kharms, Vvedensky, and Vaginov, of the nature of literary fiction, and the countless literary devices which all three writers foreground, manipulate, and defamiliarize, renders dubious the claim, made in the article, that the main aim of the group was to peel away the object's 'literary skin'. The Romantic notions of authorship which underpin the article's descriptions of the group's individual members (not least the reference to Vaginov 'warming' the poetic object with his very 'breath'!; Milner-Gulland, ' "Left Art" ', p. 71) also run strangely counter to the images of authorship to be found in much OBERIU metafiction. The references in the article to left art also deserve comment. If, as Shepherd maintains (*Beyond Metafiction*, p. 117), OBERIU as a group sought to align itself with early left art, it must be said that Kharms, Vvedensky, and Vaginov all evince a deeply ambivalent attitude towards the transformative power of the word (one of early left art's basic tenets). And while Shepherd's reading of Vaginov's *The Labours and Days of Svistonov* in line with late left-art theory is convincing, there is a certain irony in the fact that Vaginov should have articulated the views of Chuzhak, Brik, and other left-art theorists in a literary genre (the novel) which was anathema to them.

Third, what unites the work of Kharms, Vvedensky, and Vaginov goes far deeper and extends much further than their relatively brief collaboration in OBERIU. In this sense, the point made by various scholars that OBERIU was merely a makeshift association which came together for essentially practical reasons is largely irrelevant.[2] On the other hand, rather than simply see OBERIU as just one episode in the evolution of the *chinari* group (as scholars such as Sazhin and Jaccard have argued), it is equally as possible to view the philosophy of the *chinari* as just one of a number of influences on OBERIU metafiction.

Of course, Kharms, Vvedensky, and Vaginov each writes from his own particular perspective, and each has a literary style recognizably his own. Kharms, for example, questions all kinds of conventional sources of 'wisdom', in fiction which testifies to his interest in 'nonsense' ('chush''). On the other hand, Vvedensky constantly explores the nature of time, of death, and of God. And so much of Vaginov's literary output, whether poetry or prose, is pervaded by a deep sense of social and cultural crisis in the aftermath of the October Revolution. Similarly, while Kharms and Vvedensky engage in their fiction in a dialogue with the other *chinari* Lipavsky and Druskin, Vaginov's novels testify to his acquaintance with the Bakhtin circle. Moreover, Vaginov at times appears to parody both OBERIU as a group (in *The Goat's Song* and *The Labours and Days of Svistonov*), and Kharms as an individual (in *Bambocciade*). Such diversity should not surprise us however, if we recall the warning contained in the OBERIU article (penned, ironically, by the most untypical member of the group, Zabolotsky), against regarding the group as a brotherhood of like-minded 'monks'. Indeed, one is reminded of Lunts's comment concerning that other literary 'brotherhood', the Serapions: 'The Serapion Brothers, as a school, [has] never existed. What we have in common is not a manner of writing, but an attitude towards what is written.'[3]

What of the tradition in which Kharms, Vvedensky, and Vaginov were writing? OBERIU metafiction belongs to what is, as Segal and Shepherd have shown, a strong tradition of self-consciousness in Russian literature, extending back as far as Pushkin and Gogol', and including more recent writers such as Andrey Bitov and Sasha Sokolov.[4] One writer whom neither Segal nor Shepherd mentions is the Russian émigré Vladimir Kazakov, whose self-conscious fiction – drama, prose, and verse – contains a number of stylistic features remarkably close to those which I have been examining here.[5] Another who should be mentioned in this context is Valeriya Narbikova, whose oneiric metafiction comes closer to the spirit of OBERIU than practically anything else in post-Soviet Russian literature.[6]

There are also points of contact between Kharms, Vvedensky, and Vaginov and certain Western writers of metafiction. For example, by the way in which they question the authority of the author, foreground the presence of the spectator in the theatre, and explore the nature of the theatrical illusion, the plays of Kharms and Vvedensky have much in common with Pirandello's metadrama *Six Characters in Search of an Author* (*Sei personaggi in cerca d'autore*, 1921).[7] In his prose miniatures Kharms seems to be suggesting, rather like the narrator of Samuel Beckett's *The Unnamable* (*L'Innommable*, 1953), that even when there is nothing to say, 'the discourse must go on'.[8] As for Vaginov, the trouble which the 'author' experiences with his characters in *The Goat's Song* (or, for that matter, the problems which Svistonov has with *his* characters) are a much milder version of the tribulations of the 'author' in Flann O'Brien's *At-Swim-Two-Birds* (1939), whose characters rebel against him, with fatal consequences. Vaginov's self-conscious novels also anticipate certain aspects of the French New Novel, such as Nathalie Sarraute's fictional explorations of writing and reading, or Michel Butor's novelistic enquiries into the nature of representation.[9]

However, rather than produce yet another survey of twentieth-century metafiction, there is one important question which still needs to be asked – what, if anything, was *distinctive* about OBERIU? Radically challenging the authority of the writer, insisting on the co-creative role of the reader, and exploring the ontological relation between words and the world, Kharms, Vvedensky, and Vaginov substantially extended the aesthetic programme of Russian modernism and the avant-garde. OBERIU metafiction is perhaps unique within Russian literature in as much as it occupies a transitional space between modernism – evident in, for example, the obsession with time, and the early images of the writer as social outcast – and what might be called postmodernism – in particular Kharms's insistence on the primacy of language, Vvedensky's focus on the productive role of the audience, and Vaginov's aestheticization of kitsch. This should not surprise us, given the fact that the writing which I have been discussing covers the period from the late 1920s (the end of the modernist period, particularly in the Soviet Union) to the early 1940s (the dawn of what is generally held to be the postmodernist era, at least in the West).

A few scholars have in fact begun to discuss particular members of the group as precursors of postmodernism. One of the first to argue this point of view was Herta Schmidt, who saw a direct line from OBERIU through the Theatre of the Absurd in the West to three Russian playwrights whom she described as postmodernist, namely Andrey Amal'rik, Vasily Aksenov, and Aleksandr Vampilov.[10]

Some scholars have gone so far as to suggest that individual *Oberiuty* should be considered postmodernist in their own right, rather than precursors of postmodernism.[11] Nina Perlina, for example, has described the surfeit of intertextuality in Vaginov's poetry as a typically postmodernist strategy (Perlina, 'Konstantin Vaguinov', p. 475). Vaginov's last two novels have been compared by Dubravka Ugrešić to the postmodernist collage-novels of Il'ya Kabakov (Ugrešić, 'Avangard i sovremennost'').[12] The poetry of Kharms and Vvedensky has recently been compared to what many see as the Russian strain of postmodernism, namely 'Conceptualism'.[13] Anemone, for his part, has argued that the second of what he sees as the three phases in Kharms's evolution as a writer was dedicated to 'the exploration of what have come to be called post-modern problems of language and meaning' (Anemone, 'The Anti-World of Daniil Kharms', p. 88). Neil Cornwell maintains that 'Kharms, the black miniaturist, is an exponent not so much of the modernist "end of the Word" (in a Joycean sense) as of a post-modernist, minimalist and infantilist "end of the Story" (in a sense perhaps most analogous to Beckett)' (Cornwell, 'Introduction: Daniil Kharms, Black Miniaturist', pp. 18–19). Indeed, what Cornwell calls the 'skeletal terseness' of Kharms's 'Incidents' calls to mind much North American prose fiction of the 1960s and 1970s. Cornwell defends himself, moreover, from any possible charge of ahistoricism by arguing that the sense of impending apocalypse which produced Western postmodernism in the period after World War II already existed in the Soviet Union of the 1920s and the Stalinist era.[14]

The problem, of course, is that the concepts 'modernism' and (especially) 'postmodernism' are notoriously slippery. Depending on whose definition one takes, either term could apply to any of the authors whom I have been discussing. To take the case of Kharms, for example: Andre Le Vot produces what is almost a definition of the Kharmsian prose text when he argues that in postmodernist fiction, 'fragmentation and inconsequence are accepted as the rule. The illusions of memory are obliterated, causes and effects considered as reversible, logic and temporality toyed with as period pieces.'[15] Yet when Alan Wilde argues that modernist irony posits 'in opposition to its vision of disjunctiveness a complementary vision of inclusive

order',[16] this brings to mind works by Kharms as diverse as
Elizaveta Bam and 'The Connection'. A similar ambiguity
surrounds Vvedensky's writing. If Linda Hutcheon, for
example, is justified in claiming that postmodernism foregrounds history as text, then Vvedensky is a postmodernist
writer. Richard Palmer, who asserts that postmodernism is
underscored by a Heideggerean view of time and language,
would also, presumably, regard Vvedensky's work as postmodernist.[17] Yet if, as Allen Thiher suggests, 'the absurdity of
temporality' (Thiher, *Words in Reflection*, p. 36) is a quintessentially modernist concept, then we must conclude that Vvedensky is a modernist. Nor does Vaginov escape this confusion.
If we accept Matei Calinescu's claim that 'the "logic" of linear
time [...] characterizes modernity's secularized version of
Judeo-Christian eschatology', then this means that Vaginov is
primarily a modernist.[18] On the other hand, if in recent
accounts of postmodernism, 'it is the awareness of the absence
of centers, of privileged languages, higher discourses, that is
seen as the most striking difference with Modernism' (Bertens,
p. 46), then Vaginov, at least when he wrote *Harpagoniana*,
should be considered something of a postmodernist.

If anything, the plethora of available definitions actually
supports the view that OBERIU bridges the gap between these
two '-isms'. Be that as it may, my study of OBERIU metafiction
will have led, it is hoped, to a re-evaluation of the group and of
the group's place within Russian literature. It is surely time for
scholarship on OBERIU *as a group* to move forward, and
broaden its focus beyond the relatively brief period during
which OBERIU existed as a collective, beyond that collective's
'manifesto' and most famous performance, and beyond the
more accessible works of its most outlandish member, Daniil
Kharms. Only in this way can we hope to reach an adequate
understanding, not just of OBERIU itself, but also of Russian
metafiction, recent Soviet postmodernist literature, and today's
post-Soviet fiction.

Notes

INTRODUCTION; OBERIU – THE LAST SOVIET AVANT-GARDE

1 I am aware that the term 'avant-garde' is much over-used. My own understanding of the concept is borrowed largely from Charles Russell, who defines the avant-garde as that branch of modernism which believed in art as a vehicle for social change: see Charles Russell, *Poets, Prophets, and Revolutionaries*.

2 Since OBERIU is by far the best known of all the names which the group used, I shall, for the sake of simplicity, also use it when referring to the group in general. An account of the pre-history and history of the group is given by Anatoly Aleksandrov: 'Evrika Oberiutov', in Aleksandrov (ed.), *Vanna Arkhimeda*, a recently published OBERIU anthology (the first of its kind). In 1991 an entire issue of the leading Russian theatre journal was dedicated to OBERIU: *Teatr*, 11 (1991). In the late 1920s, there were plans to publish an anthology of OBERIU poetry under the 'Biblioteka poeta' imprint. This project has taken more than sixty years to reach fruition: Meilakh, Nikol'skaya, Oleinikova, and Erl' (eds.), *Poety gruppy 'OBERIU'*. This publication contains a lengthy historical account of the group: M. Meilakh, ' "Ya ispytyval slovo na ogne i na stuzhe..." '. General surveys of the group's aesthetics have been few and far between. See, for example: Anatoly Aleksandrov, 'Oberiu. Predvaritel'nye zametki'; M. Arndt, 'OBERIU'; and Anna Gerasimova, 'OBERIU. (Problema smeshnogo)'. For a bibliography on OBERIU, see Rosanna Giaquinta, 'OBERIU: per una rassegna della critica'.

Bakhterev is the only surviving member of OBERIU. A selection of his work is contained in Aleksandrov (ed.), *Vanna Arkhimeda*, pp. 412–40. Details of other publications by Bakhterev can be found in the bibliography. Some of Bakhterev's verse is also quoted in Sergej Sigov, 'Istoki poetiki Oberiu'. Bakhterev is also the author of one of the most detailed historical accounts of

OBERIU: 'Kogda my byli molodymi (Nevydumannyi rasskaz)', in Zabolotskaya, Makedonov and Zabolotsky (eds.), *Vospominaniya o N. Zabolotskom.*

3 Vladimir Markov, *Russian Futurism*, p. 382.

4 'Stolbtsy' can be translated as 'Scrolls', or as 'Columns'.

5 On Zabolotsky's life and works, see A. V. Makedonov, *Nikolay Zabolotsky* and Darra Goldstein, *Nikolai Zabolotsky*. A biography of Zabolotsky written by the poet's son has recently been published in English translation: Nikita Zabolotsky, *The Life of Zabolotsky*. For memoirs on Zabolotsky, see Zabolotskaya, Makedonov, and Zabolotsky (eds.), *Vospominaniya o N. Zabolotskom.*

6 All three, along with Oleinikov, worked for the journals *The Hedgehog* (*Ezh*), and *The Finch* (*Chizh*). On Zabolotsky's work as a children's writer, see Nikita Zabolotsky, *The Life of Zabolotsky*, chapter 3. A list of Vvedensky's publications for children is given in Aleksandr Vvedensky, *Polnoe sobranie sochinenii*, vol. II, pp. 367–75 (hereafter referred to as *PSS*). For Kharms, see Jean-Philippe Jaccard, 'Bibliographie', and Neil Cornwell and Julian Graffy, 'Selected Bibliography'. For an overview of the children's literature of OBERIU and their associates, see Elena Sokol, *Russian Poetry for Children*, pp. 122–51, and A. Makedonov, *Nikolay Zabolotsky*, pp. 163–82.

7 The fullest biographical account of Vvedensky is contained in Mikhail Meilakh, 'Predislovie'. For Kharms's life and works, see: Anatoly Aleksandrov, 'Materialy D. I. Kharmsa v rukopisnom otdele Pushkinskogo doma', 'Chudodei: lichnost' i tvorchestvo Daniila Kharmsa', and 'Kratkaya khronika zhizni i tvorchestva Daniila Kharmsa'. 'Kharms' was a pseudonym for 'Yuvachev'; see Neil Cornwell, 'Introduction: Daniil Kharms, Black Miniaturist', p. 4. The first book-length study of both writers' works was Alice Stone Nakhimovsky, *Laughter in the Void*; this is a revised version of her 'From the Language of Nonsense to the Absurdity of Life'.

8 See A. Aleksandrov and M. Meilakh, 'Tvorchestvo Daniila Kharmsa', and 'Tvorchestvo Aleksandra Vvedenskogo'. Their names first appeared in the West in R. R. Milner-Gulland, ' "Left Art" in Leningrad: the OBERIU Declaration'. The first collection of Kharms's prose was *Izbrannoe*, ed. George Gibian. A planned nine- or ten-volume edition of Kharms's works, *Sobranie proizvedenii*, has so far reached vol. IV.

9 Since the appearance in Russia in 1988 of a collection of Kharms's work, entitled *Polet v nebesa. Stikhi. Proza. Dramy. Pis'ma* (hereafter referred to as *Polet*), there have been several other publications, mostly of the writer's prose. See, for example, *Sluchai: rasskazy i*

stseny (hereafter *Sluchai*), and *Gorlo bredit britvoyu*. The first Russian edition of Vvedensky's work has recently been published: *Polnoe sobranie proizvedenii v dvukh tomakh*; this is a slightly amended version of Meilakh's original, 'Ardis' edition.

10 There have been a number of 'life and works' surveys of Vaginov published in recent years. See, for example: Leonardo Paleari, 'La letteratura e la vita nei romanzi di Vaginov'; L. Chertkov, 'Poeziya Konstantina Vaginova'; Anthony Anemone, 'Konstantin Vaginov and the Leningrad Avant-Garde: 1921–1934'; T. L. Nikol'skaya, 'K. K. Vaginov (Kanva biografii i tvorchestva)'; Nikolay Chukovsky, 'Iz vospominanii'; Anna Gerasimova, 'Trudy i dni Konstantina Vaginova'; and Aleksey Purin, 'Opyty Konstantina Vaginova'. A monograph on Vaginov's prose has recently been published: Daniela von Heyl, *Die Prosa Konstantin Vaginovs*. See also T. L. Nikol'skaya's useful bibliography, 'Dopolneniya k bibliografii K. Vaginova'.

11 T. Nikol'skaya, 'O tvorchestve Konstantina Vaginova'.

12 On Zabolotsky and OBERIU, see Goldstein, *Nikolai Zabolotsky*, pp. 26–35, her article, 'Zabolotsky and Filonov: The Science of Composition', and Fiona Björling, *Stolbcy by Nikolaj Zabolockij: Analyses*, especially chapter 1. For an attempt to define the OBERIU aesthetic based largely on Kharms's poetry, see Ljubomir Stoimenoff, *Grundlagen und Verfahren*.

13 The first conference was organized in April 1990 at the Hermitage theatre in Moscow, and the second in February 1994, at the Moscow State University. Most contributions to the former have since been published in a special issue of the journal *Teatr*, 11 (1991), while a number of papers given at the latter have appeared in *Literaturnoe obozrenie*, 9/10 (1994), 49–72. The *Teatr* publication contains just one paper devoted exclusively to Vaginov, while the issue of *Literaturnoe obozrenie* contains none.

14 By far the best account of Vaginov's literary career is contained in Anemone, 'Konstantin Vaginov and the Leningrad Avant-Garde'. See also two articles by Anemone and Ivan Martynov: 'Towards the History of the Leningrad Avant-Garde: The "Circle of Poets"', and 'The Islanders: Poetry and Polemics in Petrograd of the 1920s'.

15 On this group, and Vaginov's involvement in it, see Katerina Clark and Michael Holquist, *Mikhail Bakhtin*, pp. 95–119, and Anemone, 'Konstantin Vaginov and the Leningrad Avant-Garde', pp. 213–18. According to Clark and Holquist, Vaginov was only an 'occasional attender' at meetings of the Bakhtin circle (p. 101). In his introduction to a major collection of essays by Bakhtin, Michael Holquist has suggested that Kharms also belonged to

Bakhtin's circle of friends, although he provides no evidence to this effect: 'Introduction', in Bakhtin, *The Dialogic Imagination*, p. xxiv. Il'ya Levin has suggested that Vvedensky and Kharms may have come into contact with Bakhtin via Vaginov: 'The Collision of Meanings', p. 61. Although there is scant documentary evidence, Bakhtin may have become personally acquainted with OBERIU, if not through Vaginov, then through the pianist Mariya Yudina, who frequented both the Bakhtin circle and OBERIU. Yudina's memoirs contain information of an anecdotal nature on both Vvedensky and Kharms: M. V. Yudina, *Mariya Veniaminovna Yudina. Stat'i. Vospominaniya. Materialy*, pp. 262–77. The outlandishness, and non-conformism of OBERIU has prompted some critics to claim that the group was the modern embodiment of the carnival spirit as understood by Bakhtin. See for example A. Dorogov, 'Idei M. M. Bakhtina v istoriko-kul'turnom kontekste' (unpublished paper mentioned by O. Revzina, in *Voprosy yazykoznaniya*, 2 (1971), 160–2).

16 See the poster advertising this literary evening, which took place on 25 February 1925, in P. N. Luknitsky, *Acumiana* (unnumbered page, opposite p. 155).

17 Igor' Terent'ev (1892–1941) was a poet, critic, and experimental theatre director, most famous for his membership of the Tiflis-based group of poets, in existence between 1917 and 1920 and which also included Aleksey Kruchenykh and Il'ya Zdanevich, '41°'. For an account of the group, see Markov, *Russian Futurism*, pp. 338–63. On Terent'ev see T. Nikol'skaya, 'I. Terent'ev'. In an unpublished study on Terent'ev, S. Sigov notes that it was originally planned to include one of his plays in the OBERIU performance of 24 January 1928, known as 'Three Left Hours': see Jean-Philippe Jaccard, *Daniil Harms*, p. 456, n. 120.

18 On Druskin (1902–80), a philosopher, mathematician, and musicologist, see Lidiya Druskina's introduction to Yakov Druskin, 'Pered prinadlezhnostyami chego-libo', 'Uchitel' iz fabzavucha', and 'O kontse sveta', pp. 46–83 (pp. 46–50). Druskin's most important publication is *Vblizi vestnikov*. Druskin was also to write in the late 1930s a major study of Vvedensky's work, entitled 'The Star of Nonsense' ('Zvezda bessmyslitsy'). The fifth chapter of this study has recently been published: Yakov Druskin, 'Kommunikativnost' v tvorchestve Aleksandra Vvedenskogo'. Some material is also contained in Yakov Druskin, 'Stadii ponimaniya'. See also an essay, in English translation: 'On Daniil Kharms'.

Savel'ev was the pseudonym of L. Lipavsky (1904–41), a philosopher and children's writer. One of his major writings has recently been published: 'Issledovanie uzhasa'. For an introduction to Lipavsky's philosophy, see Jean-Philippe Jaccard, 'Strashnaya beskonechnost' Leonida Lipavskogo', and Yakov Druskin, '"Chinari"' (pp. 113–15). The latter is a revised version of Druskin's 'Stadii ponimaniya', and 'Chinari: glava iz knigi Yakova Semenovicha Druskina (1902–1980), *Son i Yav'*, 1968' (hereafter referred to as 'Son i Yav'').

19 In fact, Druskin and Lipavsky had both attended the same Leningrad school as Vvedensky, the L. D. Lentovskaya gymnasium, although they were older than Vvedensky by two years and one year respectively; see Druskin, '"Chinari"', p. 104 (Vaginov was another former pupil; see Meilakh, 'Predislovie', p. xii).

20 On the influence of this group and their philosophy on Kharms's fiction, see Jaccard, *Daniil Harms*, chapter 3, and also his 'L'impossible éternité'.

21 On the circumstances surrounding Oleinikov's arrest, see Evgeny Lunin, 'Delo Nikolaya Oleinikova'.

22 On Oleinikov, his poetry, and the relationship between his work and OBERIU literature, see for example: I. Bakhterev and A. Razumovsky, 'O Nikolae Oleinikove'; L. S. Fleishman, 'Marginaly k istorii russkogo avangarda/Oleinikov, oberiuty/'; R. R. Milner-Gulland, 'Grandsons of Kozma Prutkov'; and S. V. Polyakova, 'Tvorchestvo Oleinikova'.

Despite the fact that Oleinikov never took part in any OBERIU performances, his membership of Druskin's circle and his close friendship with Kharms in particular have led some scholars to consider him a full member of OBERIU. In a survey of recent Russian alternative fiction, Robert Porter goes so far as to claim that OBERIU was 'headed' by Oleinikov along with Kharms and Vvedensky: *Russia's Alternative Prose*, p. 39. Rosanna Giaquinta even claims that Oleinikov was one of the group's co-founders: 'I poemi drammatici di Aleksandr Vvedenskij', p. 67. On the other hand, Lidiya Zhukova asserts that the poet would have found ridiculous any suggestion that his verse was related to OBERIU: *Epilogi*, p. 162. In a recent interview, Bakhterev has stated that the question of Oleinikov's joining the group was frequently raised at OBERIU meetings. It was eventually agreed to accept him on condition that he wrote some new poems, since 'his humour did not suit' the others. Oleinikov accepted the challenge, but the poems were never written: Vadim Nazarov and Sergey Chubukin, 'Poslednii iz Oberiu', p. 54. Meilakh believes that Oleinikov actually declined their offer, perhaps out of fear of associating himself publicly with the literary avant-garde (since he was in fact a member of the Communist Party: 'Predislovie', p. xix).

23 It would appear that the group gave themselves this collective name only as long as Kharms and Vvedensky referred to themselves as 'chinar'-vziral'nik' and 'chinar' avto-ritet bessmyslitsy' respectively. The origin of the term 'chinar'' is unclear. Nakhimovsky suggests that the word comes from the Slavic root meaning 'to create' (*Laughter in the Void*, p. 10), while Milner-Gulland believes that it may be derived from the verb 'chinit'', meaning 'to devise' or 'to mend' (editorial note in Nikita Zabolotsky, *The Life of Zabolotsky*, p. 47). A brief summary of the group's activity is given by V. N. Sazhin, ' "Chinari" – literaturnoe ob"edinenie 1920–1930-x godov'. See also Jean-Philippe Jaccard, 'Chinari'. For an account of some of the group's meetings, see T. Lipavskaya, 'Vstrechi s Nikolaem Alekseevichem i ego druz'yami'. See also Lipavsky's transcripts of some of the group's conversations, 'Iz razgovorov "chinarei" ', a much-expanded version of which has recently been published: Leonid Lipavsky, 'Razgovory'. Sazhin argues that OBERIU is best regarded simply as one episode in the history of the *chinari* group: ' "…Sborishche druzei" ', p. 200.

24 See Druskin, 'Son i Yav'', pp. 397–8.

25 According to Jaccard, Evgeny Vigilyansky (1890[?]–1942[?]) also took part in the 'Radiks' and OBERIU groups as an actor, and subsequently operated as an 'administrator' for OBERIU (see *Daniil Harms*, p. 324, n. 180). On 'Radiks', see below, note 29.

26 The group was subsequently joined by two other poets, Igor' Markov, an engineer, and Venedikt Matveev, an accountant. See Jean-Philippe Jaccard and Andrey Ustinov, 'Zaumnik Daniil Kharms: nachalo puti', pp. 160–2, and Sergej Sigov, 'Orden zaumnikov'. On Tufanov and OBERIU, see Bakhterev, 'Kogda my byli molodymi', pp. 66–7. Jaccard discusses Tufanov's theories and his influence on Kharms in his *Daniil Harms*, pp. 40–57. For an overview of *zaum'* in the work of Kharms and Vvedensky, see Mikhail Meilakh, 'Oberiuty i zaum''. For details of a *zaum'* evening in which Kharms and Vvedensky took part alongside Tufanov, see Vvedensky, *PSS*, vol. II, pp. 238–9. Tufanov's *zaum'* manifesto, which originally appeared in Leningrad in 1924, has recently been republished: 'K zaumi'.

27 See Nikita Zabolotsky, *The Life of Zabolotsky*, p. 47. Bakhterev states that the 'Left Flank', containing Kharms and Vvedensky, began its existence in 1924 (Nazarov and Chubukin, 'Poslednii iz Oberiu', p. 39). This is presumably a mistake, however, since Kharms and

Vvedensky did not meet until 1925. By their predilection for the term 'left', Kharms and Vvedensky were presumably aligning themselves with the Russian left-art movement, which had its origins in pre-revolutionary Russian Futurism and Formalism, and whose adherents believed in the ability of art to transform reality. For a general account of left art, see Halina Stephan, *'LEF'*. On the pre-revolutionary origins of the left-art movement, which included Khlebnikov and the dramatist Nikolay Evreinov, see D. G. B. Piper, *V. A. Kaverin*, chapter 1.

28 Although Vaginov was not formally acquainted with the two poets at this stage, he may well have had a hand in their acceptance into the Union: see Jaccard and Ustinov, 'Zaumnik Daniil Kharms', p. 169. It is highly likely that Vaginov first heard their poetry at a 'Left Flank' evening. The article by Jaccard and Ustinov contains invaluable information on this stage of the young poets' literary careers, including the questionnaire which Kharms filled in as part of his application to join the Union, and details of their acquaintance with the agrarian poet Nikolay Klyuev (1887–1937). It was under the imprint of the Union of Poets that two of Kharms's poems appeared, namely 'Incident on the Railway' ('Sluchai na zheleznoi doroge', 1926), and 'The Verse of Petr Yashkin' ('Stikh Petra Yashkina', 1927). These were the only works, other than his children's literature, which Kharms published during his lifetime. See also V. Erl', 'Konstantin Vaginov i A. Vvedensky v Soyuze Poetov'.

29 For further information on 'Radiks', see Bakhterev, 'Kogda my byli molodymi', pp. 67–8, and M. Meilakh, 'O "Elizavete Bam"' (pp. 163–72). An abridged version of Meilakh's article exists in English translation: 'Kharms's Play *Elizaveta Bam*'. On the relationship between 'Radiks' and OBERIU theatre, see also Meilakh, 'Zametki o teatre oberiutov', and Jaccard, *Daniil Harms*, pp. 234–40. Many 'Radiks' projects were planned, but none came to fruition.

30 Levin (1905–41) wrote a number of novels on his Jewish childhood, all of which have since been lost: see Nakhimovsky, *Laughter in the Void*, pp. 20 and 172. Levin knew Kharms through Paul Marcel, the brother of Kharms's first wife, Esther. See a recently published collection of Kharms's diaries and letters: ' "Bozhe, kakaya uzhasnaya zhizn'…" ', p. 208. Substantially the same material, but with much fuller notes, is contained in Daniil Kharms, 'Dnevnikovye zapisi Daniila Kharmsa'.

31 Zabolotsky was commissioned by 'Radiks' to write a 'play in masks', a project which was never realized: see Bakhterev, 'Kogda

my byli molodymi', p. 79, and Nikita Zabolotsky, *The Life of Zabolotsky*, pp. 48–50.

32 Material concerning 'Radiks' and the play 'My Mum is Covered in Watches', including an interview with the play's director, Georgy Katsman, can be found in Vvedensky, *PSS*, vol. II, pp. 230–7.

33 There is evidence that Kharms hoped to expand 'Radiks' even further, to include a number of experimental writers and artists working in Leningrad at the time. His plan for an anthology of 'Radiks' material, drafted around this time, includes: a 'theory' section, with contributions from, among others, Shklovsky, Malevich, and Lipavsky; a 'creative' section, to be made up of work by himself, Vvedensky, Zabolotsky, Bakhterev, and Vaginov, as well as Khlebnikov and Tufanov; and artwork by Bakhterev, Zabolotsky, and Filonov, as well as members of Malevich's Institute of Artistic Culture (see Vvedensky, *PSS*, vol. II, pp. 236–7). Sadly, this project, like so many others, never came to fruition.

34 The term 'Left Flank' harked back to Tufanov's 'Order of the *zaumniki* DSO', which had changed its name on the initiative of Kharms and Vvedensky (see Bakhterev, 'Kogda my byli molodymi', p. 67). On the group's various name changes see Meilakh, 'Predislovie', pp. xviii–xx. In a notebook entry dated 10 October 1926, Kharms writes ' "Radiks" has collapsed' (Vvedensky, *PSS*, vol. II, p. 235). Yet in the same notebook he dates a 'Radiks' performance as '14 January 1927. Midnight' (ibid., p. 236). This suggests that the new group did not call themselves the 'Left Flank' immediately.

35 For more detailed accounts of these evenings see: Bakhterev, 'Kogda my byli molodymi', pp. 83–4; and Nikita Zabolotsky, *The Life of Zabolotsky*, chapter 2. The plan for one such evening, drafted in Kharms's notebook, is contained in Aleksandrov, 'A Kharms Chronology', p. 35.

36 See Igor' Bakhterev, '[Vstrecha] s Viktorom Borisovichem Shklovskim'. The Formalists Tynyanov (as prose writer) and Shklovsky (as prose writer and critic) were to have contributed along with a number of writers including Kharms, Vvedensky, and Zabolotsky, to a literary-critical anthology entitled *Archimedes' Bath* (*Vanna Arkhimeda*), which Kharms planned in spring 1929, but which never came to fruition. For details of the plans, see A. B. Blyumbaum and G. A. Morev, ' "Vanna Arkhimeda" '. Kharms's poem, 'Archimedes' Bath' refers to this project, and Kharms may well have planned to include it in the anthology: Daniil Kharms, *Sobranie proizvedenii*, vol. II, pp. 3–4.

37 After this manifesto had been read out, Shklovsky is said to have

approached the members of the group and commented, implicitly, and unfavourably, contrasting them with the Futurists: 'you couldn't even raise a scandal' (see Meilakh, 'Predislovie', p. xix).

38 Bakhterev, 'Kogda my byli molodymi', pp. 59–60. Bakhterev mistakenly refers here to Mayakovsky's journal *LEF*, which was founded in Moscow by the Futurists in March 1923, only to fold in 1925. See also Goldstein, *Nikolai Zabolotsky*, pp. 247–8, n. 65.

39 For an account of the circumstances surrounding this invitation, and details of the performance which ensued, see Bakhterev, 'Kogda my byli molodymi', pp. 86–98, and Nikita Zabolotsky, *The Life of Zabolotsky*, pp. 71–6. An eye-witness account of the 'Three Left Hours' evening which followed Baskakov's invitation is contained in B. Semenov, 'Dalekoe-ryadom'.

40 Bakhterev also points out here that the 'э' was changed back to 'e' some time later, for reasons, ironically, of what he calls 'common sense' ('Kogda my byli molodymi', p. 87).

41 See, for example, Meilakh, 'Predislovie', p. xx. Although Goldstein implies (*Nikolai Zabolotsky*, p. 27) that the performance of 24 January 1928 was one of a number given by OBERIU at the Leningrad Press Club, it was the only one given in that particular building, since the club was relocated shortly afterwards.

42 'OBERIU', *Afishi Doma Pechati*, 2 (1928) 11–13; reprinted in Milner-Gulland, ' "Left Art" ', pp. 69–74. Mikhail Meilakh claims that it is unlikely that this article was the same as the one previously drafted by Zabolotsky and Vvedensky, and read out at the Leningrad Capella in 1927 ('Predislovie', p. xxii).

43 There is, however, a considerable degree of confusion over this among OBERIU scholars. Nina Perlina, for example, claims that it was Kharms, Vvedensky, Vaginov, and Oleinikov who drafted the declaration: 'Konstantin Vaguinov', p. 479. Nakhimovsky, on the other hand, claims that Kharms and Zabolotsky wrote the whole article (*Laughter in the Void*, p. 15). Milner-Gulland maintains that Kharms was responsible for the section on theatre (' "Left Art" ', p. 75).

44 Zabolotsky, who drafted this section of the article, would have felt particular sympathy for Filonov, since he had been a part-time student at Filonov's workshop-school of analytic art at the Academy of Arts. On the influence of Filonov on Zabolotsky, see Goldstein, 'The Science of Composition' and *Nikolai Zabolotsky*, pp. 35–45, and Nikita Zabolotsky, *The Life of Zabolotsky*, pp. 50–3. On Filonov, see also Camilla Gray, *The Great Experiment: Russian Art 1863–1922*, pp. 182–4. For a comparison between Malevich's

aesthetics and those of OBERIU (and in particular Kharms), see Ilya Levin, 'The Fifth Meaning of the Motor-Car'. Jaccard maintains that Malevich played an important role not only in the development of Kharms's philosophy, but also in the elaboration of OBERIU theory (*Daniil Harms*, p. 80). Georges Nivat believes that both Filonov and Malevich may have actively participated in OBERIU performances: *Vers la fin du mythe russe*, p. 233.

45 On the OBERIU critique of Tufanov and *zaum'*, see, for example: Robin Milner-Gulland, 'Beyond the Turning-Point: An Afterword', p. 255; and Lazar Fleishman, 'On One Enigmatic Poem by Daniil Kharms', p. 160. On the other hand, some of Tufanov's poetry was to be included in the first 'Radiks' compilation: see Vvedensky, *PSS*, vol. II, pp. 236–7.

46 Quoted in Nikita Zabolotsky, *The Life of Zabolotsky*, p. 56. The letter from which the second quotation is taken is reprinted in full in Vvedensky, *PSS*, vol. II, pp. 252–3 (see also ibid., p. 256). One commentator claims that Zabolotsky was Vvedensky's 'constant opponent' (Aleksandrov, 'Chudodei', p. 25). Bakhterev offers a less objective, more nostalgic view when he suggests that, 'For several years the group appeared monolithic' ('V techenie neskol'kykh let gruppa kazalas' monolitnoi'; 'Kogda my byli molodymi', p. 65). More recently, however, he has modified this statement somewhat: 'It is difficult to say what united us. It was most likely our dissimilarity' ('Trudno skazat', chto imeno ob"edinyalo nas. Skoree vsego, nasha nepokhozhest'; Nazarov and Chubukin, 'Poslednii iz Oberiu', p. 39).

47 Despite this rejection of *zaum'* in the declaration, Kharms's play *Elizaveta Bam* contains a passage written entirely in trans-rational poetry. Examples of *zaum'* in Bakhterev's work occur as late as 1935: see his poem 'The Old Man who Hanged Himself Instead of a Lamp' ('Odin starik vmesto lampy sebya povesivshii', dated '1935 and after'), in Igor' Bakhterev, ['V magazine star'evshchika'], p. 53.

48 A. V. Razumovsky (1907–80) was a playwright and author of several children's books and a series of articles on cinema. According to Bakhterev, Razumovsky was the author of the section on film in the OBERIU article ('Kogda my byli molodymi', p. 88). After the break-up of OBERIU, he and Bakhterev co-wrote a number of plays: see the introduction to Igor' Bakhterev, '"Tak ya i zhivu..."', p. 86, and Kuz'minsky's introduction to Bakhterev, 'Starik Bakhterev', p. 19. Mints became a well-known Russian film director (see Meilakh, 'Predislovie', p. xxxi, n. 76).

49 Reprinted in Bakhterev, 'Kogda my byli molodymi', p. 92.

50 Tsimbal's participation in one of the first performances of what was to become OBERIU, on 12 November 1927, is, however, mentioned in one of Kharms's notebooks (see Aleksandrov, 'A Kharms Chronology', p. 35).

51 The only surviving work by Vladimirov (1909–31) is a very short prose text, entitled 'The Gymnast' ('Fizkul'turnik'), and written between 1929 and 1930.

52 For details of an evening devoted to a discussion of contemporary poetry, at which Kharms publicly scoffed at Zabolotsky's departure from OBERIU (in Zabolotsky's presence!), see I. Sinel'nikov, 'Molodoi Zabolotsky', p. 118.

53 This was at the performance entitled 'Vasily Oberiutov', which Vigilyansky compered, and which took place on the '12 Derkarebarya 1928': see M. Meilakh, 'O "Elizavete Bam"', pp. 192–3.

54 L. Nil'vich, 'Reaktsionnoe zhonglerstvo (Ob odnoi vylazke literaturnykh khuliganov)', reprinted in Vvedensky, *PSS*, vol. ii, pp. 247–9 (p. 249). Interestingly, the article mentions only Vladimirov's poetry and Levin's prose. This may mean that Kharms, Vvedensky, and Bakhterev were not even present (Zabolotsky and Vaginov certainly were not), which, if indeed the case, would suggest that the demise of OBERIU came much earlier than April 1930. An entry in Kharms's diary, dated 27 June 1928, shows that even at that early stage the writer believed that OBERIU was finished as a group (see Jaccard, *Daniil Harms*, pp. 442–3). Gibian, however, believes that Kharms was involved in the last OBERIU performance: 'Introduction: Daniil Kharms and Alexander Vvedensky', p. 22.

55 N. Ioffe and L. Zheleznov, 'Literaturnye dela (o "chinaryakh")' (see Aleksandrov, 'A Kharms Chronology', pp. 35–6). See also D. Tolmachev, 'Dadaisty v Leningrade'; and L. Lesnaya, 'Ytuerebo' (the latter, a review of the 'Three Left Hours' performance, is reprinted in Vvedensky, *PSS*, vol. ii, pp. 246–7).

56 Makedonov (*Nikolay Zabolotsky*, p. 165) argues that the work which the various members of OBERIU had already begun to write for children contributed to the demise of the group, since it forced them to rethink their aesthetic principles. As early as 27 July 1928 Kharms named his first wife, Esther, as the direct cause of the group's decline ('"Bozhe, kakaya uzhasnaya zhizn'..."', p. 202). Kharms's verse play 'Vengeance' ('Mest''), dated 22 October 1930, features a group of writers who timidly express the hope that since they are 'humble and quiet' ('skromny i tikhi'), their poetry and prose will not be judged harshly (Kharms, *Sobranie proizvedenii*, vol. ii, pp. 54–65 (p. 63)).

57 For an account of RAPP, see Edward J. Brown, *The Proletarian Episode.*

58 See Victor Erlich, *Modernism and Revolution*, chapter 13.

59 John E. Malmstad, 'Mikhail Kuzmin: A Chronicle of his Life and Times', p. 306; and George Cheron, 'Mikhail Kuzmin and the Oberiuty: An Overview', p. 98. Kuzmin championed Vaginov's verse (Malmstad, 'Mikhail Kuzmin', p. 260), and also held Vvedensky's poetry in high esteem (Meilakh, 'Predislovie', p. xiii).

60 See Meilakh, ' "Ya ispytyval slovo na ogne i na stuzhe…" ', p. 7, n. 2, and p. 34.

61 By the time of his death, Vaginov had published in total three collections of poetry, three novels, and two short prose works. The two prose pieces, 'The Monastery of our Lord Apollo' ('Monastyr' Gospoda nashego Apollona'), and 'The Star of Bethlehem' ('Zvezda Vifleema') were published, respectively, in the first two editions of Kuzmin's journal, *Abraksas* (both appeared in 1922). His first collection of poetry was published in 1921, and entitled *Journey into Chaos: Poems (Puteshestvie v khaos: stikhotvoreniya)*. This was followed in 1926 by a second, untitled collection, and in 1931 by *Experiments in Combining Words by Means of Rhythm (Opyty soedineniya slov posredstvom ritma)*. Two further collections of poetry, *Petersburg Nights (Peterburgskie nochi*, 1921–2), and *Likeness of Sound (Zvukopodobie*, 1929–34) remained unpublished during his lifetime, as did his long dramatic poem of 1925, 'The Year 1925' ('Tysyacha devyat'sot dvadsat' pyatyi god'). These are contained, with a few omissions, in Vaginov's *Sobranie stikhotvorenii* (ed. Chertkov). Extracts from *Zvukopodobie* were also published, with an introduction by J. Malmstad and G. Shmakov, in the anthology *Apollon"-77*, pp. 34–41 (under the title 'Poeziya'). Vaginov also published the novels, *The Goat's Song (Kozlinaya pesn')* in 1928, *The Labours and Days of Svistonov (Trudy i dni Svistonova)* in 1929, and *Bambocciade (Bambochada)* in 1931. At the time of his death, he had completed a short story, 'The End of a First Love' ('Konets pervoi lyubvi', 1931; since lost), was revising a fourth novel, *Harpagoniana (Garpagoniana)*, for publication, and working on a fifth, *1905 (1905 god)*: on these three works, see Chertkov, 'Poeziya Konstantina Vaginova', p. 227, and Nikol'skaya, 'Konstantin Vaginov, ego vremya i knigi', p. 11 respectively.

62 On the circumstances surrounding these arrests, see A. B. Ustinov, 'Delo detskogo sektora Gosizdata 1932 g.'. See also the various documents published by Igor' Mal'sky in a special edition of *Sankt-Peterburgskii Universitet*, dated 1 November 1991. Mal'sky's collection includes the transcripts of 'confessions' made by Kharms,

Vvedensky, and others, much of which is also contained in Igor′ Mal′sky, 'Razgrom OBERIU'.

63 For an example of this politicization of children's literature, see L. Kon, 'O yumore'.

64 The circumstances surrounding the deaths of Kharms and Vvedensky are far from clear. On Vvedensky, see Meilakh, 'Predislovie', pp. xxvi–xxvii. On Kharms, see Anatoly Aleksandrov, 'Mesto smerti Daniila Kharmsa – ?', and M. V. Malich, 'K istorii aresta i gibeli Daniila Kharmsa'. On the circumstances surrounding Kharms's arrest, see also Mikhail Meilakh, 'Daniil Kharms: anecdota posthuma'.

65 Two versions of this piece have been published, one in Kuz′minsky and Kovalev (eds.), *The Blue Lagoon Anthology*, vol. iva, pp. 24–6, and another in Aleksandrov (ed.), *Vanna Arkhimeda*, pp. 412–17. This latter version, considerably different and entitled 'V magazine star′evshchika' ('In the Junk Shop'), is also contained in Bakhterev, ['V magazine star′evshchika'], p. 52.

66 The full text of 'Proshchanie s druz′yami' is contained in Zabolotsky, *Stolbtsy i poemy*, pp. 234–5. A full English translation, entitled 'Goodbye to Friends', can be found in Nikita Zabolotsky, *The Life of Zabolotsky*, p. 356.

67 See for example R. R. Milner-Gulland, ' "Kovarnye stikhi" ', p. 22. On the differences between the two writers' personalities see Semenov, 'Dalekoe – ryadom' p. 182.

68 Victor Terras, 'Vaginov, Konstantin Konstantinovich', p. 500. Similarly, Wolfgang Kasack maintains that Vaginov's first three novels are 'close to the spirit of Oberiu': Kasack, 'Vaginov, Konstantin Konstantinovich', p. 434. See also Gerasimova, 'Trudy i dni Konstantina Vaginova', pp. 144–5. Anemone, on the other hand, points out that Vaginov began writing his first novel some time before he met the members of OBERIU ('Konstantin Vaginov and the Leningrad Avant-Garde', p. 14).

69 On the 'Absurd' as a feature common to the work of Kharms, Vvedensky, and Vaginov, see also George Gibian, 'Introduction', in Gibian and Tjalsma (eds.), p. 15.

70 Viktor Shirokov, 'Poet tragicheskoi zabavy', p. 16.

71 I. Oksenov, 'Leningradskie poety'.

72 David Shepherd, *Beyond Metafiction*, p. 115. For a similar argument concerning these writers' poetry, see Makedonov, *Nikolay Zabolotsky*, p. 57.

73 T. L. Nikol′skaya, 'Tragediya chudakov', p. 10.

74 See, for example: I. M. Nappel′baum, 'Pamyatka o poete', p. 94; and Chukovsky, 'Iz vospominanii', p. 102 (who notes that Vaginov

was notorious for giving his poems to anyone who would read them, regardless of group affiliation).

75 Similarly, Tjalsma maintains that in the three books of verse published during his lifetime Vaginov 'rather quickly departs from the rigors of Gumilev's Acmeism and approaches the poetry of the surrealist group, called Oberiu': 'The Petersburg Poets', p. 72.

76 Two other mutually antithetical groups to which Vaginov had belonged, although not at the same time, were Gumilev's second 'Guild of Poets' and the 'Islanders': see Anemone and Martynov, 'The Islanders'.

77 Aleksandrov, 'Oberiu. Predvaritel'nye zametki', p. 300. Similarly, Nakhimovsky talks of Vaginov's 'passing association' with OBERIU (*Laughter in the Void*, p. 173). See also Il'ya Levin, 'The Collision of Meanings', p. 57.

78 Anemone also decribes Vaginov as the group's 'outsider' ('Konstantin Vaginov and the Leningrad Avant-Garde', p. 122).

79 Quoted in Anemone, 'Konstantin Vaginov and the Leningrad Avant-Garde', p. 119. See also T. L. Nikol'skaya, 'Konstantin Vaginov, ego vremya i knigi', p. 6.

80 The list of those present at the meeting to discuss Vaginov's candidature is contained in Jaccard and Ustinov, 'Zaumnik Daniil Kharms', p. 181. Vaginov was also absent from the meeting of 8 March 1928, at which the association's future development was discussed (ibid., p. 183).

81 Milner-Gulland's contention has been echoed more recently by Jaccard, who dismisses the notion of OBERIU poetics as 'questionable' (*Daniil Harms*, p. 327), and maintains that the group was little more than a makeshift and heterogeneous association of writers, hastily assembled specifically for the 'Three Left Hours' evening (ibid., p. 137).

82 In her survey of twentieth-century metafiction, Patricia Waugh believes that the term was first used by the American critic William H. Gass in 1970 in his *Fiction and the Figures of Life*: see Waugh, *Metafiction*, p. 2. By analysing OBERIU fiction precisely as metafiction, I hope to build on Shepherd's pioneering study of Soviet metafiction (which includes a chapter on Vaginov's *The Labours and Days of Svistonov*). Although Shepherd does concede that both Vaginov and Kharms produced metafiction, he maintains that Kharms's metafiction is of 'a distinctly different character' from Vaginov's (*Beyond Metafiction*, p. 116). For a survey of scholarship on, and definitions of metafiction, see Shepherd, ibid., chapter 1. Bibliographies of critical works on metafiction can be

found in Waugh, *Metafiction*, pp. 161–9, and Shepherd, *Beyond Metafiction*, pp. 208–12.

83 Despite the presence of his name in the OBERIU declaration, there is no evidence to suggest that Vaginov took part in any of the group's performances subsequent to 24 January 1928. Accounts of the association's shows prior to the 'Three Left Hours' are extremely sketchy, and give little clue as to who actually took part in them.

1 AUTHORS AND AUTHORITY

1 'Men of the future remember me / I lived at the time when kings were ending'; Guillaume Apollinaire, *Œuvres poétiques*, p. 149.

2 See José Ortega y Gasset, 'The Dehumanization of Art'.

3 On Dada, see John D. Erickson, *Dada: Performance, Poetry and Art*.

4 For an introduction to Russian Symbolism, see Avril Pyman, *A History of Russian Symbolism*. To place modernism in opposition to Romanticism is not, however, to ignore the numerous debates which have taken place around the terms themselves. As Tjalsma points out ('The Petersburg Poets', p. 76), many critics maintain that modernism is 'just one more replay of Romanticism'.

5 On Primitivism in Russian art, see Gray, *The Great Experiment*, chapter 4. Of course, one could argue that the challenge to such notions, and in particular the Romantic concept of the artist as inspired and original 'creator', had begun to be subverted in the early nineteenth century. This period, what David Shepherd has described as 'the age of the incipient professionalization of Russian letters' (*Beyond Metafiction*, p. 72), saw the triumph, with the establishment of copyright laws and the development of commercialism, of the notion of private ownership of one's text. Indeed, Pushkin's dramatic poem of 1824, 'Conversation between a Bookseller and a Poet' ('Razgovor knigoprodavtsa s poetom'), underscores, according to David Glenn Kropf, Pushkin's dual role at the time as both 'inspirationally guided poet and mercantile bookseller': *Authorship as Alchemy*, p. 73.

6 For an account of Acmeism, and its relation to Russian Symbolism, see Justin Doherty, *The Acmeist Movement in Russian Poetry*. The best study of Russian Futurism (in all its various forms) remains Vladimir Markov's *Russian Futurism*.

7 The term 'samovitoe slovo' was first coined in what was in effect the first Futurist manifesto, *A Slap in the Face of Public Taste* (*Poshchechina obshchestvennomu vkusu*), published in December 1912, and

co-signed by Khlebnikov, Kruchenykh, David Burlyuk, and Vladimir Mayakovsky. The Russian text can be found in Markov (ed.), *Manifesty i programmy russkikh futuristov*, pp. 50–1. An English translation of *A Slap* is contained in Markov, *Russian Futurism*, pp. 45–6. For an English translation of Kruchenykh's 1913 pamphlet, *Declaration of the Word as Such* (*Deklaratsiya slova kak takovogo*), see Markov, *Russian Futurism*, pp. 130–1.

8 Kharms considered Khlebnikov one of his 'teachers', along with Vvedensky and Marshak. For a discussion of the importance of Khlebnikov for Kharms's poetic system, see Jaccard, *Daniil Harms*, pp. 32–9. Bakhterev has recently claimed that Khlebnikov was the idol of all the members of OBERIU (see Nazarov and Chubukin, 'Poslednii iz Oberiu', p. 54).

9 The full text is contained in Markov, *Russian Futurism*, p. 44. There were, of course, quite divergent views of *zaum'* amongst its practitioners. See Bernice Glatzer Rosenthal, 'Nietzsche and Russian Futurism', p. 240. On Kruchenykh, see Rosemarie Ziegler, 'Aleksey E. Kruchenykh'. For a discussion of Matyushin's aesthetic theories and their relation to Kharms's poetics, see Jaccard, *Daniil Harms*, pp. 90–7. A useful account of Khlebnikov's concept of *zaum'* can be found in Raymond Cooke, *Velimir Khlebnikov: A Critical Study*, pp. 82–94.

10 Quoted in English in the entry on 'Suprematism', in Read (ed.), *The Thames and Hudson Dictionary of Art and Artists*, p. 315. Malevich first elaborated his theory of Suprematism in 1916 in his *Ot kubizma i futurizma k suprematizmu*. A collection of Malevich's theoretical writings can be found in: K. Malevich, *Essays on Art, 1915–1928*. As Goldstein points out, the Soviet critic D. Tolmachev considered the early OBERIU verse the closest thing to Suprematism in poetry: *Nikolai Zabolotsky*, p. 38. Personally, as well as artistically, Kharms was close to Malevich. Kharms's ode to Malevich, delivered by the poet at Malevich's funeral in 1935, is contained in Kharms, *Sobranie proizvedenii*, vol. IV, p. 42. This piece, and a poem on Malevich by Bakhterev, entitled 'The Well-Known Artist' ('Znakomyi khudozhnik'), are contained in Levin, 'The Fifth Meaning of the Motor-Car', pp. 296–8. It was at one time hoped that Malevich would join OBERIU, but this came to nothing.

11 For a discussion of the link between Malevich and *zaum'*, see: Charlotte Douglas, 'Views from the New World'; and John E. Bowlt, 'Demented Words'.

12 Malevich, 'O poezii'.

13 Quoted in Boris Thomson, *Lot's Wife and the Venus of Milo*, p. 8.

14 Quoted in G. M. Hyde, 'Russian Futurism', p. 261.

15 On Mayakovsky's view of his role as poet, see Russell, *Poets, Prophets and Revolutionaries*, pp. 183–205.

16 Quoted in Vyacheslav Zavalishin, *Early Soviet Writers*, p. 147. Part 3 of Zavalishin's study contains a useful account of proletarian cultural organizations, including 'Proletkul't' and 'The Smithy'. See also Brown, *The Proletarian Episode*, chapter 1.

17 From 'The Montage of Film Attractions', in S. M. Eisenstein, *Selected Works, vol. 1: Writings, 1922–34*, p. 75. On the practical application of Eisenstein's 'montage of attractions' in his theatre and cinema work, see Peter Wollen, *Signs and Meaning in the Cinema*, chapter 1.

18 On Constructivist poetry, see Zavalishin, *Early Soviet Writers*, pp. 260–8.

19 See Mel Gordon, 'Meyerhold's Biomechanics'.

20 See Vlada Petrić, *Constructivism in Film*.

21 See Goldstein, *Nikolai Zabolotsky*, p. 45.

22 The novel, written in 1923, was published in the first two numbers of the journal *Krasnaya nov'* for 1924: see Robert A. Maguire, *Red Virgin Soil*, pp. 110–27.

23 For an introduction to the 'Serapion Brothers', see Hongor Oulanoff, *The Serapion Brothers*, and Gary Kern, 'The Serapion Brothers: A Dialectics of Fellow Travelling'. There is a weak link between OBERIU and the Serapions through the Serapion poets Nikolay Tikhonov and Elizaveta Polonskaya (the only woman in the 'brotherhood'), who had been members of the 'Islanders' group, along with Vaginov: see Anemone and Martynov, 'The Islanders: Poetry and Polemics in Petrograd of the 1920s'. Kaverin was supposed to contribute some prose to Kharms's *Archimedes' Bath* anthology: see Blyumbaum and Gorev, ' "Vanna Arkhimeda" '. The relationship between the Serapions and OBERIU has yet to be adequately explored. See, however, the chapter 'The Serapion Brethren, the Pass, and the Oberiuts', in Marc Slonim, *Soviet Russian Literature*, pp. 99–108; and Harold B. Segel, *Twentieth-Century Russian Drama*, chapter 6.

24 Lev Lunts, 'Pochemu my Serapionovy brat'ya'. An English translation of the entire article can be found in Oulanoff, pp. 26–8.

25 This is not to overlook the numerous debates and polemics between the various 'brothers' concerning the nature of the literary process: see Kern, 'The Serapion Brothers: A Dialectics of Fellow Travelling'.

26 For an account of Zoshchenko's use of *skaz*, see I. R. Titunik, 'Mikhail Zoshchenko and the Problem of *Skaz*'.

27 Shklovsky, *Tret'ya fabrika*, p. 18: quoted in English translation in Shepherd, *Beyond Metafiction*, p. 132.

28 Oulanoff has gone so far as to say that 'to draw a distinct line between Formalist thinking and the specific opinions of the Serapion Brothers presents a real difficulty' (*The Serapion Brothers*, p. 21). For a comparative study of Serapion literature and Formalist theory, see D. G. B. Piper, 'Formalism and the Serapion Brothers'.

29 V. Shklovsky, *Voskreshenie slova*. Fuller accounts of Formalism can be found in Victor Erlich, *Russian Formalism*, and Peter Steiner, *Russian Formalism: A Metapoetics*.

30 See Viktor Shklovsky, 'Iskusstvo kak priem' (a version of this essay has recently been published in Shklovsky, *Gamburgskii schet*, pp. 58–72).

31 See Shklovsky, *Gamburgskii schet*, p. 60.

32 See Yury Tynyanov, 'O literaturnoi evolyutsii'.

33 See Boris Eikhenbaum, 'Literaturnyi byt'.

34 Boris Eikhenbaum, 'Teoriya formal'nogo metoda' (quoted from the English translation, 'The Theory of the Formal Method', p. 32; my emphasis). On the crisis which affected Russian Formalist theory towards the end of the 1920s, and Eikhenbaum's personal evolution as a theorist, see Carol Any, *Boris Eikhenbaum*, chapter 4.

35 See Osip Brik, 'T. n. formal'nyi metod'.

36 On left art's call for 'literature of fact', see Vahan D. Barooshian, 'Russian Futurism in the Late 1920s'. On the call for writers to produce newspaper articles instead of novels, see Thomson, *Lot's Wife and the View of Milo*, p. 70.

37 Chuzhak (ed.), *Literatura fakta*.

38 Osip Brik, 'Uchit' pisatelei', p. 181. See also Brik's essays, 'Protiv "tvorcheskoi" lichnosti', and 'Blizhe k faktu'.

39 N. F. Chuzhak, 'Opyt ucheby na klassike', p. 175.

40 See Meilakh, 'Predislovie', pp. xvii–xviii, xxiii.

41 See Bakhtin's 1934–5 essay 'Discourse in the Novel' ('Slovo v romane').

42 The case for Bakhtin's occupying a position some way between these two sets of theory has been advanced by Tony Bennett, *Formalism and Marxism*. For the 'Formalist' Bakhtin, see Gary Saul Morson, 'The Heresiarch of *Meta*'. Those wishing to read an account of Bakhtin as a Marxist should consult Michael Gardiner, *The Dialogics of Critique*.

43 Mikhail Bakhtin, *Formal'nyi metod v literaturovedenii*, p. 44. This essay was originally published in 1928 under the name of P. N.

Medvedev, with the following sub-title: *A Critical Introduction to Sociological Poetics* (*Kriticheskoe vvedenie v sotsiologicheskuyu poetiku*). I have no intention of becoming embroiled in the controversy surrounding authorship of the various works published under the names of Medvedev or Voloshinov but frequently attributed to Bakhtin. For a discussion of the problem, see Clark and Holquist, *Mikhail Bakhtin*, pp. 146–70 (who believe Bakhtin *did* at least co-author them), and Gary Saul Morson and Caryl Emerson, *Mikhail Bakhtin: Creation of a Prosaics*, pp. 101–19 (who argue against Bakhtin's authorship). For the sake of simplicity, where authorship is disputed I shall refer throughout to 'Bakhtin'.

44 M. M. Bakhtin/V. N. Voloshinov, *Freidizm: kriticheskii ocherk*.

45 M. M. Bakhtin, *Problemy tvorchestva Dostoevskogo*.

46 Bakhtin's study of Rabelais was not published until more than twenty years later, in 1965: *Tvorchestvo Fransua Rable i narodnaya kul'tura srednevekov'ya*.

47 See Revzina's (untitled) summary of Dorogov's paper.

48 Lars Kleberg, *Theatre as Action*, p. 123. In a note to this comment (pp. 144–5, n. 8), Kleberg draws up a list of characteristics of Leningrad and Moscow cultures respectively in the 1920s and 1930s, in which both OBERIU and Bakhtin are included as characteristic of Leningrad (and in which, interestingly, OBERIU is directly contrasted to Constructivism).

49 For a fuller discussion of Bakhtin's implied views on the question of authorship, see Morson and Emerson, *Mikhail Bakhtin: Creation of a Prosaics*, chapters 4–6.

50 N. Zabolotsky, *Stolbtsy i poemy*, pp. 66–7 (p. 67).

51 Quoted in English in Nikita Zabolotsky, *The Life of Zabolotsky*, p. xix.

52 In a poem written in 1935 and addressed to Oleinikov, Kharms notes Oleinikov's habit of lampooning canonical writers such as Goethe and Dante, and comments that Oleinikov's verse contains little that could be called art: 'To Oleinikov' ('Oleinikovu'), in Kharms, *Sobranie proizvedenii*, vol. IV, p. 38.

53 On the 'infantilism' and 'primitivism' of Oleinikov's poetry, see Meilakh, ' "Ya ispytyval slovo na ogne i na stuzhe..." ', p. 46, and Polyakova, 'Tvorchestvo Oleinikova', p. 331.

54 N. Oleinikov, *Puchina strastei. Stikhi. Tsikl. Poema*, p. 13.

55 The full text of 'Koloborot' is contained in Aleksandrov (ed.), *Vanna Arkhimeda*, pp. 426–30. The text is simply dated 'The period of the [Krushchev] thaw' ('Period ottepeli').

56 This text, undated, is contained in Aleksandrov (ed.), *Vanna Arkhimeda*, pp. 430–2. The reference to 'sluchai' in the title is

perhaps a parodic allusion to Kharms's prose cycle of the same name: *Incidents* (*Sluchai*).

57 For a broader discussion of the figure of the author/narrator in Kharms's work, see: Graham Roberts, 'A Matter of (Dis)-course'; and Susan Downing Scotto, 'Daniil Xarms's Early Poetry and its Relations to His Later Poetry and Short Prose', chapter 4.

58 Kharms, *Polet*, p. 372. Unless otherwise indicated, all references to works by Kharms will be to this edition. Mikhail Zolotonosov offers an alternative interpretation of 'Four Illustrations', claiming that it represents a description of how the Soviet intelligentsia was being persecuted in the 1930s: 'Muzyka vo l'du', p. 52. J. Douglas Clayton, on the other hand, has argued that the active challenge to authority (including the authority of the poet) in Kharms's drama betrays its *balagan* origins: *Pierrot in Petrograd*, p. 194.

59 The text first appeared in *Chizh*, 7 (1935).

60 These can be found in Daniil Kharms, *Gorlo bredit britvoyu*, pp. 61–2, and 60–1 respectively.

61 Kharms's prose, which contains countless acts of violence and sadism, has been seen as anticipating more recent trends in Soviet literature. See, for example, Deming Brown, *The Last Years of Soviet Russian Literature*, chapter 7.

62 Kharms once declared that he was interested only in life's 'absurd manifestations', and that concepts such as 'ethics' and 'morality' were 'hateful' to him (quoted by Glotser in Kharms, ' "…I emu v rot zaletela kukushka" ', p. 263). Il'ya Levin, however, has argued that his prose exposes 'the nonsense of evil in the world': Il'ya Levin, 'Mir vymyshlennyi i mir sozdannyi', p. 274.

63 This text dated 27 March 1937, may have been written for a specific reader, namely Druskin, who is probably the 'philosopher' referred to at the end of the text. Virtually everything written by members of the *chinari* group will have been read out at group meetings. Hugh Maxton believes that Kharms's tendency to compose miniature vignettes was a comment on the irrelevance of many traditional literary forms: 'Kharms and Myles: an After-word', p. 96.

64 The title of this piece may be a parodic reference to Bely's 'Symphonic' novels: see V. Simina, 'Kharms i Bely'.

65 Untitled text, in Kharms, 'Neopublikovannye rasskazy i stsenki', p. 94.

66 On Kharms's subversive attitude towards the Russian literary tradition, see, also, Anthony Anemone, 'The Anti-World of Daniil

Kharms', pp. 77–8, and Aleksandr Flaker, 'O rasskazakh Daniila Kharmsa'.

67 See also 'About Pushkin' ('O Pushkine'; Russian text contained in Jaccard, 'De la réalité au texte', p. 285). The Russian Futurists' manifesto, *A Slap in the Face of Public Taste*, named Pushkin as one of the first writers, along with Dostoevsky and Tolstoy, to be 'thrown overboard from the steamer of modernity': see Hyde, *Russian Futurism*, p. 265. Some scholars have argued that by writing about Pushkin in this way Kharms was not allying himself with the iconoclastic Futurist tradition, but rather parodying (Soviet) unrefined, uncultured attitudes towards the 'greats' of Russian literature ('Anecdotes' was written in 1937, the centenary of Pushkin's death). See for example Aleksandrov, 'Materialy D. I. Kharmsa', pp. 78–9, and Sazhin, 'Literaturnye i fol'klornye traditsii', pp. 60–1. As Sazhin notes, there was a particularly strong tradition of humorous Pushkin anecdotes in nineteenth-century Russia. Many of these are contained in Z. V. Vazarin (ed.), *Nigde eshche do sikh por ne pechatnye anekdoty pro A. S. Pushkina*.

68 A similar image is contained in Kharms's poem 'The Dream of Two Swarthy Ladies' ('Son dvukh chernomazykh dam', dated 19 August 1936); in their dream, Tolstoy is beaten with an axe by Ivan the house-manager ('upravdom'), leaving behind him 'all Russian literature in a chamber pot' ('vsya literatura russkaya v nochnom gorshke'; Kharms, *Sobranie proizvedenii*, vol. IV, p. 49).

69 This text is contained in Daniil Kharms, ' "Bitva so smyslami" Daniila Kharmsa', p. 6.

70 Interestingly, Darra Goldstein notes that contemporary critics said the same thing about the (comparatively serious) Zabolotsky: *Nikolai Zabolotsky*, p. 158.

71 D. S. Likhachev and A. M. Panchenko, *'Smekhovoi mir' drevnei Rusi*, pp. 9–10. On the concept of the 'yurodvyi', and its applicability as an ethical concept to Kharms's prose, see Anemone, 'The Anti-World of Daniil Kharms', pp. 75–7.

72 Michael Holquist cites Kharms's 'Anecdotes from Pushkin's Life' as precisely the kind of thing Bakhtin had in mind by his reference to 'recent carnivalizations of legends surrounding Dante, Pushkin, etc.' (Mikhail Bakhtin, 'Epic and Novel', p. 25, note p.).

73 The full text can be found in Kharms, *Polet*, pp. 398–430.

74 The letter is contained in Kharms, *Polet*, pp. 482–5. See also Il'ya Levin', 'Mir vymyshlennyi i mir sozdannyi', p. 274. It is this sort of statement from Kharms which has led some scholars to believe that Kharms equated his own status as an artist to that of a 'magician'. See, for example, V. Sazhin, 'Tsirk Kharmsa', p. 90.

75 Evidence of Kharms's parlous material state in the mid- to late
   1930s can be found in his diary entries for this period. See
   Kharms, ' "Bozhe, kakaya uzhasnaya zhizn'..." ', pp. 215–20.
76 This poem can be found in Kharms, *Polet*, p. 249. On the
   controversy surrounding this poem, see N. Gernet, 'O Kharmse'.
77 In fact, Kharms had been prey to periodical lapses of inspiration,
   beginning around 1931. In a short autobiographical piece from
   that year, entitled 'Morning' ('Utro'), Kharms describes sitting
   down to write: 'But I did not know what to write. I didn't even
   know whether I should write a poem, or a story, or a philosophical
   essay. I did not write anything and went to bed' ('No ya ne znal,
   chto mne nado napisat'. Ya dazhe ne znal, dolzhny byt' eto stikhi,
   ili rasskaz, ili rassuzhdenie. Ya nichego ne napisal i leg spat";
   Kharms, *Polet*, pp. 440–4 (p. 442)).
78 Kharms and his family shared their communal flat for some time
   with an old woman with whom they did not get on very well. See
   A. A. Aleksandrov, 'Materialy o Daniile Kharmse i stikhi ego v
   fonde V. N. Petrova', p. 192.
79 This character may have been intended to represent Oleinikov,
   since in Kharms's manuscript he was originally called 'Nikolay
   Makarovich'.
80 Most scholars have focused on the intertextual aspects of the tale,
   and particularly the parodic allusions to Pushkin's *The Queen of
   Spades* and Dostoevsky's *Crime and Punishment*. See, for example,
   Steven Cassedy, 'Daniil Kharms's Parody of Dostoevskii' and
   Ellen Chances, 'Daniil Charms' "Old Woman" Climbs her
   Family Tree'. For approaches which focus on intertextual refer-
   ences to non-Russian works of literature, see Susan D. Scotto,
   'Xarms and Hamsun: *Starukha* Solves a Mystery?', and A. Gerasi-
   mova and A. Nikitaev, 'Kharms i "Golem" '. Parodying the
   Petersburg literary tradition, *The Old Woman* looks back to
   Kharms's play *The Comedy of the City of Petersburg* (*Komediya goroda
   Peterburga*), written in 1927 (Kharms, *Sobranie proizvedenii*, vol. I,
   pp. 84–125). On the latter, see Anatoly Vishevsky, 'Tradition in
   the Topsy-Turvey World of Two Oberiu Plays'.
81 This is not to ignore Bakhtin's caveat that 'in the narrowly
   formalist, literary parody of the modern era the link with the
   carnivalesque world view has almost totally been lost' ('V uzko-
   formal'noi literaturnoi parodii novogo vremeni svyaz' s karna-
   val'nym   mirooshchushcheniem   pochti   vovse   poryvaetsya';
   Bakhtin, *Problemy poetiki Dostoevskogo*, p. 217 (hereafter
   PPD)). However, *The Old Woman*, as I hope to show, is much more than
   merely the kind of dry exercise in intertextuality which Bakhtin

criticizes. For an alternative Bakhtinian reading of *The Old Woman*, see Margaret Dudley Simonton, 'From Solipsism to Dialogue', chapter 6.

82 Bakhtin specifically mentions scandals caused by the undead as carnivalesque (Bakhtin, *PPD*, p. 239).

83 For a discussion of this aspect of the story, see Alice Stone Nakhimovsky, 'The Ordinary, the Sacred and the Grotesque'.

84 While Bakhtin makes no mention of menippean satire in the first edition of his book on Dostoevsky, Leonardo Paleari suggests that Bakhtin may well have come across material concerning the genre during his reading in the 1920s: 'Tvorchestvo glazami tvortsa', p. xiii. According to Bakhtin, 'menippean satire' takes its name from the philosopher Menippus of Gadara, who lived in the third century BC. Bakhtin discusses the generic features of menippean satire in *PPD*, pp. 190–206. *The Old Woman* demonstrates other significant features of menippean satire, including the concern with topical issues (the housing problem, the Stalinist terror-machine); the nether world (in the theme of the 'undead'); 'inserted genres' (the conversations transcribed as dramatic dialogue); and the abnormal moral and psychic states of man.

85 On the fantastic in *The Old Woman*, see Rosanna Giaquinta, 'Elements of the Fantastic in Daniil Kharms's *Starukha*'.

86 For a reading of the novella based on the ethical philosophy of Kharms's fellow *chinar* Yakov Druskin, see Robin Aizlewood, ' "Guilt without Guilt" '.

87 By attempting to write a story about a miracle worker, Kharms's narrator may in fact himself be trying to write an example of menippean satire. As Bakhtin observes, one type of menippea was constituted by the 'aretological' genres, which were narratives about the miraculous deeds of gods or heroes (Bakhtin, *PPD*, p. 191).

88 The carnivalization of the Petersburg literary tradition continues until the very last sentence of the text, which, as has frequently been pointed out, echoes the ending of Dostoevsky's *Notes from Underground* (*Zapiski iz podpol'ya*, 1864).

89 One scholar who has also related the twin themes of the writer and God in *The Old Woman* is Neil Carrick. For Carrick, the intertextual overload in Kharms's story implies that the writer can say nothing new, that he is subordinate to God, the ultimate author of the script that is our lives. However, Carrick concludes his study by downplaying the metafictional subtext of *The Old Woman* in favour of its ethical and theological aspects: Carrick, 'A Familiar Story'.

90 Vvedensky, *PSS*, vol. 1, pp. 120–6. All references to works by Vvedensky will be from this edition.

91 Time, as Ol'ga Revzina has argued, is central to much of Vvedensky's work: O. G. Revzina, 'Kachestvennaya i funktsional'naya kharakteristika vremeni v poezii A. I. Vvedenskogo', p. 398.

92 Murder was also the theme of Vvedensky's novel *Murderers, You are Fools* (*Ubiitsy, vy duraki*). Unfortunately, this work has been lost; see Vvedensky, *PSS*, vol. 11, pp. 220–3.

93 This text is undated, although Meilakh believes that it was written 'no later than 1933' (Vvedensky, *PSS*, vol. 11, pp. 293). All quotations from Vvedensky's works will follow as far as possible the punctuation used in Meilakh's two-volume edition, which is based on the only existing manuscript versions.

94 Extracts from the 'Grey Notebook', a collection of observations and commentaries which Vvedensky made from 1932 to 1933, are contained in Vvedensky, *PSS*, vol. 11, pp. 181–90. Unless otherwise indicated, all references to Vvedensky's theoretical writings will be from this edition.

95 Nakhimovsky makes a similar point in her discussion of 'The Eyewitness and the Rat' (Nakhimovsky, *Laughter in the Void*, p. 158).

96 Vvedensky, *PSS*, vol. 1, pp. 77–101 (p. 80).

97 The full text of this work, unpublished in Vvedensky's lifetime, can be found in Vvedensky, *PSS*, vol. 1, pp. 5–21. A fragment from *Minin and Pozharsky* was published in the Union of Poets almanack, *Koster*, in 1927 (the same almanack which contained Kharms's 'The Verse of Petr Yashkin', 'Stikh Petra Yashkina'). Apart from his work for children, this was Vvedensky's only publication during his lifetime.

98 In this respect *Minin and Pozharsky* is close to Kruchenykh's *Victory over the Sun*. On the general treatment of history by OBERIU, see B. Konstriktor, 'Otkrytie Peterburga'.

99 In Vvedensky's text the surname is spelt with a soft sign, however: 'Men'shikov' ('Меньшиков').

100 The following information is taken from the entries on Minin and Pozharsky in Prokhorov (ed.), *Bol'shaya sovetskaya entsiklopediya*. See also Lionel Kochan, *The Making of Modern Russia*, p. 71.

101 There have, in fact, been two more famous Minins in Russian history. One, Sergey Konstantinovich Minin (1887–1962), was a prominent figure in the Russian Communist Party, who by 1926 was in the midst of being purged by Stalin as part of his drive against the 'new opposition'. The other, Fedor Alekseevich Minin (b. 1709; year of death unknown), was a Russian arctic explorer (a

possible explanation for the presence of the penguins in *Minin and Pozharsky*; p. 8). See the (anonymous) entries on both figures in Prokhorov (ed.), *Bol'shaya sovetskaya entsiklopediya*.

102 A more conventional, and openly patriotic account of these events was to be written in the aftermath of the Molotov–Ribbentrop pact, with which the USSR annexed Belorussia and parts of Poland: Viktor Shklovsky, *Minin and Pozharsky*.

103 The reference to the 'law of the hours' may be a parodic allusion to Khlebnikov's claim to have discovered the 'laws of time', laws, moreover, which he calculated by means of his 'string of years'. On Khlebnikov's concept of time, see Cooke, *Velimir Khlebinikov: A Critical Study*, chapter 4.

104 These characters who recount their own deaths on a battlefield also echo some of Khlebnikov's war poetry, and in particular the short poem which ends the *War in a Mousetrap* cycle: see Cooke, *Velimir Khlebnikov: A Critical Study*, p. 136.

105 On the 'dialogues of the dead' and menippean satire, see Bakhtin, *PPD*, pp. 188–9.

106 See Vishevsky, 'Tradition in the Topsy-Turvey World of Two Oberiu Plays', pp. 355–8.

107 Vvedensky would have been particularly well acquainted with *The Government Inspector*, since he played the part of Khlestakov in a school production: see Meilakh, 'Predislovie', p. xii.

108 As Vishevsky notes ('Tradition in the Topsy-Turvey World of Two Oberiu Plays', p. 358), the final line of this passage contains two Russian proverbs split to make a third, meaningless one: 'S volkami zhit', rot ne razevai' is an amalgam of 'S volkami zhit', po-volchi vyt'' ('When in Rome do as the Romans do', literally 'When you live among wolves you howl like one'), and 'Na chuzhoi karavai rot ne razevai' ('Don't try to take a bite out of someone else's pie').

109 On Kharms's use of children's counting rhymes ('schitalki'), see R. B. Kalashnikova, 'Daniil Kharms i narodnaya schitalka'.

110 Barthes, 'The Death of the Author', p. 146. See also Michel Foucault, 'What is an Author?'.

111 Similarly, Vishevsky believes ('Tradition in the Topsy-Turvey World of Two Oberiu Plays', pp. 364–5) that two of the characters in Kharms's *The Comedy of the City of Petersburg* represent Vvedensky and Kharms.

112 After his first experience of arrest and imprisonment in 1931–2, Vvedensky's understanding of time appears to have undergone an important modification. He now regarded time as linear, but in the sense of a series of non-existent seconds which ultimately

bring one to death (see Vvedensky, *PSS*, vol. ii, pp. 187–8). Such a view does not appear, however, to have altered the fundamental distinction which he drew between time before death and time after death.

113 It would be interesting to compare *Minin and Pozharsky* with the 'simultanéist' poems of German Dadaist Kurt Schwitters (1887–1948), in which Schwitters sought to create the impression of many things happening at once. On Schwitters, see Robert Short, 'Dada and Surrealism', pp. 297–8.

114 On counting rhymes, and their basis in a linear model of time, see Susan Stewart, *Nonsense*, p. 130.

115 Tat'yana Nikol'skaya, [introduction to poems by Konstantin Vaginov], p. 72.

116 Vaginov had been a member of Gumilev's second 'Guild of Poets'. On Vaginov's close personal attachment to Gumilev, see Anthony Anemone, 'Konstantin Vaginov and the Death of Nikolai Gumilev'.

117 This untitled poem is taken from the collection entitled *Petersburg Nights*, which was originally to have been published in February 1922, but which failed to appear for financial reasons. It is contained in Vaginov, [untitled], p. 72.

118 This untitled poem, dated May 1926, is published in Vaginov, [untitled], p. 73.

119 Vaginov, *Sobranie stikhotvorenii*, p. 71. Unless otherwise stated, further references to poems by Vaginov will be from this edition. See also Vaginov's long poem of 1924, 'Hermits' ('Otshel'niki', 1924; ibid., pp. 143–5).

120 This is the first half of a single-stanza poem dated April 1924, which was published in the collection *An Experiment in Combining Words by Means of Rhythm* (*Opyty soedineniya slov posredstvom ritma*), in 1931: the poem is contained in Vaginov, *Sobranie stikhotvorenii*, p. 138. The plea to a higher authority for poetic inspiration looks forward to a similar request made by Kharms in his 'Prayer Before Sleep' ('Molitva pered snom', 1931; Kharms, *Sobranie proizvedenii*, vol. iii, p. 22). The word 'Gospod'' ('Lord') is, however, missing from the version of this poem contained in the 1991 reprint of the original 1931 edition: Vaginov, *Opyty soedineniya slov posredstvom ritma*, p. 18.

121 As Anemone notes, 'Vaginov conceived of Culture as a universal and panchronic tradition which transcends the normal boundaries of time and space. The entire cultural and literary tradition of the past lives in the work of the poet, while every poem takes its meaning from its place in, and its interaction with, the

tradition' ('Konstantin Vaginov and the Leningrad Avant-Garde', pp. 154–5). Anemone compares Vaginov's views on culture with those of Mandel'shtam and T. S. Eliot.

122 On the importance of the theatre as a theme in Vaginov's work, see Ol'ga Shindina, 'Teatralizatsiya povestvovaniya v romane Vaginova "Kozlinaya pesn'"'.

123 'The Star of Bethlehem' and 'The Monastery of our Lord Apollo' are contained in Vaginov, *Kozlinaya pesn': romany* (hereafter *Romany*), pp. 491–500, and 481–90 respectively. All subsequent page references for these texts refer to this edition. They are also published together in Konstantin Vaginov, ' "Pomnyu ya aleksandriiskii zvon..." ', pp. 107–9, and 109–11 respectively. Both works were originally contained (as was Vaginov's poem 'Art') in the *Abraksas* anthology published in 1922 by Mikhail Kuzmin's 'Emotionalists' group, of which Vaginov was a member. For a discussion of these two texts, see Tat'yana Nikol'skaya's introduction to Vaginov's ' "Pomnyu ya aleksandriiskii zvon..." ' (pp. 105–7), and O. V. Shindina, 'Nekotorye osobennosti poetiki rannei prozy Vaginova'.

124 For a discussion of the motif of Christian culture and the figure of Philostratus in Vaginov's early poetry and prose, see Anemone, 'Konstantin Vaginov and the Leningrad Avant-Garde', pp. 126–34 and 155–70.

125 'The Year 1925' written in June 1925, is contained in Vaginov, *Sobranie stikhotvorenii*, pp. 107–18. It is also published, with the provisional title 'A Dramatic Poem about Philostratus' ('Dramaticheskaya poema o Filostrate'), together with a number of book reviews written by Vaginov, in K. K. Vaginov, 'Poema. Retsenzii', pp. 16–24.

126 In particular, the reference in the novel to a group of 'green youths in brocade caps with tassels' ('zeleny[e] yunosh[i] v parchevykh kolpachkakh s kistochkami'), has been interpreted as lampooning the *Oberiuty*: see M. B. Meilakh, 'Shkap i kolpak', p. 192. On possible correspondences between the novel's characters and Vaginov's intellectual milieu, see the extensive notes on the novel contained in Vaginov, *Romany*, pp. 544–61. Vaginov himself was quick to deny any intended correspondence between the novel's characters and his own acquaintances (see Gerasimova, 'Trudy i dni Konstantina Vaginova', p. 150).

127 Vaginov, *Romany*, p. 56. This version, revised by the author, differs slightly from the original 'Priboi' edition of 1928. Unless otherwise stated, all references to *The Goat's Song* (and to Vaginov's other novels) will be from the version in *Romany*, since this

edition is the most widely available. The élitist notion of cultural 'islanders' echoes the 'Islanders' ('Ostrovityane') group of poets to which Vaginov belonged in the early 1920s, which itself looked back to the short-lived journal *The Island (Ostrov)*, founded and edited by Gumilev and A. N. Tolstoy in 1909: see Anemone and Martynov, 'The Islanders'.

128 This may be an allusion to the Symbolist Vyacheslav Ivanov's habit of referring to his apartment as the 'Tower'. It was here around 1910 that Ivanov and other Symbolists held weekly meetings to discuss matters of aesthetics: see Tjalsma, 'The Petersburg Poets', p. 69.

129 This image suggests an ambivalence on Vaginov's part towards the Bolshevik régime, since it implies that, like the destruction which accompanied the advent of the Christian era, the chaos caused by the October Revolution might ultimately be creative. Such ambivalence has been described by Victor Erlich as a hallmark of the Russian *intelligentsia* as a class in the 1920s: see Erlich, *Modernism and Revolution*.

130 See, for example, Ol'ga Shindina, 'Teatralizatsiya povestvovaniya'. Dmitry Segal has placed both *The Goat's Song* and Vaginov's subsequent novel, *The Labours and Days of Svistonov*, in the Russian tradition of 'literature about literature', along with Pushkin's *Eugene Onegin (Evgenii Onegin*, 1825–32), Dostoevsky's *Diary of a Writer (Dnevnik pisatelya*, 1873–81), and two pre-revolutionary novels by Vasily Rozanov, *Solitaria (Uedinnenoe*, 1912) and *Fallen Leaves (Opavshie list'ya*, 1913–15). Segal's survey also includes Mandel'shtam's novella *The Egyptian Stamp (Egipetskaya marka*, 1927), as well as later works such as Bulgakov's *Master and Margarita (Master i Margarita*, 1928–40), Nabokov's *The Gift (Dar*, 1937–8), and Pasternak's *Doctor Zhivago (Doktor Zhivago*, 1957): 'Literatura kak okhrannaya gramota'. Shepherd discusses the metafictional aspects of *The Goat's Song* in *Beyond Metafiction*, chapter 4 (especially pp. 109–14). For details of contemporary reviews which focused on the metafictional nature of *The Goat's Song* and a number of other Soviet novels, see ibid., pp. 22–3.

131 See Vishevsky 'Tradition in the Topsy-Turvy World of Two Oberiu Plays', p. 356. This is probably an allusion to the Soviet slogan, 'Leningrad is the cradle of the Revolution'.

132 The extent to which *The Goat's Song* can be read as an attack on contemporary Soviet society has been a source of disagreement among critics. Contemporary reviewers generally felt it to paint a highly negative picture. See for example: A. Selivanovsky, 'Ostrovityane iskusstva'; D. Tal'nikov, 'Literaturnye zametki'; and

A. Manfred, 'Kladbishchenskaya muza'. See also Vyacheslav Zavalishin, 'Proza i stikhi Konstantina Vaginova', pp. 285–6. For a discussion of the novel as broadly pro-Soviet, see A. Blyum and I. Martynov, 'Petrogradskie bibliofily'. The line taken by Blyum and Martynov is basically a reiteration of the approach adopted by A. Vulis, *Sovetskii satiricheskii roman*, pp. 122–5.

133 See Anna Gerasimova, 'Trudy i dni Konstantina Vaginova', p. 148.

134 Konstantin Vaginov, *Kozlinaya pesn'* (New York, 1978), pp. 177–8 (hereafter *KP*). This quotation is taken from a chapter, omitted from the second version of the novel, and entitled 'Interword of the Established Author' ('Mezhduslovie ustanovivshegosya avtora').

135 M. M. Bakhtin, 'Avtor i geroi v esteticheskoi deyatel'nosti (fragment pervoi glavy)', p. 25.

136 Dmitry Segal has expressed most articulately this ambivalence of Vaginov's carnivalization: 'The attitude of the author to himself and his heroes includes [...] not only uncrowning and mockery, but also adulation, not only death, but revival, and resurrection' ('Literatura kak okhrannaya gramota', p. 243). The question of the relationship between Vaginov's novels and Bakhtin's concept of 'carnival' is a contentious one. According to Nikol'skaya, Bakhtin himself expressed the opinion in a private conversation that Vaginov was a genuinely carnivalesque writer ('Konstantin Vaginov, ego vremya i knigi', p. 8). Nina Perlina maintains that there are close parallels between Vaginov's novels and Bakhtin's thought, including the latter's understanding of menippean satire: Perlina, 'Vzaimootnosheniya literaturnykh teorii i poeticheskoi praktiki v literaturno-filosofskikh kruzhkakh 1920-godov'. Leonardo Paleari has argued that *The Goat's Song* conforms to all the essential characteristics of the carnivalesque genre of menippean satire as defined by Bakhtin: 'La Letteratura e la vita nei romanzi di Vaginov'. Paleari's conclusions concerning the 'carnivalesque' nature of *The Goat's Song* have, however, been contested by Anthony Anemone: 'Carnival in Theory and Practice'.

137 The novel was first published in 1983 in the USA, under the erroneous title *Harpagoniada (Garpagoniada)*. The text of *Harpagoniana* which will be referred to in this chapter is contained in Vaginov, *Romany*, pp. 371–480 (the text of the first version of the novel, excluding chapter 11, which has been lost), and 512–43 (the addenda to the second, incomplete version, including two whole new chapters). The Russian edition of the text has been preferred to the earlier, American edition since the latter is said to contain

'distortions and inaccuracies' (*Romany*, p. 579). There is very little information as to why Vaginov decided to revise the first version, after it had already been sent for publication. According to one source, however, Vaginov wished to expand the novel's social dimension: on this and other details concerning the publication of *Harpagoniana*, see Vaginov, *Romany*, pp. 579–80. See also the text of a letter concerning the novel, which Vaginov sent to his publisher: ibid., pp. 511 and 589.

138 This *mise en abyme* structure links *Harpagoniana* both to *The Labours and Days of Svistonov*, and to *Bambocciade* (see below, chapters 2 and 3).

139 These stories were added to the second version of the novel: see Vaginov, *Romany*, pp. 514–15.

140 Like the anecdotes which Anfert'ev overhears, these stories were also added to the novel at a later stage: see Vaginov, *Romany*, pp. 535–42.

141 Nina Perlina briefly mentions heteroglossia as a feature of Kharms's poetry: 'Daniil Kharms's Poetic System', p. 188.

142 On this political aspect of heteroglossia in general, see Allon White, 'Bakhtin, Sociolinguistics and the Novel', p. 127.

143 The idea that by the end of the novel the author has 'lost his voice' raises the possibility that the second version of *Harpagoniana* may have been finished, despite affirmations to the contrary from various scholars (see, for example, Vaginov, *Romany*, p. 579, and Chukovsky, 'Iz vospominanii', p. 114).

144 This is not to agree with Gerasimova's assertion that the author is absolutely absent from the text ('Trudy i dni Konstantina Vaginova', p. 163), for it is only at the end of the novel that the author's voice finally disappears. It should be pointed out that one or two scholars have produced very different readings of the fate of the author in *Harpagoniana* and Vaginov's prose in general. Perlina, for example, claims that in the novel we can hear the author's 'lyric intonation' ('Konstantin Vaguinov', p. 478). And according to D. S. Moskovskaya, in this as in all his novels, Vaginov was engaged precisely in a struggle to find his own word as an author, in an age when the word became public property: 'Sud'ba chuzhogo slova v romanakh K. Vaginova'.

145 See Shepherd, *Beyond Metafiction*, p. 120, and Segal, pp. 215–16 respectively. Although relevant to *The Goat's Song*, both scholars' conclusions primarily concern Vaginov's second novel, *The Labours and Days of Svistonov*.

146 Anthony Anemone has gone so far as to suggest that Vaginov's friendship and association with Bakhtin and his circle, which

began in 1924, was particularly influential in his decision to turn to prose ('Konstantin Vaginov and the Leningrad Avant-Garde', p. 13).

2 REREADING READING

1 See Mandel'shtam, 'O sobesednike', and Gumilev, 'Chitatel''. See also Doherty, *The Acmeist Movement*, pp. 118–22, and p. 136.
2 The term 'horizon of expectations' was first coined by German reception-theorist Hans Robert Jauss: *Toward an Aesthetic of Reception*, chapter 5.
3 Roland Barthes, *S/Z*, p. 4.
4 Vsevolod Meyerhold, *Meyerhold on Theatre*, p. 63.
5 See Clayton, *Pierrot in Petrograd*, pp. 62–4. For a full account of Evreinov's theatre, see Spencer Golub, *Evreinov*.
6 Vassily Kandinsky, *Concerning the Spiritual in Art, and Painting in Particular*, quoted in Herbert Read, *A Concise History of Modern Painting*, p. 171. The essay from which this quotation is taken was first published in Berlin in 1913.
7 Quoted in Kleberg, *Theatre as Action*, p. 78.
8 Sergei Eisenstein, *Film Form*, p. 168.
9 Quoted in Kleberg, 'The Nature of the Soviet Audience', p. 175.
10 Cathy Popkin, *The Pragmatics of Insignificance*, p. 117.
11 See Petrić, *Constructivism in Film*, p. 3.
12 Dziga Vertov, 'The Essence of Kino-Eye', from *Kino-Eye: The Writings of Dziga Vertov*, p. 49.
13 Lars Kleberg sees a similar tendency to force the spectator to engage actively with the text in Soviet theatre in the mid-1920s: 'The Nature of the Soviet Audience', p. 187.
14 See Petrić, *Constructivism in Film*, p. 252.
15 See Alan C. Birnoltz, 'El Lissitzky and the Spectator'.
16 El Lissitsky, 'Suprematism in World Reconstruction', quoted in Birnholz, 'El Lissitsky and the Spectator', p. 100.
17 On Shostakovich's rereading of Leskov, see Thomson, *Lot's Wife*, p. 66. On the opera itself, see Elizabeth Wilson, *Shostakovich: A Life Remembered*, pp. 94–100.
18 For details on Meyerkhol'd's production, see Meyerhold, *Meyerhold on Theatre*, chapter 6.
19 See Jaccard, *Daniil Harms*, pp. 229–30.
20 Erika Greber, 'The Metafictional Turn in "Russian Hoffmannism"', p. 4.
21 Greber's article contains an astute analysis of the narrative

strategies by which Kaverin underlines the interrelationship between writing and reading in this story.

22 Lev Lunts, 'Na Zapad!'; quoted in Russian in Greber, 'The Metafictional Turn in "Russian Hoffmanism"', p. 4.

23 See Viktor Shklovsky, *'Tristram Shendi' Sterna i teoriya romana*, and Yury Tynyanov, *Dostoevsky i Gogol': k teorii parodii.*

24 Shklovsky, 'Iskusstvo kak priem', in *Gamburgskii schet*, p. 63.

25 For a useful comparison of Formalism and Reception Theory, see Robert C. Holub, *Reception Theory*, pp. 15–22.

26 Carol Any, *Boris Eikhenbaum* (pp. 68–71), has recently made a similar point, arguing that Boris Eikhenbaum's model reader was a purely passive recipient of the text.

27 Quoted in Steiner, *Russian Formalism: A Metapoetics*, p. 136.

28 See David Shepherd, 'Bakhtin and the Reader' (especially pp. 98–9), and Shepherd, *Beyond Metafiction*, chapter 6.

29 V. N. Voloshinov, *Marksizm i filosofiya yazyka*, p. 87.

30 See Shepherd, *Beyond Metafiction*, pp. 166–7.

31 Mikhail Bakhtin, 'K metodologii gumanitarnykh nauk', p. 373. Although Bakhtin completed this essay in 1974, he began it as early as 1940.

32 Aleksey Medvedev, 'Skol'ko chasov v miske supa?', p. 131.

33 S. N. Chumakov, 'Galchinsky i Kharms', p. 87.

34 Robin Milner-Gulland, 'Zabolotsky and the Reader', p. 389.

35 This poem is reproduced, translated, and discussed in Goldstein, *Nikolai Zabolotsky*, pp. 69–72.

36 Fiona Björling, *Stolbcy*, chapter 2.

37 On these particular poems, see Goldstein, *Nikolai Zabolotsky*, pp. 176–90, and 229–31 respectively.

38 The full text of this (undated) poem is contained in N. Oleinikov, *Ya mukhu bezumno lyubil*, pp. 11–13. The poem comes with an epigraph from a poem by Dostoevsky's Captain Lebyadkin: 'The cockroach was caught in a glass' ('Tarakan popalsya v stakan').

39 *V kartinnoi galeree (Mysli ob iskusstve)*, in N. Oleinikov, *Puchina strastei*, pp. 23–6.

40 The full text, undated, can be found in Aleksandrov (ed.), *Vanna Arkhimeda*, pp. 417–26. All references to the story will be taken from this edition, and indicated by the page number in the text. Shklovsky discusses retardation devices in the novels of Sterne and Cervantes in his *O teorii prozy.*

41 The inclusion within a play of an audience commenting on the action is a metatheatrical device with its roots in the *commedia dell'arte*. On Russian modernist metatheatre, see J. Douglas

Clayton, 'The Play-within-the-play as Metaphor and Metatheatre in Modern Russian Drama'.

42 It is possible to interpret the reader's insult as based on a desire to liberate the text from the writer's authority in a positive way. However, one should be careful not to overlook the fact that 'Four Illustrations' was written in the 1930s, at a time when real readers, in the form of critics or censors, were challenging writers' authority over their texts in a very real and sinister manner.

43 Ann Shukman, 'Towards a Poetics of the Absurd', p. 85.

44 These stories can be found in Kharms, *Polet*, pp. 382 and 356 respectively. The narrrator's deadpan attitude towards death is also a feature of Yury Vladimirov's sole surviving text, the short story 'The Gymnast'.

45 Shukman's article, 'Towards a Poetics of the Absurd', is a general study of the ways in which Kharms subverts certain norms of communication in his prose.

46 In particular, Jean-Philippe Jaccard has defined Kharms's absurd as 'the incoherence of the world elevated to the level of the means of expressing this incoherence': 'Daniil Kharms in the Context of Russian and European Literature of the Absurd', p. 66. Other studies of Kharms which describe him as a writer of the 'absurd' include: Aleksandr Flaker, 'O rasskazakh Daniila Kharmsa'; Elena Sokol, 'Observations on the Prose of Daniil Kharms'; Wolfgang Kasack, 'Daniil Charms: Absurde Kunst in der Sowjetunion'; Jean-Philippe Jaccard, 'De la réalité au texte'; and Valery Sazhin, 'Chitaya Daniila Kharmsa'.

47 In an article penned in the 1960s, Viktor Shklovsky saw this challenge to 'common sense' as central to Kharms's art: 'O tsvetnykh snakh'.

48 Umberto Eco has seen the frustration of the reader's expectations of relevance as a characteristically twentieth-century trend: *The Role of the Reader*, p. 30. On the other hand, Cathy Popkin (*The Pragmatics of Insignificance*, chapters 4 and 5) has demonstrated that a play with notions of relevance is central to Gogol''s prose.

49 In his Formalist study of Kharms's prose, Neil Carrick has gone so far as to suggest that this amounts to the reader 'rewriting' the work: 'interpretation involves a re-ordering of the stories' narrative structure. Consequently, the reader's own analysis comes to appropriate to the act of narration itself' ('Daniil Kharms and a Theology of the Absurd', p. 22).

50 These texts can be found in Kharms, *Polet*, p. 394, *Sluchai*, pp. 39–40, and *Polet*, p. 354, respectively.

51 With their general lack of precise detail, Kharms's miniature

stories are reminiscent of popular, 'extra-literary' genres such as the fable, the parable, the anecdote, and the children's story.

52 For a fuller discussion of the kinds of endings which feature in Kharms's prose, see Ellen Chances, 'Čexov and Xarms: Story/ Anti-Story'. One Formalist who was particularly interested in endings, and plot structure in general, was Vladimir Propp, whose study of narrative patterns in folk literature, *Morfologiya skazki*, was originally published in Leningrad in 1928. If the narrative structures in Kharms's prose are evidence of an interest in the question of narrative itself, then this interest may well have been kindled by contact with Propp's book, or with Propp himself. Nakhimovsky notes that Kharms's papers include the transcript of a conversation between Propp and Lipavsky, which took place in Kharms's room, on the nature of the fairy-tale (*Laughter in the Void*, p. 79).

53 This story, untitled in Kharms's manuscript, is published as 'The Pursuit' ('Pogonya'), in Kharms, '"Moi tvoreniya, synov'ya i docheri moi..."', p. 88.

54 This is a classic example of what Shklovsky called a 'zero ending', examples of which he found in Maupassant's short stories: see Erlich, *Russian Formalism*, p. 244.

55 This text is untitled in Kharms's manuscript.

56 'The Connection', which begins as a letter to an unnamed 'philosopher', may have been addressed specifically to Yakov Druskin, as may 'Five Unfinished Narratives' ('Pyat' neokonchennykh povestvovanii'), written in the same year (1937), which begins 'Dear Yakov Semenovich' (Kharms, *Polet*, p. 498).

57 In his letter to the actress Klavdiya Vasil'evna Pugacheva, written in October 1933 (Kharms, *Polet*, pp. 482–5), Kharms talked about creating an alternative order, or a 'purity of order' ('chistota poryadka') in his art (p. 483).

58 Such information overload is reminiscent of Gogol''s prose: see Cathy Popkin, *The Pragmatics of Insignificance*, chapters 4 and 5. Moreover, this story about an office-worker purchasing a new garment contains parodic echoes of Gogol''s 'The Overcoat'.

59 This text is untitled in Kharms's manuscript. Milner-Gulland has suggested that the name 'Nikandr', which also appears in one or two poems by Kharms, may be a coded reference to Kharms's fellow-*chinar'*, Oleinikov: 'Beyond the Turning-Point', pp. 252–3.

60 Texts such as this suggest a major distinction between Kharms and two authors with whom he has been compared, namely Chekhov and Zoshchenko, since with these last two, as Cathy Popkin notes in her detailed study of narrative insignificance, 'the

"insignificant" story emerges as enormously significant' (*The Pragmatics of Insignificance*, p. 213).

61 See Jaccard, 'Daniil Kharms in the Context of Russian and European Literature of the Absurd', p. 62.

62 Jonathan Culler, *Structuralist Poetics*, p. 130.

63 Barthes discusses two types of reading, one which looks for 'the point', and one which enjoys the experience of negotiating the narrator's discourse for its own sake. See Barthes, *S/Z*, pp. 75–6, and Barthes, *The Pleasure of the Text*.

64 On 'The Connection', see Shukman, 'Towards a Poetics of the Absurd', p. 91.

65 In this way Kharms anticipates the Relevance Theory of linguists Deirdre Wilson and Dan Sperber, for whom 'relevance, and the aim of maximisating relevance, is the key to human cognition': 'An Outline of Relevance Theory', p. 30. For a fuller account of Relevance Theory, see Dan Sperber and Deirdre Wilson, *Relevance: Communication and Cognition*. If Kharms's narrative structures are evidence of a broader interest in the question of language and cognition, then this interest may have been kindled by the work of the Soviet psychologist and linguist, Lev Semenovich Vygotsky (1896–1934). Throughout his life, Vygotsky was interested in the relationship between thinking and speech, particularly in infants and children. He became involved in many of the literary-linguistic debates of post-revolutionary Russia. Although he was based in Moscow, he had many contacts in Leningrad, including the Formalists (but not, it would appear, Bakhtin). Kharms may have come into contact with some of Vygotsky's thought via Mariya Yudina, who during the 1920s was urging everyone whom she knew to read Vygotsky's *The Psychology of Art*, long before it became well known: see Clark and Holquist, *Mikhail Bakhtin*, p. 106.

66 Carrick makes a similar point: 'Daniil Kharms and a Theology of the Absurd', p. 21. Essentially, however, Carrick argues that Kharms 'lays bare the device' of narration in his stories in order to make a point, not about reading, but rather about story-telling and God's ultimate authorship of the world: 'Kharms's miniature stories may be seen as essays on the use of narrative as a means to describe the world' (ibid.).

67 Kleberg, 'The Nature of the Soviet Audience', p. 187. To paraphrase Kleberg, it could be argued that the 1930s saw a reversion in Soviet arts from pragmatics (based on the relation sign/recipient), to semantics (the relation sign/reality): see Kleberg, ibid., p. 172.

68 The full text of *Christmas at the Ivanovs'* is contained in Vvedensky,

PSS, vol. 1, pp. 157–73. All page references to the text will be from this edition.

69 Spencer Golub, 'The Curtainless Stage and the Procrustean Bed', p. 83.

70 See Kleberg, 'The Nature of the Soviet Audience', p. 188.

71 See Marc Slonim, *Russian Theater*, p. 304.

72 Quoted in Slonim, *Russian Theater*, p. 306 (my emphasis). A number of important documents concerning Socialist Realism can be found in English translation in James C. Vaughan, *Soviet Socialist Realism: Origin and Theory*.

73 See, for example, Régine Robin's excellent study, *Socialist Realism: An Impossible Aesthetic*.

74 For an overview of the Socialist Realist novel, see Katerina Clark, *The Soviet Novel: History as Ritual*. On Soviet Socialist Realist cinema, see R. Taylor and D. Spring, *Stalinism and Soviet Cinema*, and P. Kenez, *Cinema and Soviet Society, 1917–1953*, chapter 8. Accounts of Socialist Realism in the theatre can be found in: Slonim, *Russian Theater*, chapter 10; and Harold B. Segel, *Twentieth-Century Russian Drama*, pp. 239–80.

75 See Slonim, *Russian Theater*, p. 325. It was in this year that Zabolotsky began his eight-year imprisonment: see Nikita Zabolotsky, *The Life of Zabolotsky*, pp. 168–225.

76 On the parodic aspects of the play, see, for example, Milivoe Jovanovič, 'A. Vvedensky – parodist: k razboru "Elki u Ivanovykh"'.

77 Foregrounding and disrupting the conventions of theatre, *Christmas at the Ivanovs'* looks back to the deliberate 'theatricality' of Evreinov's notion of 'theatre as such' ('teatr kak takovoi') and Meyerkhol'd's 'stylized' ('uslovnyi') theatre. See, for example, Clayton, *Pierrot in Petrograd*, pp. 76–81 (this contains an account of Meyerkhol'd's famous production of Blok's *The Fairground Booth* (*Balaganchik*), which was premiered in December 1906). On the self-conscious Russian drama of this period, see also Michel Aucouturier, 'Theatricality as a Category of Early Twentieth-Century Russian Culture', and George Kalbouss, 'Russian Drama and The Self-Conscious Play'.

78 Keir Elam, *The Semiotics of Theatre and Drama*, p. 52. My account of the codes and conventions disrupted by Vvedensky is a simplification of Elam's table of conventions: see Elam, pp. 57–62.

79 See Laurence Senelick, 'Introduction', in *Russian Dramatic Theory*, p. xxxviii.

80 Andrey Bely, 'Theater and Modern Drama', p. 149.

81 See, for example, Ju. M. Lotman, 'The Stage and Painting as

Code Mechanisms for Cultural Behavior in the Early Nineteenth Century', pp. 165–6. The notion of drama as 'picture' had under-pinned a number of theoretical pronouncements on the theatre made by the Symbolists. See, for example, Fedor Solgub, 'The Theatre of a Single Will', p. 145. Mayakovsky's *The Bedbug* (*Klop*, 1929) was also divided into nine 'tableaux'.

82 At one moment in 'The Eyewitness and the Rat', Vvedensky creates similar ambivalence between the notion of 'kartina' as a real-life scene, and as a two-dimensional depiction: 'Everyone ran into an adjacent room and saw the following picture. Across the third table there was the following picture' ('Vse vbezhali v postoronnyuyu komnatu i uvideli sleduyushchuyu kartinu. Poperek tret′ego stola stoyala sleduyushchaya kartina'; Vvedensky, *PSS*, vol. I, pp. 122). See also Meilakh, ' "Ya ispytyval slovo na ogne i na stuzhe…" ', p. 41.

83 Vvedensky's intrusive narrator is reminiscent of the author figure in Blok's *The Fairground Booth*, who appears on stage in order to plead that his characters have usurped his power over his own play. In a similar vein, Nikolay Evreinov's dramatic works some-times featured characters who would directly address the audi-ence, with self-referential questions concerning the nature of the author's message, or the author's inability to end his play. See Spencer Golub, 'Mortal Masks', especially pp. 127–8.

84 The detail of the candles floating down a river may be an eschatological image of the kind which abounds in *A Certain Quantity of Conversations*. See pp. 151–6, and Meilakh 'Primecha-niya', in Vvedensky, *PSS*, vol. II, p. 328.

85 For more information on Okhlopkov's productions at his Moscow 'Realistic Theatre', see Nick Worrall, *Modernism to Realism on the Soviet Stage*, pp. 149–69.

86 Nikolay Okhlopkov, 'On Convention', p. 122.

87 On *Christmas at the Ivanovs'* as *balagan*, see Clayton, *Pierrot in Petrograd*, pp. 198–200.

88 See Waugh, *Metafiction*, pp. 28–34.

89 Mayakovsky uses a similar device in his verse-play *Vladimir Mayakovsky: A Tragedy* (*Vladimir Mayakovsky: tragediya*), where 'A Man Without an Ear' can apparently hear, and 'A Man Without a Head' is capable of muttering sounds (albeit unintelligible sounds).

90 Meilakh includes this last example in his survey of *zaum′* in OBERIU: 'Oberiuty i zaum'', p. 365.

91 See Elam, *The Semiotics of Theatre and Drama*, pp. 103–4.

92 This is not to suggest, however, that Vvedensky read Bakhtin's essay, since this is highly unlikely, given the fact that it remained

unpublished for decades, and also that Vvedensky spent much of the 1930s in the Ukraine.

93 Bakhtin, 'Slovo v romane', p. 93. While one should be extremely careful not to confuse 'dialogue' and 'dialogism', it is interesting to note that so many of Vvedensky's texts are constructed as questions-and-answers. See, for example, 'Fact, Theory, and God' ('Fakt, teoriya i bog', 1930), in Vvedensky, *PSS*, vol. II, pp. 61–3.

94 V. N. Voloshinov [M. M. Bakhtin], 'The Construction of the Utterance', p. 122. For a discussion of how Kharms subverts this particular convention in his prose, see Ann Shukman, 'Towards a Poetics of the Absurd'.

95 V. N. Voloshinov [M. M. Bakhtin], 'Discourse in Life and Discourse in Poetry', p. 21.

96 Emphasizing the productive role of the audience, Vvedensky anticipated more recent trends in the theory and practice of theatre. See Susan Bennett, *Theatre Audiences*.

97 This repudiation of naturalistic assumptions about drama links Vvedensky's play to German Expressionist theatre. See the article by Harold B. Segel (although it does not mention Vvedensky), 'German Expressionism and Early Soviet Drama', p. 196. For possible points of comparison between expressionism and OBERIU aesthetics, see Arndt, 'OBERIU'.

98 This may be a specific reference to contemporary attempts to create the illusion of seamless contiguity between the world of the play and the world of the auditorium, such as Okhlopkov's production of A. Serafimovich's play *The Iron Flood*, in which he had his actors openly 'make love' and 'defecate' on stage (see Worrall, *Modernism to Realism on the Soviet Stage*, p. 159).

99 Aleksandrov may have been influenced by the fact that Igor' Bakhterev sub-titled his 1950 mini-drama 'Tsar Makedon, or Fenya and the *Chebolveki*' ('Tsar' Makedon, ili Fenya i chebol-veki'), in which two men engage in a verbal game of domination, as 'A Performance For Reading' ('Predstavlenie dlya chteniya'; Aleksandrov (ed.), *Vanna Arkhimeda*, pp. 434–40). See also Arndt, 'OBERIU', p. 58.

100 See, for example, a review by Vladimir Mirzoev of an adaptation of *Christmas at the Ivanovs'*, Kharms's *Elizaveta Bam* and other OBERIU texts: 'Elizaveta Bam, 62 goda spustya'.

101 See Sologub, 'The Theatre of a Single Will', pp. 138–9. This was how one Moscow director, Mikhail Levitin at the Hermitage Theatre, recently produced Vvedensky's *A Certain Quantity of Conversations*, a dramatic text which also features a subjective narrative voice.

102 Quoted by Martin Esslin, 'Modernist Drama', p. 551.

103 An extract from *The Labours and Days of Svistonov* was first published in *Zvezda*, 5 (1929), 72–90. The novel was subsequently published in full in Leningrad in the same year. Unless otherwise stated, all references to the novel will be from the slightly amended version contained in Vaginov, *Romany*, pp. 162–261.

104 In a comment made in 1926, Mariya Yudina, expressed the need for aesthetic reception to involve active engagement with the work of art, and cited Vaginov as one poet who encouraged such a reader (Yudina, *Mariya Veniaminovna Yudina*, p. 335).

105 The question of possible correspondences between this novel's characters and Vaginov's real-life acquaintances is, with the passage of time, particularly difficult to answer, as Nikol'skaya admits ('Tragediya chudakov', pp. 10–11). One object of parody, however, seems to have been an OBERIU performance, as portrayed in the literary evening which Svistonov stumbles upon at the Leningrad Press Club (pp. 176–7). In particular, Meilakh believes that the poet Mar'ya Stepanova, who is described as taking part in the performance 'without knowing why' stands for Vaginov himself (' "Ya ispytyval slovo na ogne i na stuzhe..." ', p. 48). According to Shepherd, this parodic portrayal 'might be taken as a pointed indication of the distance between the novel and the group's practice' (*Beyond Metafiction*, p. 115).

106 On the diegetic confusion between Vaginov's and Svistonov's novels, see Shepherd, *Beyond Metafiction*, p. 107.

107 M. Gel'fand, 'Zhurnal'noe obozrenie', pp. 70–1. The marginally more moderate Raisa Messer included Vaginov among a number of writers whom she labelled 'neo-bourgeois': 'Poputchiki vtorogo prizyva'. In the same year, Vaginov came under attack for his poetry, with A. Manfred describing him as the 'undertaker-in-chief', inspired by a 'necrophiliac muse', of a group of reactionary poets: Manfred, 'Kladbishchenskaya muza', pp. 32–3. For a more detailed account of contemporary reception of the novel, see Shepherd, *Beyond Metafiction*, pp. 113–14.

108 See, for example, Perlina, 'Konstantin Vaguinov' (who suggests that the novel is a parody of Formalist-inspired narrative techniques used by the 'Serapion Brothers'). For other accounts of *The Labours and Days of Svistonov* as a novel about novel-writing, see Nikol'skaya, 'Konstantin Vaginov, ego Vremya i knigi', and Gerasimova, 'Trudy i dni Konstantina Vaginova'.

109 See also Perlina, who has argued that *The Labours and Days of*

Svistonov constitutes a grotesque-parodic reworking of Bakhtin's 'Author and Hero' essay: Perlina, abstract of 'Vzaimootnosheniya literaturnykh teorii i poeticheskoi praktiki', [p. 2].

110 Anemone suggests the appropriateness to *The Labours and Days of Svistonov* of Reader-Reception Theory, although he does not expand upon this observation ('Carnival in Theory and Practice', p. 10).

111 Leonardo Paleari, 'Tvorchestvo glazami tvortsa', p. iii.

112 The term is Linda Hutcheon's: *Narcissistic Narrative*, p. 34.

113 Svistonov's writing method may point, in a characteristically modernist fashion, to the dialogic nature of human subjectivity in general. As early as 1888, in the preface to his play, *Miss Julie*, the Swedish playwright August Strindberg commented, 'since they are modern characters, living in an age of transition more urgently hysterical at any rate than the age that preceded it, I have drawn them as split and vacillating [. . .] conglomerations of past and present [. . .] scraps from books and newspapers': quoted in Malcolm Bradbury and James Mcfarlane, 'The Name and Nature of Modernism', p. 47.

114 In this sense, *The Labours and Days of Svistonov* may be not so much 'about *The Goat's Song*' (Kasack, 'Vaginov'), as about the initial reception of *The Goat's Song*.

115 See Stanley Fish, *Is There a Text in This Class?*.

116 See Jacques Derrida, *Of Grammatology*.

117 This may be another autobiographical detail; Vaginov knew Old French (see Nikol'skaya, 'Tragediya chudakov', p. 10).

118 Konstantin Vaginov, *Trudy i dni Svistonova* (New York, 1984), p. 147. Interestingly, the revised version of the novel omits the references to Psikhachev and Chavchavadze from this passage, and has a different typographical layout, as a result of which we remain with Svistonov in the bar, and continue to read the framing novel, rather than the framed novel: Vaginov, *Romany*, pp. 257–8. As Shepherd points out (*Beyond Metafiction*, pp. 98–9), there is some ambiguity as to the identity of the Chavchavadze who appears in Svistonov's – and Vaginov's – novel. He may be either the Georgian poet Prince Aleksandr Chavchavadze (1786–1846), son of the Georgian ambassador to the court of Catherine II, and father-in-law of Aleksandr Griboedov, or another Georgian poet, Il'ya Grigor'evich Chavchavadze (1837–1907). On these two figures, see the articles 'Chavchavadzhe, Aleksandr Garsevanovich' and 'Chavchavadzhe, Il'ya Grigor'evich' by G. N. Abzianidze and Sh. D. Radiani respectively.

119 See also Anemone, 'Carnival in Theory and Practice', pp. 9–10.

'Slushatel'' ('listener') was one of the terms which Bakhtin used to express the concept of the 'addressee'.

120 See Anemone, 'Carnival in Theory and Practice', p. 7; and Perlina, abstract of 'Vzaimootnosheniya literaturnykh teorii i poeticheskoi praktiki', [pp. 2–3].

121 See Robert Crosman, 'Do Readers Make Meaning?'.

3 LANGUAGE AND REPRESENTATION

1 Andrey Bely, 'The Magic of Words' (1909), pp. 93–4.

2 Quoted in Russian in Doherty, *The Acmeist Movement*, p. 136.

3 See Cooke, *Velimir Khlebnikov: A Critical Study*, p. 76.

4 Quoted in Cooke, *Velimir Khlebnikov: A Critical Study*, p. 89. On the belief, held by Khlebnikov and other early left artists, in the ability of art to transform reality, see Piper, *V. A. Kaverin*, pp. 25–30.

5 Kruchenykh, *Declaration of the Word as Such*, quoted in Russian in Jaccard, *Daniil Harms*, p. 25.

6 The 'cognitive' theory of art was expressed most forcefully after the Revolution by Aleksandr Voronsky, writing in the journal *Krasnaya nov'*: see Maguire, *Red Virgin Soil*, pp. 193–8.

7 Quoted in English translation in Oulanoff, *The Serapion Brothers*, p. 28.

8 See in particular Kruchenykh's manifesto, *Declaration of Trans-rational Language* (*Deklaratsiya zaumnogo yazyka*), which describes one of the three essential functions of *zaum'* as 'revelation (naming and depicting) of invisible things' (quoted in English translation in Markov, *Russian Futurism*, pp. 345–6).

9 Quoted in Russian in Jaccard, *Daniil Harms*, pp. 45–6. Although he does not use the same term here, Tufanov may have borrowed the idea of 'broadened' perception from Matyushin. On Matyushin's notion of 'broadened vision' ('rasshirennoe smotrenie'), see p. 123.

10 The first *zaum'* production had been Kruchenykh's opera *Victory over the Sun* of 1913.

11 Jaccard compares Terent'ev's concept of 'naturizm' (based on, but distinct from 'naturalism') with the notion of 'real art', since both, he maintains, tend 'towards a representation of a here-now' (*Daniil Harms*, p. 228). Terent'ev's views on theatre as primary reality, rather than secondary representation, link him to Antonin Artaud, who was to develop his own 'Theatre of Cruelty' in France in the 1930s: see Antonin Artaud, *Artaud on Theatre*. For a critical account of Artaud's theatre, see Eric Sellin, *The Dramatic Concepts of Antonin Artaud*.

12 Malevich and Matyushin had both been members of the pre-revolutionary group of artists known as 'Union of Youth' ('Soyuz molodezhi'), which had also included Filonov. On the 'Union', see John E. Bowlt, 'The "Union of Youth"'.

13 See Jaccard, *Daniil Harms*, pp. 90–7.

14 M. Matyushin, 'Dnevnik. 1915–1916', p. 48; quoted in Russian in Jaccard, *Daniil Harms*, p. 91. Selected passages from Matyushin's memoirs and theoretical writings can be found in *K istorii russkogo avangarda*, pp. 129–87.

15 K. Malevich, *Bog ne skinut. Iskusstvo. Tserkov'. Fabrika*, p. 7; quoted in Jaccard, *Daniil Harms*, p. 125. On left art's distinction between 'being' ('byt') and 'becoming' ('bytie'), and its equation of the latter with the 'real' reality of genuine art, see Maguire, *Red Virgin Soil*, pp. 189–90.

16 See Meilakh, ' "Ya ispytyval slovo na ogne i na stuzhe..." ', pp. 9–10. A version of this work in English translation can be found in Malevich, *Essays on Art, 1915–1933*, vol. i, pp. 188–223.

17 See, for example, Shklovsky, 'O poezii i zaumnom yazyke' (recently republished in edited form in Shklovsky, *Gamburgskii schet*, pp. 45–58).

18 See Ann Jefferson, 'Russian Formalism', p. 34.

19 On Bakhtin and referentiality, see Ann Jefferson, 'Realism Reconsidered'.

20 Bakhtin, 'Iskusstvo i otvetstvennost'', p. 6.

21 Letters written by Kharms to the Lipavsky's in the early 1930s are contained in Kharms, *Polet*, pp. 463–73.

22 The fullest accounts published so far are those by Jaccard: see *Daniil Harms*, chapter 3, and his article 'Chinari'.

23 'My pytalis' postroit' novuyu nesubstantsial'nuyu eksistentsial'nuyu ontologiyu'; Druskin, 'Son i Yav'', p. 403.

24 On the importance of the zero in the works of Kharms, Vvedensky, and Oleinikov, see Jaccard, 'Chinari', pp. 83–5. Although Jaccard mentions in this context Oleinikov's poem 'On noughts' ('O nulyakh'), he fails to make the point that this text is almost certainly a parody of the *chinari* and their interest in zeroes and circles: 'Noughts are medicinal little circles, / They are doctors and medical assistants, / Without them the patient cries from [pain in] his kidney, / But with them he shouts "hurray!" ' ('Nuli – tselebnye kruzhochki, / Oni vrachi i fel'dshera, / Bez nikh bol'noi krichit ot pochki, / A s nimi on krichit "ura" '; Oleinikov, *Ya mukhu bezumno lyubil*, p. 6). A keen amateur mathematician, Oleinikov shared Kharms's interest in numbers and the numerical sequence. In his poem 'To Oleinikov' ('Oleinikovu'), dated 23 January 1935,

Kharms refers to his fellow *chinar'* as 'The conductor of numbers' ('Konduktor chisel'; *Sobranie proizvedenii*, vol. IV, p. 38). Two of Kharms's related philosophical texts, 'Null and nil (spelt in the old way)' ('Nul' i nol' (po staroi orfografii)'), and 'On the Circle' ('O kruge'), can be found in Daniil Kharms, 'Neizdannoe', pp. 141–2 and 142–3 respectively.

25 L. Lipavsky, 'Opredelennoe (kachestvo, kharakter, izmenenie...)'; quoted in Jaccard, 'Chinari', p. 81.

26 See Jaccard, 'Chinari', p. 85. Kharms also used the term 'turning-point' ('povorot'). On the importance of this term in his prose and verse, see Milner-Gulland, 'Beyond the Turning-Point'.

27 'Razgovory vestnikov'; quoted in Jaccard, 'Chinari', p. 89. Jaccard directly relates the views of Druskin and Lipavsky on the primacy of language to Kruchenykh's assertion that 'a new verbal form creates a new content' (ibid., pp. 89–90). For the *chinari*, objects and phenomena have beginnings but not ends because they exist in an eternal (i.e. endless) present. This notion of events as beginnings without endings may also help to account for Kharms's habit of disrupting his narratives, analysed in chapter 2 above, and in particular the preponderance of 'zero endings' in his prose. Lipavsky's comment, 'Plot is an unimportant thing ['Syuzhet – neser'eznaya veshch'] [...] because the real link betweeen things is not visible in their usual sequence' is also relevant in this respect (see T. Lipavskaya, 'Vstrechi s Nikolaem i ego druz'yami', p. 53).

28 For a fuller discussion of Lipavsky's 'A Theory of Words', see Jaccard, *Daniil Harms*, pp. 193–6.

29 L. Lipavsky, unpublished note, quoted in Jaccard, *Daniil Harms*, p. 196. The reference to the nineteen scenes of Kharms's play *Elizaveta Bam* as 'pieces' ('kuski') may be a conscious echo of Lipavsky's use of the word 'kusok' to describe the units into which language divides the world.

30 Lipavsky, 'Teoriya slov'; quoted in Jaccard, 'Chinari', p. 89.

31 See Yakov Druskin, 'Razgovory vestnikov' (1932). One chapter from this, entitled 'Vestniki i ikh razgovory', is contained in Druskin, *Vblizi vestnikov*, pp. 230–2. It is unclear when Lipavsky first introduced the term.

32 The downside to this, of course, was the possibility that the world only appeared to exist (part of the Petersburg myth). Both Kharms and Vvedensky asked the question 'do I exist?' in their work; see Jaccard, 'Chinari'.

33 Quoted in Henry Orlov, 'Predislovie', in Druskin, *Vblizi vestnikov*, p. 9.

34 The Russian word 'real′nyi' means 'real' precisely in the ontological sense of 'not imaginary'

35 See Nikol′skaya, 'The Oberiuty and The Theatricalisation of Life'. A photograph of Kharms masquerading as Ivan Ivanovich Kharms can be found in Kharms, *Polet*, p. 352.

36 Goldstein identifies the notion of 'concreteness' ('predmetnost′') as 'a basic principle of OBERIU aesthetics' (*Nikolai Zabolotsky*, p. 32).

37 'U iskusstva svoya logika' (Milner-Gulland, '"Left Art"', p. 71). Compare Lunts's assertion in the Serapions' manifesto that 'a work of literature must be organic, real, live its own special life' (see Oulanoff, *The Serapion Brothers*, p. 27).

38 Despite the fact that the OBERIU article contains only one reference to the concrete *word* (in the description of the group's members as 'people of a concrete world, object, and word'), Jaccard asserts that the concrete materiality of the word ('[l']objectalité des mots') is the 'cornerstone' of the OBERIU declaration (*Daniil Harms*, p. 121).

39 This poem was written at about the time that Zabolotsky began attending *chinari* meetings. No research has yet been conducted on the possible influence of *chinari* philosophy on Zabolotsky's verse. Jaccard asserts that the poems contained in Zabolotsky's *Stolbtsy* collection of 1929 (which does not include 'The Face of a Horse') constitutes the sole point of contact between *chinari* thought and Zabolotsky's aesthetics – a point which he does not substantiate, however (*Daniil Harms*, p. 136).

40 For a discussion of 'The Battle of the Elephants', see Goldstein, *Nikolai Zabolotsky*, pp. 187–9.

41 See Milner-Gulland, 'Beyond the Turning-Point', p. 254, and Goldstein, *Nikolai Zabolotsky*, pp. 103, and 127–8.

42 The full poem is contained in Oleinikov, *Ya mukhu bezumno lyubil*, pp. 6–8.

43 Despite this poem's comic tone, Druskin takes it entirely seriously, suggesting that it shows how the individual human subject can contain a 'neighbouring world' within her/himself: Druskin, 'Son i Yav′', p. 391.

44 It is, however, interesting that he should have provided the story 'The Shop with a Hole in it' with the alternative title 'the *Chinar′-Molvoka*': see Bakhterev, 'Starik Bakhterev', p. 24.

45 The full text is contained in Aleksandrov (ed.), *Vanna Arkhimeda*, pp. 433–4. There are also more obvious links here with the surrealist notion of 'surreality', predicated upon just such a conflation of dream and reality. The surrealist element in OBERIU has been the subject of a small number of generally

unsubstantiated generalizations made by scholars. See, for example, Tjalsma, 'The Petersburg Poets', p. 72 (on OBERIU as a group), Terras, 'Vaginov, Konstantin Konstantinovich' (on Vaginov's novels), and D. P. Gallagher, 'The Surrealist Mode in Twentieth-Century Russian Literature', chapter 5 (on Kharms's prose).

46 There is also what appears to be a parodic reference to this notion of a 'neighbouring world' ('mir sosednii') penetrating into our own world in the opening speech of Bakhterev's playlet 'The Ancient Greek Squabble (A Vaudeville)' ('Drevnegrecheskaya razmolvka (vodevil')').

47 For a discussion of Kharms's views on language in the context of the Russian avant-garde, see Fedor Uspensky and Elena Babaeva, 'Grammatika "absurda" i "absurd" grammatiki'.

48 See in particular Jaccard, *Daniil Harms*, pp. 247–81. Of course, Kharms does at times echo the call made by Kruchenykh or Tufanov for the poet to go beyond 'everyday' language in order to understand the true meaning of existence. See, for example, his philosophical text of 1927 entitled 'Objects and Figures Discovered by Daniil Ivanovich Kharms' ('Predmety i figury otkrytye Daniilom Ivanovichem Kharmsom'), in which he talks about the essential, or 'fifth', meaning of an object or a word (as opposed to its four 'working' meanings), which becomes apparent only when the object or word is placed in an unfamiliar context. The Russian text can be found as an appendix to Levin, 'The Fifth Meaning of the Motor-Car', pp. 299–300, and also in Kharms, '"Bitva so smyslami" Daniila Kharmsa', p. 6.

49 Kharms, '"Bozhe, kakaya uzhasnaya zhizn'…"', p. 196. On Kharms's interest in ancient alphabets and hieroglyphs, see Aleksandr Nikitaev, 'Tainopis' Daniila Kharmsa: opyt deshifrovki'.

50 The entire letter is contained in Kharms, *Polet*, pp. 482–5.

51 It is possible to interpret Kharms's use of the leitmotif of the 'turning-point' ('povorot') as another way of expressing the 'impediment'. This would explain the appearance of this leitmotif as the last word of the *Incidents* cycle (see Milner-Gulland, 'Beyond the Turning-Point'). According to this interpretation, once we go beyond the impediment/turning-point that is the text, there can be nothing but 'nothing', an absolute ontological void. It is, of course, into just such a void that Rakukin's soul falls at the end of the 'Pakin and Rakukin' story and of the cycle as a whole (it disappears 'in the distance' ['vdali'] beyond the turning-point; see Kharms, *Polet*, p. 397).

52 The full Russian text is contained in Jaccard, 'De la réalité au texte', pp. 304–6.

53 Jaccard, 'De la réalité au texte', p. 304.

54 Jaccard interprets the fairy as a *vestnik*, a messenger from another, neighbouring world: see *Daniil Harms*, p. 163.

55 The full text is contained in Kharms, *Polet*, pp. 317–18.

56 This short text can be read in a number of different ways. For an exhaustive discussion of its philosophical (and even theological) ramifications, see Neil Carrick, 'Daniil Kharms and the Art of Negation'. As Aizlewood also observes, the note 'against Kant' written under this text in Kharms's manuscript alludes to Kant's phenomenological model of understanding (essentially the belief that there exists a first-order reality, independently of our perception of it): see 'Towards an Interpretation of Kharms's *Sluchai*', p. 107. This comment notwithstanding, Aizlewood chooses to discuss this text primarily in socio-political terms, as 'an account of someone who becomes a non-person' in Stalinist Russia (ibid., p. 102). Kharms's text is also discussed briefly in Elizabeth Wright, *Psychoanalytic Criticism: Theory and Practice*, p. 179 (it also features as the epigraph to Wright's book; p. xiii).

57 On state-sanctioned terror as a series of 'language games', see Jean-François Lyotard, *The Postmodern Condition: A Report on Knowledge*.

58 This may be behind Anemone's interesting claim that towards the end of the 1930s, 'Kharms gradually becomes aware that his role, as an artist, was one of complicity in the creation of a monstrous social order' ('The Anti-World of Daniil Kharms', p. 81). Much of George Orwell's novel *1984* (1949) is devoted to the ways in which Big Brother manipulates language in order to preserve his political power. For a brief comparative study of aspects of Kharms's prose and Orwell's novel, see Carrick, 'Daniil Kharms and the Art of Negation', pp. 629–33. One typical example of this habit of speaking one's own truth came in Zabolotsky's own interrogation. In 1938, while in custody facing the charge of having participated in an anti-Soviet conspiracy led by Nikolay Tikhonov, Zabolotsky read a newspaper article which revealed not only that Tikhonov was at liberty, but that he had recently been awarded a state prize for literature; see Nikita Zabolotsky, *The Life of Zabolotsky*, chapter 4.

59 See Kharms, *Sluchai*, pp. 14–16.

60 On the 'Orwellian dimensions' of the 'crucial break between signifiers and signifieds' in this piece, see also Anemone, 'The Anti-World of Daniil Kharms', p. 86.

61 Published in Kharms, *Polet*, pp. 340–3.

62 Kharms, *Polet*, pp. 348–50 (untitled in Kharms's manuscript).

63 It was the word of a denunciator which caused Kharms to lose his own life: see Mikhail Meilakh, 'Daniil Kharms: anecdota posthuma'.

64 The following is an adapted, and much shortened version of my 'Of Words and Worlds: Language Games in *Elizaveta Bam* by Daniil Kharms'.

65 The phrase 'tragedy of language' is used by Jaccard to link Kharms's play with the later, Western Absurdist notion that human communication is impossible: *Daniil Harms*, p. 247 (see also Jaccard's 'Daniil Kharms: teatr absurda – real'nyi teatr'). However, by the association which it makes between language and power, Kharms's work belongs more closely to another tradition, one which includes plays by writers as diverse as Václav Havel, Eugène Ionesco, David Mamet and Sam Shepard. On this tradition, see Jeanette Malkin, *Verbal Violence in Contemporary Drama*.

I shall refer throughout to the 'scenic' version of the play, in which each of the nineteen sections ('kuski', a key Lipavskian concept, which means literally 'bits', or 'pieces') is given a generic title. For a brief history of the fate of the manuscripts of the two versions of the play see Meilakh, 'Kharms's Play *Elizaveta Bam*', pp. 210–12. All translations of the play are my own, and will be followed by a page reference to the original Russian 'scenic' version (or, in the case of the last scene, to the 'standard' version), as published in Meilakh, 'O "Elizavete Bam"' (pp. 220–40).

66 See, for example, Meilakh, 'Oberiuty i zaum'', p. 371.

67 Mention of the arrest of Katsman is made in Meilakh, 'O "Elizavete Bam"', p. 170. L. S. Druskina has recently refuted the view that *Elizaveta Bam* was written as a reaction to repression in the Soviet Union at this time: see her introduction to Druskin, 'Kommunikativnost'', p. 81.

68 There is some ambiguity as to the status of these headings. It is unclear whether they were written by one, or more than one person, or, indeed, whether they were written by Kharms at all; see Meilakh, 'Kharms's Play *Elizaveta Bam*', p. 202. Stelleman, on the other hand, appears to treat the section headings as part of the basic text. She believes that they were presented to the public prior to each scene, rather like the captions used in cabaret or street theatre: 'The Transitional Position of *Elizaveta Bam* between Avant-Garde and Neo-Avant-Garde', p. 228. (This is a revised version of Stelleman's article, 'An Analysis of *Elizaveta Bam*'.)

69 See Lipavsky, 'Iz razgovorov "chinarei"', p. 125.

70 The standard 'ешь' ((you) eat) is given as 'есшь' in Meilakh's publication. See however, Kharms, *Polet*, p. 191, which has 'ешь'. Nakhimovsky sees the influence of Khlebnikov in the way in which Kharms plays with language here (*Laughter in the Void*, p. 39).

71 The first scholar to suggest similarities between *Elizaveta Bam* and later West European theatre was Alicia Wŏjodźko: 'Poeci z "Oberiu"'. The first Soviet critic to do so was V. Kaverin: 'V starom dome', p. 151. For a fuller discussion of the play as 'Absurdist', see also, Bertram Müller, *Absurde Literatur in Rußland*, pp. 78–94; Jaccard, 'Daniil Kharms – teatr absurda, real'nyi teatr'; and Jenny Stelleman, *Aspects of Dramatic Communication*, chapter 6.

72 It is impossible to date many of the key *chinari* concepts. What one can say, however, is that these concepts were generally developed over a considerable time, sometimes before they were given a specific name. Such may well have been the case with those *chinari* concepts relevant to *Elizaveta Bam*.

73 For Wittgenstein's theory of language games see his *Philosophical Investigations*. Although he knew German, Kharms makes no reference to Wittgenstein in his personal notes. Wittgenstein's *Tractatus Logico-Philosophicus* was first published in the USSR in 1958. For an extended Wittgensteinian reading of *Elizaveta Bam* see my 'Of Words and Worlds'. Milner-Gulland mentions Wittgenstein's 'language games' to support his assertion that much of Kharms's poetry constitutes an investigation 'into the nature and workings of language, into its relationship or non-relationship with our conceptual world and with the real world of objects' ('"Kovarnye stikhi"', p. 32).

74 For a more Bakhtinian reading of the play, and also one which is more gender-oriented, see Graham Roberts, 'Poor Liza: The Sexual Politics of *Elizaveta Bam* by Daniil Kharms'.

75 See Druskin, 'Son i Yav'', p. 381.

76 A number of critics take this view. See, for example: Revzina, 'Kachestvennaya i funktsional'naya kharakteristika vremeni v poezii A. I. Vvedenskogo'.

77 For a discussion of this text, see M. Meilakh, 'Neskol'ko slov o "Kupriyanove i Natashe" Aleksandra Vvedenskogo'.

78 For Vvedensky's thoughts on the relationship between time and death in his 'Grey Notebook', and in particular his understanding of death as a 'miracle' affording access to the 'timelessness' of the afterlife, see the discussion of *Minin and Pozharsky* in chapter 1, above.

79 These works are contained in Vvedensky, *PSS*, vol. I, pp. 54–63 and 67–9.

80 By far the best analysis of this text published so far, and one which looks at Vvedensky's treatment of space as well as time, is Aleksandr Kobrinsky, 'Sistema organizatsii prostranstva v poeme Aleksandra Vvedenskogo "Krugom vozmozhno Bog"'. Kobrinsky maintains that *All Around Maybe God* was written as a 'play to be read', a genre which, he claims, is characteristic for Vvedensky (p. 94). In Vvedensky's use of the word 'krugom' ('all around'), there may be an echo of Matyushin's assertion that in order to represent the world adequately, 'one must learn to see everything from all around' ('neobkhodimo priuchat'sya videt' vse krugom'): quoted in Jaccard, *Daniil Harms*, p. 91.

81 Yakov Druskin, 'Kommunikativnost''. In her introduction to this article, L. S. Druskina tells us (p. 80) that it constitutes the fifth chapter of Druskin's major study of Vvedensky's work, entitled 'Zvezda bessmyslitsy' ('The Star of Nonsense').

82 On the eschatological significance of this co-identity between words and things, see also Meilakh, ' "Ya ispytyval slovo na ogne i na stuzhe..." ', p. 27.

83 The word for 'tribe', 'plemya', is written without inverted commas in Vvedensky's original. This has the effect of blurring the distinction between the word and its object, although it should be pointed out that in much of his work Vvedensky either ignored standard rules of punctuation or, as in this particular piece, used no punctuation marks at all. The question of punctuation in various works by Vvedensky has been the subject of a certain polemic amongst OBERIU scholars. Milner-Gulland believes that Vvedensky adopted punctuation 'rather suddenly after his public readings became a thing of the past' (' "Kovarnye stikhi" ', p. 28).

84 In Vvedensky, *PSS*, vol. I, p. 109, 'шепот' is misprinted as 'шопот'. The full text of this poem, written between 1931 and 1933, can be found in Vvedensky, *PSS*, vol. I, pp. 109–11.

85 As in the previous example, 'шепот' is misprinted in Vvedensky, *PSS* as 'шопот'. Like the word 'plemya' in 'Two Birds', the word 'shkaf' ('cupboard') is not written in inverted commas by Vvedensky (as if to blur the distinction between word and object). The term 'cupboard' had a similar metapoetic significance for Vvedensky as it had for Kharms: see Meilakh, 'Shkap i kolpak'.

86 See Meilakh, ' "Ya ispytyval slovo na ogne i na stuzhe..." ', p. 41.

87 Druskin does, however, analyse the semantic slippage between different pronouns as employed by Vvedensky (see 'Kommunikativnost'', pp. 86–94). For a discussion of semantics in Vvedensky's

work as a whole, see Mikhail Meilakh, 'Semanticheskii eksperiment v poeticheskoi rechi'.

88 Vvedensky, *PSS*, vol. 1, pp. 135–41.

89 Compare this with Bakhterev's verse, 'I asked: / what time? / He answered: / A white table' ('Ya sprosila: / skol′ko vremya? / On otvetil: / Belyi stol'): quoted in Sigov, 'Istoki poetiki Oberiu', p. 94.

90 In his study of Vvedensky's work, for example, Druskin suggests that the four speakers, Zumir, Kumir, Tumir, and Chumir, in 'Four Descriptions' may be *vestniki* from another, neighbouring world (Druskin, 'Son i Yav'', p. 392).

91 Vvedensky, *PSS*, vol. 1, pp. 127–8.

92 Vvedensky, *PSS*, vol. 1, pp. 47–50. This work, written during the OBERIU period, was dedicated to Zabolotsky.

93 The following section is a revised and abridged version of my 'Diabolical Dialogue or Divine Discourse?'.

94 This text, the full title of which is *A Certain Quantity of Conversations (or a completely reworked themebook)* (*Nekotoroe kolichestvo razgovorov (ili nachisto peredelannyi temnik)*), is contained in Vvedensky, *PSS*, vol. 1, pp. 142–56. Throughout the rest of this chapter the title of this text will generally be shortened to *Conversations*. Aleksandrov believes that Vvedensky intended his cycle of conversations to be comparable to Kharms's prose cycle *Incidents* (Aleksandrov, 'Evrika Oberiutov', p. 31).

95 The same could be said about *Christmas at the Ivanovs'*, written a year after the *Conversations*, in which 'real' people and events are flattened into two-dimensional representations.

96 This conversation, constructed as a language game, may be a parody of *chinari* conversations, rather like certain sections of Kharms's *Elizaveta Bam* (see above).

97 Kobrinsky sees a similar comment on the inability of human language to express the mysteries of the universe at the heart of *All Around Maybe God*: 'Sistema organizatsii prostranstva', p. 101.

98 The discussion which follows is based loosely on the communication model established by O. G. Revzina and I. I. Revzin, 'Semioticheskii eksperiment na stsene'. On the applicability of such a model to the *Conversations*, see Nakhimovsky, *Laughter in the Void*, p. 139.

99 See also Kharms's dramatic sketch, 'The Mathematician and Andrey Semenovich', in which everything which is said is repeated (Kharms, *Polet*, pp. 368–9).

100 A similar effect is achieved in 'Four Descriptions'.

101 As Druskin remarks, this comment means in effect that 'conversa-

tion is equated with non-conversation' ('Kommunikativnost'', p. 85). Examples of this abound in Vvedensky's *oeuvre*. 'Fact, Theory, and God', for example, contains the lines, spoken by/as 'fact', 'I see everything and speak / and say nothing' ('ya vizhu vse i govoryu / i nichego ne govoryu'; *PSS*, vol. 1, p. 61). And one line of the dialogue in '24 Hours' ('Sutki') is described as a 'non-existent reply' ('nesushchestvuyushchii otvet'; ibid., p. 132).

102 Aleksandr Kobrinsky briefly mentions Heidegger in connection with Vvedensky's *All Around Maybe God*: 'Sistema organizatsii prostranstva', p. 95. Vvedensky's jibe at Kant in the ninth conversation ('shame on Kant; 'Kantu styd'; p. 154) foreshadows Heidegger's critique of Kant's substantial ontology: see Allen Thiher, *Words in Reflection*, pp. 45–6.

103 Martin Heidegger, 'The Origin of the Work of Art', p. 275. The full version can be found in Martin Heidegger, *Poetry, Language, Thought*, pp. 17–87.

104 It is towards the realm of silence, argues Mikhail Epshtein, that the discursive discontinuity of a certain type of avant-garde literature ultimately points: 'The denigration of language, and the debasement of thought are ways of showing another, silent reality, for which there are not, nor can there be, any words'; Mikhail Epshtein, 'Iskusstvo avangarda i religioznoe soznanie', p. 230. The notion of the afterlife as a realm of silence is made more explicit in 'Potets', which Vvedensky wrote around the same time as the *Conversations* (*PSS* vol. 1, pp. 135–41). At the end of this text, a father, surrounded by his sons, dies: 'And the gates of heaven opened, [...] In a flash came a terrible silence' ('I vdrug otkrylis' dveri raya, [...] Vmig nastupila strashnaya tishina'; p. 140).

105 Nakhimovsky argues that Vvedensky distinguishes, in *Christmas at the Ivanovs'*, between humans and animals, on the basis that animals can understand and articulate certain existential truths; *Laughter in the Void*, p. 145.

106 On the silence of the natural world in Vvedensky's 'I am sorry that I am not a wild beast', see Meilakh's notes to the poem, in Vvedensky, *PSS*, vol. II, p. 301. On the importance given in Vaginov's poetry to the 'language' of Nature, see Anemone, 'Konstantin Vaginov and the Leningrad Avant-Garde', p. 139. Nature was also an important theme in Zabolotsky's post-OBERIU verse: see R. R. Milner-Gulland, 'Zabolotsky: Philosopher-Poet'.

107 Karsten Harries, 'Language and Silence: Heidegger's Dialogue with Georg Trakl', p. 164.

108 Martin Heidegger, quoted in English translation in Harries, 'Language and Silence', p. 165. That Heidegger here seems to echo the unknown poet in Vaginov's *The Goat Song* is ironic. If Vaginov ultimately distances himself from the unknown poet's Symbolist credo, Vvedensky might appear here to embrace that credo. However, whereas the unknown poet envisaged madness as a means of passing from one kind of life to another, the madness depicted in Vvedensky's *Conversations* leads from life to death. Moreover, the unknown poet's suicide is motivated not by the Heideggerean desire for 'holy silence', but rather by the belief that 'high' art is no longer possible in post-revolutionary Leningrad.

109 This notion of God speaking without words is also evoked in one of Kharms's poems: 'Spirit of God, speak, Thou hast no need of words' ('Dukh Bozhii govori, Tebe ne nado slov'; Kharms, *Sobranie proizvedenii*, vol. IV, p. 56).

110 Druskin discusses the notions of *vestniki* and neighbouring worlds in relation to Vvedensky's *Conversations*: 'Son i Yav'', p. 391.

111 This chronotopic aspect of Vaginov's early poetry was appreciated by contemporary reviewers. See, for example, V. R[ozhdestvensky]'s review of *Journey into Chaos*. According to Anemone, the sudden, unexpected shifts in time and space characteristic of Vaginov's poetry 'are motivated by the fantastic reality of the revolutionary era' itself ('Konstantin Vaginov and the Leningrad Avant-Garde', p. 229).

112 In the 1991 reprint of the 1931 edition of *Opyty soedineniya slov posredstvom ritma*, from which 'Hermits' is taken, there is a different typography, which implies that these lines are contained in the song which the poet hears, rather than spoken by the poet himself. Furthermore, the second quoted line ends 'quieter than doves' ('tishe golubei'; *Opyty*, p. 23).

113 Once again, there are significant textual differences between Chertkov's edition and the reprinted 1931 edition; in the latter, the section of 'The Song of Words' beginning 'Slovo v teatral'nom kostyume' is the second, not the third (*Opyty*, p. 52).

114 This interpretation is an extension of Anemone's reading of Vaginov's poetry. In his analysis of 'Hermits', for example, Anemone sees Vaginov's assertion of what he calls 'the life of the imagination' as part of the poet's belief in the possibility of transcendence through art ('Konstantin Vaginov and the Leningrad Avant-Garde', pp. 193–5). Elsewhere in his study, Anemone is more specific as to the nature of this transcendence, claiming that in his early poetry Vaginov erases temporal and spatial boundaries specifically in order to underline the fact that 'only

through Art can man hope to gain immortality' (ibid., p. 186). The poems which Anemone mentions in this respect are the two untitled pieces which begin 'Amid wondrous nocturnal wanderings' ('Sredi nochnykh blistatel'nykh bluzhdanii'), and 'Rhodes is noisy, Aleksandria does not sleep' ('Shumit Rodos, ne spit Aleksandriya'), both of which were written in 1922 (see Vaginov, *Sobranie stikhotvorenii*, p. 123 and 124 respectively).

115 Vaginov, *Romany*, p. 262. All references to *Bambocciade* will be to the edition contained in Vaginov, *Romany*, pp. 262–370, and will be marked by the page reference in the text. The term 'Bambocciata' refers to 'a genre of painting which deals with peasant life and bawdy scenes. 17th-c. Dutch and Flemish artists were particularly given to it' (Read (ed.), *The Thames and Hudson Dictionary of Art and Artists*, p. 28).

116 The rather aimless life led by most of the novel's characters has prompted one or two critics to see *Bambocciade* as a parody of the eighteenth-century adventure novel; see, for example, Nikol'skaya, 'Tragediya chudakov', p. 16, and Perlina, 'Konstantin Vaguinov', pp. 477–8.

117 Blyum and Martynov ('Petrogradskie bibliofily', p. 232) suggest that the figure of Felinflein is largely based on the contemporary Leningrad bibliophile Sergey Aleksandrovich Mukhin.

118 In this respect, Felinflein may be modelled on Vaginov himself, who, by 1931 was suffering from incurable tuberculosis (see Gerasimova, 'Trudy i dni Konstantina Vaginova', p. 158 and Nikol'skaya and Erl', 'Primechaniya', p. 576). On the other hand, he seems not to have begun visiting sanatoria until some time in the 1930s, after he had completed *Bambocciade* (see Nikol'skaya, 'Kanva biografii i tvorchestva', p. 77).

119 On the theme of play in *Bambocciade*, see Gerasimova, 'Trudy i dni Konstantina Vaginova', p. 159.

120 The simulation of an alternative reality is one of four basic types of play identified by Roger Caillois: *Man, Play and Games*. For a brief discussion of Caillois' philosophy of play, and its applicability to literature, see Waugh, *Metafiction* pp. 34–47.

121 On the thematic link between art and play in *Bambocciade*, see Gerasimova, 'Trudy i dni Konstantina Vaginova', p. 159.

122 On the importance of *mise en abyme* in Vaginov's *The Labours and Days of Svistonov*, see Shepherd, *Beyond Metafiction*, pp. 106–8.

123 One contemporary reviewer saw this society as a thinly disguised counter-revolutionary organization: K. Aleksandrova, [review of *Bambocciade*]. See also I. Bachelis, 'Melkii bes-mladshii, ili syn uchitelya Peredonova'. On the significance of the theme of kitsch

in *Bambocciade*, see Dubravka Ugrešić, 'Avangard i sovremen-nost''. Toropulo, Punshevich, and the 'Society for the Collection of Trivia' also appear briefly in Vaginov's subsequent novel, *Harpagoniana* (see above, chapter 1).

124 The cake-shop ceiling is particularly important for the way in which Vaginov's description of it blurs the distinction between the world depicted in the painting and the world of the shop itself. The ontological confusion thus generated in the text is a variety of the 'aporetic duplication' (of framed text and framing text) to be found in Vaginov's *The Labours and Days of Svistonov*, as well as in contemporary novels such as Leonid Leonov's *The Thief* (*Vor*, 1927), and André Gide's *The Counterfeiters* (*Les Faux-monnayeurs*, 1925). On these last three novels, see Shepherd, *Beyond Metafiction*, pp. 41–51. Such confusion between different diegetic levels of the text is, as Patricia Waugh suggests, a classic metafictional strategy: 'In metafiction the historical world and the alternative or fantasy world are held in tension, and the relationship between them – between "play" and "reality" – is the main focus of the text' (Waugh, *Metafiction*, p. 38).

125 This is perhaps why kitsch is so important in *Bambocciade*, for, as Matei Calinescu maintains, 'the curious semiotic ambiguity of most kitsch [...means that] such objects are intended to look both genuine and skilfully fake': *Faces of Modernity. Avant-Garde. Decadence. Kitsch*, p. 252.

126 Felinflein's confusion of the image (the 'snow-woman') and the real thing (the woman) underlines a basic fact concerning aesthetic perception; once the perceiver recognizes one element in any representation from our own world, she/he constructs a whole, an entire ontology based on that representation. What is unsaid, or not included in the representation, is mentally sketched in by the perceiver. Vaginov may have been exposed to such a theory of aesthetic perception from his reading of Philostratus' biography of Apollonius of Tyana, who was deeply interested in the psychology of art. As E. H. Gombrich puts it, paraphrasing Apollonius' view: 'The mind of the beholder [...] has its share in the imitation. Even a picture in monochrome, or a bronze relief, strikes us as a resemblance – we see it as form and expression': *Art and Illusion*, p. 155.

127 Elam, *The Semiotics of Theatre and Drama*, p. 99.

128 Eugen Fink, 'The Oasis of Happiness', p. 23.

129 The cat in question is the eponymous hero of E. T. A. Hoffmann's novel, *Tomcat Murr* (*Kater Murr*, 1820–1; see Vaginov, *Romany*, p. 578).

130 See also Gerasimova, 'Trudy i dni Konstantina Vaginova', p. 159.

131 Whereas the mirrors in *Bambocciade* emphasize that the real and imaginary worlds are not the same, Vvedensky uses mirrors to suggest that the world of the imagination is *more* real than the everyday world.

132 Fink makes this point particularly well ('The Oasis of Happiness', p. 27).

133 Christine Brooke-Rose, *A Rhetoric of the Unreal*, p. 338.

134 On the anti-mimetic thrust of the metafictional tradition, extending back to Cervantes, see Robert Alter, *Partial Magic*.

135 On Kharms's 'playful' character, see, for example: Alisa Poret, 'Vospominaniya o Daniile Kharmse'; and Nikol'skaya, 'The Oberiuty and the Theatricalisation of Life'. On play as the *modus vivendi* of the OBERIU group as a whole, see Aleksandr Ponomarev, ' "Nastoyashchee" v luchshikh ego proyavleniyakh', p. 87.

136 An interesting comparison could be drawn between *Bambocciade*, and a poem from 1928, which begins 'Slova iz pepla slepok' ('Words from the ash of moulds'). In this poem Vaginov dismisses his youthful, formalist method of composing poetry by juxtaposing words in unexpected ways and subsequently 'guessing' their meaning (an approach which the poet describes as soulless, and equates specifically with playing a game ('ya prosto tak, igrayu'; Vaginov, *Sobranie stikhotvorenii*, p. 175). On this poem, see Anemone, 'Konstantin Vaginov and the Leningrad Avant-Garde', p. 243.

137 Anemone, 'Konstantin Vaginov and the Leningrad Avant-Garde', pp. 186–7. However, Anemone reads one of Vaginov's very last poems, written in a sanatorium just three months before his death, as an affirmation of the power of art over death. Commenting on 'Leningrad', and in particular the lines, 'Alas, there is no way one can destroy / The vision of a carefree youth' ('Uvy, nikak ne istrebit' / Viden'e yunosti bespechnoi'; Vaginov, *Sobranie stikhotvorenii*, p. 207), Anemone asserts: 'At the end of his journey, Vaginov returns to his starting point, his belief in the saving power of art. He cannot free himself of his youthful faith in the power of art to overcome death, for that would mean to deny the meaning and purpose of art itself' ('Konstantin Vaginov and the Leningrad Avant-Garde', p. 269). Although, as Anemone suggests, Vaginov may have rediscovered his faith in art in the last few months of his life, in 1930, when he completed *Bambocciade*, he appeared to have abandoned it for ever.

138 The rejection of a life of play, motivated by an awareness of the

inevitability of death, is also a theme of one of Vaginov's early poems: 'Play, player. It's the cemetery for you, all the same' ('Igrai igrok. Ved' vse ravno kladbishche'); quoted in Arlen Viktorovich Blyum, *Za kulisami 'Ministerstva Pravdy'*, p. 240.

139 Gerasimova's assertion that the ontology of art is as real in *Bambocciade* as it is in *The Goat's Song* ('Trudy i dni Konstantina Vaginova', p. 159) must surely be questioned.

140 Toropulo may also have in mind those wrappers which do not depict anything immediately recognizable as 'political' or 'historical': see A. K. Zholkovsky's ideological reading of a Latvian sweet wrapper, featuring leaves and the word 'October': '19 oktjabrja 1982 g., or The Semiotics of a Soviet Cookie Wrapper'. The notion that something as banal as a sweet wrapper may indeed reflect the ideological purview of the society which produced it was expressed by a despairing Mayakovsky in a comment he made at one of his last public appearances before his suicide:

> twenty years ago we Futurists raised the subject of a new beauty. We said that the marble beauty of museums, all those Venuses of Milo with their lopped-off arms, all that Greek classical beauty, could never satisfy the millions who were now entering into a new life in our noisy cities, and who would soon be treading the path of revolution. Just now [...] our chairwoman offered me a sweet with Mossel'prom on it; and above that there was the same old Venus. So, the thing you've been fighting against for twenty years has now won. And now this lopsided old beauty is being circulated among the masses, even on sweetpapers, poisoning our brains and our whole idea of beauty all over again. (quoted in Boris Thomson, *Lot's Wife*, p. 73).

141 In particular, *Bambocciade* may be a parody of the view put forward in Bakhtin's *The Formal Method* that literature is not just an imitation of other imitations of the real world, but an ideological (in the general sense) refraction of other ideological refractions of reality.

CONCLUSION: OBERIU – BETWEEN MODERNISM AND POSTMODERNISM?

1 See Raymond Federman, 'Fiction Today or the Pursuit of Non-Knowledge', p. 122.

2 See, for example, Jaccard, *Daniil Harms*, p. 137, and Milner-Gulland, ' "Kovarnye stikhi" ', p. 17.

3 Quoted in Kern, 'The Serapion Brothers', p. 245.

4 See Segal, 'Literatura kak okhrannaya gramota', and Shepherd, *Beyond Metafiction*, chapter 1.

5 On Kazakov, see Bertram Müller, 'Zagadochnyi mir Vladimira Kazakova', introduction to Vladimir Kazakov, *Sluchainyi voin.* Müller claims that it was as writers of the Absurd that Vvedensky and Kharms influenced Kazakov ('Zagadochnyi mir', p. 7). Wolfgang Kasack makes a similar point: 'Oberiu', p. 227.

6 On Narbikova, see Riitta Pittman, 'Valeriya Narbikova's Iconoclastic Prose'.

7 On Pirandello's metatheatre, and its relation to Russian drama of the 1920s and 1930s (including works by Kharms and Vvedensky), see Clayton, *Pierrot in Petrograd*, chapter 6.

8 Samuel Beckett, *The Unnamable*, p. 7.

9 For studies of the French New Novel as metafiction, see Stephen Heath, *The Nouveau Roman: A Study in the Practice of Writing*, and Ann Jefferson, *The Nouveau Roman and the Poetics of Fiction*. Also relevant in this respect is Calvino's arch-metafictional novel *If on a Winter's Night a Traveller* (*Se una notte d'inverno un viaggiatore*, 1979). On Italian metafiction, see Gregory Lucente, *Beautiful Fables: Self-Consciousness in Italian Narrative from Manzoni to Calvino*.

10 Herta Schmidt, 'Postmodernism in Russian Drama', p. 166. Amal'rik claimed that his plays bore the influence of Kharms: 'O sebe kak pisatele p'es', p. 7.

11 One should, of course, be careful when using the term 'postmodernist' in the context of Russian literature. It is not just that, to quote Herta Schmidt, 'in the field of Slavic literatures, the concept "Postmodernism" cannot be used without qualification' ('Postmodernism in Russian Drama', p. 157). Shepherd also warns against seeing Soviet metafiction of the 1920s and 1930s as 'postmodernist', pointing out that whatever features we may ascribe to works such as Vaginov's *The Labours and Days of Svistonov* must depend on the 'postmodern' context of our own reading, as much as on the texts themselves (*Beyond Metafiction*, pp. 173–4). For an extensive and stimulating account of Russian postmodernism, see Mikhail Epstein, *After the Future*.

12 See also Sergey Kibal'nik, 'V gostyakh u vdovy Konstantina Vaginova'.

13 See Mikhail Epshtein, 'Exposing the Quagmire'; Boris Grois, 'O pol'ze teorii dlya iskusstva'; and Nikol'skaya, 'The Oberiuty and the Theatricalisation of Life', pp. 198–9. Aleksey Medvedev has recently argued that the work of Vvedensky and Kharms is in fact more 'postmodernist' than Conceptualism (although he equates 'postmodernism', with a 'rehabilitation' of more traditional aesthetic methods: 'Skol'ko chasov v miske supa?', p. 138. Bakhterev, however, denies that recent Russian literature contains anything

remotely resembling OBERIU (Nazarov and Chubukin, 'Poslednii iz Oberiu', p. 54).

14 Perhaps Cornwell's claim may need no historical justification; as Hans Bertens points out, the term 'postmodern' was first used in 1934: 'The Postmodern *Weltanschauung* and its Relation with Modernism', p. 11. Nevertheless, with the exception of Zabolotsky's post-World War II poetry, and one or two pieces by Bakhterev, such as 'Tsar Makedon' (written in 1950), OBERIU as a literary phenomenon is much closer to the modernist period than to what is conventionally accepted as the era of postmodernism (from around 1950 onwards).

15 Andre Le Vot, 'Disjunctive and Conjunctive Modes in Contemporary American Fiction', p. 51.

16 Alan Wilde, *Horizons of Assent*, p. 121.

17 See Linda Hutcheon, *A Poetics of Postmodernism. History. Theory. Fiction*, and Richard E. Palmer, 'Towards a Postmodern Hermeneutics of Performance'.

18 Matei Calinescu, 'From the One to the Many: Pluralism in Today's Thought', p. 264.

Select bibliography

PRIMARY SOURCES

OBERIU AND THE *CHINARI*

General

Aleksandrov, Anatoly A. (ed.), *Vanna Arkhimeda* (Leningrad: Khudozhestvennaya literatura, 1991).

Lipavsky, Leonid, 'Iz razgovorov "chinarei" ', *Avrora*, 6 (1989), 124–31.

'Razgovory', *Logos: filosofsko-literaturnyi zhurnal*, 4 (1993), 7–75.

Meilakh, M. B., Nikol'skaya, T. L., Oleinikova, A. N., and Erl', V. I. (eds.), *Poety gruppy 'OBERIU'* (St Petersburg: Sovetskii pisatel', 1994).

'OBERIU', *Afishi Doma Pechati*, 2 (1928) 11–13; English translation in George Gibian (trans. and ed.), *The Man in [with] the Black Coat: Russia's Literature of the Absurd. Selected Works of Daniil Kharms and Alexander Vvedensky* (Evanston, Ill.: Northwestern University Press, 1987), pp. 245–54.

Individual writers

Bakhterev, Igor', 'Starik Bakhterev', in Konstantin K. Kuz'minsky and Gregory L. Kovalev, (eds.), *The Blue Lagoon Anthology of Modern Russian Poetry*, 5 vols. (Newtonville, Mass.: Oriental Research Partners, 1980–6), vol. IV (1983), pp. 17–27.

['V magazine star'evshchika'], *Rodnik*, 12 (1987), 52–3.

' "Tak ya i zhivu..." ', *Iskusstvo Leningrada*, 2 (1990), 86–91.

'I. Bakhterev: mirakl' iz Mo-kho-go', *Teatr*, 11 (1991), 139–53.

'Drevnegrecheskaya razmolvka (vodevil')', *Bezdna*, 12 (1992), 136–8.

Druskin, Yakov, 'Razgovory vestnikov' (1932), unpublished manuscript, held in Otdel Rukopisei, Gos. Publichnaya Biblioteka imeni Saltykova-Shchedrina, St Petersburg, fond 1232, ms. 5.

Vblizi vestnikov, ed. Henry Orlov (Washington, D.C.: H. A. Frager & Co., 1988).

Kharms, Daniil, 'Rasskazy', *Grani*, 81 (1971), 65–83.

Izbrannoe, ed. George Gibian (Würzburg: Jal-Verlag, 1974).

Sobranie proizvedenii, ed. Mikhail Meilakh and Vladimir Erl' (Bremen: K-Presse, 1978–).

'Neizdannoe', *Neue Russischer Literatur-Almanach*, 2 (1979–80), 135–42.

'Proza', *Kontinent*, 24 (1980), 271–95.

'Rasskazy', *Soviet Union/Union Soviétique*, 7 (1980), 228–37.

'Iz rukopisei Daniila Kharmsa', *Russkaya mysl'* (3 January 1985), literary supplement 1, viii.

' "…I emu v rot zaletela kukushka" (iz prozy i poezii Daniila Kharmsa)', *Voprosy literatury*, 8 (1987), 262–75.

' "Moi tvoreniya, synov'ya i docheri moi…" ', *V mire knig*, 12 (1987), 83–8.

'Neopublikovannye rasskazy i stsenki', *Yunost'*, 10 (1987), 93–5.

Polet v nebesa. Stikhi. Proza. Dramy. Pis'ma, ed. A. A. Aleksandrov (Moscow: Sovetskii pisatel', 1989).

Sluchai: rasskazy i stseny, ed. Vladimir Glotser (Moscow: TsK KPSS Pravda, 1989).

'Dnevnik Daniila Kharmsa: iz dnevnika 1933–1938 gody', *Knizhnoe obozrenie* (19 January 1990), 8–9.

' "Bitva so smyslami" Daniila Kharmsa', *Leningradskii literator* (20 April 1990), 6–7.

'Ot Kharmsa – k "mit'kam"?', *Sovetskaya kul'tura* (7 June 1990), 1 and 10.

'Dnevnikovye zapisi Daniila Kharmsa', *Minuvshee*, 11 (1991), 417–583.

Gorlo bredit britvoyu. Sluchai. Rasskazy. Dnevnikovye zapisi, ed. A. Kobrinsky and A. Ustinov, *Glagol: literaturno-khudozhestvennyi zhurnal*, 4 (1991).

' "Bozhe, kakaya uzhasnaya zhizn' i kakoe uzhasnoe u menya sostoyanie". Zapisnye knizhki. Pis'ma. Dnevniki', *Novyi Mir*, 2 (1992), 192–224.

Lipavsky, Leonid, 'Opredelennoe (kachestvo, kharakter, izmenenie…)', unpublished manuscript, held in Otdel Rukopisei, Gos. Publichnaya Biblioteka imeni Saltykova-Shchedrina, St Petersburg, fond 1232 ms. 63.

'Teoriya slov', unpublished manuscript, held in Otdel Rukopisei, Gos. Publichnaya Biblioteka imeni Saltykova-Shchedrina, St Petersburg, fond 1232, ms. 58.

'Issledovanie uzhasa', *Wiener Slawistischer Almanach*, 27 (1991), 233–47.

Oleinikov, N. I. *Stikhotvoreniya*, [n. ed.] (Bremen: K-Presse, 1975).

Ironicheskie stikhi, [n. ed.] (New York: Serebryanyi vek, 1982).
Puchina strastei. Stikhi. Tsikl. Poema, ed. Vladimir Glotser (Moscow: Prometei, 1990).
Ya mukhu bezumno lyubil: izbrannye stikhotvoreniya, ed. Vladimir Glotser (Moscow: Prometei, 1990).
Puchina strastei: stikhotvoreniya i poemy, ed. A. N. Oleinikova (Leningrad: Sovetskii pisatel', 1991).
Vaginov, Konstantin, *Kozlinaya pesn'* (Leningrad: Priboi, 1928; repr. New York: Serebryanyi vek, 1978).
Trudy i dni Svistonova (Leningrad: Izdatel'stvo pisatelei, 1929; repr. New York: Serebryanyi vek, 1984).
Opyty soedineniya slov posredstvom ritma [n. ed.] (Leningrad: Izdatel'stvo pisatelei, 1931; Moscow: Kniga, 1991).
'Poeziya', in *Apollon''*-77, ed. Mikhail Shemyakin (Paris: Shemyakin, 1977), pp. 35–41.
Sobranie stikhotvorenii, ed. Leonid Chertkov (Munich: Otto Sagner in Kommission, 1982).
Garpagoniada (Ann Arbor, Mich.: Ardis, 1983).
[untitled], *Rodnik*, 6 (1989), 72–3.
' "Pomnyu ya aleksandriiskii zvon..." ', *Literaturnoe obozrenie*, 1 (1989), 105–12.
Kozlinaya pesn': romany, ed. A. I. Vaginova and V. I. Erl' (Moscow: Sovremennik, 1991).
'Poema. Retsenzii', *de visu*, 6 (1993), 15–28.
Vladimirov, Yury, 'Fizkul'turnik', *Slavica Hierosolymitana*, 4 (1979), 357–9.
Vvedensky, Aleksandr, *Polnoe sobranie sochinenii*, ed. Mikhail Meilakh, 2 vols. (Ann Arbor, Mich.: Ardis, 1980–84).
Polnoe sobranie proizvedenii v dvukh tomakh, ed. M. Meilakh and V. Erl' (Moscow: Gileya, 1993).
Zabolotsky, N. *Stolbtsy* (Leningrad: Izdatel'stvo pisatelei, 1929).
Stolbtsy i poemy. Stikhotvoreniya, ed. N. N. Zabolotsky (Moscow: Khudozhestvennaya literatura, 1989).

OTHER

Apollinaire, Guillaume, *Œuvres poétiques*, ed. Marcel Adéma and Michel Décaudin (Paris: Gallimard, 1965).
Beckett, Samuel, *The Unnamable*, trans. by the author (Grove Press: New York, 1970).
Kazakov, Vladimir, *Sluchainyi voin. Stikhotvoreniya 1961–1976. Poemy. Dramy. Ocherk >Zudesnik<* [n. ed.] (Munich: Otto Sagner in Kommission, 1978).

Mayakovsky, Vladimir, *Vladimir Mayakovsky: tragediya*, in Mayakovsky, *Sobranie sochinenii v dvenadtsati tomakh*, ed. V. V. Vorontsov, F. F. Kuznetsov, A. V. Sofronov, V. V. Makarov, S. S. Narovchatov, and V. V. Nobikov (Moscow: Pravda, 1978), vol. v, pp. 5–24.

Shklovsky, Viktor, *Minin i Pozharsky* (Moscow: Sovetskii pisatel', 1940; repr. Ann Arbor, Mich.: University Microfilms International, 1983).

Vazarin, Z. V. (ed.), *Nigde eshche do sikh por ne pechatnye anekdoty pro A. S. Pushkina* (Tiflis: [n. pub.], 1914).

CRITICAL THEORY

Bakhtin, M. M. *Problemy tvorchestva Dostoevskogo* (Leningrad: Priboi, 1929).

Tvorchestvo Fransua Rable i narodnaya kul'tura srednevekov'ya (Moscow: Khudozhestvennaya literatura, 1965); English translation, *Rabelais and His World*, trans. Hélène Iswolsky (Bloomington: Indiana University Press, 1984).

Problemy poetiki Dostoevskogo, 3rd edn (Moscow: Sovetskii pisatel', 1972); English translation, *Problems of Dostoevsky's Poetics*, trans. and ed. Caryl Emerson (Manchester University Press, 1984).

'Epos i roman (o metodologii issledovaniya romana)', in Bakhtin, *Voprosy literatury i estetiki: issledovaniya raznykh let*, ed. S. Leibovich (Moscow: Khudozhestvennaya literatura, 1975), pp. 447–83; English translation, 'Epic and Novel: Toward a Methodology for the Study of the Novel', in Bakhtin, *The Dialogic Imagination: Four Essays by M. M. Bakhtin*, ed. M. Holquist, trans. C. Emerson and M. Holquist (Austin: University of Texas Press, 1981), pp. 3–40.

'Slovo v romane', in Bakhtin, *Voprosy literatury i estetiki: issledovaniya raznykh let*, ed. S. Leibovich (Moscow: Khudozhestvennaya literatura, 1975), pp. 72–233; English translation, 'Discourse in the Novel', in Bakhtin, *The Dialogic Imagination: Four Essays by M. M. Bakhtin*, ed. M. Holquist, trans. C. Emerson and M. Holquist (Austin: University of Texas Press, 1981), pp. 259–422.

Voprosy literatury i estetiki: issledovaniya raznykh let, ed. S. Leibovich (Moscow: Khudozhestvennaya literatura, 1975).

'Avtor i geroi v esteticheskoi deyatel'nosti', in Bakhtin, *Estetika slovesnogo tvorchestva*, ed. S. G. Bocharov, 1st edn (Moscow: Iskusstvo, 1979), pp. 7–180; English translation, 'Author and Hero in Aesthetic Activity', in Bakhtin, *Art and Answerability: Early Philosophical Essays by M. M. Bakhtin*, ed. M. Holquist and

V. Liapunov, trans. V. Liapunov, (Austin: University of Texas Press, 1990), pp. 4–256.

Estetika slovesnogo tvorchestva, ed. S. G. Bocharov, 1st edn (Moscow: Iskusstvo, 1979).

'Iskusstvo i otvetstvennost'', in Bakhtin, *Estetika slovesnogo tvorchestva*, ed. S. G. Bocharov, 1st edn (Moscow: Iskusstvo, 1979), pp. 5–6; English translation, 'Art and Answerability', in Bakhtin, *Art and Answerability; Early Philosophical Essays by M. M. Bakhtin* (Austin: University of Texas Press, 1990), pp. 1–3.

'K metodologii gumanitarnykh nauk', in Bakhtin, *Estetika slovesnogo tvorchestva*, ed. S. G. Bocharov, 1st edn (Moscow: Iskusstvo, 1979), pp. 361–73; English translation, 'Toward a Methodology for the Human Sciences', in M. M. Bakhtin, *Speech Genres and Other Late Essays*, trans. Vern W. McGee, ed. Caryl Emerson and Michael Holquist (Austin: University of Texas Press, 1986), pp. 159–72.

The Dialogic Imagination: Four Essays by M. M. Bakhtin, ed. Michael Holquist, trans. Caryl Emerson and Michael Holquist (Austin: University of Texas Press, 1981).

Formal'nyi metod v literaturovedenii (New York: Serebryanyi vek, 1982); *Formal'nyi metod v literaturovedenii: kriticheskoe vvedenie v sotsiologichskuyu poetiku* (Leningrad: Priboi, 1928); English translation, M. M. Bakhtin/P. N. Medvedev, *The Formal Method in Literary Scholarship: A Critical Introduction to Sociological Poetics*, 2nd edn, trans. Albert J. Wehrle (Cambridge, Mass., and London: Harvard University Press, 1985).

'Avtor i geroi v esteticheskoi deyatel'nosti (fragment pervoi glavy)', in Bakhtin, *Literaturno-kriticheskie stat'i*, ed. S. G. Bocharov and V. V. Kozhinov (Moscow: Khudozhestvennaya literatura, 1986), pp. 5–26; English translation 'Supplementary section', in Bakhtin, *Art and Answerability: Early Philosophical Essays by M. M. Bakhtin*, ed. Holquist and Liapunov (Austin, University of Texas Press, 1990).

Art and Answerability: Early Philosophical Essays by M. M. Bakhtin, ed. Michael Holquist and Vadim Liapunov, trans. Vadim Liapunov, supplement trans. Kenneth Brostrom (Austin: University of Texas Press, 1990).

Bakhtin, M. M./Voloshinov, V. N. *Freidizm: kriticheskii ocherk* (New York: Chalidze, 1983); originally published as V. N. Voloshinov, *Freidizm: kriticheskii ocherk* (Moscow-Leningrad: Gosizdat, 1927); English translation, V. N. Voloshinov, *Freudianism: A Marxist Critique*, ed. I. R. Titunik and Neal H. Bruss, trans. I. R. Titunik (New York: Academic Press, 1976).

Barthes, Roland, *S/Z*, trans. Richard Miller (London: Cape, 1975).

The Pleasure of the Text, trans. Richard Miller (London: Farrar, Straus and Giroux, Inc, 1975; repr. Oxford: Blackwell, 1994).

'The Death of the Author' in Barthes, *Image, Music, Text*, trans. and ed. S. Heath (London: Fontana, 1977), pp. 142–8.

Brik, Osip, 'T. n. formal'nyi metod', *LEF*, 1 (1923), 213–15; English translation, 'The So-Called Formal Method', trans. Ann Shukman, *Russian Poetics in Translation*, 4 (1977), 90–1.

'Blizhe k faktu', in Chuzhak (ed.), *Literatura fakta: pervyi sbornik materialov rabotnikov Lefa* (Munich: Wilhelm Fink, 1972), pp. 78–83.

'Protiv "tvorcheskoi" lichnosti', in Chuzhak (ed.), *Literatura fakta: pervyi sbornik materialov rabotnikov Lefa* (Munich: Wilhelm Fink, 1972), pp. 75–8.

'Uchit' pisatelei', in Chuzhak (ed.), *Literatura fakta: pervyi sbornik materialov rabotnikov Lefa* (Munich: Wilhelm Fink, 1972), pp. 180–5.

Chuzhak, N. F. 'Opyt ucheby na klassike', in Chuzhak (ed.), *Literatura fakta: pervyi sbornik materialov rabotnikov Lefa* (Munich: Wilhelm Fink, 1972), pp. 165–79.

Chuzhak, N. F. (ed.), *Literatura fakta: pervyi sbornik materialov rabotnikov Lefa* (Moscow: Federatsiya, 1929; repr. Munich: Wilhelm Fink, 1972).

Derrida, Jacques, *Of Grammatology*, trans. Gayatri C. Spivak (Baltimore and London: Johns Hopkins University Press, 1976).

Eco, Umberto, *The Role of the Reader: Explorations in the Semiotics of Text* (London: Hutchinson, 1981).

Eikhenbaum, Boris, 'Teoriya formal'nogo metoda', in *Literatura. Teoriya. Kritika. Polemika* (Leningrad: Priboi, 1927; repr. Chicago: Russian Language Specialities, 1969), pp. 116–48; English translation, 'The Theory of the Formal Method', in Matejka and Pomorska (eds.), *Readings in Russian Poetics: Formalist and Structuralist Views* (Ann Arbor, Mich.: Michigan Slavic Publications, 1978), pp. 3–37.

'Literaturnyi byt', in Boris Eikhenbaum, *Moi vremennik: slovesnost', nauka, kritika, smes'* (Leningrad: Izdatel'stvo pisatelei, 1929), pp. 49–58; English translation, 'Literary Environment', in Matejka and Pomorska (eds.), *Readings in Russian Poetics: Formalist and Structuralist Views* (Ann Arbor, Mich.: Michigan Slavic Publications, 1978), pp. 56–65.

Fish, Stanley, *Is There a Text in This Class? The Authority of Interpretive Communities* (Cambridge, Mass., and London: Harvard University Press, 1980).

Foucault, Michel, 'What is an Author?', in Josué V. Harari (trans. and ed.), *Textual Strategies: Perspectives in Post-structuralist Criticism* (London: Methuen, 1980), pp. 141–60.

Heidegger, Martin, *Poetry, Language, Thought,* trans. Albert Hofstadter (New York: Harper and Row, 1971).

'The Origin of the Work of Art', trans. Albert Hofstadter, abridged in Mark C. Taylor (ed.), *Deconstruction in Context: Literature and Philosophy* (Chicago and London: University of Chicago Press, 1986), pp. 256–79.

Jauss, Hans Robert, *Toward an Aesthetic of Reception,* trans. Timothy Bathi (Brighton: Harvester Press, 1982).

Matejka, Ladislav and Pomorska, Krystyna (eds.), *Readings in Russian Poetics: Formalist and Structuralist Views* (Ann Arbor, Mich.: Michigan Slavic Publications, 1978).

Medvedev, P. N. see under Bakhtin.

Propp, Vladimir, *Morfologiya skazki* (1st edn, Leningrad: Academia, 1928; 2nd edn, Moscow: Nauka, 1969); English translation, *A Morphology of the Russian Folk Tale,* trans. Laurence Scott, (Austin and London: University of Texas Press, 1958; 2nd edn, rev. and ed. Louis A. Wagner, 1968).

Shklovsky, Viktor, *Voskreshenie slova* (Petersburg: Tipografiya Z. Sokolinskogo, 1914).

'O poezii i zaumnom yazyke', in *Sborniki po teorii poeticheskogo yazyka,* vol. I (Petrograd: OMB, 1916), pp. 1–15.

'Iskusstvo kak priem', in *Sborniki po teorii poeticheskogo yazyka,* vol. II (Petrograd: OMB, 1917), pp. 3–14; English translation, 'Art as Technique', in Lee T. Lemon and Marion J. Reis (eds.), *Russian Formalist Criticism: Four Essays* (Lincoln and London: University of Nebraska Press, 1965), pp. 3–24.

'*Tristram Shendi*' *Sterna i teoriya romana* (Petrograd: Opoyaz, 1921); reprinted as 'Parodiinyi roman. *Tristram Shendi* Sterna', in Shklovsky, *O teorii prozy,* 2nd edn (Moscow: Federatsiya, 1929), pp. 177–204; English translation, 'Sterne's *Tristram Shandy*: A Stylistic Commentary', in Lee T. Lemon and Marion J. Reis (eds.), *Russian Formalist Criticism: Four Essays,* (Lincoln and London: University of Nebraska Press, 1965), pp. 25–57.

Tret'ya fabrika (Moscow: Krug, 1926; repr. Letchworth: Prideaux Press, 1978).

O teorii prozy, 2nd edn (Moscow: Federatsiya, 1929).

Gamburgskii schet: stat'i – vospominaniya – esse (1914–1933), ed. A. Yu. Galushkina and A. P. Chudakova (Moscow: Sovetskii pisatel', 1990).

Tynyanov, Yury, *Dostoevsky i Gogol': k teorii parodii* (Petrograd: Opoyaz, 1921; repr. Letchworth: Prideaux Press, 1975).

'O literaturnoi evolyutsii', in Tynyanov, *Arkhaisty i novatory* (Leningrad: Priboi, 1929; repr. Munich: Wilhelm Fink, 1967), pp.

30–47; English translation, 'On Literary Evolution', in Matejka and Pomorska (eds.), *Readings in Russian Poetics: Formalist and Structuralist Views* (Ann Arbor, Mich.: Michigan Slavic Publications, 1978), pp. 66–78.

Voloshinov, V. N. *Marksizm i filosofiya yazyka: osnovnye problemy sotsiologicheskogo metoda v nauke o yazyke*, 2nd edn (Leningrad: Priboi, 1930; repr. The Hague and Paris: Mouton, 1972); English translation, *Marxism and the Philosophy of Language*, trans. Ladislaw Matejka and I. R. Titunik (Cambridge, Mass.: Harvard University Press, 1986).

Voloshinov, V. N. [M. M. Bakhtin], 'Discourse in Life and Discourse in Poetry', trans. John Richmond, *Russian Poetics in Translation*, 10 (1983), 5–30.

'The Construction of the Utterance', trans. Noel Owen, *Russian Poetics in Translation*, 10 (1983), 114–38.

Wittgenstein, Ludwig, *Philosophical Investigations*, trans. G. E. M. Anscombe (New York: Macmillan, 1958).

ARTISTS' AND WRITERS' THEORETICAL ESSAYS

Artaud, Antonin, *Artaud on Theatre*, ed. Claude Schumacher (London: Methuen, 1989).

Bely, Andrey, 'Theater and Modern Drama', in Senelick (trans. and ed.), *Russian Dramatic Theory from Pushkin to the Symbolists: An Anthology* (Austin: University of Texas Press, 1981), pp. 149–70.

'The Magic of Words', in Andrey Bely, *Selected Essays of Andrei Bely*, trans. and ed. Stephan Cassedy (Berkeley and Los Angeles: University of California Press, 1985), pp. 93–110.

Burlyuk, D., Khlebnikov, V., Kruchenykh, A., and Mayakovsky, V. *Poshchechina obshchestvennomu vkusu* (Moscow: G. L. Kuzmin, 1913).

Eisenstein, Sergei, *Film Form: Essays in Film Theory*, trans. and ed. Jay Leyda (New York: Harcourt, Brace and Co., 1949).

Selected Works, vol. 1: *Writings, 1922–34*, trans. and ed. Richard Taylor (London: BFI; Bloomington and Indianapolis: Indiana University Press, 1988).

Gumilev, Nikolay, 'Chitatel'', in Gumilev, *Sobranie sochinenii v chetyrekh tomakh*, ed. G. P. Struve and B. A. Filippov (Washington, D.C.: Kamkin, 1962–8), vol. IV, pp. 177–84.

Kandinsky, Vassily, *Concerning the Spiritual in Art, and Painting in Particular* (New York: Wittenborn, 1947); republished as 'On The Spiritual in Art', in Kandinsky, *Complete Writings on Art*, ed. Kenneth C. Lindsay and Peter Vergo, 2 vols. (London: Faber and Faber, 1982), vol. I, pp. 119–219.

K istorii russkogo avangarda: N. Khardzhiev, K. Malevich, M. Matyushin, [n. ed.] (Stockholm: Hylaea Prints, 1976).

Kruchenykh, Aleksey, *Deklaratsiya slova kak takovogo* (Petersburg: [pamphlet], 1913).

Deklaratsiya zaumnogo yazyka (Baku: [pamphlet], 1921).

Fonetika teatra (Moscow: 41°, 1923).

Lissitsky, El, 'Suprematism in World Reconstruction', in *El Lissitsky. Life. Letters. Texts*, ed. Sophie Lissitsky-Küppers (London: Thames and Hudson, 1968), pp. 331–4.

Lunts, Lev, 'Pochemu my Serapionovy brat'ya', in *Literaturnye zapiski* (1 August 1922), 30–1; reprinted in Lunts, *Rodina i drugie proizvedeniya*, ed. M. Vainshtein (Jerusalem: Pamyat', 1981), pp. 279–84.

'Na Zapad!', *Beseda*, 3 (1923), 259–74.

Malevich, Kazimir, *Ot kubizma i futurizma k suprematizmu (novyi zhivopisnyi realizm)* (Moscow: [n. pub.], 1916).

Bog ne skinut. Iskusstvo. Tserkov'. Fabrika (Vitebsk: Unovis, 1922).

Essays on Art, 1915–1933, ed. Troels Andersen, trans. Xenia Glowacki-Prus and Arnold Mcmillin, 2 vols., 2nd edn (Copenhagen: Borgens Forlag a-s, 1971).

'O poezii', in Konstantin K. Kuz'minsky and Gregory L. Kovalev, (eds.), *The Blue Lagoon Anthology of Modern Russian Poetry*, 5 vols. (Newtonville, Mass.: Oriental Research Partners, 1980–6), vol. II (1983), pp. 57–61.

Mandel'shtam, Osip, 'O sobesednike' in Mandel'shtam, *Sobranie sochinenii v trekh tomakh*, ed. G. P. Struve and B. A. Filippov (Washington, D.C.: Inter-Language Literary Associates, 1967–71), vol. II, 2nd edn (1971), pp. 233–40.

Markov, Vladimir (ed.), *Manifesty i programmy russkikh futuristov* (Munich: Wilhelm Fink, 1967).

Matyushin, M. 'Dnevnik. 1915–1916', *A-Ya*, 6 (1984), 48–55.

Mayakovsky, Vladimir, *How are Verses Made?*, trans. G. M. Hyde (London: Cape, 1970; reprinted, London: Duckworth/Bristol Classical Press, 1990).

Meyerhold, Vsevolod, *Meyerhold on Theatre*, trans. and ed. Edward Braun (London and New York: Methuen, 1969).

Okhlopkov, Nikolay, 'On Convention', in Mikhail Parkhomenko and Aleksandr Myasnikov (eds.), *Socialist Realism in Literature and Art: A Collection of Articles*, (Moscow: Progress, 1971), pp. 103–26.

Senelick, Laurence (trans. and ed.), *Russian Dramatic Theory from Pushkin to the Symbolists: An Anthology* (Austin: University of Texas Press, 1981).

Sologub, Fedor, 'The Theatre of a Single Will', in Senelick (trans. and ed.), *Russian Dramatic Theory from Pushkin to the Symbolists: An Anthology* (Austin: University of Texas Press, 1981), pp. 132–48.

Tolstoy, L. N. 'Chto takoe iskusstvo?', in L. N. Tolstoy, *Polnoe sobranie sochinenii*, ed. V. G. Chertkov and others, 90 vols. plus index (Moscow: Gosudarstvennoe izdatel'stvo khudozhestvennoi literatury, 1928–64), vol. XXX (1951), pp. 27–203.

Tufanov, Aleksandr, 'K zaumi. Fonicheskaya muzyka i funktsii soglasnykh fonem', in Tufanov, *K zaumi: stikhi i issledovanie soglasnykh fonem* (Petersburg: [author's edition], 1924); reprinted in Konstantin Kuz'minsky, Gerald Janaček, and Aleksandr Ochertyansky (eds.), *Zabytyi avangard. Rossiya. Pervaya tret' XX stoletiya: sbornik spravochnykh i teoreticheskikh materialov*, (Vienna: Gesell. z. Förderung Slawistischer Studien, 1988), pp. 102–25.

Vertov, Dziga, *Kino-Eye: The Writings of Dziga Vertov*, ed. Annette Michelson, trans. Kevin O'Brien (London and Sydney: Pluto, 1984).

SECONDARY SOURCES

OBERIU AND THE *CHINARI*

Bibliographies

Cornwell, Neil and Graffy, Julian, 'Selected Bibliography', in Neil Cornwell (ed.), *Daniil Kharms and the Poetics of the Absurd: Essays and Materials* (Basingstoke and London: Macmillan, 1991), pp. 268–77. [Kharms].

Giaquinta, Rosanna, 'OBERIU: per una rassegna della critica', *Ricerche Slavistiche*, 32–5 (1985–88), 213–52. [OBERIU].

Jaccard, Jean-Philippe, 'Bibliographie', in *Cahiers du monde russe et soviétique*, 26 (1985), 493–522. [Kharms].

Nikol'skaya, Tat'yana, 'Dopolneniya k bibliografii K. Vaginova', in M. O. Chudakova (ed.), *Shestye Tynyanovskie chteniya: tezisy dokladov i materialy dlya obsuzhdeniya* (Riga and Moscow: Zinatne, 1992), pp. 301–6. [Vaginov].

Contemporary reviews which mention OBERIU or its members

Aleksandrova, K. [review of Vaginov, *Bambocciade*], *Kniga – stroitelyam sotsializma: khudozhestvennaya literatura*, 5 (1932), 15–16.

Bachelis, I. 'Melkii bes-mladshii, ili syn uchitelya Peredonova', *Literaturnaya gazeta* (17 April 1932), p. 3.

Gelfand, M. 'Zhurnal'noe obozrenie', *Pechat' i revolyutsiya*, 8 (1929), 67–72.

Ioffe, N. and Zheleznov, L. 'Literaturnye dela (o "chinaryakh")', *Smena* (3 April 1927), [n. pg.].

Lesnaya, L. 'Ytuerebo', *Krasnaya gazeta* (evening edition, 25 January 1928), [n. pg.].

Manfred, A. 'Kladbishchenskaya muza', *Kniga i revolyutsiya*, 12 (1929), 31–4.

Messer, Raisa, 'Poputchiki vtorogo prizyva', *Zvezda*, 4 (1930), 203–11.

Nil'vich, L. 'Reaktsionnoe zhonglerstvo (Ob odnoi vylazke literaturnykh khuliganov)', *Smena* (9 April 1930), 5.

Oksenov, I. 'Leningradskie poety', *Krasnaya gazeta* (evening edition, 21 November 1926), [n. pg.].

R[ozhdestvensky], V. [review of Vaginov, *Journey into Chaos*], *Kniga i revolyutsiya*, 7 (1922), p. 64.

Selivanovsky, A. 'Ostrovityane iskusstva', *Na literaturnom postu*, 23 (1928), 49–58.

Sergievsky, I. [review of *The Goat's Song*], *Novyi mir*, 11 (1928), 284–5.

Tal'nikov, D. 'Literaturnye zametki', *Krasnaya nov'*, 2 (1929), 189–99.

Tolmachev, D. 'Dadaisty v Leningrade', *Zhizn' iskusstva* (1 November, 1927), p. 14.

Memoirs and historical

Aleksandrov, Anatoly, 'Mesto smerti Daniila Kharmsa – ?', *Literaturnaya gazeta*, 21 February 1990, p. 5.

Bakhterev, Igor', 'Kogda my byli molodymi (Nevydumannyi rasskaz)', in A. V. Zabolotskaya, A. V. Makedonov and N. N. Zabolotsky (eds.), *Vospominaniya o N. Zabolotskom* (Moscow: Sovetskii pisatel', 1984), pp. 57–100.

'[Vstrecha] s Viktorom Borisovichem Shklovskim', in Aleksandrov (ed.), *Vanna Arkhimeda* (Leningrad: Khudozhestvennaya literatura, 1991), pp. 441–6.

Chukovsky, Nikolay, 'Iz vospominanii', *Wiener Slawistischer Almanach*, 24 (1989), 97–114.

Gernet, N. 'O Kharmse (zametki k vecheru pamyati D. I. Kharmsa, Moskva, 1976 god)', *Neva*, 2 (1988), 201–4.

Kaverin, V. 'V starom dome', *Zvezda*, 10 (1971), 138–86.

Lipavskaya, T. 'Vstrechi s Nikolaem Alekseevichem i ego druz'yami', in A. V. Zabolotskaya, A. V. Makedonov and N. N. Zabolotsky (eds.), *Vospominaniya o N. Zabolotskom* (Moscow: Sovetskii pisatel', 1984), pp. 47–56.

Luknitsky, P. N. *Acumiana: vstrechi s Annoi Akhmatovoi. Tom 1, 1924–25gg.* (Paris: YMCA-Press, 1991). [contains references to Vaginov].

Lunin, Evgeny, 'Delo Nikolaya Oleinikova', *Avrora*, 7 (1991), 140–6.

Malich, M. V. 'K istorii aresta i gibeli Daniila Kharmsa (pis'ma M. V. Malich k N. B. Shan'ko)', *Russkaya literatura*, 1 (1991), 204–9.

Mal'sky, Igor', 'Razgrom OBERIU: materialy sledstvennogo dela', *Oktyabr'*, 11 (1992), 166–91.

Meilakh, Mikhail, 'Daniil Kharms: anecdota posthuma (posmertnye anekdoty Daniila Kharmsa)', *Russkaya mysl'* (23 June 1989), literary supplement 8, x–xi; republished as 'Devyat' posmertnykh anekdotov Daniil Kharmsa', *Teatr*, 11 (1991), 76–9.

Nappel'baum, I. M. 'Pamyatka o poete', in Chudakova (ed.), *Chetvertye Tynyanovskie chteniya: tezisy dokladov i materialy dlya obsuzhdeniya* (Riga: Zinatne, 1988), pp. 89–95.

Nazarov, Vadim and Chubukin, Sergey, 'Poslednii iz Oberiu', *Rodnik*, 12 (1987), 39 and 54 [interview with Bakhterev].

Poret, Alisa, 'Vospominaniya o Daniile Kharmse', *Panorama iskusstv*, 3 (1980), 345–59.

Sankt-Peterburgskii Universitet (1 November 1991) [special issue devoted to arrest of Kharms, Vvedensky, Tufanov, and I. Andronikov in 1931].

Semenov, B. 'Dalekoe-ryadom', *Neva*, 9 (1979), 180–5.

Sinel'nikov, I. 'Molodoi Zabolotsky', in Zabolotskaya, Makedonov, and Zabolotsky (eds.), *Vospominaniya o N. Zabolotskom* (Moscow: Sovetskii pisatel', 1984), pp. 101–20.

Ustinov, A. B. 'Delo detskogo sektora Gosizdata 1932 g.: predvaritel'naya spravka', in Morev (ed.), *Mikhail Kuzmin i russkaya kul'tura XX veka: tezisy i materialy konferentsii 15–17 maya 1990g.* (Leningrad: Sovet po istorii mirovoi kul'tury AN SSSR, 1990), pp. 125–36.

Yudina, M. V. *Mariya Veniaminovna Yudina. Stat'i. Vospominaniya. Materialy*, ed. M. A. Kuznetsov (Moscow: Sovetskii kompozitor, 1978). [contains references to various members of OBERIU].

Zabolotskaya, A. V., Makedonov, A. V., and Zabolotsky, N. N. (eds.),*Vospominaniya o N. Zabolotskom*, 2nd edn (Moscow: Sovetskii pisatel', 1984).

Zhukova, Lidiya, *Epilogi (Kniga 1aya)* (New York: Chalidze, 1983). [contains sections on OBERIU and its members].

General

Aizlewood, Robin, ' "Guilt without Guilt" in Kharms's Story "The Old Woman" ', *Scottish Slavonic Review*, 14 (1990), 199–217.

'Towards an Interpretation of Kharms's *Sluchai*', in Cornwell (ed.), *Daniil Kharms and the Poetics of the Absurd: Essays and Materials* (Basingstoke and London: Macmillan, 1991), pp. 97–122.

Aleksandrov, A. 'Oberiu. Predvaritel'nye zametki', *Československá rusistika*, 13 (1968), 296–303.

'Materialy D. I. Kharmsa v rukopisnom otdele Pushkinskogo doma', in K. D. Muratova (ed.), *Ezhegodnik rukopisnogo otdela Pushkinskogo doma 1978* (Leningrad: Nauka, 1980), pp. 64–79.

'Chudodei: lichnost' i tvorchestvo Daniila Kharmsa', in Daniil Kharms, *Polet v nebesa. Stikhi. Proza. Dramyt. Pis'ma*, ed. A. Aleksandrov (Moscow: Sovetskii pisatel', 1989), pp. 7–48.

'Kratkaya khronika zhizni i tvorchestva Daniila Kharmsa', in Daniil Kharms, *Polet v nebesa. Stikhi. Proza. Dramy. Pis'ma*, ed. A. Aleksandrov (Moscow: Sovetskii pisatel', 1989), pp. 538–55; slightly amended English translation: 'A Kharms Chronology', trans. Neil Cornwell, in Cornwell (ed.), *Daniil Kharms and the Poetics of the Absurd: Essays and Materials* (Basingstoke and London: Macmillan, 1991), pp. 32–46.

'Evrika Oberiutov', in Aleksandrov (ed.), *Vanna Arkhimeda* (Leningrad: Khudozhestvennaya Literatura, 1991), pp. 3–34.

'Materialy o Daniile Kharmse i stikhi ego v fonde V. N. Petrova', in T. Tsar'kova (ed.), *Ezhegodnik rukopisnogo otdela Pushkinskogo doma na 1990 god* (St Petersburg: Gumanitarnoe agentstvo 'Akademicheskii proekt', 1993), pp. 184–213.

Aleksandrov, A. and Meilakh, M. 'Tvorchestvo Aleksandra Vvedenskogo', in A. B. Roginsky and G. G. Superfin (eds.), *Materialy XXII nauchnoi studencheskoi konferentsii. Poetika. Istoriya literatury. Lingvistika* (Tartu: Tartuskii gosudarstvennyi universitet, 1967), pp. 105–10.

'Tvorchestvo Daniila Kharmsa', in A. B. Roginsky and G. G. Superfin (eds.), *Materialy XXII nauchnoi studencheskoi konferentsii. Poetika. Istoriya literatury. Lingvistika* (Tartu: Tartuskii gosudarstvennyi universitet, 1967), pp. 101–4.

Anemone, Anthony, 'Konstantin Vaginov and the Leningrad Avant-Garde: 1921–1934' (unpublished Ph.D. dissertation, University of California, Berkeley, 1985).

'Konstantin Vaginov and the Death of Nikolai Gumilev', *Slavic Review*, 48 (1989), 631–6.

'Carnival in Theory and Practice: Konstantin Vaginov and Mixail Bakhtin' (unpublished paper presented at *Fifth International Bakhtin Conference*, Manchester, England, July 1991).

'The Anti-World of Daniil Kharms: On the Significance of the Absurd', in Cornwell (ed.), *Daniil Kharms and the Poetics of the*

Absurd: Essays and Materials (Basingstoke and London: Macmillan, 1991), pp. 71–93.

Arndt, M. 'OBERIU', *Grani*, 81 (1971), 45–64.

Bakhterev, I. and Razumovsky, A. 'O Nikolae Oleinikove', in *Den' poezii*, ed. V. B. Azarov, S. V. Botvinnik, and N. R. Yavorskaya (Leningrad: Sovetskii pisatel', 1964), pp. 54–60.

Björling, Fiona. *Stolbcy* by Nikolaj Zabolockij: *Analyses* (Stockholm: Almqvist and Wicksell, 1973).

Blyum, A. and Martynov, I. 'Petrogradskie bibliofily: po stranitsam satiricheskikh romanov Konstantinova Vaginova', *Al'manakh bibliofila*, 4 (1977), 217–35.

Blyumbaum, A. B. and Morev, G. A. ' "Vanna Arkhimeda": k istorii nesostoyavshegosya izdaniya', *Wiener Slawistischer Almanach*, 28 (1991), 263–9.

Carrick, Neil, 'Daniil Kharms and a Theology of the Absurd' (unpublished Ph.D. dissertation, Northwestern University, 1993).

'Daniil Kharms and the Art of Negation', *The Slavonic and East European Review*, 72 (1994), 622–43.

'A Familiar Story: Insurgent Narratives and Generic Refugees in Daniil Kharms's *The Old Woman*', *Modern Language Review*, 90 (1995), 707–21.

Cassedy, Steven, 'Daniil Kharms's Parody of Dostoevskii: Anti-Tragedy as Political Comment', *Canadian-American Slavic Studies*, 18 (1984), 268–84.

Chances, Ellen, 'Čexov and Xarms: Story/Anti-Story', *Russian Language Journal*, 36 and 123–4 (1982), 181–92.

'Daniil Charms' "Old Woman" Climbs her Family Tree: "Starucha" and the Russian Literary Past', *Russian Literature*, 17 (1985), 353–66.

Cheron, George, 'Mikhail Kuzmin and the Oberiuty: An Overview', *Wiener Slawistischer Almanach*, 12 (1983), 87–101.

Chertkov, L. N. 'Poeziya Konstantina Vaginova', in Vaginov, *Sobranie stikhotvorenii*, ed. L. Chertkov (Munich: Otto Sagner in Kommission, 1982), pp. 213–30.

Chudakova, M. O. (ed.), *Chetvertye Tynyanovskie chteniya: tezisy dokladov i materialy dlya obsuzhdeniya* (Riga: Zinatne, 1988). [contains articles on Vaginov and on *chinari*].

Tynyanovskii sbornik: chetvertye Tynyanovskie chteniya (Riga: Zinatne, 1990). [contains articles on OBERIU and *chinari*].

Chumakov, S. N. 'Galchinsky i Kharms: O prirode skhodnogo khudozhestvennogo yavleniya', in V. A. Milovitsov, I. V. Kartashova, B. I. Kolesnikov, L. V. Spitsyna, and N. A. Korzina (eds.), *Tekst i kontekst: Russko-zarubezhnye literaturnye svyazi XIX–XX vv. Sbornik nauchnykh trudov* (Tver': Ministerstvo nauki, vysshei shkoly i tekhnicheskoi politiki Rossiiskoi federatsii, Tverskoi gosudarstvennyi universitet, 1992), pp. 83–96.

Cornwell, Neil, 'Introduction: Daniil Kharms, Black Miniaturist', in Cornwell (ed.), *Daniil Kharms and the Poetics of the Absurd: Essays and Materials* (Basingstoke and London: Macmillan, 1991), pp. 3–21.

Cornwell, Neil (ed.), *Daniil Kharms and the Poetics of the Absurd: Essays and Materials* (Basingstoke and London: Macmillan, 1991).

Druskin, Yakov, 'Chinari: glava iz knigi Yakova Semenovicha Druskina (1902–1980), *Son i Yav'*, 1968', *Wiener Slawistischer Almanach*, 15 (1985), 381–403.

'Stadii ponimaniya', *Wiener Slawistischer Almanach*, 15 (1985), 405–13.

'"Chinari"', *Avrora*, 6 (1989), 103–15.

'Kommunikativnost' v tvorchestve Aleksandra Vvedenskogo', intro. Druskina, *Teatr*, 11 (1991), 80–94.

'On Daniil Kharms', trans. Neil Cornwell, in Cornwell (ed.), *Daniil Kharms and the Poetics of the Absurd: Essays and Materials* (Basingstoke and London: Macmillan, 1991), pp. 22–31.

Druskina, L. [introduction to Druskin, 'Kommunikativnost' v tvorchestve Aleksandra Vvedenskogo'], *Teatr*, 11 (1991), 80–1.

[introduction to Druskin, 'Pered prinadlezhnostyami chego-libo', 'Uchitel' iz fabzavucha', and 'O kontse sveta', in V. Shubinsky and I. Vichnevetsky (eds.), *Nezamechannaya zemlya: literaturno-khudozhestvennyi al'manakh* (Moscow and St Petersburg: Novaya literatura, 1991), pp. 46–83], pp. 46–50.

Erl', V. 'Konstantin Vaginov i A. Vvedensky v Soyuze Poetov', *Wiener Slawistischer Almanch*, 27 (1991), 219–22.

Flaker, Aleksandr, 'O rasskazakh Daniila Kharmsa', *Československá rusistika*, 14 (1969), 78–84.

Fleishman, L. S. 'Marginaly k istorii russkogo avangarda/Oleinikov, oberiuty/', in Oleinikov, *Stikhotvoreniya* (Bremen: K-Presse, 1975), pp. 3–18.

'On One Enigmatic Poem by Daniil Kharms', trans. Neil Cornwell, in Cornwell (ed.), *Daniil Kharms and the Poetics of the Absurd: Essays and Materials* (Basingstoke and London: Macmillan, 1991), pp. 159–68.

Gerasimova, Anna, 'OBERIU. (Problema smeshnogo)', *Voprosy literatury*, 4 (1988), 48–79.

'Trudy i dni Konstantina Vaginova', *Voprosy literatury*, 12 (1989), 131–66.

Gerasimova A., and Nikitaev, A. 'Kharms i "Golem"', *Teatr*, 11 (1991), 36–50.

Giaquinta, Rosanna, 'Su alcuni aspetti del teatro *Oberiu*', *Annali di Ca' Foscari*, 21, 1–2 (1982), 85–97.

'I poemi drammatici di Alexander Vvedenskij *Minin i Požarskij* e *Krugom vozmožno Bog*', *Annali di Ca' Foscari*, 22, 1–2 (1983), 67–81.

'Elements of the Fantastic in Daniil Kharms's *Starukha*', in Cornwell (ed.), *Daniil Kharms and the Poetics of the Absurd: Essays and Materials* (Basingstoke and London: Macmillan, 1991), pp. 132–48.

Gibian, George. 'Introduction: Daniil Kharms and Alexander Vvedensky', in *The Man in [with] the Black Coat: Russia's Literature of the Absurd. Selected Works of Daniil Kharms and Alexander Vvedensky* (Evanston Ill.: Northwestern University Press, 1987), pp. 1–42.

Goldstein, Darra, 'Zabolotsky and Filonov: The Science of Composition', *Slavic Review*, 48 (1989), 579–91.

Nikolai Zabolotsky: Play for Mortal Stakes (Cambridge University Press, 1993).

Heyl, Daniela von, *Die Prosa Konstantin Vaginovs* (Munich: Otto Sagner in Kommission, 1993).

Jaccard, Jean-Philippe, 'De la réalité au texte: l'absurde chez Daniil Harms', *Cahiers du monde russe et soviétique*, 27 (1985), 269–312.

'Daniil Kharms: teatr absurda – real'nyi teatr. Prochtenie p'esy *Elizaveta Bam*', *Russian Literature*, 27 (1990), 21–40.

Daniil Harms et la fin de l'avant-garde russe (Bern: Peter Lang, 1991).

'Daniil Kharms in the Context of Russian and European Literature of the Absurd', trans. Neil Cornwell, in Cornwell (ed.), *Daniil Kharms and the Poetics of the Absurd: Essays and Materials* (Basingstoke and London: Macmillan, 1991), pp. 49–70.

'Strashnaya beskonechnost' Leonida Lipavskogo', *Wiener Slawistischer Almanach*, 27 (1991), 229–32.

'Chinari', *Russian Literature*, 32 (1992), 77–94.

'L'impossible éternité. Réflexions sur le problème de la sexualité dans l'oeuvre de Daniil Harms', in Leonid Heller (ed.), *Amour et érotisme dans la littérature russe du XXe siècle: actes du colloque de juin 1989 organisé par l'Université de Lausanne, avec le concours de la Fondation du 450ème anniversaire* (Bern: Peter Lang, 1992), pp. 213–47.

Jaccard, Jean-Philippe and Ustinov, Andrey, 'Zaumnik Daniil Kharms: nachalo puti', *Wiener Slawistischer Almanach*, 27 (1991), 159–228.

Jovanovič, Milivoe, 'A. Vvedensky – parodist: k razboru "Elki u Ivanovykh"', *Wiener Slawistischer Almanach*, 12 (1983), 71–86.

Kalashnikova, R. B. 'Daniil Kharms i narodnaya schitalka', in I. P. Lupanova (ed.), *Problemy detskoi literatury* (Petrozavodsk: Petrozavodskii gosudarstvennyi universitet, 1989), pp. 24–33.

Kasack, Wolfgang, 'Daniil Charms: Absurde Kunst in der Sowjet-union', *Welt der Slaven*, 21 (1976), 70–80.

'Vaginov, Konstantin Konstantinovich', and 'Oberiu', in Kasack, *Dictionary of Russian Literature Since 1917*, trans. Maria Carlson and Jane T. Hedges, rev. Rebecca Atack (New York: Columbia University Press, 1988), p. 434, and pp. 277–8.

Kibal'nik, Sergey, 'V gostyakh u vdovy Konstantina Vaginova', *Russkaya mysl'* (31 August 1990), 11, and *Russkaya mysl'* (7 September 1990), 11.

Kobrinsky, Aleksandr, 'Sistema organizatsii prostranstva v poeme Aleksandra Vvedenskogo "Krugom vozmozhno Bog"', *Teatr*, 11 (1991), 94–101.

Konstriktor, B. 'Otkrytie Peterburga: istoricheskaya tema u ober-iutov', *Sumerki*, 9 (1990), 100–6.

Levin, Il'ya, 'The Fifth Meaning of the Motor-Car: Malevich and the Oberiuty', *Soviet Union/Union Soviétique*, 5 (1978), 287–300.

'Mir vymyshlennyi i mir sozdannyi', introduction to Daniil Kharms, 'Proza', *Kontinent*, 24 (1980), 271–95.

'The Collision of Meanings: The Poetic Language of Daniil Kharms and Aleksandr Vvedensky' (unpublished Ph.D. disserta-tion, University of California, Berkeley, 1987).

Literaturnoe obozrenie, 9/10 (1994), 49–72. [articles on OBERIU].

Logos: filosofsko-literaturnyi zhurnal, 4 (1993) 7–138. [contains important OBERIU and *chinari* material].

Makedonov, A. V. *Nikolay Zabolotsky. Zhizn'. Tvorchestvo. Metamorfozy* (Leningrad: Sovetskii pisatel', 1968; 2nd rev. edn, 1987).

Malmstad, John and Shmakov G. 'O poezii Vaginova', in *Apollon"-77*, ed. Mikhail Shemyakin (Paris: Shemyakin, 1977), p. 34.

Maxton, Hugh, 'Kharms and Myles: an Afterword', in Kharms, *The Plummeting Old Women*, trans. and ed. Neil Cornwell (Dublin: Lilliput Press, 1989), pp. 93–100.

Medvedev, Aleksey, 'Skol'ko chasov v miske supa? Modernizm i real'noe iskusstvo', *Teatr*, 11 (1991), 128–38.

Meilakh, Mikhail, 'Semanticheskii eksperiment v poeticheskoi rechi', *Russian Linguistics*, 1 (1974), 271–6.

'Neskol'ko slov o "Kupriyanove i Natashe" Aleksandra Vvedens-kogo', *Slavica Hierosolymitana*, 3 (1978), 252–7.

'Predislovie', in Vvedensky, *Polnoe sobranie sochinenii*, ed. Mikhail Meilakh (Ann Arbor, Mich.: Ardis, 1980–84), vol. I, pp. ix–xxxiii.

'Primechaniya' in Vvedensky, *Polnoe sobranie sochinenii*, ed. Mikhail Meilakh (Ann Arbor, Mich.: Ardis, 1980–84), vol. II, pp. 261–362.

'O "Elizavete Bam" Daniila Kharmsa (predystoriya, istoriya

postanovki, p'esa, tekst)', *Stanford Slavic Studies*, 1 (1987), 163–246 (163–205).

'Shkap i kolpak: fragment oberiutskoi poetiki', in Chudakova (ed.), *Tynyanovskii sbornik: chetvertye Tynyanovskie chteniya* (Riga: Zinatne, 1990), pp. 181–93.

'Kharms's Play *Elizaveta Bam*', trans. Ann Shukman, in Cornwell (ed.), *Daniil Kharms and the Poetics of the Absurd: Essays and Materials* (Basingstoke and London: Macmillan, 1991), pp. 200–19.

'Oberiuty i zaum'', in L. Magarotto, M. Marzaduri, and D. Ricci (eds.), *Zaumnyi futurizm i dadaizm v russkoi kul'ture* (Bern: Peter Lang, 1991), pp. 361–75.

'Zametki o teatre oberiutov', *Teatr*, 11 (1991), 173–9.

' "Ya ispytyval slovo na ogne i na stuzhe..." ', in M. Meilakh, T. Nikol'skaya, A. Oleinikova, and V. Erl' (eds.), *Poety gruppy 'OBERIU'* (St Petersburg: Sovetskii pisatel', 1994), pp. 5–58.

Morev, G. A. (ed.), *Mikhail Kuzmin i russkaya kul'tura XX veka: tezisy i materialy konferentsii 15–17 maya 1990g.* (Leningrad: Sovet po istorii mirovoi kul'tury AN SSSR, 1990). [contains articles on members of OBERIU].

Milner-Gulland, R. R. ' "Left Art" in Leningrad: the OBERIU Declaration', *Oxford Slavonic Papers*, NS, 3 (1970), 65–74.

'Zabolotsky: Philosopher-Poet', *Soviet Studies*, 4 (1971), 595–608.

'Zabolotsky and the Reader: Problems of Approach', *Russian Literature Triquarterly*, 8 (1974), 385–92.

'Grandsons of Kozma Prutkov: Reflections on Zabolotsky, Oleynikov and their Circle', in *Russian and Slavic Literatures*, ed. R. Freeborn, R. Milner-Gulland, and C. Ward (Columbus, Ohio: Slavica, 1976), pp. 313–27.

' "Kovarnye stikhi": Notes on Daniil Kharms and Aleksandr Vvedensky', *Essays in Poetics*, 9, 1 (1984), 16–37.

'Beyond the Turning-Point: An Afterword', in Cornwell (ed.), *Daniil Kharms and the Poetics of the Absurd: Essays and Materials* (Basingstoke and London: Macmillan, 1991), pp. 243–67.

Mirzoev, Vladimir, 'Elizaveta Bam, 62 goda spustya', *Moskovskie novosti* (11 June 1989), p. 11.

Moskovskaya, D. S. 'Sud'ba chuzhogo slova v romanakh K. Vaginova', in T. Kasatkina and A. Rogachevsky (eds.), *Nachalo: sbornik rabot molodykh uchenykh*, vol. 11 (Moscow: Nasledie, 1993), pp. 181–9.

Müller, Bertram, *Absurde Literatur in Rußland: Entstehung und Entwicklung* (Munich: Otto Sagner in Kommission, 1978).

Nakhimovsky, Alice Stone, 'From the Language of Nonsense to the Absurdity of Life' (unpublished Ph.D. dissertation, University of Cornell, 1976).

'The Ordinary, the Sacred and the Grotesque in Daniil Kharms's *The Old Woman*', *Slavic Review*, 37 (1978), 203–16.

'About Vvedensky's *Conversations*', *Ulbandus Review*, 1, 1 (1979), 106–37 [includes a translation of Vvedensky's *A Certain Quantity of Conversations*, pp. 112–37].

Laughter in the Void: An Introduction to the Writings of Daniil Kharms and Alexander Vvedensky (Vienna: Institut für Slawistik der Universität Wien, 1982).

Nikitaev, Aleksandr, 'Tainopis' Daniila Kharmsa: opyt deshifrovki', *Daugava*, 8 (1989), 95–9.

Nikol'skaya, T. L. 'O tvorchestve Konstantina Vaginova', in A. B. Roginsky and G. G. Superfin (eds.), *Materialy XXII nauchnoi studencheskoi konferentsii. Poetika. Istoriya literatury. Lingvistika* (Tartu: Tartuskii gosudarstvennyi universitet, 1967), pp. 94–100.

'K. K. Vaginov (Kanva biografii i tvorchestva)', in Chudakova, M. O. (ed.), *Chetvertye Tynyanovskie chteniya: tezisy dokladov i materialy dlya obsuzhdeniya* (Riga: Zinatne, 1988), pp. 67–88.

[introduction to Konstantin Vaginov, ' "Pomnyu ya aleksandriiskii zvon…" '], *Literaturnoe obozrenie*, 1 (1989), 105–7.

[introduction to poems by Konstantin Vaginov], *Rodnik*, 6 (1989), 72–3 (72).

'Tragediya chudakova', in Vaginov, *Kozlinaya pesn'. Trudy i dni Svistonova. Bambochada*, ed. A. I. Vaginova (Moscow: Khudozhestvennya literatura, 1989), pp. 5–18.

'Konstantin Vaginov, ego vremya i knigi', in Vaginov, *Kozlinaya pesn': romany*, ed. A. I. Vaginova and V. I. Erl' (Moscow: Sovremennik, 1991), pp. 3–11.

'The Oberiuty and the Theatricalisation of Life', in Cornwell (ed.), *Daniil Kharms and the Poetics of the Absurd: Essays and Materials* (Basingstoke and London: Macmillan, 1991).

Nikol'skaya, T. L. and Erl', V. I. 'Primechaniya', in Vaginov, *Kozlinaya pesn': romany*, ed. A. I. Vaginova and V. I. Erl' (Moscow: Sovremennik, 1991), pp. 544–91.

Orlov, Henry, 'Predislovie', in Druskin, *Vblizi vestnikov* (Washington D.C.: H. A. Frager & Co., 1988), pp. 5–13.

Paleari, Leonardo, 'La letteratura e la vita nei romanzi di Vaginov', *Rassegna Sovietica*, 5 (1981), 153–70.

'Tvorchestvo glazami tvortsa: roman o pisatel'skoi kukhne', introduction to Vaginov, *Trudy i dni Svistonova* (New York: Serebryanyi vek, 1984), i–xv.

Perlina, Nina, 'Vzaimootnosheniya literaturnykh teorii i poeticheskoi praktiki v literaturno-filosofskikh kruzhkakh 1920-godov: Mikhail Bakhtin i Konstantin Vaginov' (unpublished paper presented at

Discontinuous Discourses in Russian Literature conference, Oxford, 1984).

'Konstantin Vaguinov (1899–1934)', trans. Anne de Pouvourville, in Etkind, Nivat, Serman, and Strada (eds.), *Histoire de la littérature russe: le XX siècle***. *La révolution et les années vingt* (Paris: Fayard, 1988), pp. 474–82.

'Daniil Kharms's Poetic System', in Cornwell (ed.), *Daniil Kharms and the Poetics of the Absurd: Essays and Materials* (Basingstoke and London: Macmillan, 1991), pp. 175–91.

Polyakova, S. V. 'Tvorchestvo Oleinikova', *Russian Literature Triquarterly*, 23 (1990), 327–55.

Ponomarev, Aleksandr, ' "Nastoyashchee" v luchshikh ego proyavleniyakh', *Teatr*, 11 (1991), 86–9.

Purin, Aleksey, 'Opyty Konstantina Vaginova', *Novyi mir*, 8 (1993), 221–33.

Revzina, O. G. 'Kachestvennaya i funktsional'naya kharakteristika vremeni v poezii A. I. Vvedenskogo', *Russian Literature*, 6 (1978), 397–401.

Roberts, Graham, 'Diabolical Dialogue or Divine Discourse?: A Study of *Nekotoroe kolichestvo razgovorov* by Aleksandr Vvedensky', *Essays in Poetics*, 16, 2 (1991), 24–49.

'A Matter of (Dis)course: Metafiction in the Works of Daniil Kharms', in *New Directions in Soviet Literature: Selected Papers from the Fourth World Congress for Soviet and East European Studies, Harrogate, 1990*, ed. Sheelagh Duffin Graham (Basingstoke and London: Macmillan, 1992), pp. 138–63.

'Of Words and Worlds: Language Games in *Elizaveta Bam* by Daniil Kharms', *Slavonic and East European Review*, 72 (1994), 38–59.

'Poor Liza: The Sexual Politics of *Elizaveta Bam* by Daniil Kharms', in *Gender and Russian Literature: New Perspectives*, ed. Rosalind Marsh (Cambridge University Press, 1996), pp. 244–62.

Sazhin, Valery. 'Literaturnye i fol'klornye traditsii v tvorchestve D. I. Kharmsa', in *Literaturnyi protsess i razvitie russkoi kul'tury XVIII–XX vv: tezisy nauchnoi konferentsii* (Tallinn: Tallinskii politekhnicheskii institut, 1985), pp. 23–4.

'Chitaya Daniila Kharmsa', *Daugava*, 10 (1986), 110–15.

' "Chinari" – literaturnoe ob"edinenie 1920–1930-x godov (istochniki dlya izucheniya)', in Chudakova, M. O. (ed.), *Chetvertye Tynyanovskie chteniya: tezisy dokladov i materialy dlya obsuzhdeniya* (Riga: Zinatne, 1988), pp. 23–4.

' "...Sborishche druzei, ostavlennykh sud'boyu" ', in Chudakova (ed.), *Tynyanovskii sbornik: chetvertye Tynyanovskie chteniya* (Riga: Zinatne, 1990), pp. 194–201.

'Tsirk Kharmsa', *Znanie-sila*, 2 (1993), 89–94.

Scotto, Susan Downing, 'Daniil Xarms's Early Poetry and its Relations to His Later Poetry and Short Prose' (unpublished Ph.D. dissertation, University of California, Berkeley, 1984).

'Xarms and Hamsun: *Staruxa* Solves a Mystery?', *Comparative Literature Studies*, 23 (1986), 282–96.

Shindina, Ol'ga, 'Nekotorye osobennosti poetiki rannei prozy Vaginova', in Morev (ed.), *Mikhail Kuzmin i russkaya kul'tura XX veka: tezisy i materialy konferentsii 15–17 maya 1990g.* (Leningrad, 1990), pp. 103–11.

'Teatralizatsiya povestvovaniya v romane Vaginova "Kozlinaya pesn"'', *Teatr*, 11 (1991), 161–71.

Shirokov, Viktor, 'Poet tragicheskoi zabavy: posleslovie k reprintnomu izdaniyu', afterword to Vaginov, *Opyty soedineniya slov posredstvom ritma* (Moscow: Kniga, 1991).

Shklovsky Viktor, 'O tsvetnykh snakh', *Literaturnaya gazeta* (22 November 1967), p. 16.

Shukman, Ann, 'Towards a Poetics of the Absurd: The Prose Writings of Daniil Kharms', in Henri Broms and Rebecca Kaufmann (eds.), *Semiotics of Culture: Proceedings of the Tartu-Moscow School of Semiotics, Imatra, Finland, 27th–29th July, 1987* (Helsinki, 1987), pp. 81–95; this is a revised version of 'Toward a Poetics of the Absurd: The Prose Writings of Daniil Kharms', in Catriona Kelly, Michael Makin, and David Shepherd (eds.), *Discontinuous Discourses in Modern Russian Literature*, (Basingstoke and London: Macmillan, 1989), pp. 60–72.

Sigov, Sergey, 'Istoki poetiki Oberiu', *Russian Literature*, 20 (1986), 87–95.

'Orden zaumnikov', *Russian Literature*, 22 (1987), 85–96.

Simina, V. 'Kharms i Bely', *Literaturnoe obozrenie*, 9/10 (1994), 52–3.

Simonton, Margaret Dudley, 'From Solipsism to Dialogue: A Bakhtinian Approach to Nabokov's "Lolita" and Xarms's "Staruxa"' (unpublished Ph.D. dissertation, Washington University, 1992).

Sokol, Elena, 'Observations on the Prose of Daniil Kharms', *Proceedings of the Pacific North-West Conference on Foreign Languages*, 26, 1 (1975), 179–83.

Stelleman, Jenny, 'An Analysis of *Elizaveta Bam*', *Russian Literature*, 27 (1985), 319–52.

'The Transitional Position of *Elizaveta Bam* between Avant-Garde and Neo-Avant-Garde', in Jan van der Eng and Willem G. Weststeijn (eds.), *Avant Garde*, vols. v/vi ('USSR') (Amsterdam and Atlanta: Rodopi, 1991), pp. 207–29.

Aspects of Dramatic Communication: Action, Non-Action, Interaction: (A. P. Čechov, A. Blok, D. Charms) (Amsterdam and Atlanta: Rodopi, 1992).

Stoimenoff, Ljubomir, *Grundlagen und Verfahren des Sprachlichen Experiments im Frühwerk von Daniil I. Charms: Ein Beitrag zur Definition der 'obériutischen' Ästhetik* (Frankfurt: Peter Lang, 1984).

Teatr, 11 (1991). [special issue devoted to OBERIU].

Terras, Victor, 'Vaginov, Konstantin Konstantinovich', in Terras (ed.), *Handbook of Russian Literature* (New Haven and London: Yale University Press, 1985), pp. 500–1.

Ugrešić, Dubravka, 'Avangard i sovremennost' (Vaginov i Kabakov: tipologicheskaya parallel')', *Russian Literature*, 27 (1990), 83–96.

Uspensky, Fedor and Babaeva, Elena, 'Grammatika "absurda" i "absurd" grammatiki', *Wiener Slawistischer Almanach*, 29 (1992), 127–58.

Vishevsky, Anatoly, 'Tradition in the Topsy-Turvey World of Two Oberiu Plays', *Slavic and East European Journal*, 30 (1986), 355–66.

Wójodko, Alicia, 'Poęci z "Oberiu"', *Slavia Orientalis*, 3 (1967), 219–27.

Zabolotsky, Nikita, *The Life of Zabolotsky*, ed. R. R. Milner-Gulland, trans. R. R. Milner-Gulland and C. G. Bearne (Cardiff: University of Wales Press, 1994).

Zavalishin, Vyacheslav, 'Proza i stikhi Konstantina Vaginova', *Novyi zhurnal*, 157 (1984), 283–91.

OTHER SECONDARY SOURCES

Abzianidze, G. N. 'Chavchavadze, Aleksandr Garsevanovich', in Surkov and others (eds.), *Kratkaya literaturnaya entsiklopediya*, vol. VIII (1975), pp. 421–2.

Alter, Robert, *Partial Magic: The Novel as a Self-Conscious Genre* (London and Berkeley: University of California Press, 1975).

Amal'rik, Andrey, 'O sebe kak pisatele p'es', in Amal'rik, *P'esy* (Amsterdam: Fond imeni Gertsena, 1970), pp. 5–8.

Anemone, Anthony and Martynov, Ivan, 'Towards the History of the Leningrad Avant-Garde: The "Circle of Poets"', *Wiener Slawistischer Almanach*, 17 (1986), 131–48.

'The Islanders: Poetry and Polemics in Petrograd of the 1920s', *Wiener Slawistischer Almanach*, 29 (1992), 107–26.

[Anon.], 'Minin, Fedor Alekseevich', 'Minin, Kuz'ma', and 'Minin, Sergey Konstantinovich', in Prokhorov (ed.), *Bol'shaya sovetskaya entsiklopediya* (Moscow: Sovetskaya entsiklopediya, 1969–78), vol. XVI (1974), p. 287.

Any, Carol, *Boris Eikhenbaum: Voices of a Russian Formalist* (Stanford University Press, 1994).

Aucouturier, Michel, 'Theatricality as a Category of Early Twentieth-Century Russian Culture', in Kleberg and Nilsson (eds.), *Theater and Literature in Russia 1900–1930* (Stockholm: Almqvist and Wicksell International, 1984), pp. 9–21.

Barooshian, Vahan D. 'Russian Futurism in the Late 1920s: Literature of Fact', *The Slavic and East European Journal*, 15, 1 (1971), 38–46.

Bennett, Susan, *Theatre Audiences: A Theory of Production and Reception* (London and New York: Routledge, 1990).

Bennett, Tony, *Formalism and Marxism* (London and New York: Methuen, 1979).

Bertens, Hans, 'The Postmodern *Weltanschauung* and its Relation with Modernism: An Introductory Survey', in Fokkema and Bertens (eds.), *Approaching Postmodernism* (Amsterdam and Philadelphia: John Benjamins, 1986), pp. 9–51.

Birnoltz, Alan C. 'El Lissitsky and the Spectator: From Passivity to Participation', in Stephanie Barron and Maurice Tuchman (eds.), *The Avant-Garde in Russia, 1910–1930: New Perspectives* (Cambridge, Mass. and London: MIT Press, 1980), pp. 98–101.

Blyum, Arlen Viktorovich, *Za kulisami 'Ministerstva Pravdy': tainaya istoriya sovetskoi tsenzury, 1917–1929* (St Petersburg: Gumanitarnoe agentstvo 'Akademicheskii proekt', 1994).

Bowlt, John E. 'The "Union of Youth"', in Gibian and Tjalsma (eds.), *Russian Modernism: Culture and the Avant-Garde, 1900–1930* (Ithaca and London: Cornell University Press, 1976), pp. 165–87.

'Demented Words: Kazimir Malevič and the Energy of Language', in Magarotto, Marzaduri, and Ricci (eds.), *Zaumnyi futurizm i dadaizm v russkoi kul'ture* (Bern: Peter Lang, 1991), pp. 295–311.

Bradbury, Malcolm and Mcfarlane, James, 'The Name and Nature of Modernism', in Bradbury and Mcfarlane (eds.), *Modernism: A Guide to European Literature 1890–1930* (Harmondsworth: Penguin, 1991), pp. 19–55.

Bradbury, Malcolm and Mcfarlane, James (eds.), *Modernism: A Guide to European Literature 1890–1930* (Harmondsworth: Penguin, 1991).

Brooke-Rose, Christine. *A Rhetoric of the Unreal: Studies in Narrative and Structure, especially of the Fantastic* (Cambridge University Press, 1981).

Brown, Deming, *The Last Years of Soviet Russian Literature: Prose Fiction 1975–1991* (Cambridge University Press, 1993).

Brown, Edward J. *The Proletarian Episode in Russian Literature 1928–1932* (New York: Octagon Books, 1971).

Caillois, Roger, *Man, Play and Games*, trans. Meyer Barash (London: Thames and Hudson, 1962).

Calinescu, Matei, *Faces of Modernity. Avant-Garde. Decadence. Kitsch* (Bloomington and London: Indiana University Press, 1977).

'From the One to the Many: Pluralism in Today's Thought', in Ihab Hassan and Sally Hassan (eds.), *Innovation/Renovation: New Perspectives on the Humanities* (Madison: University of Wisconsin Press, 1983), pp. 263–88.

Clark, Katerina, *The Soviet Novel: History as Ritual* (Chicago and London: Chicago University Press, 1981).

Clark, Katerina and Holquist, Michael, *Mikhail Bakhtin* (Cambridge, Mass. and London: Harvard University Press, 1984).

Clayton, J. Douglas, 'The Play-within-the-play as Metaphor and Metatheatre in Modern Russian Drama', in Kleberg and Nilsson (eds.), *Theater and Literature in Russia 1900–1930: A Collection of Essays* (Stockholm: Almqvist and Wicksell International, 1984), pp. 71–82.

Pierrot in Petrograd: The Commedia dell'Arte/Balagan in Twentieth-Century Russian Theatre and Drama (Montreal and Kingston: McGill-Queen's University Press, 1993).

Cooke, Raymond, *Velimir Khlebnikov: A Critical Study* (Cambridge University Press, 1987).

Crosman, Robert, 'Do Readers Make Meaning?', in Susan R. Suleiman and Inge Crosman (eds.), *The Reader in the Text: Essays on Audience and Interpretation* (Princeton: Princeton University Press, 1980), pp. 149–64.

Culler, Jonathan, *Structuralist Poetics: Structuralism, Linguistics and the Study of Literature* (London: Routledge and Kegan Paul, 1975).

Doherty, Justin, *The Acmeist Movement in Russian Poetry: Culture and the Word* (Oxford: Clarendon Press, 1995).

Douglas, Charlotte, 'Views from the New World. A. Kruchenykh and K. Malevich: Theory and Painting', *Russian Literature Triquarterly*, 12 (1975), 353–70.

Elam, Keir, *The Semiotics of Theatre and Drama* (London and New York: Methuen, 1980).

Epshtein, Mikhail, 'Exposing the Quagmire', *Times Literary Supplement* (7 April 1989), p. 366.

'Iskusstvo avangarda i religioznoe soznanie', *Novyi mir*, 12 (1989), 222–35.

[Epstein] *After the Future: The Paradoxes of Postmodernism and Contemporary Russian Culture*, trans. Anesa Miller-Pogacar (Amherst, Mass.: University of Massachusetts Press, 1995).

Erickson, John D. *Dada: Performance, Poetry and Art* (Boston: Twayne, 1984).

Erlich, Victor, *Russian Formalism: History-Doctrine*, 3rd edn (New Haven and London: Yale University Press, 1981).

Modernism and Revolution: Russian Literature in Transition (Cambridge, Mass., and London: Harvard University Press, 1994).

Esslin, Martin, 'Modernist Drama: Wedekind to Brecht', in Bradbury and Macfarlane (eds.), *Modernism: A Guide to European Literature 1890–1930* (Harmondsworth: Penguin, 1991), pp. 527–60.

Federman, Raymond, 'Fiction Today or the Pursuit of Non-Knowledge', *Humanities in Society*, 1, 2 (1978), 115–31.

Fink, Eugen, 'The Oasis of Happiness: Toward an Ontology of Play', *Yale French Studies*, 41 (1968), 19–30.

Fokkema, Douwe, and Bertens, Hans, *Approaching Postmodernism*, (Amsterdam and Philadelphia: John Benjamins, 1986).

Gallagher, D. P. 'The Surrealist Mode in Twentieth-Century Russian Literature' (unpublished Ph.D. dissertation, University of Kansas, 1975).

Gardiner, Michael, *The Dialogics of Critique: M. M. Bakhtin and the Theory of Ideology* (London and New York: Routledge, 1992).

Gass, William H. *Fiction and the Figures of Life* (New York: Alfred A. Knopf, 1970).

Gibian, George, 'Introduction', in Gibian and Tjalsma (eds.), *Russian Modernism: Culture and the Avant-Garde, 1900–1930* (Ithaca and London: Cornell University Press, 1976), pp. 9–17.

Gibian, G. and Tjalsma, H. W. (eds.), *Russian Modernism: Culture and the Avant-Garde, 1900–1930*, (Ithaca and London: Cornell University Press, 1976).

Golub, Spencer, *Evreinov: The Theatre of Paradox and Transformation* (Ann Arbor, Mich.: UMI Research Press, 1984).

'Mortal Masks: Yevreinov's Drama in Two Acts', in Russell and Barrett (eds.), *Russian Theatre in the Age of Modernism* (Basingstoke and London: Methuen, 1990), pp. 123–47.

'The Curtainless Stage and the Procrustean Bed: Socialist Realism and Stalinist Theatrical Eminence', *Theatre Survey*, 32 (1991), 64–84.

Gombrich, E. H. *Art and Illusion: A Study in the Psychology of Pictorial Representation*, 5th edn (Oxford: Phaidon Press, 1977).

Gordon, Mel, 'Meyerhold's Biomechanics', *Drama Review*, 63 (September 1974), 73–88.

Gray, Camilla, *The Great Experiment: Russian Art 1863–1922* (London: Thames and Hudson, 1962).

Greber, Erika, 'The Metafictional Turn in "Russian Hoffmannism"': Veniamin Kaverin and E. T. A. Hoffmann', *Essays in Poetics*, 17, 1 (1992), 1–34.

Grois, Boris, 'O pol'ze teorii dlya iskusstva', *Literaturnaya gazeta* (31 October 1990), p. 5.

Harries, Karsten, 'Language and Silence: Heidegger's Dialogue with Georg Trakl', in William V. Spanos (ed.), *Martin Heidegger and the Question of Literature: Toward a Postmodern Literary Hermeneutic* (Bloomington and London: Indiana University Press, 1979), pp. 155–71.

Heath, Stephen, *The Nouveau Roman: A Study in the Practice of Writing* (London: Elek, 1972).

Hirschkop, Ken, and Shepherd, David (eds.), *Bakhtin and Cultural Theory* (Manchester and New York: Manchester University Press, 1989).

Holquist, Michael, 'Introduction', in Bakhtin, *The Dialogic Imagination: Four Essays by M. M. Bakhtin*, ed. M. Holquist, trans. Emerson and Holquist (Austin: University of Texas Press, 1981), pp. xv–xxxiv.

Holub, Robert C. *Reception Theory: A Critical Introduction* (London and New York: Methuen, 1984).

Hutcheon, Linda, *Narcissistic Narrative: The Metafictional Paradox* (London and New York: Methuen, 1983).

A Poetics of Postmodernism. History. Theory. Fiction (London and New York: Methuen, 1988).

Hyde, G. M. 'Russian Futurism', in Bradbury and Macfarlane (eds.), *Modernism: A Guide to European Literature 1890–1930* (Harmondsworth: Penguin, 1991), pp. 259–73.

Jefferson, Ann, *The Nouveau Roman and the Poetics of Fiction* (Cambridge University Press, 1980).

'Realism Reconsidered: Bakhtin's Dialogism and the "Will to Reference"', *Australian Journal of French Studies*, 23 (1986), 169–84.

'Russian Formalism', in Jefferson and Robey (eds.), *Modern Literary Theory: A Comparative Introduction* (London: B. T. Batsford, 1986), pp. 24–45.

Jefferson, Ann and Robey, David (eds.), *Modern Literary Theory: A Comparative Introduction* (London: B. T. Batsford, 1986).

Kalbouss, George, 'Russian Drama and The Self-Conscious Play', *Russian Language Journal*, 32 (1978), 107–21.

Kenez, P. *Cinema and Soviet Society, 1917–1953* (Cambridge University Press, 1992).

Kern, Gary, 'The Serapion Brothers: A Dialectics of Fellow Travelling', *Russian Literature Triquarterly*, 2 (1972), 223–47.

Kleberg, Lars, 'The Nature of the Soviet Audience: Theatrical Ideology and Audience Research in the 1920s', in Russell and Barrett (eds.), *Russian Theatre in the Age of Modernism* (Basingstoke and London: Macmillan, 1990), pp. 172–95.

Theatre as Action: Soviet Russian Avant-Garde Aesthetics (Basingstoke and London: Macmillan, 1993).

Kleberg, Lars, and Nilsson, Nils Åke (eds.),*Theater and Literature in Russia 1900–1930: A Collection of Essays* (Stockholm: Almqvist and Wicksell International, 1984).

Kochan, Lionel, *The Making of Modern Russia*, (Harmondsworth: Penguin, 1962).

Kon, L. 'O yumore', *Detskaya literatura*, 8 (1937), 6–13.

Kropf, David Glenn, *Authorship as Alchemy: Subversive Writing in Pushkin, Scott, Hoffmann* (Stanford: Stanford University Press, 1994).

Le Vot, Andre, 'Disjunctive and Conjunctive Modes in Contemporary American Fiction', *Forum*, 14, 1 (1976), 44–55.

Likhachev, D. S. and Panchenko, A. M. *'Smekhovoi mir' drevnei Rusi* (Leningrad: Nauka, 1976).

Lotman, Ju. M. 'The Stage and Painting as Code Mechanisms for Cultural Behavior in the Early Nineteenth Century', trans. Judith Armstrong, in Ju. M. Lotman and B. A. Uspensky, *The Semiotics of Russian Culture*, ed. Ann Shukman (Ann Arbor, Mich.: Michigan University Press, 1984), pp. 165–76.

Lucente, Gregory, *Beautiful Fables: Self-Consciousness in Italian Narrative from Manzoni to Calvino* (Baltimore and London: Johns Hopkins University Press, 1986).

Lyotard, Jean-François, *The Postmodern Condition: A Report on Knowledge*, trans. Geoff Bennington and Brian Massumi (Manchester: Manchester University Press, 1984).

Magarotto, Luigi, Marzaduri, Marzio, and Ricci, Daniela (eds.), *Zaumnyi futurizm i dadaizm v russkoi kul'ture* (Bern: Peter Lang, 1991).

Maguire, Robert A. *Red Virgin Soil: Soviet Literature in the 1920's* (Princeton University Press, 1968).

Malkin, Jeanette R. *Verbal Violence in Contemporary Drama: From Handke to Shepard* (Cambridge University Press, 1992).

Malmstad, John E. 'Mikhail Kuzmin: A Chronicle of his Life and Times', in M. A. Kuzmin, *Sobranie stikhov*, ed. J. E. Malmstad and V. Markov, 3 vols. (Munich: Wilhelm Fink, 1977–8), vol. III (1977), pp. 7–319.

Markov, Vladimir, *Russian Futurism: A History* (Berkeley and Los Angeles: University of California Press, 1968).

Morson, Gary Saul, 'The Heresiarch of *Meta*', *PTL: A Journal for the Descriptive Poetics and Theory of Literature*, 3 (1978), 407–27.

Morson, Gary Saul and Emerson, Caryl, *Mikhail Bakhtin: Creation of a Prosaics* (Stanford University Press, 1990).

Müller, Bertram, 'Zagadochnyi mir Vladimira Kazakova', introduction to Kazakov, *Sluchainyi voin. Stikhotvoreniya 1961–1976. Poemy. Dramy. Ocherk >Zudesnik<* (Munich: Otto Sagner in Kommission, 1978), pp. 5–13.

Nazarov, V. D. 'Pozharsky, Dmitry Mikhailovich', in Prokhorov (ed.), *Bol'shaya sovetskaya entsiklopediya* (Moscow: Sovetskaya entsiklopediya, 1969–78), vol. XIX (1975), p. 360.

Nikol'skaya, T. 'I. Terent'ev', *Russian Literature*, 22 (1987), 75–84.

Nivat, Georges, *Vers la fin du mythe russe* (Lausanne: L'Age d'Homme, 1982).

Ortega y Gasset, José, 'The Dehumanization of Art', in Ortega y Gasset, *The Dehumanization of Art, and Other Writings on Art and Culture* (New York: Doubleday, 1956), pp. 1–50.

Oulanoff, Hongor, *The Serapion Brothers: Theory and Practice* (The Hague and Paris: Mouton, 1966).

Palmer, Richard E. 'Towards a Postmodern Hermeneutics of Performance', in Michel Benamou and Charles Caramello (eds.), *Performance in Postmodern Culture* (Madison: University of Wisconsin Press, 1977), pp. 19–32.

Petrić, Vlada, *Constructivism in Film. The Man with the Movie Camera: A Cinematic Analysis* (Cambridge University Press, 1987).

Piper, D. G. B. 'Formalism and the Serapion Brothers', *Slavonic and East European Review*, 47 (1969), 78–93.

    V. A. Kaverin: A Soviet Writer's Response to the Problem of Commitment: The Relationship of 'Skandalist' and 'Khudozhnik Neizvesten' to the Development of Soviet Literature in the Late Nineteen-Twenties (Pittsburgh: Duquesne University Press, 1970).

Pittman, Riitta H. 'Valeriya Narbikova's Iconoclastic Prose', *Forum for Modern Language Studies*, 28 (1992), 376–89.

Popkin, Cathy, *The Pragmatics of Insignificance: Chekhov, Zoshchenko, Gogol* (Stanford University Press, 1993).

Porter, Robert, *Russia's Alternative Prose* (Oxford and Providence: Berg, 1994).

Prokhorov, A. M. (ed.), *Bol'shaya sovetskaya entsiklopediya*, 30 vols., 3rd edn (Moscow: Sovetskaya entsiklopediya, 1969–78).

Pyman, Avril, *A History of Russian Symbolism* (Cambridge University Press, 1994).

Radiani, Sh. D., 'Chavchavadze, Il'ya Grigor'evich', in Surkov and others (eds.), *Kratkaya literaturnaya entsiklopediya*, vol. VIII (1975), pp. 422–4.

Read, Herbert, *A Concise History of Modern Painting*, 3rd edn (London: Thames and Hudson, 1988).

Read, Herbert (ed.), *The Thames and Hudson Dictionary of Art and Artists* (London: Thames and Hudson, 1985).

Revzina, O. [summary of Dorogov, A. 'Idei M. M. Bakhtina v istoriko-kul'turnom kontekste' (unpublished paper presented at a conference to mark Bakhtin's 75th birthday at Moscow University)], *Voprosy yazykoznaniya*, 2 (1971), 160–2.

Revzina, O. G. and Revzin, I. I. 'Semioticheskii eksperiment na stsene (Narushenie postulata normal'nogo obshcheniya kak dramaturgicheskii priem)', *Trudy po znakovym sistemam*, 5 (1971), 232–54.

Robin, Régine, *Socialist Realism: An Impossible Aesthetic*, trans. Catherine Porter (Stanford University Press, 1992).

Roginsky A. B. and Superfin, G. G. (eds.), *Materialy XXII nauchnoi studencheskoi konferentsii. Poetika. Istoriya literatury. Lingvistika* (Tartu: Tartuskii gosudarstvennyi universitet, 1967).

Rosenthal, Bernice Glatzer, 'Nietzsche and Russian Futurism', in Peter I. Barta (ed.), *The European Foundations of Russian Modernism* (Lewinston, Queenston, Lampeter: Edwin Mellen Press, 1991), pp. 219–50.

Russell, Charles, *Poets, Prophets, and Revolutionaries: The Literary Avant-Garde from Rimbaud through Postmodernism* (New York and Oxford: Oxford University Press, 1985).

Russell, Robert, and Barrett, Andrew (eds.), *Russian Theatre in the Age of Modernism* (Basingstoke and London: Macmillan, 1990).

Schmidt, Herta, 'Postmodernism in Russian Drama: Vampilov, Amalrik, Aksenov', in Fokkema and Bertens (eds.), *Approaching Postmodernism* (Amsterdam and Philadelphia: John Benjamins, 1986), pp. 157–84.

Segal, Dmitry, 'Literatura kak okhrannaya gramota', *Slavica Hierosolymitana*, 5–6 (1981), 151–244.

Segel, Harold B. *Twentieth-Century Russian Drama: From Gorky to the Present* (New York: Columbia University Press, 1979).

'German Expressionism and Early Soviet Drama', in Russell and Barrett (eds.), *Russian Theatre in the Age of Modernism* (Basingstoke and London: Methuen, 1990), pp. 196–218.

Sellin, Eric, *The Dramatic Concepts of Antonin Artaud* (Chicago and London: Chicago University Press, 1968).

Senelick, Laurence, 'Introduction', in Senelick (trans. and ed.), *Russian Dramatic Theory from Pushkin to the Symbolists: An Anthology* (Austin: University of Texas Press, 1981), pp. xv–lv.

Shepherd, David, 'Bakhtin and the Reader' in Hirschkop and Shepherd (eds.), *Bakhtin and Cultural Theory* (Manchester and New York: Manchester University Press, 1989), pp. 90–102.

Beyond Metafiction: Self-Consciousness in Soviet Literature (Oxford: Clarendon Press, 1992).

Short, Robert, 'Dada and Surrealism', in Bradbury and Macfarlane (eds.), *Modernism: A Guide to European Literature 1890–1930* (Harmondsworth: Penguin, 1991), pp. 292–308.

Slonim, Marc, *Russian Theater: From the Empire to the Soviets* (London: Methuen, 1963).

Soviet Russian literature: Writers and Problems, 1917–1977, 2nd edn (Oxford and New York: Oxford University Press, 1977).

Sokol, Elena, *Russian Poetry for Children* (Knoxville: University of Tennessee Press, 1984).

Sperber, Dan and Wilson, Deirdre, *Relevance: Communication and Cognition* (Oxford: Blackwell, 1986).

[Wilson and Sperber], 'An Outline of Relevance Theory', in *Encontro de Linguistas: Actas* [n. ed.] (Braga: Universidade de Minho, 1986), pp. 19–41.

Steiner, Peter, *Russian Formalism: A Metapoetics* (Ithaca and London: Cornell University Press, 1984).

Stephan, Halina, *'LEF' and the Left Front of the Arts* (Munich: Otto Sagner, 1981).

Stewart, Susan, *Nonsense: Aspects of Intertextuality in Folklore and Literature* (Baltimore and London: Johns Hopkins University Press, 1979).

Surkov, A. A. and others (eds.), *Kratkaya literaturnaya entsiklopediya*, 9 vols. (Moscow: Sovetskaya entsiklopediya, 1962–78).

Taylor, R. and Spring, D. *Stalinism and Soviet Cinema* (London: Routledge, 1993).

Terras, Victor (ed.), *Handbook of Russian Literature* (New Haven and London: Yale University Press, 1985).

Thiher, Allen, *Words in Reflection: Modern Language Theory and Postmodern Fiction* (Chicago and London: University of Chicago Press, 1984).

Thomson, Boris, *Lot's Wife and the Venus of Milo: Conflicting Attitudes to the Cultural Heritage in Modern Russia* (Cambridge University Press, 1978).

Titunik, I. R. 'Mikhail Zoshchenko and the Problem of *Skaz'*, *California Slavic Studies*, 6 (1971), 83–96.

Tjalsma, H. W. 'The Petersburg Poets', in Gibian and Tjalsma (eds.), *Russian Modernism: Culture and the Avant-Garde, 1900–1930* (Ithaca and London: Cornell University Press, 1976), pp. 65–84.

Vaughan, James C. *Soviet Socialist Realism: Origin and Theory* (New York: St Martin's Press, 1973).

Vulis, A. *Sovetskii satiricheskii roman: evolyutsiya zhanra v 20-e – 30-e gody* (Tashkent: Nauka, 1966).

Vygotsky, Lev, *The Psychology of Art*, trans. Scripta Technica (Cambridge, Mass. and London: MIT Press, 1971).

Waugh, Patricia, *Metafiction: The Theory and Practice of Self-Conscious Fiction* (London and New York: Methuen, 1984).

White, Allon, 'Bakhtin, Sociolinguistics and the Novel', in Frank Gloversmith (ed.), *The Theory of Reading* (Brighton and Totowa: Harvester Press, 1984), pp. 123–47.

Wilde, Alan, *Horizons of Assent: Modernism, Postmodernism, and the Ironic Imagination.* (Baltimore and London: Johns Hopkins University Press, 1981).

Wilson, Elizabeth, *Shostakovich: A Life Remembered* (London: Faber and Faber, 1994).

Wollen, Peter, *Signs and Meaning in the Cinema*, 3rd edn (London: Secker and Warburg, 1972).

Worrall, Nick, *Modernism to Realism on the Soviet Stage: Tairov – Vakhtangov – Okhlopkov* (Cambridge University Press, 1989).

Wright, Elizabeth, *Psychoanalytic Criticism: Theory and Practice* (London and New York: Methuen, 1984).

Zavalishin, Vyacheslav, *Early Soviet Writers* (New York: Frederick A. Praeger, 1958).

Zholkovsky, A. K. '19 oktjabrja 1982 g., or The Semiotics of a Soviet Cookie Wrapper', *Wiener Slawistischer Almanach*, 11 (1983), 341–54.

Ziegler, Rosemarie, 'Aleksey E. Kruchenykh', *Russian Literature*, 19 (1986), 79–104.

Zolotonosov, Mikhail, 'Muzyka vo l'du', *Iskusstvo Leningrada*, 1 (1989), 37–41 and 45–56.

Since this book went to press, a major study of carnival and Russian literature has appeared, with sections on Kharms and Vaginov.

Brandist, Craig, *Carnival Culture and the Soviet Modernist Novel* (Macmillan: Basingstoke and London, 1996).

Index

Titles of works are listed in English under the names of the authors

ABDEM, 17
Absurd, literature of the, 2, 97, 142, 176,
    211 n.46, 225 n.65, 235 n.5
Acmeism, 23, 75, 121, 128
active understanding (*see* Bakhtin)
addressee (*see* Bakhtin)
Akhmatova, Anna, 2, 4, 23
Aksenov, Vasily, 176
Amal'rik, Andrey, 2, 176, 235 n.10
Apollinaire, Guillaume, 22
Apollonius of Tyana, 232 n.126
aporetic duplication, 232 n.124
Aristotle, 105, 168
Artaud, Antonin, 2, 219 n.11
art
    'trans-rational' (*see* zaum')
    visual, 159–70
audience, theatre, 94–105, 176, 216 n.96
author, 22–74, 75, 157
avant-garde, 179 n.1
    Soviet, 30, 128, 176

Bakhterev, Igor', 1–21, 32–3, 84, 94, 130,
    173, 179–80 n.2, 186 n.33, 188 n.46,
    236 n.13
    'The Ancient Greek Squabble (A
        Vaudeville)', 223 n.46
    'The Eternally Standing', 130
    'I asked: / what time? . . .', 228 n.89
    'An Incident in "The Crooked
        Stomach"', 33
    'In the Junk Shop', 191 n.65
    'Koloborot', 32–3
    'The Old Man who Hanged Himself
        Instead of a Lamp', 188 n.47
    'Only a Pintle', 84–5

'The Shop with a Hole in it', 14, 222
    n.44
'Tsar Makedon, or Fenya and the
    Chebolveki', 130, 216 n.99, 236 n.14
'The Well-Known Artist', 194 n.10
'A Winter Stroll', 12
Bakhtin, Mikhail, 2, 4, 18, 29–30, 33, 63,
    69–70, 81–3, 104, 107, 113, 124–5,
    169, 172, 174–5, 181–2 n.15, 196–7
    n.43, 199 n.72, 200–1 n.81, 208–9
    n.146, 218 n.109, 234 n.141
    active understanding, 20, 82, 106, 171
    addressee, 19, 75, 81, 97, 104, 105, 110,
        219 n.119
    carnival, 30, 38, 40–4, 70, 73, 125, 145,
        171, 201 n.82, 207 n.136
    dialogism, 30, 81–2, 103, 105–19, 171,
        216 n.93
    heteroglossia, 30, 72–3, 169, 171
    menippean satire, 40–4, 49, 201 n.84,
        201 n.87
    polyphony, 30
Bakhtin circle (*see* Bakhtin, Mikhail)
balagan, 51, 56, 101, 198 n.58, 215 n.87
Barthes, Roland, 51, 76, 93, 110, 213 n.63
Baskakov, A. A., 7
Beckett, Samuel
    The Unnamable, 175
Bely, Andrey, 98, 120–1
Bitov, Andrey, 175
Blok, Aleksandr,
    A realibus ad realiora, 120
    The Fairground Booth, 214 n.77, 215 n.83
Bolsheviks, 61, 64, 124, 157, 169
Brik, Osip, 2, 6, 28, 43–4, 174
Brooke-Rose, Christine, 168

'Brotherhood of Fools', 3
Bulgakov, Mikhail, 2
   Master and Margarita, 206 n.130
Butor, Michel, 176

Calinescu, Matei, 178, 232 n.125
Calvino, Italo
   If on a Winter's Night a Traveller, 235 n.9
carnival (*see* Bakhtin)
Chavchavadze, Aleksandr
   Garsevanovich, 218 n.118
Chavchavadze, Il'ya Grigor'evich, 218
   n.118
Chekhov, Anton, 94, 97, 212–13 n.60
chinari, 4, 14, 18, 20, 46, 125–8, 130, 131,
   139, 141–2, 150, 151, 156, 158, 168,
   174, 184 n.23, 198 n.63, 220–1 n.24,
   221 n.27, 222 n.39, 226 n.72, 228 n.96
Chuzhak, Nikolay, 28, 43–4, 174
cognition, art as, 23, 24, 56, 80, 122, 128,
   213 n.65, 219 n.6
commedia dell'arte, 76, 211 n.41
Communist Party, 13, 77–8, 95, 122, 184
   n.22
Conceptualism, 2, 177, 235 n.13
concrete object, 222 n.36, 222 n.38
Constructivism, 25–6, 77
cultural materialism, 63

'Dada', 22
Darwin, Charles, 22
death, 40, 44–56, 86, 96, 97, 119, 145–7,
   153–6, 161, 164–7
defamiliarization (*see* Formalism, Russian)
Derrida, Jacques, 114
dialogism (*see* Bakhtin)
Dostoevsky, Fedor, 97
   Crime and Punishment, 200 n.80
   Diary or a Writer, 206 n.130
   Notes from Underground, 201 n.88
Druskin, Yakov, 4, 20, 125–7, 133, 142,
   145, 147–8, 149, 150, 174, 182 n.18,
   183 n.19, 198 n.63, 221 n.27, 222 n.43
   'minor error' ('pogreshnost''), 126
Druskina, L. S., 225 n.67

Eikhenbaum, Boris, 4, 6, 27, 80
Einstein, Albert, 123
Eisenstein, Sergey, 25, 77
embedded representation (*see* mise en
   abyme)
'Emotionalists', 3–4, 205 n.123

eschatology, 148, 150–6, 178, 215 n.84, 227
   n.82
Evreinov, Nikolay, 76, 95, 185 n.27, 214
   n.77, 215 n.83
Expressionism, German, 216 n.97

'41°', 182 n.17
Fedin, Konstantin, 4, 26
Filonov, Pavel, 9, 26, 186 n.33, 187–8
   n.44, 220 n.12
Finch, The (Chizh), 7, 180 n.6
Fish, Stanley, 114
Formalism, Russian, 2, 4, 6, 18, 27–8, 29,
   33, 80–1, 83, 103, 107, 124–5
   defamiliarization, 19, 38, 76, 80, 83–4,
   97, 103, 124
   retardation device, 84
   zero ending, 212 n.54, 221 n.27
Foucault, Michel, 51
Futurism, 105
   Russian, 1, 23, 75–6, 121–2, 124, 193–4
   n.7, 199 n.67

Gastev, Aleksey, 25
Gide, André
   The Counterfeiters, 232 n.124
Gladkov, Fedor,
   Cement, 26
God, 20, 39, 41, 43, 44, 89, 126, 133, 145,
   146, 147, 150, 151, 155–6, 201 n.89,
   213 n.66
Gogol', Nikolay, 37, 56, 84, 94, 175
   The Government Inspector, 49, 50, 79,
   122–3
   'Nevsky Prospect', 33
   'The Overcoat', 212 n.58
   Taras Bul'ba, 50
Gombrich, E. H., 232 n.126
Goncharova, Nataliya, 23
Griboedov, Aleksandr
   Woe From Wit, 86
'Guild of Poets', 3, 17, 192 n.76, 204 n.116
Gumilev, Nikolay, 17, 23, 75, 79, 204 n.116

Havel, Václav, 225 n.65
Hedgehog, The (Ezh), 7, 180 n.6
Heidegger, Martin, 2, 20, 154–6, 178, 229
   n.102, 230 n.108
heteroglossia (*see* Bakhtin)
Hinton, Charles, 123
Hoffmann, E. T. A., 122
   Tomcat Murr, 232 n.129

'holy fool in Christ', 37–8

Ibsen, Henrik, 97
ideology, 29, 63, 95, 97, 102, 125, 169, 234
   n.140, 234 n.141
imagination, reality of, 150
intelligentsia, 57, 64, 206 n.129
intertextuality, 19, 23, 51, 55, 57, 79, 117,
   177, 200 n.80, 201 n.89
Ionesco, Eugène, 225 n.65
irony, 41–2, 66, 166, 169, 177
'Islanders', 3, 192 n.76, 206 n.127
Ivanov, Vsevolod, 26
Ivanov, Vyacheslav, 206 n.128

Kabakov, Il'ya, 177
Kandinsky, Vasily, 76–7
Kant, Immanuel, 126, 224 n.56, 229 n.102
Katsman, Georgy, 5, 141
Kaverin, Veniamin, 26–7
   The Purple Palimpsest, 79
Kazakov, Vladimir, 2, 175
Kharms, Daniil, 1–21, 32, 33–44, 47, 49,
   52, 57, 74, 77, 83, 85–94, 99, 102,
   103, 105, 107, 108, 110, 119, 123, 124,
   125, 126, 128, 131–45, 156, 158, 159,
   166, 168, 169, 171–8, 182 n.15, 186
   n.33, 194 n.8, 194 n.10, 198 n.62, 221
   n.27, 221 n.32, 223 n.49, 224 n.58,
   225 n.63
   'impediment' ('prepyatstvie'), 126,
     133–4, 139, 142, 223 n.51
   'turning point' ('povorot'), 221 n.26, 223
     n.51
   'Anecdotes from Pushkin's Life', 36–7,
     38, 39–40
   'Archimedes' Bath', 186 n.36
   Archimedes' Bath, 186 n.36, 195 n.23
   'The Artist and the Watch', 93
   'At two o'clock in the afternoon . . .',
     93
   'The Beginning of a Beautiful Day (A
     Symphony)', 88
   'Blue Notebook No. 10', 136–7
   'The Bronze Look', 90
   'The Career of Ivan Yakovlevich
     Antonov', 90
   The Comedy of the City of Petersburg, 51,
     85–6, 102
   'Comprehensive Research', 137–8
   'The Connection', 90–1, 93, 178
   'The Drawback', 139

'The Dream of Two Swarthy Ladies',
   199 n.68
Elizaveta Bam, 20, 139–45, 156, 178, 188
   n.47, 221 n.29
'A Fairy Story', 34
'The Fate of the Professor's Wife', 37
'Fedya Davidovich', 87
'Five Unfinished Narratives', 35–6, 212
   n.56
'Four Illustrations', 34, 86
'Grigor'ev and Semenov', 88
'I cannot think uninterruptedly . . .',
   230 n.109
'Incident on the Railway', 185 n.28
'Incidents', 88
Incidents, 198 n.56, 223 n.51, 228 n.94
'Ivan Yakovlevich Bobov woke up . . .',
   91
'I have forgotten . . .', 36
'Knights', 34–5
[letter to K. V. Pugacheva], 39, 93,
   132–3, 145, 212 n.57
[letter to Nikandr Andreevich], 92
'Mashkin Killed Koshkin', 88–9
'The Mathematician and Andrey
   Semenovich', 92, 228 n.99
'A Meeting', 92–3
'Morning', 200 n.77
'Null and nil (spelt in the old way)', 221
   n.24
'Objects and Figures Discovered by
   Daniil Ivanovich Kharms', 223 n.48
The Old Woman, 18, 38–44, 49
'Ol'ga Forsh . . .', 37
'On the Circle', 221 n.24
'On the Death of Kazimir Malevich',
   194 n.10
'On Equilibrium', 91–2, 135
'On Phenomena and Existences No. 2',
   135–6
'On Time, Space, and Existence', 134
'Out of a House walked a Man', 39
'Pakin and Rakukin', 223 n.51
'Petrakov's Problem', 90
'The Plummeting Old Women', 86
'Power', 138–9
'Prayer Before Sleep', 204 n.120
'The Pursuit', 89
'Pushkin and Gogol'', 37
'The Story of the Fighting Men', 89–90
'Symphony No. 2', 35–6
'Vengeance', 189 n.56

'They Call me the Capuchin', 34–5
'To Oleinikov', 197 n.52, 220–1 n.24
'The Verse of Petr Yashkin', 185 n.28
'What they're Selling in the Shops
 these Days', 86
'A Winter Stroll', 12
Khlebnikov, Velimir, 23–4, 76, 121, 185
 n.27, 186 n.33, 194 n.8, 203 n.103,
 219 n.4, 226 n.70
 Victory over the Sun, 24, 219 n.10
 War in a Mousetrap, 203 n.104
kitsch, 163, 169, 176, 232 n.125
Klyuev, Nikolay, 185 n.28
Kogan, P. S., 24
Kropachev, Nikolay, 11
Kruchenykh, Aleksey, 23–4, 76, 121, 182
 n.17, 194 n.7, 202 n.98, 219 n.8, 221
 n.27, 223 n.48
 'Dyr bul shchyl', 23
 Victory over the Sun, 24, 57, 219 n.10
Kuzmin, Mikhail, 4, 13

language
 games, 139–45, 224 n.57
 materiality of (*see* word)
 ontological status of, 120–70
 primacy of, 126–45, 176, 221 n.27
Larionov, Mikhail, 23
LEF, 187 n.38
left art, 2, 8, 24, 28–9, 34–5, 43, 57, 107,
 122, 125, 132, 174, 185 n.27, 219 n.4,
 220 n.15
'Left Flank', 5, 185 n.28
'Left Front of the Arts' (*see* left art)
Leonov, Leonid
 The River Sot', 26
 The Thief, 232 n.124
Leskov, Nikolay
 'Lady Macbeth of the Mtsensk
 District', 79
Levin, Boris, 5, 6, 8, 10, 11, 12, 14, 16, 185
 n.30
Likhachev, D. S., 37–8
Lipavsky, Leonid, 4, 20, 125–7, 133, 142,
 145, 174, 183 n.18, 183 n.19, 186 n.33,
 212 n.52, 221 n.27, 221 n.29, 221 n.31,
 225 n.65
 vestniki, 127, 130, 224 n.54, 228 n.90, 230
 n.110
 'neighbouring world' ('sosednii mir'),
 130, 223 n.46
 'The Ox of Buddah', 4

Lissitsky, El
 'Beat the Whites with a Red Wedge',
 78
 Abstract Cabinet, 78
'literature of fact', 28
Lobachevsky, Nikolay, 123
Lunts, Lev, 26, 80, 122, 175, 222 n.37

Malevich, Kazimir, 4, 5, 9, 23–4, 123–4,
 186 n.33, 187–8 n.44, 194 n.10, 220
 n.12
 'Black Square', 23
 'Cow and Violin', 24
 'Englishman in Moscow', 24
Mamet, David, 225 n.65
Mandel'shtam, Osip, 13, 23, 75, 121
 The Egyptian Stamp, 206 n.130
Marinetti, Filippo, 105
Markov, Igor', 184 n.26
Marshak, Samuil, 7, 194 n.8
Marx, Karl, 22
Matveev, Venedikt, 184 n.26
Matyushin, Mikhail, 123, 219 n.9, 220
 n.12, 227 n.80
Mayakovsky, Vladimir, 6, 13, 76, 234
 n.140
 The Bedbug, 215 n.81
 'Homeward!', 23–4
 Vladimir Mayakovsky: A Tragedy, 215 n.89
menippean satire (*see* Bakhtin)
metadiscourse (*see* metafiction)
metafiction, 18, 32, 33, 57, 87, 94, 101, 107,
 130, 131, 140, 147, 148, 150, 151, 156,
 159, 168, 171–8, 192–3 n.82, 210 n.41,
 227 n.85, 232 n.124
metapoesis (*see* metafiction)
metatheatre (*see* metafiction)
Meyerkhol'd, Vsevolod, 25, 76, 79, 95, 214
 n.77
Meyer-Lipavskaya, Tamara, 125
mimesis, 98, 99, 105, 124, 166–9
Minin, Fedor Alekseevich, 202–3 n.101
Minin, Sergey Konstantinovich, 202–3
 n.101
Mints, Klementy,
 'Film No. 1: Meatgrinder', 11
mise en abyme, 71–3, 161–4
modernism, 176–8, 218 n.113
 Russian, 22–7, 75–80, 119, 120–4, 176
Molière, Jean-Baptiste
 The Miser, 70–1
Mukhin, Sergey Aleksandrovich, 231 n.117

Nabokov, Vladimir
The Gift, 206 n.130
Narbikova, Valeriya, 2, 175
Naturalism, 98, 99, 104, 105
'neighbouring world' (*see* Lipavsky)
New Novel, French, 2, 176
Nietzsche, Friedrich, 22
non-existence, 126–7, 134, 135–6, 150, 160,
    221 n.32
nonsense, 86–7, 145, 150, 174
New LEF, 6

OBERIU, 1–21, 30, 32, 43, 63, 82–4,
    125, 127–8, 148, 168, 171–8, 189
    n.54, 189 n.56, 197 n.48, 217 n.105,
    233 n.135
    article, 8–11, 31, 34, 57, 83, 173–4, 187
    n.42, 187 n.43
    'Three Left Hours' ('Tri levykh chasa'),
    7–12, 52, 139, 141
O'Brien, Flann
    At-Swim-Two-Birds, 176
Okhlopkov, Nikolay, 95, 100, 216 n.98
Oleinikov, Nikolay, 4, 6, 14, 17, 18,
    32–3, 173, 183–4 n.22, 197 n.52, 197
    n.53, 200 n.79, 212 n.59, 220–1
    n.24
    'A Change of Surname', 130
    'The Cockroach', 84
    In an Art Gallery, 84
    'On noughts', 220 n.24
    [trailer for *The Wedding*], 32
OPOYAZ (*see* Formalism, Russian)
'Order of the *zaumniki* DSO' (*see* Tufanov)
Orwell, George
    1984, 224 n.58
Ostrovsky, Nikolay
    How the Steel was Tempered, 26

Panchenko, A. M., 37–8
Pasternak, Boris
    Doctor Zhivago, 206 n.130
Philostratus, 62
Pil'nyak, Boris, 13, 105
    Materials for a Novel, 26
Pirandello, Luigi
    Six Characters in Search of an Author, 175
Plato, 167
play, 160–1, 165–6, 233 n.135, 233–4 n.138
    verbal, 23, 26, 80, 121, 149
Polonskaya, Elizaveta, 195 n.23
polyphony (*see* Bakhtin)

postmodernism, 2, 176–8, 235 n.11, 235
    n.13
primitivism, 23
'Production Novel', 26
proletarian literature, 25, 34 (*see also*
    RAPP)
'Proletkul't', 25
Propp, Vladimir, 212 n.52
Pushkin, Aleksandr, 36–8, 50, 56, 175
    'Conversation between a Bookseller
    and a Poet', 63, 193 n.5
    Eugene Onegin, 206 n.130
    'Ruslan and Lyudmila', 49, 84
    'The Golden Cockerel', 49
    The Queen of Spades, 200 n.80

'Radiks', 5–6, 141, 186 n.33
    'My Mum is Covered in Watches', 5–6
RAPP ('Russian Association of
    Proletarian Writers'), 13, 95, 105
Razumovsky, Aleksandr, 11, 12, 188 n.48
    'Film No. 1: Meatgrinder', 11
Reader-Reception Theory, 83, 218 n.110
reading, 75–119
realism, 86, 94, 95, 101, 105, 108, 110
    Realism, Socialist, 77, 86, 94–105
relevance, 85–94, 211 n.48, 213 n.65
retardation device (*see* Formalism,
    Russian)
'Ring of Poets in Honour of K. M.
    Fofanov', 3
Rodchenko, Aleksandr, 26
Romanticism, 2, 31, 62, 63, 67, 68, 70, 74,
    158, 173, 193 n.5
Rozanov, Vasily
    Fallen Leaves, 206 n.130
    Solitaria, 206 n.130

Sarraute, Nathalie, 176
Saussure, Ferdinand de, 127
Savel'ev, Leonid (*see* Lipavsky, Leonid)
Schwitters, Kurt, 204 n.113
self-consciousness, literary (*see* metafiction)
self-reflexiveness, literary (*see* metafiction)
'self-sufficient word', 23, 121, 193–4 n.7 (*see
    also* Futurism, Russian)
Serafimovich, A., 216 n.98
'Serapion Brothers', 26–7, 79–80, 122,
    175, 195 n.23, 217 n.108
Shaginyan, Marietta
    Hydrocentral, 26
Shepard, Sam, 225 n.65

Shklovsky, Viktor, 6, 13, 26–7, 80, 84, 124, 186 n.33, 186 n.36, 186–7 n.37, 211 n.47
  Minin and Pozharsky, 203 n.102
  The Third Factory, 27
Shostakovich, Dmitry
  Lady Macbeth of the Mtsensk District/ Katerina Izmailova, 79
Shvarts, Evgeny, 6
skaz, 32
Socialist Realism (*see* Realism, Socialist)
Sokolov, Sasha, 175
Sologub, Fedor, 4, 104–5
Sorokin, Vladimir, 2
'Sounding Shell', 3
Stalin, Iosif, 7, 95, 137, 141
Stanislavsky, Konstantin, 98
Strindberg, August, 218 n.113
Suprematism, 23
surrealism, 222–3 n.45
Symbolism, Russian, 23, 75, 98, 105, 120–2, 215 n.81

Tatlin, Vladimir
  'Relief Constructions', 25
Terent'ev, Igor', 4, 9, 79, 122–3, 182 n.17, 219 n.11
Theatre of the Absurd (*see* Absurd, literature of the)
theatricality, 105, 168, 214 n.77
Tikhonov, Nikolay, 195 n.23, 224 n.58
time, 44–56, 96, 100–1, 118, 123, 126, 129, 130, 145–50, 156, 157, 166, 202 n.91, 203–4 n.112
Tolstaya, Tat'yana, 2
Tolstoy, Lev, 22–3, 37
Tomashevsky, Boris, 6
tradition, literary, 36, 40, 65, 198 n.63, 200 n.80, 201 n.88, 204–5 n.121
Tret'yakov, Sergey, 77
Tsimbal, Sergey, 5, 6, 12, 189 n.50
Tufanov, Aleksandr, 5, 122, 186 n.33, 188 n.45, 219 n.9, 223 n.48
  'Order of the *zaumniki* DSO', 5, 186 n.34
Turgenev, Ivan
  A Nest of Gentlefolk, 111
Tynyanov, Yury, 4, 6, 27–8, 80, 186 n.36

Union of Poets, 5, 6, 13, 185 n.28, 202 n.97
'Union of Youth', 220 n.12
Uspensky, Petr, 123

Vaginov, Konstantin, 1–21, 31, 32, 33, 57–74, 83, 105–19, 120, 128, 156, 157–70, 171–8, 181–2 n.15, 183 n.19, 185 n.28, 186 n.33, 190 n.61, 191–2 n.74, 204 n.116, 204–5 n.121, 208–9 n.146, 217 n.104, 217 n.105, 217 n.107, 218 n.117, 229 n.106, 231 n.118
  membership of OBERIU, 15–17, 192 n.80, 193 n.83
  [untitled collection of poems, 1926], 190 n.61
  1905, 190 n.61
  'Amid wondrous nocturnal wanderings ...', 231 n.114
  'Art', 59–61
  Bambocciade, 20, 159–70, 175
  'Black is the endless morning ...', 158
  'The End of a First Love', 190 n.61
  Experiments in Combining Words by Means of Rhythm, 190 n.61
  The Goat's Song, 12, 19, 63–70, 74, 106, 107, 115, 116, 157, 158, 164, 168, 175, 206 n.130, 206–7 n.132, 230 n.108
  'Glory to you, Apollo, glory! ...', 58
  Harpagoniana, 19, 70–4, 107, 169, 178, 207–8 n.137, 208 n.143
  'Hermits', 157, 230 n.112, 230 n.114
  'I live as a hermit ...', 58–9
  'It is morning once again ...', 57–8
  Journey into Chaos: Poems, 190 n.61
  The Labours and Days of Svistonov, 19, 83, 105–19, 120, 157, 175, 206 n.130, 235 n.11
  'Leningrad', 233 n.137
  'Like a fierce bull ...', 60–1
  Likeness of Sound, 158, 190 n.61
  'The Monastery of our Lord Apollo', 61–3, 190 n.61
  'O, make into a ringing statue ...', 59
  Petersburg Nights, 190 n.61
  'Play, player ...', 233–4 n.138
  'Rhodes is noisy ...', 231 n.114
  'The Song of Words', 61, 157, 230 n.113
  'The Star of Bethlehem', 61–2, 157, 190 n.61
  'Words from the ash of moulds', 233 n.136
  'The Year 1925', 63, 157, 190 n.61
Vampilov, Aleksandr, 176
Vertov, Dziga, 77–8
  Man with a Movie Camera, 26, 78
vestniki (*see* Lipavsky)

Vigilyansky, Yevgeny, 5, 6, 184 n.25, 189 n.53
Vishnevsky, Vsevolod
  The Final Battle, 95
Vladimirov, Yury, 12
  'The Gymnast', 189 n.51, 211 n.44
Voloshinov, Valentin, 29, 104
Voronsky, Aleksandr, 219 n.6
Vrubel', Mikhail, 23
Vvedensky, Aleksandr, 1–21, 32, 33,
    44–57, 74, 82, 83, 89, 94–105, 107,
    110, 119, 123, 125, 127, 128, 141,
    145–56, 157, 158, 159, 166, 168, 169,
    171–8, 183 n.19, 186 n.33, 187 n.42,
    194 n.8, 203–4 n.112, 215–16 n.92,
    220 n.24, 221 n.32, 233 n.131
  '24 Hours', 146, 229 n.101
  All Around Maybe God, 46, 52, 146, 147,
    149–50, 227 n.80, 228 n.97, 229 n.102
  A Certain Quantity of Conversations, 20,
    150, 151–6, 230 n.108
  Christmas at the Ivanovs', 19, 83, 94–105,
    107, 110, 119, 146, 216 n.101, 228 n.95,
    229 n.105
  'The Eyewitness and the Rat', 44–5,
    146, 149, 215 n.82
  'Fact, Theory, and God', 147, 216 n.93,
    229 n.101
  'Four Descriptions', 146–7, 228 n.90
  'The Gods' Answer', 146
  'Grey Notebook', 45–6, 52–3, 55–6,
    150, 202 n.94, 226 n.78
  'The Guest on a Horse', 148
  'I am sorry that I am not a wild beast
    ...', 147, 148–9, 229 n.106
  'An Invitation to Think Me', 150
  'Kupriyanov and Natasha', 146
  'The Meaning of the Sea', 147
  Minin and Pozharsky, 19, 46–57, 62, 117
  'The Mirror and the Musician', 150

  'The Ox of Buddah', 4
  'Potets', 149, 229 n.104
  'The Saint and his Followers', 147
  'Two Little Birds, Grief, the Lion, and
    Night', 148
  'When.Where.', 146
Vygotsky, Lev, 213 n.65

Wittgenstein, Ludwig, 2, 145, 154, 226
    n.73
word, materiality of, 147–9, 157–8

Yudina, Mariya, 182 n.15, 213 n.65, 217
    n.104
'yurodivyi' (*see* 'holy fool in Christ')

Zabolotsky, Nikolay, 1–21, 26, 31–3, 57,
    83–4, 125, 128–30, 173, 175, 185 n.31,
    186 n.33, 187 n.42, 189 n.52, 199
    n.70, 214 n.75, 222 n.39, 224 n.58,
    228 n.92
  'An Evening Bar', 84
  'Art', 31, 128–9
  'The Battle of the Elephants', 129
  'Dinner', 84
  'The Face of a Horse', 129
  'Farewell to Friends', 14–15
  'Football', 84
  'The Mad Wolf', 84
  Scrolls, 12
  'The Thistle', 84
  'The Triumph of Agriculture', 31
Zamyatin, Yevgeny, 13, 105
zaum', 5, 9, 12–13, 23, 24, 79, 121–3, 124,
    131, 140, 188 n.47, 194 n.9, 219 n.8
Zdanevich, Il'ya, 182 n.17
zero ending (*see* Formalism, Russian)
Zhdanov, Andrey, 95
Zoshchenko, Mikhail, 4, 26–7, 77, 94,
    212–13 n.60

Dostoyevsky and the process of literary creation
JACQUES CATTEAU

The poetic imagination of Vyacheslav Ivanov
PAMELA DAVIDSON

Joseph Brodsky
VALENTINA POLUKHINA

Petrushka – the Russian carnival puppet theatre
CATRIONA KELLY

Turgenev
FRANK FRIEDEBERG SEELEY

From the idyll to the novel: Karamzin's sentimentalist prose
GITTA HAMMARBERG

The Brothers Karamazov *and the poetics of memory*
DIANE OENNING THOMPSON

Andrei Platonov
THOMAS SEIFRID

Nabokov's early fiction
JULIAN W. CONNOLLY

Iurii Trifonov
DAVID GILLESPIE

Mikhail Zoshchenko
LINDA HART SCATTON

Andrei Bitov
ELLEN CHANCES

Nikolai Zabolotsky
DARRA GOLDSTEIN

Nietzsche and Soviet culture
edited by BERNICE GLATZER ROSENTHAL

Wagner and Russia
ROSAMUND BARTLETT

Russian literature and empire
Conquest of the Caucasus from Pushkin to Tolstoy
SUSAN LAYTON

Jews in Russian literature after the October Revolution
Writers and artists between hope and apostasy
EFRAIM SICHER

Contemporary Russian satire: a genre study
KAREN L. RYAN-HAYES

Gender and Russian literature: new perspectives
edited by ROSALIND MARSH